Lecture Notes
in Business Information Processing   **396**

Series Editors

Wil van der Aalst ⓘ
RWTH Aachen University, Aachen, Germany

John Mylopoulos ⓘ
University of Trento, Trento, Italy

Michael Rosemann ⓘ
Queensland University of Technology, Brisbane, QLD, Australia

Michael J. Shaw
University of Illinois, Urbana-Champaign, IL, USA

Clemens Szyperski
Microsoft Research, Redmond, WA, USA

More information about this series at http://www.springer.com/series/7911

Maria Paasivaara · Philippe Kruchten (Eds.)

Agile Processes in Software Engineering and Extreme Programming – Workshops

XP 2020 Workshops
Copenhagen, Denmark, June 8–12, 2020
Revised Selected Papers

Springer

Editors
Maria Paasivaara
IT University of Copenhagen
Copenhagen, Denmark

Philippe Kruchten
University of British Columbia
Vancouver, BC, Canada

ISSN 1865-1348   ISSN 1865-1356   (electronic)
Lecture Notes in Business Information Processing
ISBN 978-3-030-58857-1   ISBN 978-3-030-58858-8   (eBook)
https://doi.org/10.1007/978-3-030-58858-8

This Springer imprint is published by the registered company Springer Nature Switzerland AG
The registered company address is: Gewerbestrasse 11, 6330 Cham, Switzerland

Preface

This volume contains papers from the research workshops, the agile education and training track, the doctoral symposium, as well as summaries of the research workshops and a panel presented at the 21st International Conference on Agile Software Development (XP 2020), held June 8–12, 2020. Although it was planned to take place at the IT University of Copenhagen, Denmark, due to the COVID-19 pandemic, the conference was very successfully held online.

XP is the premier agile software development conference combining research and practice. It is a unique forum where agile researchers, practitioners, thought leaders, coaches, and trainers get together to present and discuss their most recent innovations, research results, experiences, concerns, challenges, and trends. XP conferences provide an informal environment to learn and trigger discussions and welcome both people new to agile and seasoned agile practitioners.

The XP 2020 research papers were published in the conference proceedings, volume LNBIP 383. This companion volume, published after the conference, contains selected workshop papers and workshops summaries, as well as three papers from the doctoral symposium, two papers from the agile education and training track, and one panel summary.

The research workshops, the agile education and training track, and the doctoral symposium provide a highly relevant, friendly, and interactive platform to share and discuss emerging and late-breaking research findings as well as educational experiments and experiences. They represent smaller, close communities of passionate, emerging and established researchers, and a psychologically safe environment to provide and receive feedback. The publication of the post-conference proceedings allows the researchers and educators to submit their papers, feedback, and lessons learned from their participation in the conference and workshop sessions.

In 2020, the following six workshops took place:

- Third International Workshop on Software-Intensive Business
- 8th International Workshop on Large-Scale Agile Development
- Second European Symposium on Serverless Computing and Applications
- Second International Workshop on Agile Transformation
- First International Workshop on Agility with Microservices Programming
- Third International Workshop on Autonomous Agile Teams

In addition to the workshop papers and summaries, these post-conference proceedings include papers from:

- Agile education and training track
- Doctoral symposium

Finally, we include a summary of a panel discussion:

- COVID-19's Influence on the Future of Agile

We would like to extend our sincere thanks to all the people who contributed to XP 2020: the authors, reviewers, chairs, and volunteers. Finally, we would like to express our gratitude to the XP Steering Committee and the Agile Alliance for their ongoing support.

July 2020

Maria Paasivaara
Philippe Kruchten

Organization

Conference Chair

Maria Paasivaara   Technical University of Denmark, Denmark

Program Co-chairs

Viktoria Stray   University of Oslo, SINTEF, Norway
Rashina Hoda   Monash University, Australia

Workshop Co-chairs

Hubert Baumeister   Technical University of Denmark, Denmark
Mansooreh Zahedi   The University of Adelaide, Australia

Publication Chair

Philippe Kruchten   The University of British Columbia, Canada

Third International Workshop on Software-Intensive Business

Xiaofeng Wang   Free University of Bozen-Bolzano, Italy
Paul Grünbacher   Johannes Kepler University, Austria
Sami Hyrynsalmi   LUT University, Finland
Kari Smolander   LUT University, Finland

Eighth International Workshop on Large-Scale Agile Development

Julian Bass   University of Salford, UK
Abdalla Salameh   University of Salford, UK

Second European Symposium on Serverless Computing and Applications

Davide Taibi   Tampere University, Finland
Josef Spillner   Zürich University of Applied Science, Switzerland
Fellong Wang   Catalyst Cloud, New Zealand

Second International Workshop on Agile Transformation

Leonor Barroca   The Open University, UK
Noel Carroll   Lero, Ireland

Peggy Gregory   University of Central Lancashire, UK
Diane Strode   Whitireai Polytechnic, New Zealand

First International Workshop on Agility with Microservices Programming

Saverio Giallorenzo   University of Southern Denmark, Denmark
Marco Peressotti   University of Southern Denmark, Denmark
Filipe Correia   University of Porto, Portugal
Kati Kuusinen   Technical University of Denmark, Denmark

Third International Workshop on Autonomous Agile Teams

Nils Brede Moe   SINTEF, Norway
Viktoria Stray   University of Oslo, SINTEF, Norway

Agile Education and Training Track

Martin Kropp   FHNW, Switzerland
Maari Laanti   Nitor, Finland

Doctoral Symposium

Peggy Gregory   University of Central Lancashire, UK
Kati Kuusinen   Technical University of Denmark, Denmark

Contents

**Second European Workshop on Serverless Computing
and Applications**

Second International Workshop on Agile Transformations

**First International Workshop on Agility
with Microservices Programming**

Panel

Third International Workshop
on Software-Intensive Business

Unleashing the Business Potential of Software: A Summary of the Third International Workshop on Software-intensive Business

Xiaofeng Wang[1], Paul Grünbacher[2], Sami Hyrynsalmi[3], and Kari Smolander[3]

[1] Free University of Bozen-Bolzano, Bolzano 39100, Italy
xiaofeng.wang@unibz.it
[2] Johannes Kepler University Linz, Linz 4040, Austria
paul.gruenbacher@jku.at
[3] LUT University, Lappeenranta 53850, Finland
{sami.hyrynsalmi,kari.smolander}@lut.fi

Abstract. Software-intensive companies face the challenges of changing demands, rapidly evolving technology, and dynamic business ecosystems, which urge them to rethink their business models to benefit from current and future technological trends. These challenges pose interesting and significant research problems that require multi-disciplinary approaches. The International Workshop on Software-intensive Business (IWSiB) aims to bring together different research communities working on relevant topics, to jointly investigate the challenges, and to bridge the gap between these communities. The third IWSiB featured two keynote talks contemplating the business of quantum computing and the trend and impact of public cloud services. Seven research presentations both hit the main research themes, e.g., platforms and software startups, and address new topics such as product roadmapping, and Initial Coin Offerings (ICOs) enabled by Blockchain. The participants suggested other interesting topics for future workshops, including the impact of AI on software business, and new software-driven business models.

Keywords: Software-intensive business · Software ecosystems · Software startups

1 Introduction to the Workshop

"There's no business like software business" [1]. The role of software-intensive business solutions is still, after decades, ever-growing in our society. There is hardly a field or an industrial domain where software-intensive solutions have not revolutionized the business. In this context, software producing organizations face the challenges of changing demands, rapidly evolving technology, and a dynamic ecosystem in which their products and services need to operate. Organizations need to rethink their operating models and benefit from current and future trends. For instance, design thinking and lean startup approaches enable them to rapidly identify and validate the business value of their software solutions, while agile engineering practices and DevOps techniques allow them to respond swiftly to changes in their environment, thus embracing uncertainty.

The challenges to make these organizations successful are multi-disciplinary. First, there exist software engineering and technology challenges, such as eliciting and prioritizing requirements, dealing with platforms and technology standards, and operating in complex technology landscapes that constrain and enable their technology. Secondly, there exist adoption challenges: organizations need to find ways to convince their target users to adopt their technologies and to coordinate evolving technologies to provide the most valuable end-user experience. Thirdly, there exist business model challenges and organizations must find ways to maximize profit from their innovations and technologies. Because of the pervasiveness of software, the challenges are observed everywhere in the economy, whether it is logistics, online marketing, or e-health. Furthermore, they are applicable to organizations in every stage of development, whether it is a software startup or a software giant that has influenced or dominated the market consistently for decades [2].

The scientific field of software-intensive business investigates sustainable software-based value creation, capture, and delivery through arrangements and methods i) within organizations (e.g., product management, business models, agility) and ii) between organizations (e.g. ecosystems, platforms, app stores, OSS communities). There are many researchers and practitioners whose work is related to the field of software-intensive business. However, they are often not fully aware of each others work as the research is scattered to many small sub-fields such as software engineering economics, software product management, software ecosystems, technology management, software platforms, or software startups. The International Workshop on Software-intensive Business (IWSiB) strengthens the ties between these sub-fields and researchers working in different but strongly related topics. The specific goals of IWSiB are to:

- Provide a venue for members of the software engineering and business research communities to discuss issues of common interest;
- Provide a venue for sharing early work and work-in-progress to obtain feedback from the wider community.

To achieve these goals, IWSiB is open to a wide range of topics, including

- Business-oriented software development practices
- Business practices in software development
- Software product management
- Software development practices in software startups
- Business models of software startups
- Business aspects of continuous, agile and lean development
- Organizational practices in software businesses
- Software engineering economics
- Interweaving product and business development
- Software ecosystem and platform architectures, evolution and lifecycle
- Ecosystem and platform orchestration and governance
- API economy solutions and challenges
- Observations of software industry and its trends

– Impact of new technological and business model trends on software-intensive
businesses

This year's workshop is the third edition of IWSiB, and a further implementation of
the above-stated vision. The fact that it was co-located with XP2020 helped to highlight
the theme of this edition - unleashing the business potential of software, as delivering
business value is one of the core tenets of agile software development. It is also worth
mentioning that, due to the Covid-19 pandemic situation, the workshop was run
completely virtually using the tele-conferencing solution chosen by the hosting conference. Therefore, it offered different but new and interesting experience to the
workshop participants. One positive consequence of going virtual was that we have
seen a larger number of participants in comparison to the past two editions, and they
spread wider geographically, including countries such as the United States and Brazil
which were not represented in the past. In addition, there was a good mix of academics
and practitioners attending the workshop. To stimulate the discussion among workshop
participants and ensure that the presenting authors to receive feedback on their work,
we have assigned one discussant to each paper before the workshop, whose duty was to
read the paper beforehand, and lead the discussion of the paper during the workshop. Since interaction online is more challenging than that in physical format, the role
of discussant guaranteed a minimal level of interaction in an evenly distributed manner.

2 Presentations at the Workshop

The workshop featured two keynote talks. Following them were seven presentations
based on the accepted research papers, which could be roughly divided into two
categories: continuing the main themes of IWSiB, and suggesting new research
directions.

2.1 Keynote Talks

Michael Cusumano, MIT Sloan School of Management professor and author of several
seminal books and articles of the software business research area (e.g. [3]), kicked off
the workshop presentations with his keynote "Quantum Computing as the Next Software Applications Platform". Firstly, Michael explained what a quantum computer is.
Quantum computers mimic nature by using quantum bits (qubits) as their logic or
operating circuits, which can represent various states of 0, 1, or both (called super-
position). Qubits can interact at a distance (called entanglement) and cancel out wrong
solutions (called interference). The essential excitement over the quantum computing is
because correlated qubits represent an exponential increase in potential computing
power - "300 qubits can store and process information equal to the estimated number of
particles in the known universe". Based on the notion that now may be a good time to
ponder on the business of quantum computing, Michael provided an overview of the
key players in the business of quantum computing, such as D-Wave, IBM, and many
startups innovating in this area, and of the areas where quantum computing can generate business impact, including materials, finance, pharmaceutical and computational

fluid dynamics (CFD). However, the keynote reminded us that we were still in the early days of quantum computing, and there was still quite a long way to go before we could see general-purpose, universal quantum computers (more than 20 years), and they were not meant to be substitutes of conventional computers that we used in our daily lives. The keynote envisioned quantum computing as the next software applications platform, and encouraged people to "get feet wet" by playing various software development kits (SDK) and cloud services made available by the key players.

The second keynote, "Advances in Public Cloud Technology as Foundation for Global Software-Intensive Businesses", was given by Christoph Bussler, solution architect from Google, Inc., who is also an active contributor to the software-intensive business research community. Christoph asserted that current technology advances in public clouds fundamentally changed the abstractions of computing, storage and services such as machine learning, and the new computing abstractions in turn changed in significant ways the foundation of software architecture and the software development process. Through highlighting the currently available cloud technology advances of Google Cloud, the keynote talk demonstrated how global software-intensive businesses confronted with an ever increasing competition can significantly benefit from the new abstractions. One of the interesting arguments made during the talk was that, with increasing levels of abstractions and with more details of infrastructure and technology taken care of by public cloud services, software developers are freed up to focus more on the business and value aspects of software development. However, as Christoph admitted, it was a challenging task to guide software developers to focus more on business value generation activities in software development.

2.2   Paper Presentations Continuing the Main Themes

Four presented papers could fall into this category, as they addressed the topics related to software platforms, ecosystems and startups, which are the focal areas of software-business intensive research.

Andreas Kaselow, Dimitri Petrik and Sven Feja presented their paper entitled "Success Factors for a Launch of an Algorithmic Consulting Platform". They argued that, for the consulting industry, digital platforms offered the potential to win new customer groups who had not previously purchased consulting services. In their study, they examined the launch of digital platforms for the algorithmic consulting approach because of its promising market potential. Through a qualitative analysis of electronic documents on the actions of three successful crowdsourcing platforms, the authors identified 14 success factors for the platform launch, including the open nature of platform design in the areas of customer access, cooperation with other platforms, interfaces, and communication.

"API Utilization and Monetization in Finnish Industries" was co-authored and presented by Saeid Heshmatisafa and Marko Seppänen. The paper was based on the observation that many companies have joined the trend to expose their business assets through open (web) Application Programming Interface (API), and they appear to adopt API technology due to the need and demand of their customers. However, the pressure from the industry to develop, implement, and maintain API products and services could cause neglect from companies' side to better understand the true benefits behind the API development, and consequently they might not be able to exploit these business assets in monetary or non-monetary manners. The study explored the status of the API development and API economy in Finnish industries. using publicly available information from 226 companies and organizations which represent a wide variety of industries such as industrials, consumer goods, and services. Their study provided a comprehensive view of the current status regarding factors such as API readiness, types, protocols, and monetization models.

Jorge Melegati, Rafael Chanin, Afonso Sales and Rafael Prikladnicki presented a position paper called "Towards specific software engineering practices for early-stage startups". Their goal was to argue the need of specific software development practices for early-stage startups. In order to reach this goal, they discussed the consequences of innovative and market-driven contexts, which are two of the key elements used to describe software startups. They also argued that these practices could be applied to innovative initiatives within established companies since they shared similar characteristics and challenges as startups.

Kelson Silva, Eduardo Guerra and Jorge Melegati took an interesting angle and investigated how non-software-intensive companies approach software-intensive innovation projects. The main motivation behind their paper, "An Approach for Software-Intensive Business Innovation Based on Experimentation in Non-Software-Intensive Companies", was that companies whose business were not centered on technology might fail to innovate and lose to their competitors. The authors observed a knowledge gap in the literature, that is, although experimentation was described as an essential aspect of an innovation process and Software Engineering studies have explored experimentation, there was a paucity of studies focusing on software-intensive innovative projects in non-software-intensive companies which had rigid structures in comparison to fast-changing software-intensive companies. The authors proposed an experiment-oriented process, as well as roles involved, to implement innovation in non-software-intensive companies, and demonstrated positive evaluation results through three innovation projects of a cleaning and maintenance company.

2.3   Paper Presentations Suggesting New Directions

The other three paper presentations enlarged the workshop boundary and enriched its themes with their different takes on software-intensive business research. Two papers from the same group of authors, Gabriella Laatikainen, Alexander Semenov, Yixin Zhang and Pekka Abrahamsson, investigated a current and intriguing phenomenon: initial coin offerings (ICOs). Their work was set against the backdrop that blockchain technologies disrupted industries by enabling decentralized and transactional data sharing across a network of untrusted participants, and provided means to develop services that were secure, transparent and efficient by nature. New business opportunities emerged in the form of Initial Coin Offerings (ICOs), which was a novel way of crowdfunding through which blockchain-enabled businesses managed to raise a huge amount of fund in a remarkably short time. In one paper, the authors asked "What key aspects do ICOs reveal about their businesses?" given the observed knowledge gap that there was a lack of understanding of the ICO phenomenon especially related to the business aspects. In this paper, the authors described the results of an exploratory study of 91 ICOs. They identified the key business model elements that ICOs revealed in their websites and whitepapers, and noted the immaturity and lack of transparency of the business aspects behind these ICO campaigns. In the other paper entitled "ICO Crowdfunding: Incentives, Pricing strategy, Token Strategy and Crowd Involvement", the authors continued to investigate the 91 ICOs through a content analysis, and identified the ICO types, including equity-based, rewards-based, subscription-based or a combination of these.

Last but not least, in the paper "Product Roadmap Alignment – Achieving the Vision Together: A Grey Literature Review", Stefan Trieflinger, Jürgen Münch, Emre Bogazköy, Patrick Eißler, Jan Schneider and Bastian Roling set the goal of gaining a better understanding of product roadmap alignment by identifying measures, activities and techniques used to align different stakeholders around a product roadmap. Product roadmap is an important tool in product development and sets the strategic direction in which a product is to be developed to achieve the company's vision. For product roadmaps to be successful, it is essential that all stakeholders agree on the company's vision and objectives and are aligned and committed to a common product plan. The authors reviewed grey literature and discovered several approaches to gain alignment, such as defining and communicating clear objectives based on the product vision, conducting cross-functional workshops, shuttle diplomacy, mission briefing, as well as a "Behavioural Change Stairway Model" suggesting five steps to gain alignment by building empathy and a trustful relationship.

3   Future Focuses of IWSiB

The third edition of IWSiB concluded with a question to all workshop participants: "what topics/issues would you like to see in our next workshop?" While some suggestions were well in line with the defined themes of IWSiB, others hint on several interesting new directions that the future editions of IWSiB could focus on. There are also suggestions on the types of research that the participants would like to see more in the future. Table 1 summarizes the suggestions from the workshop participants.

In the future, IWSiB will continue the implementation of its vision, raising awareness of this research community and its different facets. It will also support the building of a common research agenda for the emerging area of software-intensive business to address the complex interactions of software development and business and to propose new avenues for research. Besides facilitating inter-group knowledge exchange in this research context, we will also better design the workshop to make it a desirable venue for researchers to share learning related to research rigor in the field and receive early feedback to improve their ongoing research.

Table 1. The future research focuses suggested by the workshop participants

Category	Topic
Corresponding to the existing themes of IWSiB	- Business ecosystems (vs. software ecosystems) - Software vs. digital innovations - Digital platform - Impact of software engineering practices in business - (New) Software-driven business model
New focuses	- Impact of AI on software businesses - AI ethics - Machine learning and software business - What happened when "software ate the world" - How to deal with giant corporations in innovation - Intellectual Property Rights (IPR) issues for software (governance, etc.)
Types of research	- More studies with narrative and other qualitative methods studies - Case study of successful business model on top of public API

References

1. Jansen, S.: There's no business like software business: trends in software intensive business research. In: Hyrynsalmi, S., Suoranta, M., Nguyen-Duc, A., Tyrväinen, P., Abrahamsson, P. (eds.) ICSOB 2019. LNBIP, vol 370, pp. 19–27. Springer, Cham (2019). https://doi.org/10.1007/978-3-030-33742-1_3
2. Abrahamsson, P., Bosch, J., Brinkkemper, S., Mädche, A.: Software business, platforms, and ecosystems: fundamentals of software production research (Dagstuhl seminar 18182). Dagstuhl Rep. **8**(4), 164–198 (2018)
3. Cusumano, M. A.: The Business of Software: What Every Manager, Programmer, and Entrepreneur Must Know to Thrive and Survive in Good Times and Bad. The Free Press, USA (2004)

An Approach for Software-Intensive Business Innovation Based on Experimentation in Non-software-Intensive Companies

Kelson Silva[1], Eduardo Guerra[2], and Jorge Melegati[2(✉)]

[1] Instituto Nacional de Pesquisas Espaciais, São José dos Campos, Brazil
`kelson@jetsoft.com.br`
[2] Free University of Bozen-Bolzano, Bolzano, Italy
`guerraem@gmail.com`, `jmelegatigoncalves@unibz.it`

Abstract. Several companies whose businesses are not centered on technology might fail to innovate and get advantages over their competitors. For them, meaningful innovations are not necessarily related to the usage of new technologies but the optimization of some business process. In the literature, experimentation is described as an essential aspect of the innovation process. Although software engineering studies have explored experimentation, none has focused on software-intensive innovative projects in non-software-intensive companies, which consists of a contrast between the fast-changing environment in software-intensive to rigid structures in consolidated businesses. This paper proposes an experiment-oriented process to identify and implement innovation in this kind of company, including the roles involved in such processes. It has steps to identify business bottlenecks, search for solution alternatives, implement a fast and functional software proof of concept, create a plan for evolution, and migrate to a regular project to continue that idea. This paper also presents an evaluation of this process in a company focused on outsourced services, such as cleaning and maintenance. As a result, several internal procedures in a year were improved and received software support.

Keywords: Innovation · Software-intensive business · Experimentation

1 Introduction

In an increasingly competitive world, the innovation-ability has to be developed in order to be able to survive in the long run, even in a non-high technological market. Although not being the focus of these companies, in many cases, the software may represent a way to non-software-intensive companies to innovate. Innovation is generally linked to a discontinuity in the marketing and/or technological process either in a macro (new to the world or industry) or micro-level (to the customer or the firm) [1].

© The Author(s) 2020
M. Paasivaara and P. Kruchten (Eds.): XP 2020 Workshops, LNBIP 396, pp. 9–17, 2020.
https://doi.org/10.1007/978-3-030-58858-8_1

In the literature, experimentation is a crucial activity to innovation [2]. Therefore, practices to promote experimentation are valuable to improve innovation. Based on experimentation, several practitioners oriented frameworks (e.g., Lean Startup [3]) have focused on innovation in companies developing a wide range of products. Recently, several studies proposed models to describe experimentation in software-intensive contexts (e.g., RIGHT [4] and HYPEX [5]). However, one context has received less attention: a non-software-intensive company pursues innovation through implementing a novel software system. There are several studies that investigate the usage of software development practices on companies in which software is not its primary focus [6,7]. None of these studies clearly define the differences from this kind of company, but we assume that such a context may represent unique challenges due to the difference in culture that is significant for practices related to innovation. Consequently, this study will be guided by the following research question: **How can software-intensive business innovation be pursued in a non-software-intensive company?**

To answer the RQ, we proposed a framework to implement a software innovation process based on experimentation, including steps and roles. Given that the boundary between the framework implementation and the company operation is blurred, a case study is a proper research method choice. Such an option is standard while evaluating artifacts in software engineering research [8]. As an initial evaluation, we performed a case study in a Brazilian company called Guima ConSeCo. We present three internal innovation projects that were used as units of analysis: introduction of a recruitment portal, usage of a distance algorithm to reduce transportation costs, and a software-aided process for cleaning of hospital beds. Our results showed that the company succeeded in creating software-intensive innovations supporting the usefulness of the framework.

2   Background and Related Work

The literature provides some examples of experimentation models. Olsson and Bosch [5] proposed the HYPEX (Hypothesis Experiment Data-driven Development). It consisted of six practices: generation of features that could be possibly valuable to the users; selection of highest priority features and creation of hypotheses about it; extraction of the so-called minimum viable feature or MVF: the smallest part that adds value to the customer; analysis of the difference between expected and actual behavior; in case of difference, development of hypotheses to explain it; and, finally, analysis of the hypotheses created and definition of what to do further.

Fagerholm et al. [4] proposed another model: RIGHT (Rapid Iterative value creation Gained through High-frequency Testing). It consists of cycles that start with the analysis of the learning obtained in previous cycles and the company's business model and vision. Following, the team identifies and prioritizes hypotheses. Then, the team develops an MVP (Minimum Viable Product) or MVF to test a subset of hypotheses and update the instrumentation. Once the experiment is executed and its results are analyzed, the team reaches a decision-making stage. Based on what it learned, the team may persevere in the idea (implementing/optimizing, scheduling for deployment) or pivot it/change assumptions, etc.

Sveningson et al. [9] investigated the use of continuous experimentation in companies with low control of roadmap. The authors argued that there is a relationship among the control of the roadmap and the distance to the users to the use of continuous experimentation.

Melegati et al. [10] argued that these models follow a similar cycle consisted of the following steps: 1) identify, specify, and prioritize hypotheses, 2) design an experiment, 3) execute it, and 4) analyze its results. These results will lead to learning that will be used to feed the process by, if needed, updating the hypotheses.

Nevertheless, to the best of our knowledge, there is no systematic approach to perform software-intensive innovation in non-software intensive companies, highlighting the research gap we are diving into.

3 Experiment-Driven Business-Oriented Innovation Approach

In this section, we present a proposed approach for software-intensive business innovation based on experimentation, including the roles needed. To describe it, we will detail each of the experimentation process steps identified by Melegati et al. [10] could be performed.

3.1 Roles

In the context where a non-software-intensive company wants to innovate, the first thing that should be done is to form an innovation team. This group will be responsible for identifying the opportunities for improvement and for following the results and the initial implementation. This team should include a business specialist that understands the market where the company is included. Additionally, there should also be someone with good company knowledge, that knows and understands its current main problems and difficulties. Both roles might be played by the same person or not.

The team should also have technology experts who can propose and design new solutions, including elements for software support. The expertise should be on the design of software systems but not necessarily implementation since, for the project execution, another team should be assigned. Since the company's primary focus is not technology, it might internally do not have an appropriate person for this role. In this case, it can be an external consultant or someone from a technology partner company. It is also advised to have someone with a research background to structure the projects and experiments to ensure they gather the appropriate data to evaluate the business goals' suitability.

This innovation team does not need to be full-time because their members would not necessarily work on the projects, but they will identify and prioritize the innovation projects, evaluate the results, and make decisions. Because of that, the team should also have someone with the power to make decisions inside the company. The level of hierarchy required depends on the company, but there should be someone on this team that can assign for the innovation projects the necessary resources, especially to allocate the time of persons in key positions of the company that is important for a given project.

3.2   Steps

The first step is the identification of hypotheses about a possible innovation. In this step, the innovation team has to identify opportunities for improvement. One kind of these opportunities can be related to the company's recurrent problems in some process or area. As an example, it can be a process that is not fulfilling its goals or spending more resources than it should. The target process might also not be considered with problems, but it could have points that can be improved and optimized. It can also be an opportunity to expand the company business by developing a new product or expanding the market for an existing one. The identified opportunities are prioritized, and the innovation team should define what projects should be initiated.

Once a project is chosen, in the next step, a team should be assigned to design and perform an experiment. This team might include members from inside the innovation team, and also include others from outside, even from the target company, independent consultants, and partner company. It is essential to perform a feasibility check, verifying if the team has the necessary technical and business skills and knowledge to execute the project.

For each innovation project, it should be clear the scope and how much time the team has to work. Each project should be short, usually from one to three months. Due to the uncertainty of the results, it is better to fragment projects with a broader scope, defining at first a small one with a more limited scope and chain it with another defined based on the initial results. Usually, the output for each project can be either a critical answer to move on a relevant company issue or a functional proof-of-concept that can be implemented or evaluated even with some limitations.

In this step, the team assigned to work on the innovation project should search for solution alternatives that can solve the target problem. The solution can involve a change in the work procedure and the adoption of new techniques; however, it often involves the usage of the software that can support the adoption of the new approach. Before proposing the development of new software, it should be investigated if there is a product that can fulfill even partially those needs in the market and how they can be integrated with the existing solutions. After the possible solutions are evaluated, they are presented to the innovation team, giving their feedback and approval to proceed to an experimentation phase.

In the next step, the team implements a proof-of-concept to evaluate the proposed solution. It can be the installation of existing software or the creation of a prototype of a new one. Even when existing software is used, it is usually necessary for some development effort to integrate it with the existing applications and databases. The resulting products of this phase should be developed in small iterations and frequently delivered to get feedback from the company's business side. Members of the innovation team should also follow these results.

When the innovation team judges that the solution was explored enough, it follows to the final step: analyze the results accomplished. Based on that, they make a final decision if the company is going to move forward in that direction or not. With a positive response, the project leaves the innovation team and become a regular company initiative. New related innovation projects might be created. However, the part already well established might now be managed as a regular project.

For various reasons that can be related to results, budget, or even focus, an innovation project might be abandoned. In this scenario, the innovation team should keep the knowledge obtained in the project in a way that can be used in the future, preserving valuable findings by applying Knowledge Management techniques. For instance, it is not rare for an idea that is not viable to be implemented in the present to be practicable later due to technological advances.

4   Case Study

To evaluate the proposed approach, we performed a case study. This research approach has been used in software engineering literature to the research purpose of improvement [8], like our study.

The proposed approach was applied in a Brazilian company called Guima-ConSeCo, focused on outsourcing services, such as cleaning and maintenance engineering. During our study, the company developed three innovation projects using the proposed approach. Each one is a unit of analysis. Data collection consisted of participant observation and the analysis of the project's documentation.

The company currently has around 10.000 employees and provides services in several public and private facilities. The company has plans to grow in size, and its managers feel the need to innovate in certain aspects to make the company more competitive and enable sustainable growth.

The company aims to take advantage of a Brazilian incentive law for innovation[1]. Several countries also have similar laws to incentivize companies to develop innovation. In Brazil, the company can use a small percentage of its taxes to invest in this kind of project. To get the benefit, the company should document and submit the project to the authorities.

The innovation team was composed of members of a partner technology company named Jetsoft. The third-party company was responsible for proposing and implementing this process in the target company. Jetsoft started performing a mapping study of all the business processes from the target company, identifying problems and potential points for improvement. The team works with a tool named Genexus [11], which allows fast development and generates code to

---

[1] Law No 10.973 2nd December 2004 - http://www.planalto.gov.br/ccivil_03/_ato2004-2006/2004/lei/l10.973.htm.

several platforms such as Java and .NET. The speed provided by this tool was important for fast prototyping the solutions.

In all projects described, granular experiments happened, proposing solutions to parts of the problem and validating them quickly. In many cases, the solutions were discarded for not passing in an initial evaluation. The approved solutions were put in practice on a small scale, being refined until being mature enough for being deployed to production.

4.1   Units of Analysis

Recruitment Portal: As a company that manages outsourcing services for a high number of employees, human resources is a crucial area, especially recruitment. The motivation for this innovation project was that a high number of candidates delivered their resume in a paper, which was generating much manual work, and nevertheless, many of them were not being processed. This innovation project proposed the creation of a recruitment portal were the candidates can add their resume. Additionally, an internal application was developed to allow a search through this resume database. The initial experiments generated a working prototype, and further, this solution was evolved to become a company product. After two months of the start of this innovation project, an initial version was online. As a result, the human resources manual work reduced, and now the company has a more suitable tool to search for potential job candidates for a given position. Currently, the application database has around 18k resumes.

Distance Algorithm: The company manages employees working in different areas of the city. Some of them worked in places far from their home, even having alternatives close to where they live. This mismatch generates costs for the company like transportation, possible delays due to traffic, and a drop in employee's quality of life. This project proposed an algorithm to calculate the distance between the workplace and the candidate's address to be used in the recruitment process. An experiment was performed executing the algorithm direct on the data. After its validation, it was integrated into the recruitment portal mentioned in the previous section. The automation of this distance calculation is currently being used in the recruitment process, and it is considered, as a next step, to be used for workplace optimization of current employees.

Cleaning of Hospital Beds: The cleaning of hospitals is one of the services provided by the target company. Several problems occurred in this service because the contracting hospital supervisor often evaluated the service after an extended period, which can lead to divergences. An opportunity for improvement was detected with the proposal of a tool that can be used to manage the requests for cleaning and supervision, allowing the capture of images that can register the service performed by the employee and problems found by the supervisor. The company also considered that with this data, it would be possible to evaluate the efficiency from different angles and perform actions to optimize the work. In this innovation project, the first step was to search for products that could fulfill those needs. Some potential matches were found, and meetings with their companies were made to get knowledge about them. It was found that two of them could partially fulfill the requirements, the central problem being the integration with the current systems. An experiment with these two different solutions was done in different clients, and both are currently being used in production after adjustments from the providers.

5   Discussion and Conclusions

In each analysis unit, it was possible to observe that the company successfully implemented an innovation. Such achievements were reached either by implementing prototypes or by selecting a solution already existent in the market and then experimenting and evaluating the results. Looking to the case considering the target research question: "**How can software-intensive business innovation be pursued in a non-software-intensive company?**", we can conclude that the proposed approach can be a valid way for that. The target company was able to innovate in some of its critical areas for its business, and intend to keep applying this process continuously.

We considered the focus on business problems as one of the critical success factors of this approach. Innovation can be seen wrongly as the usage of breaking edge technologies, however, with the focus on business, the use of simpler software technology could solve the problem if it is appropriate for the demands. Another critical point for the success in the studied case was the partnership of the non-software-intensive company with a company specialized in business process mapping and software development. That created a synergy where each one focuses on its field of specialization but collaborates to reach a common goal.

Although the innovation projects described do not represent anything new to the world, they can be described as micro-level innovations [1]. That is, the solutions proposed represented novelty at the firm level, and its development consisted of a challenge to the company. The novelty of the proposed approach when compared to previous experimentation models and Lean Startup is its focus on the dichotomy software-intensive innovation in a non-software-intensive context. Such target allowed the description of specific roles and activities. It is important to highlight that this work is still in progress and our goal is to tackle the lack of operationalization of Lean Startup, as previously recognized in the literature (e.g., [12]).

The proposed approach starts with identifying problems and opportunities for improvement, creating a team that identifies potential solutions, and validates them through experiments. It was evaluated through a case study in a company focused on outsourcing of cleaning and maintenance. The results of the case study imply that the proposed approach is feasible and suitable since it helped a non-software-intensive business company pursue innovation based on software-intensive business solutions.

As future work, we will collect more data in the presented case study through interviews with different actors involved in the process. The goal is to acquire information about the main difficulties and try to identify other lessons learned. We intend to implement the same process in other companies, intending to generalize practices, and identify difficulties that can arise in a different context. Another future study could identify the differences and peculiarities from non-software-intensive companies relevant for innovation projects.

References

1. Garcia, R., Calantone, R.: A critical look at technological innovation typology and innovativeness terminology: a literature review. J. Prod. Innov. Manage. **19**(2), 110–132 (2002)
2. Thomke, S.H.: Managing experimentation in the design of new products. Manage. Sci. **44**(6), 743–762 (1998)
3. Eric, R.: The Lean Startup: How Today's Entrepreneurs Use Continuous Innovation to Create Radically Successful Businesses. Crown Business, New York (2011)
4. Fagerholm, F., Guinea, A.S., Mäenpää, H., Münch, J.: The RIGHT model for continuous experimentation. J. Syst. Softw. **123**, 292–305 (2017)
5. Olsson, H.H., Bosch, J.: From opinions to data-driven software R&D: a multi-case study on how to close the 'open loop' problem. In: 2014 40th EUROMICRO Conference on Software Engineering and Advanced Applications, pp. 9–16. IEEE, August 2014
6. Gustavsson, T.: Benefits of agile project management in a non-software development context : a literature review. In: Project Management Development - Practice and Perspectives : Fifth International Scientific Conference on Project Management in the Baltic Countries, pp. 114–124. Latvijas Universitate (2016)
7. Conforto, E.C., Salum, F., Amaral, D.C., da Silva, S.L., de Almeida, L.F.M.: Can agile project management be adopted by industries other than software development? Proj. Manage. J. **45**(3), 21–34 (2014)
8. Runeson, P., Höst, M.: Guidelines for conducting and reporting case study research in software engineering. Empirical Softw. Eng. **14**(2), 131–164 (2009). https://doi.org/10.1007/s10664-008-9102-8
9. Sveningson, R., Mattos, D.I., Bosch, J.: Continuous experimentation for software organizations with low control of roadmap and a large distance to users: an exploratory case study. In: Franch, X., Männistö, T., Martínez-Fernández, S. (eds.) PROFES 2019. LNCS, vol. 11915, pp. 528–544. Springer, Cham (2019). https://doi.org/10.1007/978-3-030-35333-9_37
10. Melegati, J., Wang, X., Abrahamsson, P.: Hypotheses engineering: first essential steps of experiment-driven software development. In: 2019 IEEE/ACM Joint 4th International Workshop on Rapid Continuous Software Engineering and 1st International Workshop on Data-Driven Decisions, Experimentation and Evolution (RCoSE/DDrEE), pp. 16–19. IEEE, May 2019
11. Castagnet, N.: Software factories para construir sistemas de información con genexus. Technical report, Instituto de Computación, Facultad de Ingeniería, Universidad de la República. Informe del proyecto de grado (2007)
12. Bosch, J., Holmström Olsson, H., Björk, J., Ljungblad, J.: The early stage software startup development model: a framework for operationalizing lean principles in software startups. In: Fitzgerald, B., Conboy, K., Power, K., Valerdi, R., Morgan, L., Stol, K.-J. (eds.) LESS 2013. LNBIP, vol. 167, pp. 1–15. Springer, Heidelberg (2013). https://doi.org/10.1007/978-3-642-44930-7_1

Towards Specific Software Engineering Practices for Early-Stage Startups

Jorge Melegati[1]([✉]) [ID], Rafael Chanin[2] [ID], Afonso Sales[2] [ID],
and Rafael Prikladnicki[2] [ID]

[1] Faculty of Computer Science, Free University of Bozen-Bolzano, Bolzano, Italy
`jmelegatigoncalves@unibz.it`
[2] School of Technology, PUCRS, Porto Alegre, Brazil
{`rafael.chanin,afonso.sales,rafaelp`}`@pucrs.br`

Abstract. In this position paper, our goal is to argue the need for specific software development practices to early-stage startups. In order to reach this goal, we discuss the consequences of innovative and market-driven contexts, which are two of the key elements when describing software startups. We also argue that these practices could be applied to innovative initiatives within established companies since they share similar characteristics and challenges as those from startups.

Keywords: Early-stage startups · Innovation · Market-driven

1 Introduction

The definition of a startup is blurry in scientific research. There are two systematic mapping studies (SMS) performed on the topic, and both discussed how authors had defined the term. Back in 2014, Paternoster et al. [13] analyzed 43 primary studies and, as one of their results, grouped in themes the descriptions used by papers' authors to characterize these companies. The list consisted of 15 themes where the most common were: 1. lack of resources; 2. highly reactive; 3. innovation; 4. uncertainty; 5. rapidly evolving; 6. time pressure.

In 2018, Berg et al. [3] repeated the analysis, including papers published in the period. They concluded that the rigor had increased, but there was not still a consensus on the term. However, in the period between the SMSs, the most common themes were innovation, uncertainty, small teams, lack of resources, and little or no operating history.

Startups follow a life-cycle composed of four stages: inception, stabilization, growth, and maturity [11]. Inception starts with the idea conception and ends with the first release. In the stabilization stage, the startup prepares to scale regarding technical and operational aspects. These two stages are the early-stages where the focus is on finding a relevant problem and solution. In the growth stage, the startup aims to reach the desired market participation, and, in the last stage, it progresses into an established company.

© The Author(s) 2020
M. Paasivaara and P. Kruchten (Eds.): XP 2020 Workshops, LNBIP 396, pp. 18–22, 2020.
https://doi.org/10.1007/978-3-030-58858-8_2

In a divisive paper, Klotins [10] argued that there is no characteristic unique to startups that are not observed in other teams developing innovative, market-driven, software-intensive products. To reach his conclusions, he reviewed the literature regarding themes identified by Paternoster et al. [13]. Below, we oppose this argument arguing that innovation and market-driven are necessary and sufficient elements to characterize startups. Still, this combination has slightly been touched in the software engineering literature. Finally, we show that current research to tackle problems in this context is still in its infancy and which avenues could be explored further.

2   Necessity: Innovation and Market-Driven Context as a Challenge for Software Development in Startups

Innovation is an ambiguous term in the literature. To tackle this issue, Garcia and Calantone [7] reviewed studies on market, engineering, and new product development disciplines. The review showed that the term comprehends a discontinuity in marketing, technological, or both processes. In this context, ventures operate through several trials and errors along various dimensions of the business model [2]. This uncertain environment leads to challenges in software development like unstable requirements, compromised testing, and lack of written architecture specification [13]. These challenges exist, especially in market-driven contexts that are characterized by the software being developed to an open market with many customers instead of according to what is dictated by a paying customer (the so-called bespoke development).

A natural choice to deal with a dynamic context is to use agile methodologies since they embrace higher rates of change [15]. Nevertheless, agile methods may not be the final answer for software startups. Agile methods tackle changes through quick iterations with customer feedback [15]. However, these contact points are not available since, many times, even the customers are not known in the early-stages of a software startup. The lack of customer availability is a known challenge for teams applying these methods in market-driven environments [1,9]. Therefore, the combination of innovation and a market-driven context leads to a situation where a specific set of practices would be useful. Figure 1 summarizes this argument.

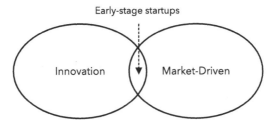

Fig. 1. Early-stage startups: combining innovative and market-driven contexts.

3   Sufficiency: Innovation on Software-Intensive Market-Driven Products as Startups

In this section, we argue that a team developing a new innovative, software-intensive, market-driven product is a software startup. Although this aspect contradicts common themes to describe software startups, such as lack of resources and lack of experience [13], teams in large companies formed to develop innovative products face similar problems as those from startups. Regardless of the context of the innovation process, uncertainty, time pressure, and the need to be highly reactive is always a part of the initiative. These characteristics require a particular way of tackling the idea being developed. A large organization cannot deal with uncertainty, for instance, just by adding more resources; the right approach needs to be implemented to transform the questions (or hypothesis) into facts.

To support our argument, we can mention the research on internal startups, in which teams develop innovative software-intensive products inside large companies. For instance, Edison et al. [5] investigated the use of Lean Startup in large companies, arguing that it facilitated the software product innovation in this context. That is, teams developing software-intensive innovative products, even in large companies, can use methods tailored to startups.

In this sense, we intend to formulate a set of best practices or a framework that could be applied in any scenario in which innovation on software-intensive market-driven products is being developed. We acknowledge that large organizations naturally differ from small ones. However, we can also find differences among small organizations: they may face different regulatory elements, competition, technical challenges, and so on. If the literature does not indicate that startups should apply different approaches depending on their characteristics, there is no reason not to include innovation software-intensive market-driven products or services being developed on large organizations.

4   Current Proposals and Future Directions

Based on the arguments above, software startups would benefit from a set of practices tailored to an innovative process. Up to now, although a broad literature on the topic are being raised in the last years [3], there are no scientific studies proposing specific practices for these companies. Academic authors focused on describing the context including currently used practices (e.g., [8,11,12]) and faced challenges (e.g., [11,14]).

Nevertheless, in the industry, some methodologies, like Lean Startup and Customer Development, are well-known. Although described based on anecdotal evidence and the authors' own experience, several academics argued the influence and importance of experimentation to the core arguments of these practices, e.g., [4,6]. Besides that, scientific studies in innovation and entrepreneurship literature have argued the value of experimentation in these contexts. Therefore, similar approaches seem a reasonable way to follow.

Our goal is to further explore our hypothesis by gathering data from initiatives in large organizations as well as from early-stage startups. By confirming our assumptions, we will work towards a set of software engineering practices for these teams. Of course, such endeavor is a huge challenge and, instead of a small team work, we expect this position paper acts as a call for the whole community to go towards this end. The literature described above will inform the creation of these practices.

5   Conclusions

This position paper initiated a discussion on software engineering practices tailored to early-stage startups. Based on the fact that innovation and market-driven are usually used to define software startups, we argue that these aspects are decisive to characterize this context. Besides that, we claim that these aspects are also relevant to teams in other contexts, such as large companies. We hope that this discussion can encourage further investigation of specific practices for early-stage startups in any given context.

Acknowledgments. This work is partially funded by FAPERGS (17/2551-0001/205-4).

References

1. Ramesh, B., Cao, L., Baskerville, R.: Agile requirements engineering practices and challenges: an empirical study. Inf. Syst. J. **20**(5), 449–480 (2007)
2. Andries, P., Debackere, K., van Looy, B.: Simultaneous experimentation as a learning strategy: business model development under uncertainty. Strateg. Entrepreneurship J. **7**(4), 288–310 (2013). https://doi.org/10.1002/sej.1170
3. Berg, V., Birkeland, J., Nguyen-Duc, A., Pappas, I.O., Jaccheri, L.: Software startup engineering: a systematic mapping study. J. Syst. Softw. **144**(February), 255–274 (2018)
4. Bortolini, R.F., Nogueira Cortimiglia, M., Danilevicz, A.d.M.F., Ghezzi, A.: Lean startup: a comprehensive historical review. Manag. Decis. (2018). https://doi.org/10.1108/MD-07-2017-0663
5. Edison, H., Smørsgård, N.M., Wang, X., Abrahamsson, P.: Lean internal startups for software product innovation in large companies: enablers and inhibitors. J. Syst. Softw. **135**, 69–87 (2018). https://doi.org/10.1016/j.jss.2017.09.034
6. Frederiksen, D.L., Brem, A.: How do entrepreneurs think they create value? A scientific reflection of Eric Ries' Lean Startup approach. Int. Entrepreneurship Manag. J. **13**(1), 169–189 (2016). https://doi.org/10.1007/s11365-016-0411-x
7. Garcia, R., Calantone, R.: A critical look at technological innovation typology and innovativeness terminology: a literature review. J. Prod. Innov. Manage **19**(2), 110–132 (2002). https://doi.org/10.1016/S0737-6782(01)00132-1
8. Gralha, C., Damian, D., Wasserman, A.I.T., Goulão, M., Araújo, J.: The evolution of requirements practices in software startups. In: Proceedings of the 40th International Conference on Software Engineering - ICSE 2018, pp. 823–833. ACM Press, New York (2018). https://doi.org/10.1145/3180155.3180158

9. Inayat, I., Salim, S.S., Marczak, S., Daneva, M., Shamshirband, S.: A systematic literature review on agile requirements engineering practices and challenges. Comput. Hum. Behav. **51**, 915–929 (2015)
10. Klotins, E.: Software start-ups through an empirical lens: are start-ups snowflakes?. In: CEUR Workshop Proceedings, vol. 2305, pp. 1–14 (2018)
11. Klotins, E., et al.: A progression model of software engineering goals, challenges, and practices in start-ups. IEEE Trans. Software Eng. **13**(9), 1 (2019)
12. Melegati, J., Goldman, A., Kon, F., Wang, X.: A model of requirements engineering in software startups. Inf. Softw. Technol. **109**(2018), 92–107 (2019). https://doi.org/10.1016/j.infsof.2019.02.001
13. Paternoster, N., Giardino, C., Unterkalmsteiner, M., Gorschek, T., Abrahamsson, P.: Software development in startup companies: a systematic mapping study. Inf. Softw. Technol. **56**(10), 1200–1218 (2014)
14. Wang, X., Edison, H., Bajwa, S.S., Giardino, C., Abrahamsson, P.: Key challenges in software startups across life cycle stages. In: Sharp, H., Hall, T. (eds.) XP 2016. LNBIP, vol. 251, pp. 169–182. Springer, Cham (2016). https://doi.org/10.1007/978-3-319-33515-5_14
15. Williams, L., Cockburn, A.: Agile software development: it's about feedback and change. Computer **36**(6), 39–43 (2003)

API Utilization and Monetization in Finnish Industries

Saeid Heshmatisafa and Marko Seppänen[(✉)]

Unit of Information and Knowledge Management, Tampere University,
Kanslerinrinne 1, 33014 Tampere, Finland
{saeid.heshmatisafa,marko.seppanen}@tuni.fi

Abstract. Many companies have followed the trend toward exposing their business assets through open (i.e., Web) application programming interfaces (APIs). However, these firms appear to have adopted API technology largely to meet their customers' needs and demands. The pressures on industries to develop, implement, and maintain API products and services can prevent companies from gaining a greater awareness of API development's benefits. Firms may thus miss out on related monetary or non-monetary exploitation of their business assets.

This study explored the status of the API economy and development among Finnish industries. The dataset comprised publicly available information from 226 private and public organizations representing a variety of industries, such as industrial, consumer goods, and services sectors. The current status of API readiness, types, protocols, and monetization models is presented to provide a more comprehensive overview.

Keywords: API · API economy · Web service · Explorative study

1 Introduction

In recent years, many companies have started to take advantage of the application programming interface (API) economy. Web APIs have caused disruption because firms can now operate, promote innovation, and create additional value from their business assets with much lower overhead costs [1, 2]. The number of publicly available APIs has thus grown significantly. For instance, ProgrammableWeb reports that over 22,000 APIs are registered on its platform and, on average, 220 new APIs are added every month [3].

Concurrently, developers perceive API as an enabler of software architecture flexibility, efficiency, and agility [4], while API providers seek to seize this as an opportunity to transform their existing business models [5]. For example, Salesforce, a pioneer in customer relations management, offers APIs to increase companies' system capabilities and integration into their customers' systems. This transformation of Salesforce's business model has empowered the firm to handle approximately 60% of its customers' transactions or about 1.3 billion daily calls through APIs instead of traditional graphical user interfaces. The strategy has generated a new revenue stream of more than five billion United States dollars annually. Another example is the

M. Paasivaara and P. Kruchten (Eds.): XP 2020 Workshops, LNBIP 396, pp. 23–31, 2020.
https://doi.org/10.1007/978-3-030-58858-8_3

Amadeus IT Group, which operates a travel technology business and generates more than six billion euros in revenue mostly from different API-based solutions.

More recently, API has become a means of developing new business strategies [6]. For instance, eBay's APIs allow third party users to list auctions and bid, which is responsible for 60% of this company's annual revenue. In addition, significant proportions of other firms' revenue, such as 90% of Expedia and 100% of Amazon Web Services, are being generated through APIs [7]. One reason for the API paradigm's success is its ability to expand ecosystems and increase innovation by embracing the outside-in practice of open innovation. These features allow third-party consumers to create new products or services from one API or a combination of available APIs, thereby enabling new approaches to capturing and creating value [8]. APIs are, therefore, becoming the corporate world's central focus.

This paper presents the initial results of a study that explored the current status of the API economy in various industries and sectors. Previous research has focused on large multi-national companies, so scant attention has been paid to small and medium-sized enterprises (SMEs) in this context. The API economy's development within SMEs was thus included in the present study. An explorative analysis was also conducted to assess the popularity of this phenomenon by addressing the following questions:

- How many organizations have adopted APIs?
- What are the most common API types and protocols?
- What monetization models are used?

2   Background

The buzzword "API economy" has recently started to attract much attention among scholars and practitioners, but the concept of API is not new. This term was initially coined in 1968 with reference to a framework or library for a specific programming language [9]. In the 2000s, the advent of service-oriented architecture (SOA) created an opportunity for companies to build business-to-business relationships using standard interfaces via a simple object access protocol (SOAP) [7]. The concept of SOA was then developed further by employing Web-based technologies such as representational state transfer (REST) [10].

With the evolution of REST, Web API shifted developers' approach to constructing and publishing applications over the Internet and created the culture of reusability by adapting create, read, update, and delete interfaces. Currently, software as a service, platform as a service, and infrastructure as a service enable developers to publish and manage application composites using key access. Developers have moved into a new era focused on speed rate, innovation, and performance while becoming better at controlling costs and risks [11].

In general, API is a way for two applications to communicate with each other over a network using a common bilateral language [6]. Thus, API acts as a control point at which a compilation of services is exposed to potential users in a controlled, managed manner [11]. In the context of the API economy, API, Web API, and business API are used interchangeably, functioning as a meta concept. Obtaining economic benefits from API is often referred to as the "API economy," which is defined as "an economy in which companies expose their (internal) business assets or services in the form of (web) APIs to third parties with the goal of unlocking additional business value" [12]. Consequently, a more appropriate definition of Web API is an Internet-based software interface that publishes specific business assets in a controlled manner [12].

Typically, this new economic model consists of three key players: API providers, API consumers, and end-users [2]. Providers expose their business assets (i.e., products, services, or/and data) over an API, and consumers are the businesses that take advantage of one API or a combination of APIs to develop new products, services, or results. End-users, in turn, are users who have a direct relationship with consumers.

Diverse and yet compatible API business models have been created [13], including free, paid, and indirect models. In paid business models, the developers either pay or get paid for API usage, while, in indirect business models, consumers are subject to business models such as content acquisition and content syndication. In this context, consumers can become the providers' direct customers by using the exposed utility services. In addition, providers may sell core products through an API, while consumers play the role of resellers [2]. Providers can exploit APIs in a great number of ways, and many of these fit into both categories or in between.

What makes APIs unique is that providers often operate in a black box and expose their business assets without being aware of the business opportunities that APIs offer and the ways that consumers can use APIs to innovate. The potential benefits of the API economy are as follows [1]:

- Reducing development costs and time
- Staying relevant in the market
- Reaching diverse platforms and devices
- Focusing on core values by outsourcing production to API consumers
- Capitalizing on new partnerships
- Entering new customer bases
- Increasing brand loyalty
- Inspiring industry standards and user expectations

Regarding types of APIs, the most common classifications are open data, open and/or public or partner, and internal and/or private APIs [14]. Open data APIs are openly accessible information mostly provided for "free" from organizations such as governments and schools. Open APIs are associated with Web APIs, which are the present study's focus and which include public and partner APIs. Open public APIs are publicly available as they can be accessed by anyone without establishing a business relationship. Conversely, partner APIs are only accessible with a key after a partnership or customer agreement is signed.

3   Research Method

Given this research's aims, a quantitative descriptive statistics method was chosen to explore the characteristics of the API economy within the sample of organizations. First, the dataset was collected from diverse private and public organizations operating in Finland, resulting in a final dataset on 226 organizations, a list of which is available upon request in a Google sheet format. The first category in the dataset comprises the top 100 companies in Finland based on their turnover in 2019 [15]. The second category includes 126 convenience sample-based SMEs to provide a more comprehensive overview of the topic under study.

Second, four variables—API readiness, types, protocols, and monetization models —were selected to define the dataset's demographics. Third, secondary data such as publicly available white papers and companies' official websites were carefully examined. Last, the content analysis's results were evaluated and associated with the findings for the defined variables. When a company did not clearly mention any of the variables, the keyword "unknown" was used.

The required data were gathered in March 2020, and the results were processed and stored in Microsoft Excel spreadsheets. Next, data wrangling was applied to clean the dataset by removing different errors, nulls, and duplications. The purified dataset was further analyzed by creating pivot tables to represent the variables' demographics. Finally, the relevant tables were constructed using Tableau software to validate and facilitate a more in-depth examination of the results.

4   Results

Information was gathered from 226 companies and organizations from different industries such as industrial, consumer goods, and services sectors. The results show that, out of 226 firms, only one-third (number [n] = 77, 34%) have open APIs, and two-thirds (n = 149, 66%) do not participate in APIs publicly (see Table 1).

The distribution of APIs indicates that the public sector is at the top of open API development with 20 organizations, whereas the healthcare sector, with its vast potential and high volume of data, has not yet invested in this technology substantially. However, technology companies have produced the most APIs or approximately 40% (n = 112) of the total. Notably, some organizations have several APIs (see Fig. 1). Consumer services firms come second with a total number of 49 open APIs. In addition, none or only one API was identified in six industries: basic materials, healthcare, telecommunications, utilities, materials, and oil and gas.

Table 1. Distribution of APIs across industries.

	With API	Without API	Total
Industrial	18	56	74
Consumer goods	3	31	34
Consumer services	10	23	33
Public	20	1	21
Technology	15	5	20
Financial	5	6	11
Basic materials	1	8	9
Healthcare	1	7	8
Materials	0	6	6
Oil and gas	0	3	3
Utilities	1	2	3
Consumer services	2	0	2
Telecommunications	1	1	2
Total	**77**	**149**	**226**

Companies apparently tend toward investing in one API type. Firms have also published more open public APIs (n = 38) compared to any other types. The second most common API type is open partner APIs (n = 18). Only a small fraction of the companies under study have APIs in both public and partner formats (n = 8). Thirteen companies did not explicitly state their type of API in any of the documents examined.

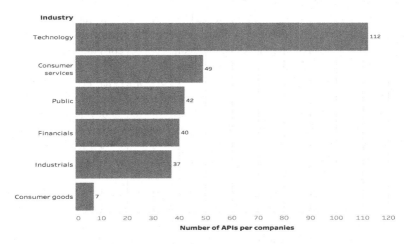

Fig. 1. API distribution across selected industries (more than one API).

Regarding monetization models, the most common revenue model in the sample is "free" with 39 companies, which means that no direct earnings or pricing is linked to API usage. A further 32 cases fall into the category of "unknown," indicating that a monetization model was not specified. Evidently, companies tend to use APIs as a facilitator and an added value to offer their existing customers.

The matrix in Table 2 shows that the 31 companies with open public APIs are exposing their business assets for free. Only a small number of the organizations in question have any monetization models linked with their APIs. All the API types and monetization models counted, totaling six organizations, are shown in italics in Table 2. Surprisingly, 12 companies did not mention their type of API or revenue model. In total, 32 organizations did not clarify their revenue model and so were coded as "unknown."

Table 2. Matrix of API classifications and monetization models.

	Unknown	Free	Free & Freemium	Free & Freemium & Premium	Free & Premium	Premium	Total
Open API (Public)	7	31	*0*	*0*	*0*	*0*	**38**
Open API (Partner)	11	6	*0*	*0*	*0*	*1*	**18**
Unknown	12	1	*0*	*0*	*0*	*0*	**13**
Open API (Partner & Public)	2	1	*1*	2	*1*	*1*	**8**
Total	**32**	**39**	*1*	**2**	*1*	**2**	**77**

Overall, the results indicate that companies do not clearly determine a revenue model. In most cases, consumers are mandated to fill out an application or contact the providers directly to receive detailed information about the type of contract and pricing models. In addition, in freemium models, companies expect consumers to upgrade to a premium model after a specific number of calls.

Similar to the findings for revenue models, API customers are also left ambiguous. Most publicly available APIs (n = 45) do not target specific market segments, and companies are unclear about whether the assets are offered to developers and/or their business partners. However, 17 open APIs expose business assets as an added value offered to partners, whereas only 3% (n = 9) of the APIs are used to collaborate with both developers and business partners. Furthermore, six public APIs explicitly aimed to serve developers.

Private companies also devote a portal to provide documentation on their APIs, but this is true of less than one-fifth (18%) of these firms. About half of the companies publish their business assets through third-party platforms such as GitHub, so the results show that only one out of six (16%) private companies dedicate an official portal to providing documentation and examples to consumers.

One-third (33%) of providers further do not clarify where consumers can access the APIs mentioned. Notably, most of the companies' information was collected for this study from their annual report, blogs, help portal, or even GitHub. This poor documentation of official information on companies' assets reflects the high level of uncertainty firms experience concerning their business assets.

In addition, SOAP architecture is more prevalent among open public APIs (see Fig. 2), while REST architecture is more common among partners and hybrid APIs. At least two firms with open partner APIs also appear to offer two different API styles (i.e., protocols) to consumers to increase the information's flexibility and usability.

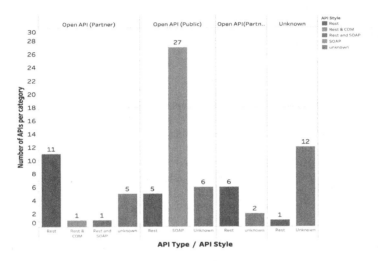

Fig. 2. API types versus style.

5 Conclusion

This paper provides an overview of public APIs and their monetization models among Finnish industries, based on a broad sample of 226 private and public organizations. Despite the growing trend toward developing open APIs, the results show that only one-third of these firms provide public access to their Web APIs. Industrial companies are pioneers in this area, but, rather surprisingly, even high potential sectors such as healthcare do not show much sign of making APIs generally available.

In terms of monetization, the findings include that the most popular revenue model among the firms under study is still "free," so direct monetization has not yet been established. Companies appear to provide APIs as an added value to their business partners, as well as to remain relevant in the market. In addition, even though documentation and protocols are some of the effective ways to encourage and engage with consumers, the results of the study indicate that companies have invested rather little on the subject matter.

This study had a few limitations that are worth mentioning. First, given the exploratory nature of the research, the results are only preliminary and are not generalizable to any great extent. Second, the data selection process was based on convenience and accessibility. Last, the results are descriptive and based on publicly available sources. Therefore, the dataset did not allow an assessment of to what extent the organizations in question may use APIs internally. Further studies using case study or survey data could help to shed light on this internal use. In addition, future research may benefit from a more theoretical approach to monetization strategies and causal relationships between monetization and organizations' performance.

References

1. Gat, I., Succi, G.: A Survey of the API Economy. Cutter Consortium Agile Product & Project Management Executive Update, vol. 14, no. 6 (2013)
2. Gat, I., Remencius, T., Sillitti, A., Succi, G., Vlasenko, J.: The API economy: playing the devil's advocate. Cutter IT J. **26**, 6–11 (2013)
3. Santos, W.: APIs show Faster Growth Rate in 2019 than Previous Years (2019). https://www.programmableweb.com/news/apis-show-faster-growth-rate-2019-previous-years/research/2019/07/17. Accessed 26 Apr 2020
4. Cois, C.A.: Devops Case Study: Amazon AWS (2015)
5. Wulf, J., Blohm, I.: Service innovation through application programming interfaces - towards a typology of service designs. In: Transforming Society with Digital Innovation, ICIS 2017, pp. 1–12 (2018)
6. Jacobson, D., Woods, D., Brail, G.: APIs: A Strategy Guide. O'Reilly Media (2011)
7. Vukovic, M., Laredo, J., Muthusamy, V., Slominski, A., Vaculin, R., et al.: Riding and thriving on the API hype cycle. Commun. ACM **59**, 35–37 (2016)
8. Doerrfeld, B., Wood, C., Anthony, A., Sandoval, K., Lauret, A.: The API Economy: Disruption and the Business of APIs. Nordic APIs (2016)
9. Cotton, I.W., Greatorex Jr., F.S.: Data structures and techniques for remote computer graphics. In: Proceedings of the Fall Joint Computer Conference, part I, 9–11 December 1968, pp 533–544 (1968)
10. Fielding, R.T., Taylor, R.N.: Architectural Styles and the Design of Network-based Software Architectures. University of California, Irvine (2000)
11. Brown, A., Fishenden, J., Thompson, M.: API economy, ecosystems and engagement models. In: Digitizing Government. Business in the Digital Economy, pp 225–236. Palgrave Macmillan, London (2014). https://doi.org/10.1057/9781137443649_13
12. Janes, A., Remencius, T., Sillitti, A., Succi, G.: Towards understanding of structural attributes of web APIs using metrics based on API call responses. In: Corral, L., Sillitti, A., Succi, G., Vlasenko, J., Wasserman, Anthony I. (eds.) OSS 2014. IAICT, vol. 427, pp. 83–92. Springer, Heidelberg (2014). https://doi.org/10.1007/978-3-642-55128-4_11
13. Musser, J.: API Business Models (2013). https://www.slideshare.net/jmusser/j-musser-apibizmodels2013. Accessed 23 June 2020

14. Moilanen, J., Niinioja, M., Seppänen, M., Honkanen, M.: API Economy 101: Changes Your Business. BoD-Books on Demand (2019)
15. The largest companies by turnover in Finland (2016). http://www.largestcompanies.com/toplists/finland/largest-companies-by-turnover. Accessed 25 June 2020

ICO Crowdfunding: Incentives, Pricing Strategy, Token Strategy and Crowd Involvement

Gabriella Laatikainen[1]([✉]), Alexander Semenov[1], Yixin Zhang[2],
and Pekka Abrahamsson[1]

[1] Faculty of Information Technology, University of Jyväskylä,
Jyväskylä, Finland
{gabriella.laatikainen,alexander.semenov,pekka.
abrahamsson}@jyu.fi
[2] Swedish Center for Digital Innovation, University of Gothenborg,
Gothenborg, Sweden
yixin.zhang@ait.gu.se

Abstract. Blockchain technologies provide means to develop services that are secure, transparent and efficient by nature. Unsurprisingly, the emerging business opportunities has gained a lot of interest that is realized in form of successful Initial Coin Offerings (ICOs) that are able to raise billions of USD through crowdfunding campaign. In this exploratory research we study 91 ICOs through content analysis in order to investigate the special characteristics of ICO crowdfunding as business models towards the possible investors. We found that ICOs can be described through (1) the model for providing incentives for investment, (2) the pricing strategy, (3) the token strategy and (4) the activities for crowd involvement in value co-creation.

Keywords: ICO · Blockchain · Crowdfunding · ICOs as business models

1 Introduction

The emergence of blockchain technologies disrupts industries by providing means for decentralization and making data processing more secure and more efficient [1, 2]. Furthermore, it allows both the creation and re-invention of services in different sectors by providing a decentralized environment for value creation. In a blockchain-enabled business environment, nobody has full control and lying about past events is impossible; thus, the role of regulatory actors and intermediaries disappears. Smart contracts (i.e., self-executing digital contracts) and smart properties (i.e., intelligent assets that are controllable through internet) enable the emergence of new types of businesses where organizations operate in a network with limited or no human interactions [3–5].

Initial Coin Offerings (ICOs) represent an unregulated fundraising model for startups that use blockchain technologies [1, 6]. That is, they enable projects to be funded via a crowdfunding model that can be seen as an open call for funds, evaluated and supported by a group of individuals (the crowd) [7]. To date, the most successful

M. Paasivaara and P. Kruchten (Eds.): XP 2020 Workshops, LNBIP 396, pp. 32–40, 2020.
https://doi.org/10.1007/978-3-030-58858-8_4

ICO, Filecoin was able to collect more than $257 million while ICOs raised a total of almost $11.4 billion in 2019 [8].

However, despite of their importance, ICOs are poorly understood [9, 10] and they represent a high-risk investment for investors. First, ICOs exist in an environment with no regulation, and this allows the founders to design any business model that makes their offering attractable without bearing any future consequences. Second, the underlying cryptocurrencies have a high volatility. Third, the health of the blockchain ecosystem depends on the crowd sentiments as well as it is exposed to speculations and manipulation [6, 11].

Recent literature has studied ICOs as a special type of crowdfunding (e.g. [7, 9, 10] and as revenue streams through which firms intend to collect funds for their business ideas [12]. However, in this research, we argue that ICOs can be seen as business models towards the possible investors. First, in case of ICOs the distinction between customers and investors is rather blurry. For example, in case of utility tokens the investors fund the service development for usage rights in return. Furthermore, besides a fundraising model, ICOs also incorporate many other elements that enable the founders to co-create and capture value in collaboration with possible investors. For example, ICOs often provide incentive programs through which investors have a great role in marketing and promoting the service. Thus, in this research, we look at ICOs from a business perspective and our research question is: *What are the key elements of ICOs as business models towards the possible investors?* In order to answer this question and understand the ICO phenomenon better, we collected a sample of 91 ICOs from 14 ICO enlisting sites and studied them through content analysis. The contribution of this study is two-fold. First, the study contributes to the ICO, crowdfunding and business model literature by conceptualizing ICOs as business models towards possible investors and identifying the key constituents. Second, this work has managerial implications by providing an overview of the key elements that practitioners have to make decisions on.

2 Related Work

Crowdfunding represents a way to raise funds for innovative projects by linking directly capital-seeking agents and a crowd of capital-giving agents through an open call via internet [13, 14]. ICOs represent a special type of crowdfunding where founders aim to raise capital for blockchain-enabled services; thus, they can be seen as revenue models towards the crowd [12]. In ICO model, founders organize a token sale when they provide tokens or coins for the initial funders at a discounted price. These tokens may have financial value (i.e., equity or security token), functional value (i.e., utility token) and speculative value (i.e., the value resulting from the impact of token trading on the exchange of cryptocurrencies) [15, 16]. However, there are a couple of special characteristics of ICO campaigns as compared to classical crowdfunding projects. First, the tokens/coins can often be traded before the service is launched [10]. Second, in classical crowdfunding projects the founders and investors are matched via crowdfunding platforms that serve as intermediaries while ICOs are based on P2P interactions without intermediaries [14].

In the literature, different crowdfunding categories exist based on the funders' incentives. Mollick [17] described four contexts in which individuals fund projects. First, some crowdfunding projects, such as humanitarian projects, adopt the *patronage model* where individuals donate and do not expect return. Second, in *lending model*, individuals expect some return on the capital invested. Third, in *reward-based crowdfunding*, individuals receive some kind of reward for supporting the project. The reward can be purchasing products at discounted prices, and in this way the supporters are early customers. Forth, in the *equity model*, crowdfunding supporters become investors, and they can receive equity stake for their funding.

Other categorizations of crowdfunding archetypes include the crowdfounding categories by Belleflame et al. [13]: pre-ordering and profit-sharing, and by Bradford [18]: donation, rewards, pre-ordering, lending and equity. Furthermore, Hemer identified the following crowdfunding types: donation, sponsoring, pre-ordering, membership fees, crediting, lending and profit-sharing [19].

Recent literature on ICO crowdfunding found that the investors are heterogenous and their main motives can be classified into ideology, technology, and financial motives [20]. Moreover, Fridegen et al. identified the following archetypes using cluster analysis: geographically restricted ICOs with hard funding caps and private pre-sales, geographically restricted ICOs with fiat money-oriented pricings and staking tokens, uncapped global foundation ICOs with native blockchain tokens and Global ICOs with hard funding caps [10].

3 Methodology

In order to identify the special characteristics of ICO crowdfunding, we studied the business models of 91 ICOs in May and June 2018. We collected the data by running crawling scripts that gathered the name and the link of the ICOs and the category from each ICO listing site. We aimed to crawl all sites whose primary task was to enlist ICOs. After some exploratory analysis, the crawling scripts were running on the same day in the following sites: bestcoins, coingecko, coinmarketplus, icohotlist, thetokener, icorating, icomap, topicohotlist, coinschedule, icowhatchlist, icotracker, icobazaat, listico and icobench. After identifying the sample frame, we eliminated the duplicates and as a result, the data contained 4127 ICOs. Then we grouped the data by ICO categories[1]. As a final step, we identified the final data sample of 91 ICOs by choosing *randomly* at least three ICOs from each category in order to increase the industry coverage of the sample data.

We used content analysis in the data analysis phase [21]. First, we manually collected and reviewed the available information on the sample ICOs. We reviewed the ICOs websites, the whitepapers and executive summaries as well as read the

---

[1] We grouped our data into the following ICO categories: Internet, Tourism, Cryptocurrency, Business services, Platform, Retail, Investment, Infrastructure, Financial services, Trading, Entertainment, Casino Gambling, Energy, Smart contract, Manufacturing, Media, Communication, Banking, Charity, Virtual Reality, Electronics, Software, Business services, Data analytics, Sports, Real estate and Health.

information on the ICO listing sites. In the first phase of the content analysis, we identified more than 30 ICO characteristics. Then we clustered homogeneous elements and identified the key aspects that are special for blockchain-enabled businesses. In the second phase, we calculated the descriptive statistics. Some of the characteristics could not be found for each ICO. In the calculations, these missing values were not taken into account, i.e. the percentages were calculated so that 100% is the number of ICOs with available data.

During the empirical analysis, we paid special attention to the reliability and validity of the study in each step. First, the listing sites were identified and discussed by two authors. Second, the content analysis was carried out by three authors. Many ICOs were coded by two different persons. In these cases, the results were compared and discussed and the differences were negligible.

4   Findings

Our study revealed that only 84% of the ICOs websites were active after a two-month period, and only 72% were active after two years. Furthermore, based on our findings, even though the quality of the whitepapers differed significantly, in general, the amount of information about the ICOs strategy, vision and operations was rather limited. The whitepapers aimed to describe the ICO's goals and motivation, the underlying blockchain technology, the details of the ICO's financial roadmap, the target customer segments, the key partners, the risks, etc. However, most of the whitepapers lacked some of the information, they were not transparent and not detailed enough. One of the common problems was that they did not contain clear financial roadmap or information on detailed risk assessment.

In this study we looked at ICOs as business models towards possible investors and found that they could be described through the following key characteristics: their approach for providing incentives for investment, their pricing strategy, their token strategy and the activities for crowd involvement in value co-creation. In what follows, we describe each of these elements in more details.

4.1   Strategy for Providing Incentives for Investment: Crowdfunding Types

Based on the possible investors' motives in our sample ICOs, we could differentiate between the following ICO crowdfunding types:

Equity-based ICO crowdfunding: In this model, the investors buy shares from the business and their goal is to make profit. In this case, the majority of the tokens are allocated to the ICOs investors.

Rewards-Based ICO crowdfunding: In this model, the investors get rewards, such as special usage of the service. For example, in case of ICO Wystoken the investors got discounts on the ICO's marketplace on special products.

Subscription-based ICO crowdfunding: In this model, the investors buy the possibility to use the service. For example, the ICO Oneroot provided a set of digital asset infrastructure. Their token did not provide ownership and it could not be exchanged for money; instead, buying their token gave the investors rights to use the service.

A combination of these: For example, the ICO WorldTurtleCoin offered a game platform where the investors could enhance their user experience while using the ICO's tokens in micropayments. This ICO attracted game lovers that bought tokens to use it in payments for the service (i.e., subscription-based ICO crowdfunding); however, the primary incentive for investors was to gain profit (equity-based crowdfunding).

In our data, 72% of the ICOs applied equity-based crowdfunding, 7% reward-based crowdfunding, 4% subscription-based crowdfunding and 17% some kind of combination of these.

4.2 Pricing Strategy: Time-Based Token Valuation

The founders of ICOs organize token sales, through which they offer tokens for the possible investors. These token sales consist of Pre-Sale, Sale and Post-Sale Periods. During these periods the tokens are sold through *time-based token valuation*. This refers to a time-based second type price discrimination technique [22]. During the sale periods, the possible investors can buy the tokens for a discounted price and this price is increasing over time; thus, ICOs apply a market penetration strategy.

At operational level, ICO founders should decide on some additional properties: soft cap and hard cap, country restrictions, accepted currencies, minimum and maximum purchase. The *soft cap* refers to the minimum amount of capital that the ICO needs to gather in order to be considered as successful and to start to develop its service. On the other hand, the *hard cap* is the maximum amount of capital that the ICO aims to collect. It has to be noted that some ICOs are *uncapped* and they collect as much capital as they can. In our sample data, the greatest hard cap was about 30 millions USD.

Another operational aspect is the *country restrictions*. Some of the countries (e.g. U.S., China, Israel, Singapore) have very strict investment regulations that allows only accredited investors to participate in the ICO token sales. Thus, ICOs can choose to follow the regulations and offer the tokens only for accredited investors; or, they can open the sale for everyone and restrict the investors coming from the countries that have strict laws regarding the security of investments. However, in many cases, investors are able to find a workaround to bypass these restrictions, e.g. by using VPN. In our sample, the restricted countries included U.S. (92%), China (66%), Singapore (18%), Canada (7%) and South Korea (7%).

Another characteristic of ICOs is the *accepted currencies*. The investors can pay through different cryptocurrencies as well as, in some cases, in fiat money. In our sample data, 85% of the ICOs accepted ETH as a cryptocurrency, 45% BTC, while fiat money was accepted in 9% of the ICOs. The maximum number of accepted currencies was 45 in our data sample (ICO FeastCoin).

ICOs define the amount of *minimum and maximum purchase* that refers to the minimum and maximum amount of tokens that can be purchased. In our data sample, the maximum amount of tokens was not usually restricted. The minimum amount typically varied between 0.01 and 1 ETH (in cases that ETH was the accepted main currency - this was the case in 85% of our sample data).

4.3   Token Strategy: Sell, Burn, Exchange, Give

The primary goal of ICOs is *selling* tokens. However, in case the hard cap is not reached, the founders typically *burn* the unused tokens or leave them *unburned*. Burning the token makes it non-existent that cannot be bought or sold anymore and thus, it reduces the total supply of available tokens. Leaving the tokens unburned returns the tokens to the founders. In some cases, ICOs redistribute the unused tokens proportionally through *Airdrop* program; thus, the tokens are given away for free. In our sample data, there was only one ICO that had an Airdrop program.

Founders may decide on the possibility to exchange the tokens into other cryptocurrencies or fiat money (i.e., *token liquidity*). Our findings reveal that most of the ICOs did not enclose detailed information regarding this in their whitepaper. In such cases there was no lock-in period but the tokens could be exchanged right after the ICO ended. In other cases, the ICOs described clearly that their tokens could not be exchanged to other currencies. These tokens could then be used only for payments for the service that the ICO developed. Finally, in some cases, the token exchange was restricted during a so-called holding period (e.g. 3 months after the ICO ends) and this temporary restriction kept away speculators.

4.4   Strategy for Crowd Involvement in Value Co-creation: Bounties and Referral Programs

Blockchain-enabled ecosystems provide a distributed environment where the different actors co-create value. ICO founders may involve the crowd in value co-creation through *bounty* programs where they incite investors to perform small tasks and gain some reward (usually in form of tokens) in return. The bounty tasks vary greatly among ICOs; they can be related to marketing, bug reporting, development, promotion, translation, proofreading, website design, etc. We found that 60% of our sample ICOs used bounties.

Another common strategy for crowd involvement in value co-creation is the use of *referral program* as a channel through which customers are reached and targeted. ICOs typically offer the investors the possibility to gain tokens by advertising the ICO to their friends and family, or through their websites or different social media sites. The ICO benefits from this program in three ways. First, due to network effect, the value of their service increases as the number of users increase. Second, the word-of-mouth builds trust in new customers. Third, the program brings cost reduction by decreasing the marketing and advertising costs. In our sample data, 90% of the ICOs had some kind of loyalty program.

5 Discussion and Conclusions

In this study, we took a sample of 4127 ICOs collected from 14 ICO enlisting sites and investigated the key aspects of 91 ICOs by analyzing the information available in the ICO enlisting websites, the ICOs' websites and their whitepapers. We looked at ICOs as business models towards possible investors, and found that ICO founders should decide on the following key elements: (1) what incentives the ICO offers, (2) the details of the pricing strategy, (3) the token strategy, and (4) the programs to involve the crowd in value co-creation.

Related to the first element, in 72% of the cases in our sample, the possible investors had financial motives and the most used crowdfunding type was equity-based. However, some ICOs used reward-based crowdfunding by incenting investors to give funds and get some rewards in return. As a third option, some ICOs sold their tokens as a subscription for their service. That is, investors could use and pay for the services with the ICO's own tokens.

Related to the pricing strategy, this study found that the most used pricing strategy was time-based token validation that could be seen as a market penetration strategy using second-degree price discrimination. Other operational pricing aspects consisted of soft cap and hard cap, accepted currencies, country restrictions and minimum and maximum purchase.

ICOs typically wanted to sell tokens; however, their token strategy determined also whether and under what conditions the tokens should be burned or left unburned, given for free or exchanged into fiat money (i.e., token liquidity). Finally, ICO founders typically used bounties (60% of the cases) and referral programs (90% of the cases) to incite the crowd to actively support value co-creation.

This study contributes to ICO and crowdfunding literature by conceptualizing ICOs as business models towards possible investors where the founders and investors create and capture value together. Furthermore, this research contributes to business model literature by identifying the key elements of ICOs as special type of business models. Finally, this study has managerial implications by identifying key elements that practitioners have to make decisions on.

This study is an exploratory study that has some limitations. First, the sample was collected in a limited period of time that had a limitation on the generalizability of the results because of the fast changes of the market. Second, some of the information on the websites and in the whitepapers were changed during the two-month period that the empirical study was carried out. Furthermore, the available information was not concrete and detailed enough that lead to missing values.

The research area of blockchain technology and ICOs is rather new; thus, it opens many opportunities for further research. As an example, the underlying dynamics of ICOs' success and failures could be investigated using different research methods. Furthermore, the incentives of the ICO investors and the concept of trust in blockchain environment could be studied as well. Finally, the ICO phenomenon could be investigated from the viewpoint of IEEE's ethical design guidelines.

References

1. Fenu, G., Marchesi, L., Marchesi, M., Tonelli, R.: The ICO phenomenon and its relationships with ethereum smart contract environment. In: 2018 International Workshop on Blockchain Oriented Software Engineering (IWBOSE) (2018)
2. Sinegl, J.: Blockchain: disruption by decentralization? MorningStar (2018). http://www.morningstar.com/articles/868019/blockchain-disruption-by-decentralization.html
3. Davidson, S., De Filippi, P., Potts, J.: Economics of blockchain (2016). Available at SSRN 2744751
4. Wright, A., De Filippi, P.: Decentralized blockchain technology and the rise of lex cryptographia (2015). https://papers.ssrn.com/sol3/papers.cfm?abstract_id=2580664
5. Marchesi, M., Ortu, M., Tonelli, R.: Smart contracts vulnerabilities: a call for blockchain software engineering? In: 2018 International Workshop on Blockchain Oriented Software Engineering (IWBOSE) (2018)
6. Ibba, S., Pinna, A., Baralla, G., Marchesi, M.: ICOs overview: should investors choose an ICO developed with the lean startup methodology? In: Garbajosa, J., Wang, X., Aguiar, A. (eds.) XP 2018. LNBIP, vol. 314, pp. 293–308. Springer, Cham (2018). https://doi.org/10.1007/978-3-319-91602-6_21
7. Danmayr, F.: Archetypes of Crowdfunding Platforms: A Multidimensional Comparison. Gabler Verlag, Wiesbaden (2014)
8. ICO statistics (2020). https://www.fundera.com/resources/ico-statistics. Accessed 29 Apr 2020
9. Panin, A., Kemell, K.-K., Hara, V.: Initial coin offering (ICO) as a fundraising strategy: a multiple case study on success factors. In: Hyrynsalmi, S., Suoranta, M., Nguyen-Duc, A., Tyrväinen, P., Abrahamsson, P. (eds.) ICSOB 2019. LNBIP, vol. 370, pp. 237–251. Springer, Cham (2019). https://doi.org/10.1007/978-3-030-33742-1_19
10. Fridgen, G., Regner, F., Schweizer, A., Urbach, N.: Don't slip on the initial coin offering (ICO): a taxonomy for a blockchain-enabled form of crowdfunding (2018)
11. Yadav, M.: Exploring signals for investing in an initial coin offering (ICO) (2017). Available at SSRN 3037106
12. Morkunas, V.J., Paschen, J., Boon, E.: How blockchain technologies impact your business model. Bus. Horiz. **62**(3), 295–306 (2019). https://doi.org/10.1016/j.bushor.2019.01.009
13. Belleflamme, P., Lambert, T., Schwienbacher, A.: Individual crowdfunding practices. Venture Capital **15**(4), 313–333 (2013)
14. Haas, P., Blohm, I., Leimeister, J.M.: An empirical taxonomy of crowdfunding intermediaries. In: ICIS (2014)
15. de Quénetain, S.: Token economics: how to value tokens? https://www.blockchains-expert.com/en/token-economics-how-to-value-tokens/. Accessed 23 Jun 2020
16. Holden, R., Malani, A.: The ICO paradox: transactions costs, token velocity, and token value (no. w26265). National Bureau of Economic Research (2019). https://doi.org/10.3386/w26265
17. Mollick, E.: The dynamics of crowdfunding: an exploratory study. J. Bus. Ventur. **29**(1), 1–16 (2014)
18. Bradford, C.S.: Crowdfunding and the federal securities law. Columbia Bus. Law Rev. **2012**(1) (2012)
19. Hemer, J.: A snapshot on crowdfunding (2011)
20. Fisch, C., Masiak, C., Vismara, S., Block, J.: Motives and profiles of ICO investors. J. Bus. Res. (2019). https://doi.org/10.1016/j.jbusres.2019.07.036

21. Ackland, R.: Web Social Science: Concepts, Data and Tools for Social Scientists in the Digital Age. Sage, Thousand Oaks (2013)
22. Anderson, S.P., Renault, R.: Price discrimination, processed. University of Virginia and Université de Cergy-Pontoise (2008)

What Key Aspects Do ICOs Reveal About Their Businesses?

Gabriella Laatikainen[1]([✉]), Alexander Semenov[1], Yixin Zhang[2],
and Pekka Abrahamsson[1]

[1] Faculty of Information Technology, University of Jyväskylä,
Jyväskylä, Finland
{gabriella.laatikainen,alexander.semenov,
pekka.abrahamsson}@jyu.fi
[2] Swedish Center for Digital Innovation, University of Gothenburg,
Gothenburg, Sweden
yixin.zhang@ait.gu.se

Abstract. Blockchain technologies disrupt industries by enabling decentralized and transactional data sharing across a network of untrusted participants, among others. Initial Coin Offerings (ICOs) are a novel form of crowdfunding through which hundreds of blockchain-enabled businesses manage to raise billions of dollars in total only in United States. However, there is a lack of understanding of the ICO phenomenon especially related to the business aspects. In this paper, we describe the results of an exploratory study of 91 ICOs and identify the key business model elements that ICOs reveal in their websites and whitepapers. Furthermore, we also note the immaturity and lack of transparency of the business aspects of businesses behind the ICO campaigns.

Keywords: ICO · Blockhain · Business models

1 Introduction

The emergence of blockchain technologies sparked a lot of interest towards the blockchain technology. Initial Coin Offerings (ICOs) represent an unregulated fundraising model that enable blockchain-based projects to be funded via crowd-funding model [1, 2]. To date, the most successful ICO, Filecoin was able to collect more than 257 million USD while the average ICO raised a total of almost $11.4 billion in 2019 [3]. It has to be noted that besides providing an easy opportunity to gain great profits, ICOs are often frauds that fund scams.

ICOs are poorly understood and there is a need for more research in this area [4, 5]. Earlier research discusses how blockchain technology impacts the business models of existing companies using case study methodology and literature review (e.g. [6, 7]). However, research is still nascent related to the means of possible ICO investors to get an overview of how the business behind the ICO makes money (i.e., the business model). Thus, this study focuses on blockchain-enabled business models and aims to answer the following research question: *What business model characteristics do blockchain-enabled businesses reveal in their ICO's websites and whitepapers?* To

M. Paasivaara and P. Kruchten (Eds.): XP 2020 Workshops, LNBIP 396, pp. 41–49, 2020.
https://doi.org/10.1007/978-3-030-58858-8_5

answer this question, we collected a sample of 91 ICOs from 14 ICO enlisting sites and studied the business model aspects of these ICOs through content analysis. This study contributes to the growing body of blockchain literature by identifying the revealed business model elements of blockchain-enabled businesses that aim to raise funds through ICOs. These insights can be used both in further research and in practice.

2   Related Work

A firm's business model is a conceptual model of a business: a description of how a company organizes itself, operates, and creates value [8, 9]. It is an abstract concept; it can be seen as a representation of a company or as a tool that provides a picture of a firm's competitiveness [10]. Business models are often viewed from a component-oriented perspective. Despite the business models' importance, researchers have not formed a consensus regarding either the core components of business models or their level of abstraction [11]. However, most researchers agree that business models contain the following key components: (1) *value proposition* (i.e., the product and/or service portfolio), (2) *revenue logic* (i.e., a top-level description of a business's revenue sources) and (3) *activities* (i.e., actions in order to create and deliver values to customers) [8, 10–12].

Blockchain can be seen as a distributed database that maintains a continuously growing list of records linked to each other [13]. Blockchain database is secure by design, and once the block is recorded there, it cannot be modified retroactively. Blockchain relies on a peer to peer (p2p) network without any central coordinating node. Technically, each transaction contains a small piece of code that allows complex cryptographic validation of transactions. This code presents a smart contract that is defined as "complex application involving having digital assets being directly controlled by a piece of code implementing arbitrary rules" [14]. Thus, these self-executing digital contracts (i.e. smart contracts) and intelligent assets that are controllable through internet (i.e., smart properties) enable the emergence of new types of businesses where organizations operate in a network with limited or no human interactions [15].

Blockchain technologies affect the business models in different ways, such as by authenticating traded goods, via disintermediation and via lowering transaction costs [7]. Related to the value proposition, Morkunas et al. found that blockchain technology can provide verifiability, access to new products and services, faster or less expensive transactions, and fewer middle layers [6]. The greatest revenue stream for blockchain-enabled businesses is the possibility to raise funds through ICOs; however, other revenue sources are transaction fees and service or platform fees [6]. Key activities include transforming the business processes and the key resource is the peer-to-peer network [6].

3   Methodology

We studied the business aspects of 91 ICOs in May and June 2018 in order to identify the special characteristics of blockchain-enabled business models. In the next sub-section we describe the data sample and the data collection. Then, we overview the details of the data analysis.

3.1   Data Sample

To ease the process of the data collection, we run crawling scripts that collected the ICOs name, link and category from each ICO listing sites. We aimed to crawl all the sites whose primary task is to enlist ICOs and we used Google search to identify these. After some exploratory exercises, the crawling scripts for 14 websites were running on the same day. We gathered the data from the following websites: Bestcoins, Coingecko, Coinmarketplus, Icohotlist, the tokener, icorating, icomap, topicohotlist, coinschedule, icowhatchlist, icotracker, icobazaat, listico and icobench.

After identifying the sample frame, we eliminated the duplicates and the resulting dataset contained 4127 ICOs. Then, we grouped the data by the ICOs categories[1]. As a final step, we identified the final data sample by choosing randomly at least three ICOs from each category in order to increase the industry coverage of the sample data.

3.2   Content Analysis

In the data analysis phase, we used content analysis [16]. First, we manually collected information on the sample ICOs' business models. We used the ICOs websites, the whitepapers and executive summaries as well as data on the ICO listing sites as data sources. In the first phase of the content analysis, we identified the characteristics of the ICOs business models. The gathered information included more than 30 business model characteristics, out of which many aspect could not be found for many ICOs. In the second phase, we clustered homogeneous elements and identified the business model aspects that are special for blockchain-enabled businesses.

Second, we calculated the descriptive statistics. Some of the characteristics could not be find in case of every ICO. In the calculations, these missing values were not taken into account, i.e. the percentages were calculated so that 100% is the number of ICOs with available data.

During our empirical analysis, we paid special attention to the reliability and validity of the study in each step. First, the listing sites were identified and discussed by two authors. Second, the content analysis were carried out by three authors. In order to avoid coder bias, we cross-validated the results and some of the ICOs were coded by

---

[1] We grouped our data into the following ICO categories: Internet, Tourism, Cryptocurrency, Business services, Platform, Retail, Investment, Infrastructure, Financial services, Trading, Entertainment, Casino Gambling, Energy, Smart contract, Manufacturing, Media, Communication, Banking, Charity, Virtual Reality, Electronics, Software, Business services, Data analytics, Sports, Real estate and Health.

two different persons. In these cases, the results were compared and discussed and the differences were negligible.

4   Findings

Our study revealed that after a two-month period, only 84% of the ICOs websites were active and only 72% after two years. Furthermore, based on our findings, even though the quality of the whitepapers differed significantly, in general, the amount of information about the ICOs strategy, vision and operations was rather limited. The whitepapers aimed to describe the ICO's goals and motivation, the underlying blockchain technology, the details of the ICO's financial roadmap, the target customer segments, the key partners, the risks, etc. However, most of the whitepapers lacked some of the information, they were not transparent and not detailed enough. One of the common problems was that they did not contain clear financial roadmap or information on detailed risk assessment. However, in what follows, we describe the common patterns on different aspects of the ICO's business models.

4.1   The Value Proposition

The ICOs described the value proposition in their whitepaper (i.e., the blockchain-enabled service that they developed) through two common aspects: the service characteristics and the benefits of blockchain technology. It has to be noted, that in some cases, the advantages of blockchain-based service as compared to a similar service that uses alternative technologies remained unclear.

Service Characteristics. One of the important aspects of the service that they develop is the underlying blockchain *platform* that they build their solution on. Our results showed that the most used platform was the Ethereum platform and the tokens were ERC20 tokens. In our sample, 89% of the ICOs used Ethereum as a base platform. The second most used platform in our sample data was Bitcoin, followed by Waves, Lisk, MultiChain, Pivx, etc.

Some of the ICOs do not use *public* blockchain, but they build their own *private* network. That is, instead of allowing everyone to participate in the network, and encouraging more participants to join, joining a private blockchain requires an invitation and complying with a set of rules. This restriction on the participants can be regulated by existing nodes, a regulatory authority or a consortium. The greatest advantage of using a private blockchain as compared to the public one is that it requires less computational power due to the smaller number of nodes and it assures higher level of privacy and security requirements. In our sample, there was only one ICO whose value proposition was based on a private blockchain.

Benefits of Blockchain Technology. Based on the sample data, the value of the offering was mainly described through the benefits of blockchain technology.

First, ICOs promised to provide a quality service that was more secure and confident because of the use of blockchain technology. For example, the ICO Adamant provided a private messenger platform where the blockchain technology ensured that no one had access to private data except of the owner.

Second, businesses could take use of the transparency and resistance to data manipulation that the blockchain technology provided. For example, the ICO Affchain offered a marketing protocol and a marketplace where businesses and affiliates met and made deals in online advertising. The ICO provided a cryptographically verifiable value distribution mode that increased the level of trust and enabled cost-reduction for the parties because of automatic verification without human interactions.

Third, businesses could offer cost reduction because of the distributed network where intermediaries were not needed. In blockchain-enabled businesses users could find and contact each other directly that lead to reduced transaction costs. For example, the ICO Lotuscore provided a game platform and the players were able to trade games with friends while the developers earned 100% of the revenue derived from selling their digital game.

Forth, blockchain-enabled services could provide more power for the users. In a blockchain-enabled network there was no centralized influence and thus, the control was distributed. For example, the ICO OneRoot proposed a platform that enabled building relationships based on equal co-operation and common development instead of an ecosystem with centralized entities.

Fifth, blockchain-enabled services benefitted from the self-executing smart contracts where no or limited human interactions were needed to ensure different processes. This simplified work processes and thus, it caused cost-reduction. For example, the ICO VLux proposed a renewable energy trading solution that promised cost reduction due to trading at optimal times.

Sixth, in some cases, blockchain-enabled services allowed users to pay anonymously in order to ensure their privacy. For example, the ICO Clean SL8 provided a communication platform for life coaching where the users valued privacy and the ability to stay anonymous.

Seventh, blockchain-enabled services provided the possibility of using cryptocurrencies as payments for the ICOs service. For example, in an ICO project Lunar, the founders proposed online dating services. Users needed to pay in cryptocurrency in order to communicate with other users.

Eighth, some of the value proposition of ICOs were unique because they were related to blockchain technologies or the cryptocurrencies. Indeed, new businesses emerged that addressed the possible investors' interest in blockchain. For example, the ICO Takeprofit provided a platform where experienced traders offered their advice on cryptography investments for inexperienced users.

4.2 Revenue Logic

In this study, we found that in most cases, the revenue logic of ICOs towards the customers was not well described. The ICOs gave some hints on the ways that the business might bring profits; however, the detailed concrete description on the revenue sources and the magnitude of the revenues was frequently missing in the sample we collected.

As a general note, the results of this study showed that the commonly used pricing models did not differ significantly from the businesses that offered a similar service without the use of blockchain technology. In other words, the pricing models depended mostly on the type of the service that the ICOs offered. The most used pricing models in our sample were the following: (1) *pay-per-use* (customers are charged a so-called transaction fee each time they use the service), (ii) *advertisement model* (customers use the service for free and advertisers pay for their advertisements that are shown to the users), (iii) *micropayments* (In ICOs that provide gaming platforms, micropayments are used to enhance the players' user experience) and (iv) *price discrimination* (different prices are charged depending on customers' characteristics, such as financial status or country [17]).

4.3   Activities

The activities that ICOs promised to perform could be investigated from the data on the usage of funds that described the activities and other cost factors that the collected money would be used for. In order to create and deliver values to their customers, the ICOs had to develop their service, market it to the customers, provide maintenance and administrative services, solve legal conflicts, and so on.

One of the special characteristics of blockchain-enabled business model is the importance of the ecosystem around the service where the actors jointly create value. One example could be the *bounty* program that ICOs provide to incite investors to perform small tasks and gain some reward (usually in form of tokens) in return. The bounty tasks vary greatly among ICOs; they can be related to marketing, bug reporting, development, promotion, translation, proofreading, website design, etc. We found that 60% of our sampled ICOs used bounties.

Another example of value co-creation is the use of *referral program* as a channel through which customers are reached and targeted [18]. ICOs typically offer the investors the possibility to gain tokens by advertising the ICO to their friends and family, or through their websites or different social media sites. The ICO benefits from this program in three ways. First, due to network effect, the value of their service increases as the number of users increase. Second, the word-of-mouth builds trust in new customers. Third, the program brings cost reduction by decreasing the marketing and advertising costs. In our sample data, 90% of the ICOs had some kind of loyalty program.

5   Discussion and Conclusions

In this study we took a sample of 4127 ICOs collected from 14 ICO enlisting sites and investigated the business model aspects of 91 ICOs by analyzing the ICO enlisting websites, the ICOs' websites and their whitepapers. We found that the amount of available information on the ICOs business models was rather limited. That is, the websites and the whitepapers lacked important details and concrete data on the business strategy. However, our study found common patterns that blockchain-enabled businesses revealed about their business models in the whitepapers of their ICO.

In Table 1, the business model aspects of blockchain-enabled businesses are summarized. The findings revealed that ICOs built their value proposition on the benefits of the blockchain technology, such as security, transparency, confidentiality. In blockchain-enabled businesses middlemen were not needed, and this might cause cost reduction. The self-executing smart contracts simplified processes because they eliminated or mitigated the need for human interactions. Furthermore, in a blockchain-enabled service different cryptocurrencies could be used for payments.

The revenue logic towards the customers was based on the type of the service rather than on blockchain characteristics. For example, game platforms used micropayments while electronic marketplaces got their revenues from advertisements.

In blockchain-enabled businesses, the actors of the ecosystem (e.g. investors, users) were involved in different activities that the service required to create and deliver value. For example, the referral programs provided incentives for the actors to advertise the service to their friends, family and other individuals. Besides, everybody could perform specific tasks related to development and marketing of the service and get some rewards in return.

Table 1 Blockchain-enabled business models aspects revealed from ICOs' whitepapers

Value proposition	*Service and platform characteristics*: Ethereum (89% of the ICOs), Bitcoin, Waves, Lisk, MultiChain, Pivx *Technology-enabled benefits*: security, transparency, confidentiality, no intermediaries, simplified processes, possible cost reduction, using cryptocurrencies as payments, possibility to stay anonymous
Revenue logic	Common revenue models include pay-per-use, advertisements, micropayments
Activities	Service development, marketing, maintenance and administrative services, solving legal conflicts, implementing referral programs and bounties (60% of the sample had bounties)

This study found that only 84% of the ICOs websites were active after a two-months period and only 72% were active after two years. The reasons for an ICO not to continue its business can vary. First, if it does not get the amount of funds required for the development of the service (Soft Cap), then the money can be returned to the investors and stop the business. Second, there is no guarantee that ICOs give the investors' money back. Thus, it can happen, that ICOs shut down their websites and take the money they received as funds without any consequences. This is the consequence of the unregulated environment where ICOs are not bound to economic regulations and laws and thus, ICOs provide easy means for frauds.

This study is an exploratory study that has some limitations. First, the sample was collected in a limited period of time that had a limitation on the generalizability of the results because of the fast changes of the market. Second, some of the information on the websites and in the whitepapers were changed after the two-month period that the empirical study was carried out. Furthermore, the available information was not concrete and detailed enough. Thus, there is a need for additional research in this area that allows us to compare the results and give us further insights. For example, the ICOs studied in this research could be analyzed again to investigate how their business model changed based on longitudinal data.

References

1. Fenu, G., Marchesi, L., Marchesi, M., Tonelli, R.: The ICO phenomenon and its relationships with Ethereum smart contract environment. In: 2018 International Workshop on Blockchain Oriented Software Engineering (IWBOSE) (2018)
2. Ibba, S., Pinna, A., Baralla, G., Marchesi, M.: ICOs overview: should investors choose an ICO developed with the lean startup methodology? In: Garbajosa, J., Wang, X., Aguiar, A. (eds.) XP 2018. LNBIP, vol. 314, pp. 293–308. Springer, Cham (2018). https://doi.org/10.1007/978-3-319-91602-6_21
3. ICO Statistics (2020). https://www.fundera.com/resources/ico-statistics. Accessed 29 Apr 2020
4. Panin, A., Kemell, K.-K., Hara, V.: Initial coin offering (ICO) as a fundraising strategy: a multiple case study on success factors. In: Hyrynsalmi, S., Suoranta, M., Nguyen-Duc, A., Tyrväinen, P., Abrahamsson, P. (eds.) ICSOB 2019. LNBIP, vol. 370, pp. 237–251. Springer, Cham (2019). https://doi.org/10.1007/978-3-030-33742-1_19
5. Fisch, C., Masiak, C., Vismara, S., Block, J.: Motives and profiles of ICO investors. J. Bus. Res. (2019, in press)
6. Morkunas, V.J., Paschen, J., Boon, E.: How blockchain technologies impact your business model. Bus. Horiz. 62(3), 295–306 (2019). https://doi.org/10.1016/j.bushor.2019.01.009
7. Nowiński, W., Kozma, M.: How can blockchain technology disrupt the existing business models? Entrep. Bus. Econ. Rev. 5(3), 173–188 (2017)
8. Massa, L., Tucci, C.L., Afuah, A.: A critical assessment of business model research. Acad. Manage. Ann. 11(1), 73–104 (2017)
9. Magretta, J.: Why business models matter. Harv. Bus. Rev. 80, 86–87 (2002)
10. Laatikainen, G.: Financial Aspects of Business Models: Reducing Costs and Increasing Revenues in a Cloud Context. Jyväskylä Studies in Computing, p. 278 (2018)
11. Luoma, E.: Examining Business Models of Software-as-a-Service Firms. Jyväskylä Studies in Computing (2013)
12. Zott, C., Amit, R.: Business model design: An activity system perspective. Long Range Plan. 43(2–3), 216–226 (2010)
13. Yli-Huumo, J., Ko, D., Choi, S., Park, S., Smolander, K.: Where is current research on blockchain technology?—a systematic review. PLoS ONE 11(10), e0163477 (2016)
14. Ethereum whitepaper. https://github.com/ethereum/wiki/wiki/White-Paper. Accessed 5 June 2018

15. Davidson, S., De Filippi, P., Potts, J.: Economics of Blockchain (2016)
16. Ackland, R.: Web Social Science: Concepts, Data and Tools for Social Scientists in the Digital Age. Sage (2013)
17. Anderson, S.P., Renault, R.: Price discrimination. University of Virginia and Université de Cergy-Pontoise (2008)
18. Ciaian, P., Rajcaniova, M., Kancs, D.: The economics of BitCoin price formation. Appl. Econ. **48**(19), 1799–1815 (2016)

Product Roadmap Alignment – Achieving the Vision Together: A Grey Literature Review

Stefan Trieflinger[1](✉), Jürgen Münch[1], Emre Bogazköy[1],
Patrick Eißler[1], Jan Schneider[1], and Bastian Roling[2]

[1] Reutlingen University, Alteburgstraße 150, 72762 Reutlingen, Germany
{stefan.trieflinger,
juergen.muench}@reutlingen-university.de,
{emre.bogazkoey,patrick_denis.eissler,
jan_philip.schneider}@student.reutlingen-university.de
[2] Viastore Software GmbH, Magirusstraße 13, 70469 Stuttgart, Germany
b.roling@viastore.com

Abstract. Context: A product roadmap is an important tool in product development. It sets the strategic direction in which the product is to be developed to achieve the company's vision. However, for product roadmaps to be successful, it is essential that all stakeholders agree with the company's vision and objectives and are aligned and committed to a common product plan. **Objective:** In order to gain a better understanding of product roadmap alignment, this paper aims at identifying measures, activities and techniques in order to align the different stakeholders around the product roadmap. **Method:** We conducted a grey literature review according the guidelines to Garousi et al. **Results:** Several approaches to gain alignment were identified such as defining and communicating clear objectives based on the product vision, conducting cross-functional workshops, shuttle diplomacy, and mission briefing. In addition, our review identified the "Behavioural Change Stairway Model" that suggests five steps to gain alignment by building empathy and a trustful relationship.

Keywords: Product management · Product roadmap · Stakeholder alignment · Business agility · User experience · Objectives and key results

1 Introduction

An essential aspect for achieving product success in the software-intensive business is that all stakeholders, i.e., all internal and external people who are involved in the product development and related activities (such as engineering, user experience, marketing, sales, suppliers etc.) are aligned and committed around a common product plan. Usually this plan is visualized in the product roadmap. A product roadmap describes how an organization intends to achieve a product vision. It should focus on the value it aims to deliver to its customers and the organization itself in order to rally support and coordinate effort among stakeholders [1]. Consequently, the main purpose of a product roadmap is to provide a high-level view of the direction of the product planning incorporating all key perspectives that supports the strategic dialogue about

M. Paasivaara and P. Kruchten (Eds.): XP 2020 Workshops, LNBIP 396, pp. 50–57, 2020.
https://doi.org/10.1007/978-3-030-58858-8_6

the future product portfolio. The concept of a product roadmap has changed significantly in recent years. New ways of working such as DevOps, continuous delivery and the increasing use of customer data require to have much more flexible product roadmap formats. Alignment around the product roadmap is important to ensure that each employee is involved in achieving the goals in the product roadmap, so that all activities within product development contribute to achieving the product vision [1]. Alignment means a concerted effort to help people understand the issues and what their respective roles are. Therefore, the product roadmaps will not fulfill its purpose without alignment and buy-in of the key stakeholders. In practice, however, it can be observed that most companies still work in silos, i.e. there is poor communication and cooperation between the different departments of a company [2]. Moreover, stakeholders often do not have consistent and department-specific representations of a common high-level product roadmap that reflects their information needs (e.g., the department product management requires different information on the product roadmap than the department engineering) [3]. One consequence of this situation is that often each department identifies and pursues its own goals and creates its own roadmap independently of the larger goals of the company. Thereby, individual goals are often placed above corporate goals. As a result, not every product activity contributes to achieving the company's vision and goals, thus wasting important organizational resources [2, 4].

The current scientific literature provides only little knowledge on how alignment can be achieved around a product roadmap [5]. In order to close this gap, the aim of this paper is to identify measures, methods and techniques that help companies to achieve alignment based on the analysis of the so-called "grey literature" (i.e., white papers, articles, blogs, business bocks etc.). It should be stressed that this article refers to alignment of different stakeholders around product roadmaps and not roadmaps in general.

2 Related Work

In the scientific literature, few approaches for gaining alignment around a product roadmap can be found. In the following, selected examples are sketched. Khurum and Gorschek [6] describe a method to evaluate the degree of alignment between success-critical stakeholders with respect to the understanding and interpretation of a product strategy. The method also covers misalignments and enables the identification of leading causes. Furthermore, Luftman [7] presents a "strategic alignment maturity assessment tool" which consists of 38 alignment practices grouped into six categories. An organization can evaluate its current maturity level of alignment by giving a score for each alignment practice, averaging the scores for each category and summing up the corresponding average scores. The authors point out that the most valuable part of the assessment is not the assessment itself but understanding its impact on the entire organization and what needs to be done to improve alignment. Barney et al. [8] present a case study in order to understand different levels of alignment between key stakeholders with respect to software quality attributes. As the main reason for the low alignment between different stakeholders, the authors identified among other things insufficiently defined quality requirements and a culture that does not question management decisions. Moreover Lehtola et al. [9] report lessons learned from one software product company that introduced roadmapping processes in order to tie the business viewpoint to requirements engineering decision making and to improve the communication between different stakeholder groups. The authors indicate that if just one person or one function is responsible for the roadmapping process, the other stakeholders may not see the benefits from their viewpoints and therefore feel unmotivated. Finally, Suomalainen et al. [10] point out that typically 1–5 person should participate in the roadmapping process and identified the following as the most important stakeholders of the product roadmapping process: 1) product management, 2) marketing, 3) customer and partner representatives and 4) development including manufacturing and engineering.

3 Research Approach

In order to conduct the study in a systematic and repeatable manner, the study at hand follows the guidelines according to Garousi et al. [11]. These guidelines consider three mains phases: 1) planning the review, 2) conducting the review, and 3) reporting the review. The individual phases are described below.

3.1 Planning the Review

Identification of the Need of a Grey Literature Review (GLR): First, we assessed whether a GLR is the appropriate method for our study. For this purpose, we used the checklist developed by Garousi et al. [11]. A recent review of the scientific literature about product roadmaps has shown that most scientific articles do not address product roadmaps operationally or refer to modern product management practices [5]. Furthermore, an initial review of the grey literature on product roadmapping in general and the conduction of expert interviews [4, 12] indicate that the topic product roadmap alignment is highly relevant and of great interest for practitioners. In order to obtain more insights, the conduction of a grey literature review is an appropriate approach and contributes to the transfer of practical knowledge in the scientific community.

Formulation of the Research Question: Based on the study goals we have defined the following research question:

- **RQ1:** Which measures, methods and techniques are reported in the grey literature in order to achieve alignment around the product roadmap?

Identification of the Search String: Our search term was developed in a brainstorming session that aimed at identifying grey literature about product roadmapping in general. In order to obtain sufficient results and cover our objectives we evolved the search term iteratively. At the end of the search process we identified "alignment around the product roadmap" as one of five main issues. Detailed information about the search process can be found in [13]. After evaluating different options, we have defined the following search terms:

A1: Innovation; A2: Product*; A3: Product Management; A4: Agile; A5: Outcome* driven; A6: Outcome* oriented; A7: Goal* oriented; A8: Theme*; A9: Roadmap*

The complete search string used in our study was:

(A1 OR A2 OR A3 OR A4 OR A5 OR A6 OR A7 OR A8) AND A9

Definition of the Inclusion/Exclusion Criteria: In order to filter relevant from irrelevant articles, we defined the inclusion and exclusion criteria as shown in Table 1.

Table 1. Inclusion and exclusion criteria

Inclusion	• The article discusses the application of product roadmapping in practice
	• The article was published in English
	• The URL is working and freely available
Exclusion	• The source is non text-based
	• The article contains duplicated content of a previously examined article
	• The article is not suitable for software-intensive businesses

3.2   Conducting the Review

Conduction of the Study Selection Process. The data retrieval process was performed by using the predefined search string and applying it to the Google search engine (google.com). In order to avoid biased results based on past activities the search was conducted in the incognito mode of the browser. Further, a VPN service was used to anonymize the location from which the search was conducted. Moreover, the relevance ranking was applied, which ranks the results according to the Google PageRank algorithm. To increase the amount of available URL's the Google option to include similar results was activated. The search was conducted on January 17th, 2020 and yielded in 426 hits. In addition to the search process, we conducted snowballing (i.e., considering further articles that are recommended in an article). This led to 53 further articles. After the application of the selection process (1) scan title, (2) removal of duplicates, (3) applying inclusion and exclusion criteria, (4) scan abstract, (5) scan full text) we obtained 170 relevant articles which address the main topic product roadmapping in a dynamic and uncertain market environment. On this basis we have categorized the 170 articles according to five subject areas: (1) product roadmap formats, (2) product roadmapping processes, (3) product roadmap prioritization techniques, (4) alignment of different stakeholders around the product roadmap, and (5) challenges and pitfalls regarding product roadmapping). This led to 16 relevant articles that deal with the topic alignment of different stakeholders around the product roadmap. Five of these articles are presented in this article. A list of the remaining 11 articles can be found on Figshare [14].

Quality Assessment: The criterion for the quality assessment was that the reviewers were able to comprehend the suggested approach based on their practical experience. In addition, all steps of the selection procedure were carried out individually by two reviewers. In the case that the individual reviews led to different results, the process was carried out by a third reviewer to make a final inclusion/exclusion decision.

4 Threats of Validity

We use the framework based on Wohlin et al. [15] as the basis for the discussion of the validity of our study. **Construct validity:** First the construct validity is threatened by the Google search engine regarding the accessibility of search results. After the application of the search string Google returns 78.300.000 articles, but we have only access on 426 articles. We cannot know whether these 426 articles were representative of the total search result of 78.300.000 articles. Moreover, there may be articles that deal with product roadmapping but use the terms that were not covered by our search string. **Internal validity**: In order to mitigate this thread, the quality assessment was conducted by two reviewers independently to limit confirmation bias and interpretation bias. In the case that the individual reviews led to different results, the process was repeated by a third reviewer in order to make a final decision. **External Validity:** The results and conclusion relate to product roadmapping in a dynamic market environment with high uncertainties (e.g., the software-intensive business). Therefore, the results are not directly transferable to other industry sectors. **Conclusion validity**: In order to mitigate this risk, we have presented and discussed our findings with practitioners of the software-intensive business. In this context no major ambiguities or inconsistencies were found [15, 16].

5 Results

In order to answer our research question, we analyzed the relevant articles and identified the following measures, methods and techniques that can be used to gain alignment around the product roadmap.

Foster Alignment with Shared Vision and Goals (OKRs). Khanna [17] presents an approach to reach vertical and horizontal alignment. Vertical alignment means to make sure that everyone's goals are aligned across the different layers of a company. In contrast, horizontal alignment represents the collaboration between product teams with other stakeholder such as design, engineering, operation and marketing. In order to achieve a vertical and horizontal alignment, the author recommends as a first step the definition of a clear vision and strategy and its communication throughout the company. Based on the product vision, objectives and key results (OKRs) should be defined, which are broken down and communicated across the different levels of the company. The aim of this activity is that everyone truly understands what strategic direction the company wants to take and how everyone can contribute to the larger goal of the company. In this context, Harke [18] recommends using a mixture of a top-down and bottom-up approach. Besides the definition of a clear vision, Khanna [17] suggests utilizing the following activities: 1) the conduction of weekly progress updates between the management and the product teams in order to ensure that the product activities are focused towards institutional objectives, while fostering transparency across the different levels of the company, 2) the performance of regular cross-functional meetings on the operative level to discuss the future product strategy and eliminate ambiguities regarding the direction of the future product portfolio, and 3) the publication and communication of a product roadmap that lets product teams and stakeholders know which direction the company will take in the future and which topics can be expected.

Lombardo et al. [1] propose shuttle diplomacy, meetings and workshops, and software applications (or some combination thereof) as means to achieve alignment and buy-in around the product roadmap.

Shuttle Diplomacy. Shuttle diplomacy involves the conduction of one-on-one meetings with each stakeholder to manage and coordinate their expectations and reach agreement on what the current and future product will be. The idea of this approach is to identify the individual's goals, priorities as well as other considerations by discussing a draft of the roadmap and reflect whether the stakeholders' views are in line with the organization's goals and vision. The one-on-one meetings foster the trust of each stakeholder by listening to them and asking questions why and how things are important for them.

Meetings and Co-creation Workshops. The presentation of recommendations at a meeting or the conduction of co-creation workshops can support alignment under certain conditions (e.g., if a culture exists that encourages constructive disagreement). Co-creation workshops are less about presenting a plan and more an interactive event to create a plan. Care should be taken to ensure that the workshops have clearly defined outcomes and a plan for achieving these outcomes before it takes place. A co-creation workshop can follow a shuttle diplomacy effort. However, in some situations (e.g., small teams) it might be useful to skip the one-on-one meetings and go straight to the workshops.

Software Applications. Since geographically distributed teams and remote work are becoming increasingly common, it might be difficult to conduct one-on-one shuttle diplomacies or co-creation workshops. Therefore, Lombardo et al. recommend using software applications such as "Roadmunk", "Aha!" or "ProductPlan". The combination of such tools with other communications and tracking tools (such as "JIRA"; "Slack", "GoogleDocs", "Asana" or "Trello") can help to create alignment by allowing the teams to agree on topics. The tools also help to raise, manage and track issues and prioritize/reprioritize as necessary.

Mission Briefing. Stephen Bungay [19] proposes to create a "mission briefing" as a means to reach alignment. Ideally, the entire product team works out the various sections of the mission letter jointly and iteratively. Since decisions made in one section strongly influence the other sections, it is advisable to work through each section before moving on to the next section. The mission briefing consists of the following five elements: 1) context, 2) higher intent, 3) team intent, 4) key implied tasks, and 5) boundaries. The section "context" describes the current market situation, the problem the product addresses and possible next steps regarding the evolution of the product. The section "higher intent" outlines the overarching corporate strategy and its relationship to specific activities. The identification of customer and business outcomes including appropriate metrics is addressed in the section "team intend". Within the section "key implied tasks" the forthcoming challenges as well as the persons who act as a contact person for the respective challenges are identified. Finally, the overall scope for the other sections is described in the section "boundaries".

Behavioural Change Stairway Model. Pichler [20] points out that a good way to gain alignment is to carefully listen to the stakeholders, empathise with the stakeholders, and build a trustful relationship. Therefore, the author suggests using the so-called "Behavioural Change Stairway Model" that intends to take the negotiator from listening to influencing the behaviour of other persons. The model consists of the following five stages: 1) active listening (i.e., make an effort to empathically listen to other person while suspending judgement), 2) empathy (i.e., understand the perspective, needs and interests of each individual), 3) rapport (i.e., build rapport and establish trust) 4) influence (i.e., help other persons let go of their position and look for a solution that at least partially addresses the needs of each individual involved), 5) behavioural change (i.e., agree on an acceptable solution).

6   Summary

Alignment with a product roadmap is extremely important to ensure that all product development activities contribute to the achievement of corporate goals. The results of the grey literature review presented in this article have in common that achieving alignment should start with a clear vision. Then the vision should be transformed into a strategy with clear goals that can be integrated into a product roadmap and communicated across the organization. This should involve all relevant stakeholders. The aim is that every involved person identifies with this vision and directs his or her activities towards achieving this vision. Besides this, the grey literature review helped to identify several approaches and tactics to gain alignment around the product roadmap. Before applying any of these methods, it should be ensured that the expected results and the purpose of applying the method are clearly defined and communicated to the participants and that the way to achieve the results is well structured.

References

1. Lombardo, C.T., McCarthy, B., Ryan, E., Conners, M.: Product Roadmaps Relaunched - How to Set Direction while Embracing Uncertainty. O'Reilly Media Inc., Sebastopol (2017)
2. Lencioni, P.: Silos, Politics and Turf Wars: A Leadership Fable About Destroying the Barriers that Turn Colleagues into Competitors. Jossey-Bass, San Francisco (2006)
3. Münch, J., Trieflinger, S., Lang, D.: The product roadmap maturity model DEEP: validation of a method for assessing the product roadmap capabilities of organizations. In: Hyrynsalmi, S., Suoranta, M., Nguyen-Duc, A., Tyrväinen, P., Abrahamsson, P. (eds.) ICSOB 2019. LNBIP, vol. 370, pp. 97–113. Springer, Cham (2019). https://doi.org/10.1007/978-3-030-33742-1_9
4. Münch, J., Trieflinger, S., Lang, D.: What's hot in product roadmapping? Key practices and success factors. In: Franch, X., Männistö, T., Martínez-Fernández, S. (eds.) PROFES 2019. LNCS, vol. 11915, pp. 401–416. Springer, Cham (2019). https://doi.org/10.1007/978-3-030-35333-9_29
5. Münch J., Trieflinger S., Lang, D.: Product roadmap – from vision to reality: a systematic literature review. In: International Conference on Engineering, Technology and Innovation, ICE/IEEE ITMC. IEEE (2019)

6. Khurum, M., Gorschek, T.: A method for alignment evaluation of product strategies among stakeholders (MASS) in software intensive product development. J. Soft. Maint. Evol. Res. Pract. **23**(7), 494–516 (2011)

7. Luftman, J.: Assessing IT/business alignment. Inf. Syst. Manage. **20**(4), 9–15 (2003)

8. Barney, S., Wohlin, C., Chatzipetrou, P., Angelis, L.: Offshore insourcing: a case study on software quality alignment. In: Proceedings of IEEE Sixth International Conference on Global Software Engineering, pp. 146–155 (2011)

9. Lehtola, L., Kauppinen, M., Kujala, S.: Linking the business view to requirements engineering: long-term product planning by roadmapping. In: Proceedings of the 13th IEEE International Conference on Requirements Engineering, pp. 439–443 (2005)

10. Suomalainen, T., Salo, O., Abrahamsson, P., Similä, J.: Software product roadmapping in a volatile business environment. J. Syst. Softw. **84**(6), 958–975 (2011)

11. Garousi, V., Felderer, M., Mäntylä, M.V.: Guidelines for including grey literature and conducting multivocal literature reviews in software engineering. Inf. Softw. Technol. **106**, 101–121 (2019)

12. Münch J., Trieflinger S., Lang, D.: Why feature-based roadmaps fail in rapidly changing markets: a qualitative survey. In: International Workshop on Software-Intensive Business: Start-ups, Ecosystems and Platforms (SiBW), pp. 202–218. Ceur-WS (2018)

13. Münch, J., Trieflinger, S., Bogazköy, E., Eißler, P., Roling, B., Schneider, J.: Product roadmap formats for an uncertain future: a grey literature review. Accepted at SEAA (2020). https://bit.ly/prformats. Accessed 30 June 2020

14. Published on Figshare. https://figshare.com/articles/Product_Roadmap_Alignment_Extended_references/12587759. Accessed 30 June 2020

15. Wohlin, C., Runeson, P., Hörst, M., Ohlsson, B., Regnell, B., Wesslen, A.: Experimentation in Software Engineering: An Introduction. Kluwer Academic Publishers (2000)

16. Runeson, P., Höst, M.: Guidelines for conducting and reporting case study research. Empir. Softw. Eng. **14**(2), 131–164 (2009)

17. Khanna, P.: How to run a product team. https://medium.com/pminsider/how-to-run-a-product-team-fdbee3385c3a. Accessed 1 May 2020

18. Harke, M.I.: OKR Alignment with OKR examples. https://blog.weekdone.com/okr-alignment-with-examples/. Accessed 1 May 2020

19. Bungay, S.: The Art of Action: How Leaders Close the Gaps Between Plans, Actions and Results. Nicholas Brealey Publishing, London (2011)

20. Pichler, R.: How to Lead in Product Management – Practices to Align Stakeholders. Pichler Consulting (2020)

Exploring the Success Factors for a Launch of an Algorithmic Consulting Platform

Andreas Kaselow[1], Dimitri Petrik[2]([⊠]) [iD], and Sven Feja[3]

[1] Mercedes-Benz AG, 71063 Sindelfingen, Germany
andreas.kaselow@daimler.com
[2] University of Stuttgart, 70174 Stuttgart, Germany
dimitri.petrik@gsame.uni-stuttgart.de
[3] adesso SE, 70173 Stuttgart, Germany
sven.feja@adesso.de

Abstract. Even the rather traditional consulting industry is not spared from digitization. Digital platforms are known to foster convergence and generativity. For the consulting industry, digital platforms offer the potential to win new customer groups who have not previously purchased consulting services before. If digital platforms for the mediation of consulting services are established by incumbent consulting companies, the new platform-based business models for the consulting market will appear. Since network effects fuel platforms, the launch phase of a platform is a serious challenge. In this paper, we examine the launch of a digital platform for the algorithmic consulting (AC) approach, due to its promising market potential. In order to research the adaptability of digital platforms for AC consulting, we perform a qualitative study of electronic documents on the actions of three successful crowdsourcing platforms. The preliminary results comprise 14 success factors for the platform launch that will be validated in a follow-up practical application. The open nature of platform design in the areas of customer access, cooperation with other platforms, interfaces, and communication appeared to be particularly important for a successful platform launch. All identified success factors can be applied to AC services and the consulting market in the future.

Keywords: Algorithmic consulting · Digital platforms · Consulting platforms

1 Introduction

Contributing a technical infrastructure, platforms usually connect independent companies, fostering generative activities [1]. Generativity is a characteristic of platform-centric markets, whereby digital technologies foster unprompted value creation through the recombination of various capabilities provided by independent companies [2]. Generativity reshapes markets and challenges the incumbent companies since the competition rules change [3, 4]. Platforms rely on the attraction of third-party companies, resulting in a platform-based ecosystem. Affected by network effects, the attractiveness of the platform and the aligning ecosystem are dependent on the number of complements, the number of complementors, and their value contribution [5].

M. Paasivaara and P. Kruchten (Eds.): XP 2020 Workshops, LNBIP 396, pp. 58–66, 2020.
https://doi.org/10.1007/978-3-030-58858-8_7

In general, digitization opens up new possibilities for solving consulting-specific problems by handing them over to be solved by a large number of people with the appropriate expertise. This is exactly where the idea of consulting platforms comes into play, where agents with problems meet agents with solutions [6]. We are not aware of any integrative research on the platformization of the consulting business. While there are some case studies on digital consulting and consulting platforms in practice, the amount of scientific and academic literature is still rather small [7, 8].

Our paper analyses the application of platform-based business models to the consulting market using algorithmic consulting (AC) as an exemplary but promising digital business model in the consulting market. Market research in the German consultancy industry by Nissen et al. reveals that the supply of AC-related solutions is rather low, whereas the customer acceptance in contrast to other digital business model approaches is nearly the same [9]. Therefore, we conclude that the establishment of an AC consulting platform has the highest potential among all the consulting approaches [9]. Using secondary data, we apply a case study research design to research the question of *which success factors could help to implement the platform-based approach for algorithmic consulting business models*. For this purpose, we examine three existing platforms to extract success factors (SF) from their actions related to the dynamics of platform establishment. The preliminary results consist of 14 SFs regarding the platform launch, distributed over three levels of consideration. Further research on the validity of the derived SFs needs to be performed through a practical application by incumbent consulting companies. This article contributes to the body of knowledge on chicken-or-egg problems in platform context [10]. This problem is a significant challenge for new platforms to overcome, thus indicating the relevance of the conducted research when adding the perspective of incumbent consulting companies, who would like to establish platforms in the consulting market.

2   Related Concepts

This paper draws on the theoretical concepts of digital platforms [11] and the concept of platform evolution [10]. In this section, we introduce the concepts of digital platforms, followed by a description of an algorithmic consulting business model to develop a theoretical pre-understanding of how platforms can facilitate the consulting market. Evans conceptualized platforms from an economic perspective, defining them as multi-sided markets to connect multiple sides of a market and manage their relationships, fostering generativity and convergence [11]. Similarly, a consulting platform primarily targets two customer segments, further described as seeker and solver. The seeker describes the customer segment that has a problem and is looking for a solution to reduce their costs, benefit from external expertise, or profit from external capabilities. In practice, seekers may be represented by big as well as small and medium-sized enterprises, startups, or private individuals. The customer segment of solvers is willing to offer solutions to the seeker problems. The solvers can be categorized as consultants, project managers, developers, or testers. Solvers seek to join the platform to acquire new projects and get in contact with new customers, for whom traditional consulting is too expensive. From the technological perspective, platforms usually have a modular architecture and are, therefore, extendable regarding their range of functions [10, 11].

Against this background, new consulting platforms are affected by the chicken-or-egg-problem as well. The establishment of a platform-based ecosystem may be constrained by the absence of seeking or solving customer segments [10].

Algorithmic Consulting is described by the automation of components of the consulting process. Especially data analysis components are suitable for algorithmic calculations to support the consulting process. The goal of AC is to substitute the consultant by algorithms that propose a solution for the customer. This enables scalability and leads to a consulting-based business model with exponential growth. For instance, algorithms can be used to analyze process data in transactional systems automatically and detect abnormalities. The AC software can trigger interventions when abnormalities are detected and then automatically generates reports and allocates decisional guidance. That is how AC shifts the consultant's role into a supervisory role with the possibility to give further advisory support if needed. Another example are automated reports for executives based on structured data. These reports are able to determine and visualize trends and critical processes that can help to make faster decisions [12]. Further examples of suitable use cases can be found at McKinsey Solutions, which provides a collection of data-driven solutions in the context of AC [13]. An *AC platform* is characterized by a platform where different AC software and solutions are provided to solve customer problems with the use of algorithms as well as additional consulting services to support the customer.

3   Research Approach

As mentioned in the first section, we chose three case studies to study the introduction of platforms to establish an AC platform in the market. The chosen companies are Upwork, Topcoder, and Innocentive. A brief overview of their financial metrics is depicted in Table 1, and the full list of used sources is available online at: https://bit.ly/2JRVAsx.

The reason to choose these three platforms can be explained with their success. During preliminary market research, we found that all three platforms represent successful platforms on the basis of key financial figures. All three platforms have successfully built multi-sided communities around their platforms. For instance, Topcoder still provides consulting services, but they established a platform-based business model in the area of crowdsourcing, matching solvers, and seekers in challenges for competitive programming. All of the examined companies offer at least a four-digit amount of challenges. Hence, certain levels of financial success and maturity make it possible to derive factors on how to establish a business model for platform-based AC for an incumbent consulting company.

Table 1. A brief overview of the financial metrics of the studied platform companies

Platform	Profile	Year founded	Approx. revenue in 2019 (Mio USD)	Community size
Upwork	Focus on the mediation of freelancers and problem solvers	1999	300	14000000+
Topcoder	Focus on solving the problems in the software domain conducting challenges and tournaments	2001	19	1200000+
Innocentive	Focus on the solution of scientific problems, also organizing challenges and tournaments	2001	10	400000+

Methodically we rely on the longitudinal case study analysis to track the platform evolution based on event streams related to a specific investigation object. The first step consists of the search and selection of publicly available secondary data resulting from the analysis of blog posts and press releases of the platform websites, technical blog websites, scientific articles, and archival versions of the platform websites. The examined articles, as well as the archived versions of platform websites, provided information on how the examined companies proceeded to launch a platform in their initial period. In addition, the timestamps of the analyzed articles helped to select only the articles about the initial phase. The analyzed dataset consists of 37 articles in a timespan between 2001 and 2020 (https://bit.ly/2JRVAsx). The second step is concerned with the content analysis of the data obtained to determine SFs. Thus, the data collection and the analysis approaches are inspired by Bowen's document analysis. This qualitative research method helps to capture the context of the analyzed data, adding background, and historical insight [14]. Similarly, we use the contextual data of each platform to capture their specific contexts and understand how they succeeded to establish platforms and form communities. We derive the SFs by interpreting what we notice during the analysis of the secondary data sources. Additionally, the inclusion of additional and comparable case studies should ensure the completeness and generalizability of our interpretations of the SFs. The main difference between the approach in this paper and the case study conducted by Skog et al. [15] is that no phases are determined to explain the evolution of a digital platform over time, but SFs are explicitly identified for the introduction phase of a consulting platform. The introduction phase describes the entering of a market that follows the R&D phase and transitions into the ascent phase [10]. This difference was relevant in the analysis procedure since it is possible to extract phase-independent SFs from late phases that may be relevant for the introduction phase. Overall, we are confident that the utilization of secondary data in multiple specific contexts of each case study is suitable to generate valid insights, comparable with interviews or observations [14, 16].

To structure the content analysis in the electronic data, we used Tiwana's vision of the evolutionary development of platforms due to its comprehensiveness and clustered the SFs in three levels of consideration: **strategy**, **architecture**, and **governance**.

According to Tiwana, design and organization of platform ecosystems are affected by adapting these three dimensions [10, 17] and cover the aspects of an AC platform, being a modularly extendable software platform to mediate different parties (i.e., seekers and solvers). By assigning the actions of the observed platform companies to these three dimensions, we design a structured design framework on platform launches.

4 Results

The following section provides an overview of the extracted SFs for a platform launch, which will be further described in more detail. The sources for each SFs, summed up as a table, are available online at: https://bit.ly/2JRVAsx.

Strategy: (1) The first SF suggests *Focusing on one specific value proposition* and building up expertise in that domain. Therefore, an owner of an AC Platform has to focus on the specific approach of AC and develop know-how in AC as well as Artificial Intelligence (AI). (2) One means for *Customer acquisition* describes the utilization of existing partnerships, publishing their AC-related challenges on the platform. This increases the number of seekers and challenges, which constitutes an incentive for solvers to migrate on the platform. In addition, partnerships to universities can be built to acquire students for challenge solving or to encourage them to develop and publish their own AC software on the platform. Another means includes the usage of internal consultants and developers with knowledge of AI (if available), who can be assigned to solve customer challenges on the platform. Other effective means are customer referral programs to subsidize the customer groups (solver & seeker) as well as online challenge-solving competitions to attract solvers to the platform. (3) *Customer loyalty* can be achieved by collecting and reacting to customer feedback. One means is to establish online forums where customers can write feedback articles about value proposition, price structures, or strategic decisions. A further means is founding a community advisory board (CAB), which consists of both customers and representatives of the platform to discuss improvement proposals. (4) *Marketing* provides means to use the existing communication channels (Social Media channels like Facebook, Youtube, Instagram etc.) to increase publicity and to get their followers to visit & join the platform. Also, the own corporate blog can be used to publish longer and more detailed insights of the technical functions as well as use cases of the platform. In addition, search engines can be used through adverts and keyword optimization to raise the traffic of the platform website. Moreover, exhibitions and events offer the opportunity to get physical contact with potential customers, where questions can be answered individually in person. (5) The *Expansion in emerging markets* intends to focus on one specific market where the platform owner is well informed at first. New markets can be explored and engaged afterwards. (6) *Openness* is meant to create an open strategic alignment of the platform, which impacts the dimensions of architecture and governance that need to follow this openness. One means is the definition of rules to steer the openness of the platform. The other means is the monitoring of whether the rules are obeyed. (7) The *Platform competition* recommends collaborating with other platforms to extend the value proposition by the value proposition of other platforms.

This constitutes synergies between both platforms to gain more customers and extend the value proposition portfolio of the collaboration platform.

Architecture: (8) The *Selection of the value proposition* describes which propositions the AC platform should supply. The recommendations for the selected value proposition of the platform include an AC app store, the execution of AC-related challenges, and additional consulting services. The AC app store describes a marketplace offered as an online-website platform where solvers are able to supply their developed AC-Applications. The model for this app store is constituted by the web-based platform *Solutions* [13], which follows a closed design. Since the strategic advice is to follow an open approach, it is recommended to create an open design that allows easy usage of the applications through the online platform. The second value proposition describes the ability to publish challenges on the platform to solve customer-specific AC-related problems that are not covered by the available applications in the app store. The models for the challenge-based approach are Innocentive and Topcoder. It is conceivable that solutions could be hosted in the app store in a way to award the seeker & solver for future usage. This would mean an extension of the app store supply where the platform owner, as well as a new seeker, will benefit. The third value proposition is represented by additional consulting services, which can be provided by the consultants of the platform owner. One offered service could be assisting in identifying a suitable application within the app store, which fits the needs of the seeker precisely. Another consulting service could be defining and processing challenges in the name of the seeker. **(9)** *Modularity* means in the case at hand for the AC platform that the online-website constitutes the core component, whereas the AC-applications and services of the solver are the peripheral components. The premise for the integration of peripheral applications and services is an open platform architecture that allows solvers to offer their AC-related solutions via the online website. Therefore, open interfaces are required to ensure the technical integration of the solutions. **(10)** The results of the case studies showed that *Design* is an important function for the customers. Therefore, the UI-Design should be clear and able to be operated intuitively.

Governance: (11) The *Access* is influenced by strategic orientation and *Openness* (6). Therefore, the organizational restrictions imposed on access for new customers should be as low as possible. The case study analysis has shown that this factor directly helps to ensure critical customer mass. To fulfill these factors, possible means could include an easy registration process and importing customer data from other profiles (Google, LinkedIn, GitHub etc.). An additional means could be to design a short registration form with the possibility to provide necessary profile data after following the registration. Furthermore, an AC platform provider should not implement strict standards or requirements that would prevent new customers from joining the AC platform if they do not meet them. **(12)** *Interfaces* determine the extent to which solvers can integrate their own applications and services into the platform or the integration of platform functionalities into external applications and websites. A provision of a publicly available and well-documented API is required. Therefore, as with Upwork and Topcoder, an API library should be published in an easily accessible way on the online portal for all interested parties. **(13)** The *Price structure* should be dependent on the customer segment. In customer acquisition, the focus is initially on the seeker, since solvers are initially available if an incumbent consulting company launches the platform. Therefore, in the introductory phase, the aim is to subsidize the seekers by waiving fees for the use of platform functions. This includes, for example, the costs for consulting services or fees for challenge tenders, which would have to be paid to the platform owner. The seeker only pays for the use or purchase of apps and services used by the solver, from which the payment is transferred in full to the solver. As an example, an AC platform company could charge solvers with commission fees from application purchases or challenge prizes. **(14)** *Communication* contributes to communicating information and decisions regarding the platform to customers. The existing social media and marketing channels, as well as the corporate blog of the incumbent company, can be used for this. A further means is having the founded CAB be in direct contact with customer representatives and to record their needs regarding platform relevant changes.

5 Discussion

Results

In conclusion, in this preliminary paper, we pursue the goal of identifying important SFs for practical application on the basis of real events. With this, we generated a generally applicable list of SFs for the platform launch, derived from actions of already established crowdsourcing platforms.

The identified SFs hold dependencies between each other. Generally, the strategic SFs have an effect on the design of the architectural and governance-related SFs. The distinction can be divided into sequential and technical dependencies. Sequentially, the SF *Openness* shapes the platform's alignment to open up *Access, Interfaces, Communication,* and *Platform Competition* for the customer segments as well as other platforms to collaborate with. Technically, the *Modularity* of a platform's architecture affects the *Selection of value proposition, Design, Access,* and *Interfaces* to facilitate the integration of components into the platform.

Limitations

These findings, however, only allow us to conduct logical interpretations of the steps the three observed platform companies undertook. The results do not allow extracting cause-and-effect relationships between the actions and their effects in practice. For this step, more research is required in the area of ecosystems engineering [18] to identify the barriers of entry for solvers and seekers and to evaluate how practicable and comprehensive the derived SFs are. Moreover, the identified SF list does not hold the claim of completeness since the analysis is limited to the given data sources.

Future Research

In the future, we will address this with a field study, applying the derived SF list to adesso SE, an incumbent consulting company, to help it to start a platform-based business model in AC. In addition to that, more research is required for the integrity of the identified SF list. For example, the quality of the engaged solver may have a significant impact on the success of a platform. However, it is not considered in the current state of the paper and has to be examined meticulously in the future. During this step, we will also pursue the goal of transforming the SFs into a domain-specific design framework to assist practitioners in the application of the identified SFs with guidance on best practice and implementation approaches. Furthermore, additional research is required to observe AC platform companies regarding how they implement the recommendations. The practical application of the derived SFs will help to review what cause-and-effect relationships they have to launch a successful AC platform. For instance, Upwork, which is the most successful platform in terms of sales and registered profiles, stands out due to its open nature in the areas of customer access, cooperation with other platforms, interfaces, and communication. *Openness* and its related SFs seem to play a more important role than the other extracted SFs. Therefore, we are convinced that these SFs, as well as Upwork need to be studied in more detail.

References

1. Hein, A., et al.: Digital platform ecosystems. Electron. Mark. **30**(1), 87–98 (2019). https://doi.org/10.1007/s12525-019-00377-4
2. Nambisan, S., Wright, M., Feldman, M.: The digital transformation of innovation and entrepreneurship: progress, challenges and key themes. Res. Policy **48**(8), 103773 (2019)
3. De Reuver, M., Sorensen, C., Basole, R.C.: The digital platform: a research agenda. J. Inf. Technol. **33**(2), 124–135 (2018)
4. Porter, M.E., Heppelmann, J.E.: How smart connected products are transforming competition. Harv. Bus. Rev. **92**(11), 64–68 (2014)
5. Iansiti, M., Levien, R.: The Keystone Advantage: What the New Dynamics of Business Ecosystems Mean for Strategy, Innovation, and Sustainability. HBS Press, Boston Mass (2004)
6. Werth, D., Greff, T., Scheer, A.W.: Digitale Beratung, ein Modell für den Mittelstand. IM +io Fachzeitschrift, pp. 82–87 (2016)
7. Stummer, C., Kundisch, D., Decker, R.: Platform launch strategies. Bus. Inf. Syst. Eng. **60**(2), 167–173 (2018). https://doi.org/10.1007/s12599-018-0520-x
8. Lindner, D. Beratung 4.0 - Mittelstand berät Mittelstand, Working Paper (2017)
9. Nissen, V., Füßl, A., Werth, D., Gugler, K., Neu, C., Unternehmensberater, B.D.: Zum aktuellen Stand der dig. Transformation im deutschen Markt für Unternehmensberatung (2018)
10. Tiwana, A.: Platform Ecosystems: Aligning Architecture, Governance, and Strategy. Morgan Kaufmann, Amsterdam (2014)
11. Gawer, A.: Bridging differing perspectives on technological platforms: toward an integrative framework. Res. Policy **43**, 1239–1249 (2014)
12. Nissen, V., Seifert, H.: Digital Transformation of the Consulting Industry – Extending the Traditional Delivery Model. Springer, Cham (2018). https://doi.org/10.1007/978-3-319-70491-3
13. Christensen, A., Wang, D., Van Bever, D.: Consulting on the cusp of disruption. Harv. Bus. Rev. **91**(10), 106–114 (2013)
14. Bowen, G.A.: Document analysis as a qualitative research method. Qual. Res. J. **9**(2), 27–40 (2009)

15. Skog, D.A., Wimelius, H., Sandberg, J.: Digital service platform evolution: how spotify leveraged boundary resources to become a global leader in music streaming. In: Hawaii International Conference on System Sciences, pp. 4564–4573 (2018)
16. Yin, R.K.: Case Study Research: Design and Methods. SAGE Publications, LA (2003)
17. Tiwana, A., Konsynski, B.: Complementarities between organizational it architecture and governance structure. Inf. Syst. Res. **21**(2), 288–304 (2010)
18. Hurni, T., Huber, T.: The interplay of power and trust in platform ecosystems of the enterprise application software industry. In: 22nd European Conference on Information Systems, Tel Aviv (2014)

Eighth International Workshop on Large-Scale Agile Development

Agile at Scale: A Summary of the 8th International Workshop on Large-Scale Agile Development

Julian M. Bass and Abdallah Salameh

University of Salford, 43 Crescent, Salford M5 4WT, UK
j.bass@salford.ac.uk, a.salameh@edu.salford.ac.uk

Abstract. The Large-Scale Agile Development workshop explored the main research challenges in large-scale software development. We considered multisite organisations with large-scale projects that include a large number of teams adopting agile methods. Such topics include inter-team coordination, knowledge sharing, large project organisation, agile transformation, agile teamwork quality, project models that facilitate several self-organising teams, and practices for scaling agile methods. We accepted five full research papers, which are included in this volume. The accepted papers report empirical research studies using surveys, observations and case studies. Also, an interactive online discussion session was conducted to compare the two approaches, SAFe and Spotify. The workshop participants, which were around a hundred people, joined this discussion to compare the two approaches and suggest some future research questions about the hybridisation of SAFe and Spotify. This workshop summary contributes as a current snapshot of research along with some results from an interactive discussion about SAFe and Spotify.

Keywords: Large-scale agile software development · Software engineering · SAFe · Spotify · Inter-team coordination · Agile transformation · Agile teamwork quality · Organisational change · Autonomous teams

1 Introduction

The goal of Large-Scale Agile Development workshop was to explore the main research challenges in conducting large-scale software development programmes using agile methods. How to apply agile methods to large-scale projects was identified as the "top burning research question" by practitioners at XP2010 and has since then attracted increasing interest among agile practitioners and researchers. The first of this workshop series was organised at XP2013. The workshop was planned to be conducted during the XP conference in Copenhagen in June 2020. However, the workshop was conducted online because of the Coronavirus disease (i.e., COVID-19) outbreak. Despite the pandemic, around a hundred attendees joined the workshop, which is more than double the attendance last year.

Agile methods are conventionally applied in small colocated software development teams. Since many organisations with small collocated teams have realised successful implementation of software projects, agile methods became increasingly attractive for researchers and practitioners to apply agile software development to large-scale projects [5].

Large-scale projects are challenging because several teams need to work closely together to release a single software project [1, 4]. This workshop addressed research challenges in large-scale agile development and identified topics such as inter-team coordination, knowledge sharing, large project organisation, agile transformation, agile teamwork quality, project models that facilitate several self-organising teams, and practices for scaling agile methods.

2   Workshop Contributions

The workshop comprised speakers selected following submission of short papers, which were peer-reviewed by members of the program committee, and an interactive online discussion session about the differences between SAFe and Spotify.

2.1   Research Papers

For the 2020 workshop we had seven submissions, of which five were accepted as full research paper presentations. The first paper, "Transitioning from a First Generation to Second Generation Large-Scale Agile Development Method: Towards understanding Implications for Coordination" [2] reported preliminary insights on the coordination impact when an organisation moves from first (combined agile methods with traditional project management frameworks) to a second generation (using large-scale agile frameworks). The authors used four theories of coordination from different fields to analyse the findings and explain changes in coordination. They found that two of the theories are well suited to characterising the phases of the transition, providing answer to how coordination was done. While two other theories provide answers to why the coordination changes occurred and could help explaining the success of such transition.

The second paper, "Exploring the Product Owner Role within SAFe Implementation in a Multinational Enterprise" [10] compares previously identified activities of Product Owners outside the context of SAFe with activities of Product Owners in an examined SAFe implementation to improve the understanding of the Product Owner role within the context of SAFe. The authors found that the Product Owners role in the SAFe deviates from the previous understanding of the role outside the context of SAFe as the range of Product Owner activities are narrowed. They attribute the narrowed activities of Product Owners at SAFe to the introduction of a new form of management-driven top-down approach with the fragmentation of the roles.

The third paper, "A systematic approach to agile development in highly regulated environments" [8] describes an approach, called Levels of Done-Product Quality Risk (LoD-PQR), to align agile teams and ensure that teams meet regulatory requirements and product specific quality while retaining as much autonomy as possible. The authors claim that this approach enabled the autonomous teams, in the case study organisation, to realise efficiency by design and to share techniques on how to implement compliance requirements. This in turn has streamlined the development processes in the case study organisation and led to a positive impact on process performance.

The fourth paper, "Evaluation of Agile Team Work Quality" [9] presents an approach to measure "agile Team Work Quality (aTWQ)", which enables teams in improving their agile mindset and practices without external assessments. This approach includes measurement indicators, which are based on extending the team-work quality construct that are developed by previous research. The paper presents also how the case study organisation has made use of findings on teamwork to create a usable "Toolbox" for internal process improvement.

Finally, the fifth paper, "Operationalizing Agile Methods: Examining Coherence in Large-Scale Agile Transformations" [3] explores coherence in operationalising large-scale agile methods by presenting the results of a comparison between a successful and a failed large-scale agile transformation. Also, the paper describes challenges in understanding the rationale, differences, values, and roles associated with the methods to support successful large-scale agile transformation. In addition, the authors highlight factors that contribute to failed large-scale agile transformations.

2.2   SAFe vs Spotify - A Short Discussion

Both the SAFe framework and the Spotify model, which was initially introduced by Kniberg and Ivarsson [6, 7], are increasingly attracting agile practitioners in organisations of different context [4, 10–12]. The workshop participants were asked to provide similarities and differences between SAFe and Spotify by using an online Metro Retro board. Also, the participants were asked to provide possible future research directions for the hybrid of SAFe and Spotify.

The discussion did rise some aspects of importance when comparing SAFe to Spotify. These aspects are highlighted in Table 1.

The participants highlighted very few similarities between SAFe and Spotify compared to what differences they have provided. The mentioned similarities include the utilisation of communities of practice, falling back to the agile mindset to pinpoint what is needed, and trying to copy the agile approach. However, the participants highlighted many differences between SAFe and Spotify. For example, SAFe is a knowledge base (i.e., toolbox) of integrated principles, practices, and competencies for Lean, Agile, and DevOps that range from scrum teams to portfolio. According to some

Table 1. The rised aspects from the discussion – comparing SAFe to Spotify

	SAFe	Spotify
Process/culture	Knowledge base (toolbox)	Culture & interactions
Inter-team dependencies	High	Low
Innovation	Inhibitor	Enabler
Completeness	Detailed and complete	Abstract
Adoption	Easy	Complicated
Tailoring & improving	Hard	Easy

participants, SAFe implementation is complicated, includes unnecessary process, plan focused, bureaucratic, and dis-empowers team autonomy. Hence, SAFe is characterised as anti-agile. On the contrary, the authors of the Spotify model do not want to develop a big toolbox but rather to emphasise the need to create interactions between the teams through an Agile culture. This Agile culture focuses on enabling teams' autonomy by aligning the teams to each other to common product goals and objectives.

Participants considered SAFe suitable for projects and environments that have many dependencies among teams. Such dependencies, in turn, result in spending considerable resources to plan and coordinate work. SAFe is appropriate when the need for innovation among the developers is not a high priority because SAFe favours command and control, and teams are not highly empowered compared to the Spotify teams. The teams in the Spotify model have high autonomy to increase their creativity and innovation.

SAFe offers a complete course for its implementation and certification path to creating coaches of the framework. Whereas, the Spotify model is considered abstract and provides high-level details. Consequently, everything needed to implement SAFe is almost ready. Yet, it will require following its strict recommendations for the implementation, which are difficult to set up but not difficult to implement. On the other hand, adopting the Spotify model is perceived as an adventure where there are plenty of rooms for agile process tailoring, which in turn demands to have senior agile coaches to implement it. Such experienced agile coaches need to help autonomous squads to tailor their Agile processes, align all squads together and to project objectives, set up portfolio or program part, and define the Spotify communities (i.e., Squads, Chapters, Tribes, and Guilds [6]) and their content. Unlike the Spotify model, everything is already defined for SAFe, which makes it complicated to improve and adapt.

The participants were asked to provide possible future research directions for the hybrid of SAFe and Spotify. Interestingly, three participants in our discussion revealed encountering such hybrids in the industry nowadays. Also, the workshop participants provided few research directions for such hybrids, as follows:

- Why should we have a hybrid Agile development approach from SAFe and Spotify?
- How SAFe and the Spotify can be hybridised in the industry?
- How about a comparison of organically evolved approaches with prescriptive frameworks and models (SAFe vs Spotify)?
- What are prerequisites for inter-team coordination through practices such as "big room planning" in SAFe?

3   Programme Committee

Many thanks to the members of the programme committee many of whom have also contributed to previous workshops. The members' name are ordered alphabetically by last name, as follows:

- Finn Olav Bjørnson, Norwegian University of Science and Technology, Norway.
- Torgeir Dingsøyr, Norwegian University of Science and Technology, Norway.

- Denniz Donmez, Enabling Structures, Switzerland.
- Jutta Eckstein, IT communication, Germany.
- Peggy Gregory, UCLAN, UK.
- Tomas Gustavsson, Karlstad university, Sweden.
- Andrew Haxby, Competa IT BV, Netherlands.
- Aymeric Hemon, University of Nantes, France.
- Helena Holmström Olsson, University of Malmo, Sweden.
- Eric Knauss, Chalmers University, Sweden.
- Philippe Kruchten, University of British Columbia, Canada.
- Maarit Laanti, Nitor Delta, Finland.
- Carl Marnewick, University of Johannesburg, South Africa.
- Nils B. Moe, Sintef, Norway.
- Parastoo Mohagheghi, NAV, Norway.
- John Noll, University of Hertfordshire, UK.
- Maria Paasivaara, IT University of Copenhagen & Aalto University, Denmark & Finland.
- Yvan Petit, ESG UQAM, Canada.
- Jan Pries-Heje, Roskilde University, Denmark.
- Scarlet Rahy, University of Salford, UK.
- Knut H. Rolland, University of Oslo, Norway.
- Darja Smite, Blekinge Institute of Technology, Sweden.
- Christoph Stettina, Leiden University, Netherlands.
- Klaas-Jan Stol, Lero, UK.
- Viktoria Stray, University of Oslo, Norway.
- Ömer Uludag, Technical University of Munich, Germany.

Without the valuable support of these programme committee members the workshop would not have been possible. Thanks to Hubert Baumeister and Mansooreh Zahedi, the workshop co-chairs for XP 2020. Thanks also to Maria Paasivaara, the conference chair for XP 2020.

4   Conclusions

The Large-Scale Agile Development workshop successfully created an opportunity for researchers and practitioners to consider the latest trends in large-scale agile software development. The accepted papers in this proceeding and the interactive discussion session contribute as a snapshot of the start-of-the-art in the field of large-scale agile software development. The authors presented evidence of approaches being used to enable agile development in large-scale contexts. Yet, an incomplete adoption of some presented approaches was provided since the authors share preliminary findings of their conducted research. The workshop participants joined an interactive discussion to compare SAFe and Spotify and suggest future research questions about their hybridisation.

References

1. Bass, J.M.: Future trends in agile at scale: a summary of the 7th international workshop on large-scale agile development. In: Hoda, R. (eds) Agile Processes in Software Engineering and Extreme Programming – Workshops. XP 2019. LNBIP, vol. 364, pp. 75–80. Springer, Cham (2019). https://doi.org/10.1007/978-3-030-30126-2_9
2. Bjørnson, F.O., Dingsøyr, T.: Transitioning from a first generation to second generation large-scale agile development method: towards understanding implications for coordination. In: Kruchten, P. (ed.) Agile Processes in Software Engineering and Extreme Programming – Workshops. Springer International Publishing (2020)
3. Carroll, N., Bjørnson, F.O., Dingsøyr, T., Rolland, K., Conboy, K.: Operationalizing agile methods: examining coherence in large-scale agile transformations. In: Kruchten, P. (ed.) Agile Processes in Software Engineering and Extreme Programming – Workshops. Springer International Publishing (2020)
4. Conboy, K., Carroll, N.: Implementing large-scale agile frameworks: challenges and recommendations. IEEE Softw. **36**(2), 44–50 (2019)
5. Dikert, K., Paasivaara, M., Lassenius, C.: Challenges and success factors for large-scale agile transformations: a systematic literature review. J. Syst. Softw. **119**, 87–108 (2016)
6. Kniberg, H.: Spotify squad framework, March, 2017. https://medium.com/project-management-learnings/
7. Kniberg, H., Ivarsson, A.: Scaling agile spotify with tribes, squads, chapters & guilds, October, 2012. https://blog.crisp.se/wp-content/uploads/2012/11/SpotifyScaling.pdf
8. Poth, A., Jacobsen, J., Riel, A.: Systematic agile development in regulated environments. In: Yilmaz, M., Niemann, J., Clarke, P., Messnarz, R. (eds.) EuroSPI 2020. CCIS, vol. 1251, pp. 191–202. Springer, Cham (2020). https://doi.org/10.1007/978-3-030-56441-4_14
9. Poth, A., Kottke, M., Riel, A.: Evaluation of agile team work quality. In: Kruchten, P. (ed.) Agile Processes in Software Engineering and Extreme Programming – Workshops. Springer International Publishing (2020)
10. Remta, D., Doležel, M., Buchalcevová, A.: Exploring the product owner role within safe implementation in a multinational enterprise. In: Kruchten, P. (ed.) Agile Processes in Software Engineering and Extreme Programming – Workshops. Springer International Publishing (2020)
11. Salameh, A., Bass, J.M.: Spotify tailoring for promoting effectiveness in cross-functional autonomous squads. In: Hoda, R. (eds.) Agile Processes in Software Engineering and Extreme Programming – Workshops. XP 2019. LNBIP, vol. 364, pp. 20–28. Springer, Cham (2019). https://doi.org/10.1007/978-3-030-30126-2_3
12. Salameh, A., Bass, J.M.: Heterogeneous tailoring approach using the spotify model. In: Proceedings of the Evaluation and Assessment in Software Engineering, EASE'20, pp. 293–298. Association for Computing Machinery, New York (2020)

Operationalizing Agile Methods: Examining Coherence in Large-Scale Agile Transformations

Noel Carroll[1(✉)], Finn Olav Bjørnson[2], Torgeir Dingsøyr[3],
Knut-Helge Rolland[4], and Kieran Conboy[1]

[1] Lero, National University of Ireland Galway, Galway, Ireland
noel.carroll@nuigalway.ie
[2] Norwegian University of Science and Technology, Trondheim, Norway
[3] SINTEF Digital, Trondheim, Norway
[4] University of Oslo, Oslo, Norway

Abstract. Following the highly pervasive and effective use of agile methods for software development, attention has now turned to the much more difficult challenge of applying these methods in large scale, organization-wide development. However, identifying to what extent certain factors influence success and failure of sustaining large-scale agile transformations remains unclear and there is a lack of theoretical frameworks to guide such investigations. By adopting Normalization Process Theory and specifically 'coherence', we compare two large-scale agile transformation case studies and the different perspectives individuals and teams had when faced with the problem of operationalizing the agile method as part of their large-scale agile transformation. The key contributions of this work are: (i) this is a first attempt to present the results of a comparison between a successful and failed large-scale agile transformations; and (ii) we describe the challenges in understanding the rationale, differences, value, and roles associated with the methods to support the large-scale agile transformation. We also present future research for practitioners and academics on large-scale agile transformation.

Keywords: Large-scale agile transformation · Normalization Process Theory · Coherence · Case study · Organizational change · Autonomous teams

1 Large-Scale Agile Transformation

Agile methods have been well received by practitioners and academics over the past two decades. Given the success of agile approaches at the team level, many large software organizations have begun to scale these methods to a large-scale and often enterprise-wide context [1]. We adopt the description of "transformation" from [2] which explains how the concept of transformation and "scaling up" are very closely related to describing how development organizations with small agile practices (e.g. a single agile team in a large setting) scale their agile practices to at least 50 people or 6 teams (i.e. large-scale agile practices). However, such large-scale adoption has proven challenging [3, 4], with very few successful cases reported across literature which

M. Paasivaara and P. Kruchten (Eds.): XP 2020 Workshops, LNBIP 396, pp. 75–83, 2020.
https://doi.org/10.1007/978-3-030-58858-8_8

hampers the research community in learning about specific factors of large-scale agile transformation processes. The literature identifies particular challenges such as the complexity and uncertainty introduced when a method tries to enable radical and continuous change across a fragmented set of teams and projects across an organization [2], the confusion caused by numerous variants and misinterpretations of that method [5], as well as the limitations of both top-down (management-driven) or bottom-up (team-driven) agile method transformations [2, 5]. The objective of this study is to explore coherence as one key part of normalization and in operationalizing large-scale agile transformations. Coherence is the process of sensemaking that individuals and organizations undergo in order to promote or inhibit the routine embedding of a practice (i.e. determining specifically "what is the work?"). We achieve this by (i) comparing coherence across two separate case studies (a successful and failed large-scale agile transformation); (ii) reporting on the key lessons learned around the need to consider coherence of a large-scale agile transformation; and (iii) presenting a summary of recommendations for organizations on scaling agile methods as a continuum rather than a change in state which the notion of transformations can imply.

2 Normalization Process Theory

Normalization Process Theory (NPT) is a derivative sociological theory on the implementation, embedding and integration of new technologies and organizational innovations [6] which allows us to challenge assumptions around embedding change during transformations [7]. NPT provides a rich theoretical lens to explain a transformation process since it allows us to uncover whether practices become routinely embedded in their social contexts as the result of people working, individually and collectively, to enact them. There are four main NPT constructs which explain normalization:

1. **Coherence:** the meaningful qualities of a specific practice
2. **Cognitive participation:** enrolment and engagement of individuals and groups
3. **Collective action:** interaction with already existing practices
4. **Reflexive monitoring:** how a new practice is understood and assessed by implicated actors

Each NPT construct comprises of four theoretical components, i.e. 16 components in total [7]. Within each of the core theoretical constructs, we can examine the normalization of large-scale agile transformations and shed new insights on organizing structures, social norms, group processes and conventions, i.e. work relating to assessing patterns of work and outcomes. NPT provides practical insights on specific phenomena both qualitatively and quantitatively such as examining the sustainability of large-scale agile methods [7]. NPT allows us to unpack the dynamic nature of large-scale agile transformations by focusing on the social organization of the work (implementation) of making practices routine elements of everyday life (embedding), and of sustaining embedded practices in their social context (integration). For the large-scale agile transformation case study comparison in this study, we focus on the coherence. We focus on coherence because it uncovers four key components of initiating and operationalizing new practices:

1. **Differentiation:** Comparing differences in an old and new set of practices
2. **Communal specification:** Building a shared understanding of the vision, aims, objectives, and expected benefits of a set of practices.
3. **Individual specification:** Assessing individual perceptions on their specific tasks and responsibilities around a new set of practices.
4. **Internalization:** Evaluating team members perception on the value, benefits, and importance of a new set of practices.

Specifically, coherence is a critical stage of large-scale agile transformations as it enables us to focus on sensemaking carried out individually and collectively when faced with the problem of operationalizing a set of practices, i.e. in this research context, operationalizing a large-scale agile transformation method. This also allows us to examine the rationale and drivers to transform an organization's practices and compare how people make sense of (re)defining and (re)organizing practices.

3 Research Method

Comparative case studies involve the analysis and synthesis of the key similarities, differences and emerging patterns across two or more cases [8]. This method is suitable to explore new topic areas which focus on 'how' or 'why' questions around a contemporary set of events.

Table 1. Comparative case study summary

Description	FinanceCo	PublicOrg
Sector	Financial Services	Public Services
Employees	50,000	20,000
Locations	USA, Ireland, India, China	Norway
Agile method (before transformation)	Customized	Customized (based on [10])
Large-scale agile method	Spotify	Multidisciplinary semi-autonomous teams
Result	Method abandoned after two years in favor of SAFe	Method in use with good results
Study timeframe of transformation	2017–2018	2016–2020
No. of interview participants	8 development teams (50 participants)	10 development teams (39 participants)
Data collection method(s)	Semi-structured interviews; observations; access to systems, documents, reports, meetings	Semi-structured interviews; observations; access to systems, documents, reports, meetings

This study compares two large-scale agile transformation projects using the FinanceCo [7] and PublicOrg [9] case studies. In the context of this research, both cases share a common research objective in understanding an organization's experience in undertaking a large-scale agile transformation (Table 1). Both cases were selected based on a specific criteria [2] in that the organizations with small agile practices scales their agile practices to at least 50 people or 6 teams (i.e. large-scale agile practices). In the context of the case studies, both qualitative and quantitative methods were adopted to better understand the context which influences the success and failure of a transformation process.

4   Findings

This section presents a summary of the key findings on the four components of coherence to explain efforts on the normalization of the two large-scale agile transformations. We compare how each of these components were operationalized and contributed to the success and failure of normalizing a large-scale agile transformation.

4.1   Differentiation

By examining *differentiation*, we can compare how FinanceCo and PublicOrg managed the initial stages of the large-scale transformation. For FinanceCo, there was no clear evidence that their teams attempted to differentiate the new practices associated with the large-scale agile transformation strategy. Management considered high-level differences and used sweeping claims to promote the potential of the Spotify model in terms of outcomes. Management presented ideas around how the Spotify model would address some ongoing business challenges, for example through a new software development culture, fluid team structures, and continuous software development flow. However, Squads were tasked with operationalizing the Spotify model with little guidance or expectation on how to differentiate the new practice to old ways of working.

In contrast, PublicOrg demonstrated evidence of a planned induction period to inform all stakeholders on the implications and expectations from the large-scale agile transformation. This included both consultants from two different suppliers and the developers from PublicOrg. More concretely a work group consisting of representatives working on business needs, software architecture, and development recommended to change deployment model from a bimodal model to a model of multidisciplinary semi-autonomous teams. The group delivered a 24-slide presentation to the project manager with a joint proposal, which sought to align development practice in the project with a future way of working in PublicOrg. The group considered the deployment model after identifying dependencies, suitability for continuous deployment, cross-functional teams, time criticality and user value.

4.2   Communal Specification

By focusing on *communal specification*, we compared how teams built a shared understanding of the vision, aims, objectives, and expected benefits of the large-scale agile transformation. Within FinanceCo, Squads perceived that the Spotify model had imposed changes to divisional structures and created a separation of powers. However, management had reported that team restructuring was imposed in an effort to build and sustain relational work through self-organized teams and autonomy to drive change. For FinanceCo, the overall objective to transform was to improve software team productivity and performance (guided by software flow metrics). However, a Squad Lead viewed the Spotify model as a way to remove predictability of team performance and control across relational work: *"It's difficult to make sense of the Spotify model. You want certainty, predictivity, and control on the management side. Yet, you adopt the Spotify model because you have admitted that you don't want predictability or control for the transformation process."*

PublicOrg, however, launched a four-month subproject prior to introduction of the new deployment model in order to *"build competence on agile methods"* in the project. The main vision described by PublicOrg was to transition from a delivery model based on phases and handovers to a flow-based model where the division between customer and supplier is invisible. The change involved end-to-end automatic testing, toggling of features, one shared stream of code, and an improved deployment pipeline. The change project aimed to minimize *"work in progress"* and to establish a code base per product to minimize complexity of development. The expected benefits described in the report included "higher quality and user value", "earlier realizations of business value", "more time to develop solution, less time on reporting and documentation", "a more motivating workday for employees". PublicOrg also hired two agile coaches to assist in the transition process. One of the Technical Leads described how: *"The agile coach we had – without him the whole process would have been a lot more painful!"*.

4.3   Individual Specification

By focusing on *individual specification*, we compare how individuals across both case studies perceived their specific tasks and responsibilities imposed by the large-scale agile method. From a managerial perspective at FinanceCo, the Spotify model provided a roadmap for the roles and responsibilities required to improve organizational-wide agility and software team performance and productivity. However, there was a lack of clarity in terms of how it would be operationalized and it was not always well received by software developers. As one software developer within the Platform Chapter of a Squad at FinanceCo explained: *"not only are we forced to change roles but now we are held to account to reach new performance targets in these roles…"*.

At PublicOrg, a work group was established and recommended: *"The degree of autonomy must be adapted to each domain, based on need of collaboration, dependencies, and the connection to the central administrative system team, and this might change over time."* Preparation for a new model started early, a product owner stated, *"I was aware that this change was coming since I was assigned to the project in 2017. So, the first thing I did was to attend one of those two-days agile workshops. That was two months before I started this project.*" A functional advisor experienced a varying clarity of roles: "*The thing is, my role is very vaguely defined. The product owner, that role is very specified, you attribute a lot of responsibility to that role, really. Too much if you ask me, and then me and another is in the role of functional advisor which is very vaguely defined, just supporting the product owner, really.*"

4.4   Internalization

For *internalization*, we explored team members perception on the value, benefits, and importance of the new agile method. Within a FinanceCo transformation context we probed whether value, benefits, and importance related to topics such as financial, business, cultural, or personal. However, the concepts of 'value', 'benefits', and 'importance' were considered to be a vague or elusive from both a management and team perspectives and efforts were placed on developing metrics to represent how work should be prioritized. A Senior Business Intelligence Developer in the Business Intelligence Chapter stated: "*Our progress or lack of progress is probably best reflected in the amount of unplanned work we are faced with which makes it difficult to understand the value of using the Spotify model.*"

PublicOrg, on the other hand, present evidence of more optimism around the transformation process and their transition using a large-scale agile method. For example, a Technical Lead (previous Scrum Master) explains: "*It's not really much of a difference. I see it as a good idea, and it's good to have shorter decision paths*" In addition, a Tester at PublicOrg described their experience by stating: "*Summing up the transition, I'm happy that we transitioned to such an agile way of working. It makes my workday easier and more fun, if I'm allowed to say that. Less stressful and I feel more ownership and responsibility for the functionality we deliver as a team.*"

5   Discussion

This research focuses on coherence as a critical stage of large-scale agile transformations and compares how two organizations faced the problem of operationalizing a new set of practices. Table 2 presents a summary of our comparative findings. We summarize how FinanceCo had a relatively weak foundation and attempted to adopt a "*scale and learn approach*". This approach was largely based on many weak assumptions around operationalizing the Spotify model which eventually led to growing tensions across the organization and failure in their transformation efforts. In contrast, we learned how PublicOrg had a strong foundation and implemented an agile culture and adopted a "*learn and scale approach*" which proved to be very successful in operationalizing the reorganization into autonomous teams. The key contribution of examining coherence is that we identify tensions between management expectations and teams operationalizing new practices.

We identify how complexity and uncertainty emerge when organizations try to instigate change across an organization [2] due to the lack of clarity on a large-scale transformation process and weak assumptions on how to manage the process. We uncover some of the key tensions which go unreported throughout literature regarding

Table 2. Summary of comparative findings on operationalizing large-scale agile methods

Coherence	FinanceCo	PublicOrg
Differentiation	Weak foundation in terms of competencies in place and poor communication to differentiate the transformation method and goals	Strong foundation in terms of competencies in place and excellent communication to differentiate the transformation method and goals
	Lack of agile training prior to transformation to instill an agile culture and mindset	Planned induction of agile training provided prior to transformation and implementation of an agile culture
Communal specification	Sense of imposed changes to divisional structures and created a separation of powers	Introduced a project to build competence on agile methods
	Improvements on software team productivity and performance were guided by software flow metrics	Recruitment of two agile coaches to assist in the transition process
Individual specification	Method provided a roadmap for the roles and responsibilities required to improve organizational-wide agility and software team performance and productivity	Emphasis on need of collaboration, dependencies, and the connection to the central administrative system team
	Lack clarity across teams on how the new method would be operationalized in practice	Awareness of change brought about by the methods a number of years prior to the transformation
Internalization	Concepts of 'value', 'benefits', and 'importance' were considered to be a vague or elusive from both the management and team perspectives	Evidence of value in large-scale transformation, e.g. shorter decision paths
	Efforts placed on developing metrics to represent how work should be prioritized	Improved sense of satisfaction in an agile way of working and more ownership and responsibility as a team

the top-down (management-driven) or bottom-up (team-driven) agile method transformations [2, 5]. Our findings indicate the need for organizations to become more proactive by introducing a large-scale agile transformation induction period to embed an agile culture and mindset across the organization before undergoing any transformation process. While communication is often documented as a generic yet key factor for large-scale agile transformation throughout literature [10], we identify the need to specifically focus on coherence in order to compare differences in an old and new agile method and to have a shared understanding of the vision, aims, objectives, and expected benefits of a large-scale agile transformation.

By focusing on coherence, we also identify the importance of providing dedicated resources to support the transformation, for example, agile coaches being available at team level to understand how to operationalize a scaling agile method. There is little

82   N. Carroll et al.

comparative research on how organizations assess individual perceptions of specific tasks and responsibilities around a large-scale agile transformation. This research demonstrates how critical it can be to evaluate team members perception of a large-scale agile transformation at the very early stages [5].

6 Conclusion

We present two clear contributions from this research: (i) present the results of a comparison between a successful and failed large-scale agile transformations; (ii) we describe the challenges in understanding the rationale, differences, value, and roles associated with the methods to support and sustain a successful large-scale agile transformation and factors which contribute to failed transformations. While we adopt NPT to focus on one of the theoretical constructs of coherence, we present future research for practitioners and academics on large-scale agile transformation on the NPT framework which explains how practices become implemented, embedded, integrated, and evaluated. As part of our future research, we will focus on comparing additional cases on assumptions associated with large-scale agile transformations. NPT could set new directions for research on large-scale agile development [3], agile transformation [4], and extending into other research developments on IT-enabled and digital transformations [11].

Acknowledgements. This work was supported, in part, by Science Foundation Ireland grant 13/RC/2094 and by the Research Council of Norway through grant 236759.

References

1. Laanti, M., Salo, O., Abrahamsson, P.: Agile methods rapidly replacing traditional methods at Nokia: a survey of opinions on agile transformation. Inf. Softw. Technol. **53**(3), 276–290 (2011)
2. Dikert, K., Paasivaara, M., Lassenius, C.: Challenges and success factors for large-scale agile transformations: a systematic literature review. J. Syst. Softw. **119**, 87–108 (2016)
3. Bass, J.M.: Future trends in agile at scale: a summary of the 7th international workshop on large-scale agile development. In: Hoda, R. (ed.) XP 2019. LNBIP, vol. 364, pp. 75–80. Springer, Cham (2019). https://doi.org/10.1007/978-3-030-30126-2_9
4. Barroca, L., Dingsøyr, T., Mikalsen, M.: Agile transformation: a summary and research agenda from the first international workshop. In: Hoda, R. (ed.) XP 2019. LNBIP, vol. 364, pp. 3–9. Springer, Cham (2019). https://doi.org/10.1007/978-3-030-30126-2_1
5. Conboy, K., Carroll, N.: Implementing large-scale agile frameworks: challenges and recommendations. IEEE Softw. **36**(2), 44–50 (2019)
6. May, C., Finch, T.: Implementing, embedding, and integrating practices: an outline of normalization process theory. Sociology **43**(3), 535–554 (2009)
7. Carroll, N., Conboy, K.: Applying normalization process theory to explain large-scale agile transformations. In: 14th International Research Workshop on IT Project Management (2019)
8. Miles, M.B., Huberman, A.M., Huberman, M.A., Huberman, M.: Qualitative Data Analysis: An Expanded Sourcebook. Sage (1994)

 9. Bjørnson, F.O., Vestues, K., Rolland, K.H.: Coordination in the large: a research design. In: Proceedings of the XP2017 Scientific Workshops, pp. 1–5 (2017)
10. Dingsøyr, T., Moe, N.B., Fægri, T.E., Seim, E.A.: Exploring software development at the very large-scale: a revelatory case study and research agenda for agile method adaptation. Empir. Softw. Eng. **23**(1), 490–520 (2018)
11. Carroll, N.: Theorizing on the normalization of digital transformations. In: Twenty-Eight European Conference on Information Systems, ECIS2020 (2020)

Transitioning from a First Generation to Second Generation Large-Scale Agile Development Method: Towards Understanding Implications for Coordination

Finn Olav Bjørnson[1(✉)] and Torgeir Dingsøyr[2]

[1] Norwegian University of Science and Technology, Trondheim, Norway
bjornson@ntnu.no
[2] SINTEF Digital, Trondheim, Norway

Abstract. This paper reports our initial findings from a longitudinal case study within a large development project in a public organization in Scandinavia. We focus on changes in coordination practices as the development project moved from a 1st to a 2nd generation large-scale agile development methodology. Building on four theories of coordination from different fields, we investigate how each theory illuminates our case and what insight they might provide. We find that two of the theories are well suited to characterizing each phase, providing answer to *how* coordination was done. While two other theories can provide answers to *why* these changes occurred.

Keywords: Large-scale agile · Coordination

1 Introduction

Large-scale agile software development has received significant interest in the last years [1, 2]. In particular, the topic of how to coordinate many development teams has been seen as critical to the success of agile development at scale. A previous study identified coordination challenges in large-scale agile development due to misaligned planning at inter-team levels [3]. The introduction to the special issue on large-scale agile development in *IEEE Software,* describes two generations of large-scale agile development methods:

The first generation of large-scale agile development methods combined agile methods at team level with traditional project management frameworks such as PRINCE2. *A second generation* of large-scale agile development methods are currently taken up globally. These methods which include Disciplined Agile Delivery, Large-Scale Scrum, the Scaled Agile Framework and the Spotify model [2] prescribe new arenas as well as roles in order to ensure coordination.

Agile methods have significant impact on coordination practices. They *"de-emphasize traditional coordination mechanisms such as forward planning, extensive documentation, specific coordination roles, contracts, and strict adherence to a pre-defined specified process"* [4]. In a previous article, we argued that coordination has to be re-thought [5] in order to emphasize a number of characteristics of large-scale agile

M. Paasivaara and P. Kruchten (Eds.): XP 2020 Workshops, LNBIP 396, pp. 84–91, 2020.
https://doi.org/10.1007/978-3-030-58858-8_9

development including focus on oral communication, work in teams, a high level of interdependencies, uncertainty in tasks, many people involved, relations between individuals and that coordination needs change over time.

Today, many organisations and projects are transitioning from a first to a second-generation method for large-scale agile development. In this paper, we discuss the following research question: *How can theories on coordination explain changes in coordination when moving from a first- to a second generation large-scale agile development method?*

We draw on a longitudinal case study of a development project in a large public organization in a Scandinavian country. The project started with a first generation large-scale agile method. However, in the last phase of the project, they changed to a second-generation model with autonomous teams. In the following, we first present theory which has previously been used to study coordination in large-scale agile development, then our case study method, some initial results from the case study and then a discussion of around using identified theory in analysing this case. We conclude with what we see as preliminary recommendations for studying transitions of coordination practices in large-scale agile development.

2 Theory

A previous article [5] identified four theories we believe are relevant in order to develop research-based advice for the software industry on coordination. In Table 1 below, we briefly present each theory with key reference and with reference to studies using this theory on large-scale agile development. Note that the theories have very different origins. The theory from Strode [4] and from Salas et al. [6] have basis in single teams, while Van de ven [7] and Jarzabkowski [8] focuses on organisations.

3 Method

Our data is based on a longitudinal case study of a development project in PublicOrg. In order to explain the setting, we first provide an overview of PublicOrg and the development project, before commenting briefly on our research method for understanding the case.

3.1 Case

The fieldwork was conducted within a development project at PublicOrg, a large Scandinavian organization for public services. The IT department develops, operates, and manages IT solutions that support close to 20,000 employees in their work, and provide solutions for about 800,000 active users. The IT department has approximately 700 employees and 400 consultants and maintains and operates close to 300 applications.

One of the core systems was originally developed in 1978. To accommodate legislative changes and support increased automation of work, the organization began a

Table 1. Four coordination theories, adapted from [5]

Field	Description	References
Software Engineering (Strode et al.)	A coordination strategy consists of three components: Synchronization: In arenas such as daily meetings where team members meet at the same time and place. Structure: Physical closeness, team member availability and that team members can substitute others. Boundary spanning: Activities, artefacts and roles to coordinate with other people or units beyond the project	Key reference: [4]
Sociology (van de Ven et al.)	Coordination is done through persons ("personal mode") or through artefacts ("impersonal mode"). If coordination is done through persons, it could be done individually or in groups. Impersonal coordination is "programmed" or "codified" for example through plans or written coding standards	Key reference: [7] Used in: [9–11]
Organizational Psychology (Salas et al.)	Mechanisms for coordination on team level are seen as relevant for inter-team coordination in multiteam systems. Three coordination mechanisms: Shared mental models: Common understanding of tasks, work process and knowledge of others. Closed-loop communication: Senders of messages ensure that messages are received correctly. Mutual trust: Shared belief that team members will perform roles and protect interests of teammates	Key reference: [6] Used in: [12–14]
Management Science (Jarzabkowski et al.)	Management Science researchers refer to the process of Coordinating to underscore the dynamic and emergent characteristics of coordination mechanisms. Jarzabkowski et al. argue that coordinating mechanisms are subject for change, are established, fall apart, and are transformed over time	Key reference: [8]

series of modernization projects in 2012. The projects would replace the old system in three increments. The first of these projects failed, and the failure resulted in massive media attention. When the second project began in 2016, stakeholders were therefore determined to avoid failure at any cost. This project, the "Beta" project, which is the one we are studying, had an estimated cost of 130 million Euro. At the start of our fieldwork, PublicOrg's strategy for IT development was to outsource software development projects to external suppliers. The suppliers, usually consultancy companies, would then be responsible for development and maintenance, while PublicOrg was responsible for coordination and operations. The IT department at PublicOrg employed a staged development method, with formal handovers between stages.

Our unit of analysis is the Beta project, the project was organized and run by PublicOrg according to their traditional model. They created a project group and hired one consultancy company to help them with formulating requirements and another consultancy company to implement the solution. At the height of the project group including the consultancy companies involved approximately 200 people.

Since the previous project had been a failure, much attention was given to control mechanisms and to ensure accountability within this second project. At the same time, the IT-department at PublicOrg hired a new leader who had new ideas of how PublicOrg should manage their IT strategy. They would move away from the previous regime of outsourcing and more towards inhouse development, taking ownership of their own systems. However, while the head of PublicOrg IT was talking about lean business driven development in autonomous teams in an environment of trust and openness, the project was still underway under the old regime of control and formal handovers. This change in strategy by PublicOrg IT would affect the Beta project gradually.

3.2 Research Method

The study of the Beta project has been organized as a longitudinal case study. Several researchers have been involved with gathering data over a period of two years. Our material consists of observations, project documents, and over 30 semi-structured interviews usually lasting from 30 min to two hours. The interviews were recorded and transcribed. Our main source of informants were the people from the consultancy company hired to develop the solution, but we also conducted interviews with key people in PublicOrg and in the consultancy company hired to assist with the requirements.

We are currently in the process of organizing and coding the material. The findings in this paper is based on our initial understanding of the case and the material before beginning a thorough analysis. Our analysis will consist of combination of bottom up and top down coding, and this paper outlines some key theories and constructs which will be used in the top down part of the analysis.

4   Results

During the *first phase* of the development project, which was based on the first generation "Perform model" [15, 16], there were several structures designed to promote coordination at the inter team level. We have identified around 20 arenas and tools used during this phase. Formal meetings like the upstart meetings in the beginning of each iteration, and Scrum of Scrums intended to keep the teams in the loop on what was happening in other teams. Architectural forums and test forums sought to keep the specialized roles in each team in touch with each other. Artefacts such as the overall architecture and dependency map contributed to handling of dependencies between teams. In addition, many team members were rotated between teams as the project was scaling up in order to promote knowledge sharing between developers. Contact between the developers and PublicOrg was largely formal, each team had a "functional architect" from their consultancy company that was the contact person towards the product owners and solution architects at PublicOrg. The product owners and solution architects were situated in another part of the building. We label this first part of the project "First generation agile development methodology", since the agility of the development teams takes place in strict boundaries within a framework of project management and waterfall methodology.

For the *second phase* of the project not much was changed for the core development teams. They were scaling up eventually ending up with seven teams. There were some changes relating to how they communicated with PublicOrg, as the product owners and solution architects were moved physically closer to the teams they were working with, but handover of user stories was still much based on a "relay race" approach. The larger change for this phase was that a part of the system was spun off from the larger solution and given to a dedicated multidisciplinary team, "Team Bravo". This was in addition to the seven core teams. Team Bravo was not locked into the reporting, testing and deployment regime of the core teams, they had autonomy to deploy to production at will. This team was not part of any of the coordination arenas the core teams were using to coordinate their dependencies, and dependencies with the core system was handled on an ad hoc basis, leading to some frustration as expressed by a project manager: *"We were not quite in phase when it came to coordination, I'd say. And I bet they thought we were daft, and we thought they were a bit daft too. But such things pass easy, given some time"*. This second phase of the project we've labeled "Bimodal", since the core teams are continuing with their original methodology, while team Bravo is trying out a new way of working.

During the second phase of the project, the decision was made to change the entire organization of the project, this happened in the *third phase* Everybody should now work in multidisciplinary teams. A change that was characterized as *"Changing the engine of an airplane in flight with 200 passengers aboard"*. Every team had autonomy to decide their own work structure, and most of the coordination arenas across teams was dropped in addition to several middle management roles being removed. PublicOrg hired two agile coaches that would advise the teams on how they could work. From two major deployments a year, they would now move to daily deployments. The teams were structured around functional areas of the overall system so every team had a dedicated area to develop and support. We characterize this third phase of the development project as a "second generation agile development model" as in this phase the teams have a much larger degree of both agility and responsibility.

5 Discussion

We return to our initial research question: *How can theories on coordination explain changes in coordination when moving from a first generation to a second generation large-scale agile development method?*

From the theoretical perspective of Strode [4] we see that the synchronization has been left to the teams in the new structure. Very little emphasis has been on synchronization structures across teams and six months after the change, informants were expressing needs for more synchronization arenas across teams. Structure has been well kept in that all members of teams are sitting together and they are physically close to the other teams. However, team member availability across teams can be a challenge, as can teams' ability to substitute each other since every team is now specialized within an application area. Boundary spanning is where we can see a clear lack of structure in the new organization, which might have implications later. However, six months after phase three began, we saw new boundary spanning mechanisms emerging to meet this need.

Looking at the case with the theoretical perspective of van de Ven [7], we see a move from group mode of personal coordination towards individual mode of personal coordination. In addition, we see a move within group mode coordination from scheduled to unscheduled meetings. Since decisions are moved towards the team level, we see a decline in impersonal modes of coordination across teams since teams are no longer bound by guidelines developed by other teams.

The theoretical lens of Salas [6] allows us to explain why we continue to see good coordination between teams despite removing many arenas of cross team coordination. The main explanation lies in the development of a shared mental model during the first phases of the project. With this in mind, developers are able to coordinate across teams because they know what the other teams are doing. It will be interesting to see if the new structure will lead to a decline in the shared mental model over time, which some informants were indicating signs of six months after the transition to phase three. With the teams being given much autonomy, trust is probably the second most influential factor. The management trusts the teams and the teams trust each other. The shared mental model and trust might also be key constructs in explaining the poor coordination between the first autonomous team and the rest of the developing teams during the second phase of the project.

Finally, the theoretical perspective of Jarzabkowski [8] allows us to understand the process of rebuilding the coordination arenas after they were removed during the change in the project organization. After the reorganization most of the focus was on establishing coordination at the intra team level, but when we visited the project six months after the transition, multiple respondents expressed interest in re-establishing some of the coordination mechanisms at the inter team level.

It seems like these four theories align themselves along two major lines of questions for this case. Strode and van de Ven are useful to characterize the phases and answer questions relating to *how* coordination practices were organized during the project. The theories of Salas and Jarzabkowski are useful to describe *why* these changes occurred, and the apparent success of the transition.

The main limitation of this paper is that we are presenting initial findings before the main analysis is done. We do, however, believe the findings are important and interesting in that they are guiding our work on structuring the analysis, and what types of questions each theory might provide answers to. Other researchers may find the constructs from the identified theories useful in guiding their own research towards coordination in large-scale development methods. Practitioners may find it useful to use the constructs of Strode and van de Ven to map their own current practices and keep the constructs of Salas and Jarzabkowski in mind when designing a transition strategy.

6   Conclusion and Further Work

In this paper we have reported on some of our initial findings relating to coordination from a large scale development project that transitioned from a first to a second generation development methodology during the project.

We used four different theoretical perspectives, originally put forward in [5], to analyse our findings. We found that two theories [4, 7] were useful for characterizing the phases of the transition and answer questions relating to *how* coordination was done. The other two theories [6, 8] were useful to describe *why* the changes occurred, and could help us explain the apparent success of the transition. From our initial findings, a well developed shared mental model and sufficient degree of trust seems to be key factors in the successful coordination while transitioning from one generation to the next.

From a research point of view, the identified concepts might be useful in informing new studies of coordination in large-scale software development. From a practitioner point of view we offer guidance on how to categorize the current strategy and offer some key concepts to keep in mind when designing a transition strategy.

Moving forward, we will continue to analyse the material from our longitudinal study more in depth from the different theoretical perspectives we have identified, we might also broaden our study with the theory of Relational Coordination, recently suggested in [17] or specifically focus on coordination artefacts [18]. Our aim is to both provide input to practitioners looking for evidence-based advice on scaling their agile methods, as well as continuing our discourse on rethinking coordination in large-scale software development.

Acknowledgement. This work was supported by the project Agile 2.0 supported by the Research Council of Norway through grant 236759 and by the companies DNV GL, Equinor, Kantega, Kongsberg Defence & Aerospace, Sopra Steria, and Sticos.

References

1. Bass, J.M.: Future trends in agile at scale: a summary of the 7th international workshop on large-scale agile development. In: Hoda, Rashina (ed.) XP 2019. LNBIP, vol. 364, pp. 75–80. Springer, Cham (2019). https://doi.org/10.1007/978-3-030-30126-2_9
2. Dingsøyr, T., Falessi, D., Power, K.: Agile development at scale: the next frontier. IEEE Softw. **36**, 30–38 (2019). https://doi.org/10.1109/MS.2018.2884884
3. Bick, S., Spohrer, K., Hoda, R., Scheerer, A., Heinzl, A.: Coordination challenges in large-scale software development: a case study of planning misalignment in hybrid settings. IEEE Trans. Softw. Eng. **44**(10), 932–950 (2018). https://doi.org/10.1109/TSE.2017.2730870
4. Strode, D.E., Huff, S.L., Hope, B.G., Link, S.: Coordination in co-located agile software development projects. J. Syst. Softw. **85**, 1222–1238 (2012)
5. Dingsøyr, T., Bjørnson, F.O., Moe, N. B., Rolland, K., Seim, E.A.: Rethinking coordination in large-scale software development, Gothenburg, Sweden, pp. 91–92 (2018). https://doi.org/10.1145/3195836.3195850
6. Salas, E., Sims, D.E., Burke, S.C.: Is there a "Big five" in teamwork? Small Group Res. **36**, 555–599 (2005)

7. Van de Ven, A.H., Delbecq, A.L., Koenig Jr., R.: Determinants of coordination modes within organizations. Am. Sociol. Rev. **41**(2), 322–338 (1976)

8. Jarzabkowski, P.A., Le, J.K., Feldman, M.S.: Toward a theory of coordinating: creating coordinating mechanisms in practice. Organ. Sci. **23**, 907–927 (2012). https://doi.org/10.1287/orsc.1110.0693

9. Moe, N.B., Dingsøyr, T., Rolland, K.: To schedule or not to schedule? An investigation of meetings as an inter-team coordination mechanism in large-scale agile software development. Int. J. Inf. Syst. Proj. Manage. **6**, 45–59 (2018)

10. Dingsøyr, T., Moe, N.B., Seim, E.A.: Coordinating knowledge work in multi-team programs: findings from a large-scale agile development program. Proj. Manage. J. **49**, 64–77 (2018). https://doi.org/10.1177/8756972818798980

11. Nyrud, H., Stray, V.: Inter-team coordination mechanisms in large-scale agile. In: Proceedings of the XP2017 Scientific Workshops, pp. 1–6 (2017)

12. Bjørnson, F.O., Wijnmaalen, J., Stettina, C. J., Dingsøyr, T.: Inter-team coordination in large-scale agile development: a case study of three enabling mechanisms. In: XP2018, Porto, Portugal, pp. 216–231 (2018)

13. Scheerer, A., Hildenbrand, T., Kude, T.: Coordination in large-scale agile software development: a multiteam systems perspective. In: 2014 47th Hawaii International Conference on System Sciences, pp. 4780–4788 (2014)

14. Scheerer, A., Kude, T.: Exploring coordination in large-scale agile software development: a multiteam systems perspective. In: Proceedings of the International Conference on Information Systems (2014)

15. Dingsøyr, T., et al.: Key lessons from tailoring agile methods for large-scale software development. IEEE IT Prof. **21**, 34–41 (2019). https://doi.org/10.1109/MITP.2018.2876984

16. Dingsøyr, T., Moe, N.B., Fægri, T.E., Seim, E.A.: Exploring software development at the very large-scale: a revelatory case study and research agenda for agile method adaptation. Empir. Softw. Eng. **23**(1), 490–520 (2017). https://doi.org/10.1007/s10664-017-9524-2

17. Berntzen, M., Moe, N.B., Stray, V.: The product owner in large-scale agile: an empirical study through the lens of relational coordination theory. In: Kruchten, P., Fraser, S., Coallier, F. (eds.) XP 2019. LNBIP, vol. 355, pp. 121–136. Springer, Cham (2019). https://doi.org/10.1007/978-3-030-19034-7_8

18. Zaitsev, A., Gal, U., Tan, B.: Coordination artifacts in agile software development. Inf. Organ. **30**, 100288 (2020)

Exploring the Product Owner Role Within SAFe Implementation in a Multinational Enterprise

Daniel Remta[(✉)] ⬤, Michal Doležel ⬤, and Alena Buchalcevová ⬤

University of Economics, Prague, Czech Republic
{xremd03,michal.dolezel,alena.buchalcevova}@vse.cz

Abstract. [Context] Agile development methods are highly popular across software organizations. To leverage benefits in larger enterprises, Agile development methods have to be scaled. Scaled Agile Framework (SAFe) is the most commonly used scaling framework. Performing of the Product Owner role has been identified as crucial in project success in large-scale environments. Staffing the right Product Owner is one of the challenges of adopting SAFe. [Motivation] Research papers focused on Product Owner in SAFe are scarce. Our study outcomes help enterprises to understand the Product Owner role in SAFe and therefore contribute to the removal of challenges with finding the right Product Owners. Additionally, we aim to improve the research community's understanding of the Product Owner role within the context of SAFe. [Method] Qualitative data were collected through three semi-structured interviews and analyzed using deductive content analysis. [Results] This paper presents the initial results of a single case study. We found out that many activities identified for Product Owners in previous research are not carried out by Product Owners in this particular SAFe implementation.

Keywords: Product Owner · Responsibilities · Functions · Scaled Agile Framework · SAFe · Large-scale agile methods

1 Introduction

Agile, as a set of iterative and incremental software engineering methods [1], becomes commonplace in many large organizations [2], where agile practices have to be scaled [3]. Scaling Agile was identified as an important research topic [4], and more and more large organizations are transitioning towards Agile [1, 2]. During this process, new roles are introduced to the enterprise environment, such as the Product Owner (PO) role. The PO role originates from the Scrum method [5] and has been identified to play a crucial role in project success [1]. The PO role is also present in the frameworks for large-scale Agile, such as Scaled Agile Framework (SAFe) [6], which is the most commonly used framework for scaling Agile [7]. However, staffing the right PO was identified as one of the challenges of adopting SAFe [8]. Surprisingly, research papers with a focus on the PO role in SAFe are scarce. A better understanding of the role in SAFe will help enterprises to acknowledge requirements to people assigned to the PO role and therefore help with the success of their SAFe adoption. In our research, we

M. Paasivaara and P. Kruchten (Eds.): XP 2020 Workshops, LNBIP 396, pp. 92–100, 2020.
https://doi.org/10.1007/978-3-030-58858-8_10

address the following research question (RQ): Which of the activities described for Product Owners in previous research are performed by the Product Owners in the examined enterprise that follows SAFe?

The paper is organized as follows. Following Introduction, Sect. 2 provides a literature review and a taxonomy of PO functions mapped to SAFe roles. In Sect. 3, the adopted research method and the context of the study are described. Section 4 provides findings from the semi-structured interviews. Section 5 concludes the paper with a discussion and a summary of key take-aways.

2 Background

In this section, we provide a literature review and present a taxonomy of PO functions. We use the term "function" to refer to a designated group of coupled activities.

Large-Scale Agile. Scaling Agile was identified as an important topic [4]. Dikert et al. [1] identified challenges and success factors for large-scale Agile transformations, focusing on large-scale organizations with 50 or more people. The agile practices have to be scaled [3], and POs must cope with a range of new activities [9].

Product Owner. Originally, Scrum defined the PO role relatively simply as the sole person responsible for managing the Product Backlog [5]. Yet, the adequate performing of Product Owners was identified as one of the critical success factors for projects [1], and a wide range of other activities performed by PO was described [3, 10–14]. The PO role has been examined in previous research. Bertzen and Moe [15] identified the importance of frequent communication and interaction between POs in large-scale Agile. Paasivaara et al. [3] described the differences in approaches to scaling the PO role. Bass carried out an empirical research [9, 10] on the PO activities in a large-scale Agile environment. Yet, only a limited amount of papers focus on the PO role in SAFe.

SAFe. SAFe provides prescriptive guidelines for implementing enterprise-scale Lean-Agile development, and a number of companies that have applied SAFe have reported significant benefits from it [6]. Interestingly, the popularity of SAFe seems unaffected by concerns about Agile principles and values in the top-down approach, and SAFe's strong emphasis on process rather than on people [16, 17].

SAFe and PO. Despite some existing research on SAFe [8], papers focused on the PO role in SAFe are still scarce. The study of Paasivaara et al. [2] states that implementing SAFe results in closer collaboration and communication between POs and Product Managers (PM). However, the study focus was on SAFe adoption in general. Overall, little is known about the PO in SAFe.

PO in SAFe. SAFe adopted the PO role but, in contrast to Scrum, assumes that a single person cannot handle product and market strategy while also being dedicated to agile teams. It was confirmed in [9, 10] that in large-scale Agile environments, the scope of activities goes beyond the capacity of one person acting as PO. PO and PM share responsibilities for working with customers [6]. We have identified some of the PO activities from [3, 10–14] in the descriptions of activities performed by other SAFe roles. The System Architect (SA) creates an architectural vision and aligns teams around a shared technical direction [6]. Aside from development, during planning, the Agile Team (AT) identifies risks and impediments [6]. The risks are actively managed by the Release Train Engineer (RTE) [6]. Specialty roles, people, and services to cover customer training, support, and compliance audits are represented in Shared Services [6]. Scrum Master (SM) ensures that the agile processes and guidelines are followed [6].

Taxonomy of PO Functions. To understand the fragmentation of PO activities, we extracted the taxonomy of the PO functions from the previous research on POs outside the context of SAFe [3, 10–14]. Next, we mapped the activities from the taxonomy to the descriptions of roles provided in SAFe [6]. The results are presented in Table 1. The functions described by Bass [10, 11] were used in accordance with his descriptions. When adding functions from [3, 12–14], we followed the example of the descriptions of functions in [10, 11]. Added functions from [3, 12–14] are written in italics.

Table 1. PO functions taxonomy mapped to SAFe. (Synthetized from [3, 6, 10–14].)

Function	Activity	Role in SAFe
Prioritizer [10]	Prioritizes requirements in the product or sprint backlog and ensures requirements bring value to the business.	PO/PM
Groom [10]	Makes sure product backlog is continuously evolving and registers requirements from clients. Clarifies the details of product backlog items and their respective acceptance criteria.	PO/PM
Release Master [10]	Manages and approves release schedules.	PM
Technical Architect [10]	Designs, implements, and disseminates a reference architecture, provides architecture coordination on large projects.	SA
Governor [10]	Provides a technical governance framework to project teams working on a program and ensures project compliance with corporate guidelines and policies.	RTE/SM/SA
Communicator [10]	Ensures that global teams are in sync and bridges onshore and offshore geographical distribution.	SM/PO
Traveler [10]	Travels to clients to get first-hand knowledge of the client's needs and gathers an understanding of it by spending time onshore at customer sites.	PM/PO
Intermediary [10]	Has extensive experience in the system business domain and acts as an interface to senior executives.	PM
Risk Assessor [10]	Performs risk management and mitigation when needed, especially with focus on technical complexity.	AT/RTE
Gatekeeper [11]	Determines feature or story completeness for inclusion in the release.	PO
Customer Relationship Manager [11]	Provides technical support to customers, assists with site preparation and product installation, and conducts product training.	Shared Services
Entrepreneur [12]	*Develops business/product plan and service planning.*	PM
Motivator [13]	*Motivates the team and finds ways to get the team more involved.*	SM
Leader [14]	*Leads the development teams.*	SM
Negotiator [3]	*Negotiates with different stakeholders to avoid conflicts.*	PM/PO

The mapping in Table 1 indicates the fundamental difference between the PO role in SAFe and the PO role examined in previous research by showing a visible fragmentation of previously identified PO activities to other SAFe roles.

3   Research Method

Context. The single-case study has been conducted in a division of multinational enterprise that delivers mainframe software. The examined value stream specifically focuses on workload automation software, written mostly in low-level programming languages. For newer components (e.g. modern user interfaces), higher languages like C, Java, or JavaScript are used. The division follows the Portfolio SAFe configuration [6] and claims to follow SAFe on the team and program level "by the book". The development teams work in 2- to 4-week sprints. Overall, the environment can be characterized as a very large-scale Agile with 30 teams and 250+ team members.

Data Collection. Three POs have participated in the initial phase of the study. Table 2 shows the length of their experience in the role, the number of teams they concurrently work with, the number of development team members they work with, their previous position, and overall experience in the field of mainframe enterprise software. Additional interviews with 6–7 respondents are planned to complete the study.

Table 2. Research participants

PO	Months in the role	Teams	Members	Previous position	Years in field
PO_A	14	3	16	Developer, Scrum Master	3
PO_B	12	2	16	Developer	5
PO_C	10	1	16	Software support engineer	22

The interviews were done in person, audio-recorded, and transcribed. The interview guide is available at https://rebrand.ly/4ylvsbo. The interviews consisted of 54 questions, 3 to 4 per each function, and took from 65 to 85 min to complete. Our aim was to identify if the activity of the function had been performed, to what extent, how often, typically followed by a request to provide an example to validate the previous answers. All recordings and transcripts were given codes and stored separately from any names or other direct identification of participants.

Data Analysis. A deductive content analysis [18] was used. We used the functions from the taxonomy introduced in Table 1 as categories for the analysis. Next, we manually open coded, analyzed, and matched data into these categories. As the last step, we have interpreted the results.

4   Results

In this section, we provide the preliminary results from the examined SAFe implementation. The comparison of each PO function from the taxonomy introduced in Table 1 with the findings from the semi-structured interviews showed that POs in the selected enterprise SAFe implementation perform the activities of Prioritizer, Groom, Communicator, Traveler, Gatekeeper, and Motivator. In the rest of the functions, POs are only partially involved. In Table 3, we present evidence for each function in the form of quotations or merged findings. The functions confirmed as being performed by POs are written in bold.

Table 3. PO Functions in SAFe – findings. Source: Interviews

Function	Commentary
Prioritizer	*"PI objectives are our highest priority [...] if we have some customer interest in the feature or the story, it will get prioritized higher. I try to keep my thoughts out of it. I try to prioritize first based on customer, then on business needs."* [PO_C]
Groom	*"[...] continuously going through the backlog, seeing if there are stories to be delivered and updated, as we are learning about new technologies and based on the feedback from the customer I go through the stories and change them or update them, and move into the direction we want to go."* [PO_C]
Release master	PO's main activity in the release process is ensuring completion of the release checklist, which has to be signed off by involved stakeholders representing different business units. PO_A described PM as the only one responsible. *"Release dates, numbering, names, all of this stuff goes to the product manager, and it is his responsibility."* [PO_A]
Technical architect	All POs stated that architectural activities and decisions are not in the scope of PO activities. As evident from PO_C's answer, they try to avoid any architectural involvement as much as possible. *"I try very hard to exclude myself from any involvement with architectural decisions. And I also try very hard to avoid anything in the description of the user stories that will imply any suggestion for architectural decision."* [PO_C]
Governor	Different roles perform governance activities. POs mentioned: SA, Legal, Functional Managers, and SMs. For POs, the delivery of the item is the primary concern. POs only make sure that the frameworks are followed and, in case not, inform other roles to take action. *"I raise a point or question when I believe it is appropriate to raise the point, but I don't see myself as a policeman being on guard, or anything [like that]."* [PO_B]
Communicator	*"I have team members in Texas, in Pittsburg, North Virginia, and Sydney, and it is very difficult to manage the team across so many different time zones."* [PO_C]

(continued)

Table 3. (*continued*)

Function	Commentary
Traveler	*"[...] mostly technical conferences, and this year I want to continue in US and Europe. I am also expecting to do a few customer visits. [PO_C]"*
Intermediary	All POs felt experienced in the domain of enterprise software development, but PO_B and PO_C were not that confident in the domain of Product Ownership. POs confirmed communications with senior executives; however, as the senior executives, they understand PMs, customer Account Managers, and Business Owners. *"[...] in general PM and upper product management, while I talk most of the time with PM." [PO_B]*
Risk assessor	All POs do identify and articulate potential risks but do not participate in risk mitigation. The mitigation is understood as belonging to other roles. *"Other people will go and take care of this. It is not a product owner's responsibility to solve it; it is a PO's responsibility [just] to raise it." [PO_A]*
Gatekeeper	*"I consider it complete when engineers will demo it, will show to me and the other stakeholders what they did, elect feedback, and I don't consider it complete when there will not be proper QA [Quality Assurance] testing on it to make sure what we have is working in that front." [PO_A]*
Customer relationship manager	All POs clearly stated that there are dedicated support and education teams, so POs are not directly involved in providing support nor training to the customers. PO activities in this area are limited to providing internal training sessions and materials to support and education teams. *"I got the skillset, but it is not what I do. I will not sit with the client and show him how to install the product." [PO_B]*
Entrepreneur	All POs are involved and are contributing by providing information to, and having discussions with, PM. The decisions and plans are made by PM, who also owns the product roadmap. *"As PO I just discuss what customer want, reflect this to the management, and then the decisions will come from the management, not the product owner." [PO_A]*
Motivator	All POs stated motivating the team, and people is part of their job. *"[...] give KUDOS to people who deserve it, always pull out someone and say 'Hey, good job!', in case they did a good job. If someone did an outstanding job, you should communicate this to their managers and directors. [PO_A]*
Leader	None of the POs identified himself as the leader of the team. *"No. I don't consider myself being a leader to the team. But I don't even know who the leader for the team is." [PO_B]*
Negotiator	POs seem to be positioned as mediators, but not the negotiators *per se*. *"I would consider myself a mediator between different stakeholders and trying to find the source of the conflict and initiator of it." [PO_C]*

5 Discussion and Summary

Examining the Scaled Agile Framework [6] and its concrete implementation in a multinational enterprise, we addressed the RQ: "Which of the activities described for Product Owners in previous research are performed by the Product Owners in the examined enterprise using SAFe?". We found out that many activities identified for PO in previous research are not carried out by POs in this SAFe implementation. Specifically, our preliminary research findings demonstrated that PO in this particular SAFe implementation is *not*: leading the teams; mitigating identified risks; designing, implementing and disseminating technical architecture; providing governance frameworks; ensuring compliance with corporate guidelines; communicating with senior executives; nor providing support and customer training. This is surprising because previous research conducted outside the context of SAFe assumed that PO responsibilities are very broad. Below, we offer a hypothesis about the reason for the inconsistency.

The mapping provided in Table 1 indicated that there is a complex relationship between the previously identified PO functions and roles in SAFe, where the performing of the activities is fragmented among multiple roles. Supported by the outcomes from the conducted semi-structured interviews, which indicate that in SAFe, the original PO role functions have undergone significant modifications, it is evident that PO functions in SAFe are different from the functions of the PO role identified in previous research. In our research, the close collaboration between PO and PM described in [2] was confirmed. In fact, PO's decisions about priorities and requirements for development are strongly influenced by PM, who, in reality, drives and develops business and product plans. This PM activity contradicts the prime Scrum definition of PO as the sole person responsible for managing the Product Backlog [5]. Therefore, the PO's accountability for product leadership fades away.

We offer a possible explanation. SAFe provides rigorous descriptions for the implementation of Agile processes on a large-scale and put the emphasis on the process [15]. This *de-facto* leads to a new form of the management-driven top-down approach [16] with the fragmentation of the roles. We support this statement by evidence from the interview: *"As PO I just discuss what customer want, reflect this to the management, and then the decisions will come from the management, not the product owner."* [PO_A]

Conclusion. The PO role in the examined SAFe implementation deviates from the previous understanding of the role outside the context of SAFe, as the range of PO activities is narrowed. We attribute it to the top-down approach criticized by practitioners and confirmed during our single-case study. We identified PM as the person accountable for, and steering, the product.

Limitations and Threats to Validity. The presented results were obtained in one division of a large multinational enterprise and, therefore, might be influenced by the local context. Achieving a validity in a single case study is a known challenge, thus plausible, rival explanations or triangulation methods should be used in further research to strengthen validity of our findings [19]. The study provides only preliminary outcomes from the three interviews. Hence, it is too soon generalize the PO role in SAFe. Two papers [12, 13] used in our taxonomy did not explore a large-scale environment context. Still, we identified similar activities appearing in the examined environment.

Future Works. As this research is ongoing, another 6–7 interviews will follow to validate the preliminary findings. Our next steps will be to gather, analyze, and incorporate more data from POs with different experience and from different parts of the organization, which will help to understand the real-life PO functions in SAFe implementations. More case studies exploring further enterprise SAFe adoptions are needed to confirm the findings presented in this study.

Acknowledgment. This work was supported by an internal grant funding scheme (F4/23/2019) administered by the University of Economics, Prague.

References

1. Dikert, K., Paasivaara, M., Lassenius, C.: Challenges and success factors for large-scale agile transformations: a systematic literature review. J. Syst. Softw. **119**, 87–108 (2016)
2. Paasivaara, M.: Adopting SAFe to scale agile in a globally distributed organization. In: ICGSE, pp. 36–40 (2017)
3. Paasivaara, M., Heikkila, V.T., Lassenius, C.: Experiences in scaling the product owner role in large-scale globally distributed scrum. In: ICGSE, pp. 174–178 (2012)
4. Dingsøyr, T., Moe, N.B.: Research challenges in large-scale agile software development. SIGSOFT Softw. Eng. Notes **38**, 38 (2013)
5. Schwaber, K., Sutherland, J.: The Definitive Guide to Scrum: The Rules of the Game (2017). https://www.scrumguides.org/docs/scrumguide/v2017/2017-Scrum-Guide-US.pdf
6. SAFe: Scaled agile framework (2019). http://www.scaledagileframework.com/
7. CollabNet VersionOne: The 13th State of Agile Survey (2019). https://www.stateofagile.com/
8. Putta, A., Paasivaara, M., Lassenius, C.: Adopting scaled agile framework (SAFe): a multivocal literature review. In: XP'18, pp. 39:1–39:4 (2018)
9. Bass, J.M., Haxby, A.: Tailoring product ownership in large-scale agile projects: managing scale, distance, and governance. IEEE Softw. **36**, 58–63 (2019)
10. Bass, J.M.: How product owner teams scale agile methods to large distributed enterprises. Empir. Softw. Eng. **20**, 1525–1557 (2015)
11. Bass, J., Beecham, S., Razzak, M.A., et al.: Poster: an empirical study of the product owner role in scrum. In: ICSE, pp. 123–124 (2018)
12. Oomen, S., Waal, B.D., Albertin, A., Ravesteyn, P.: How can Scrum be succesful? Competences of the scrum product owner. In: ECIS, pp. 130–142 (2017)
13. Raithatha, D.: Making the whole product agile – a product owners perspective. In: XP, pp. 184–187 (2007)
14. Kristinsdottir, S., Larusdottir, M., Cajander, Å.: Responsibilities and challenges of product owners at spotify - an exploratory case study. In: HCSE/HESSD, pp. 3–16 (2016)
15. Berntzen, M., Moe, N.B., Stray, V.: The product owner in large-scale agile: an empirical study through the lens of relational coordination theory. In: XP, pp. 121–136 (2019)
16. Jeffries, R.: Issues with SAFe (2014). https://ronjeffries.com/xprog/articles/issues-with-safe/. Accessed 22 Mar 2020

17. Elssamadisy, A.: Has SAFe Cracked the Large Agile Adoption Nut? (2013). https://www.infoq.com/news/2013/08/safe/#. Accessed 22 Mar 2020
18. DeFranco, J.F., Laplante, P.A.: A content analysis process for qualitative software engineering research. Innov. Syst. Softw. Eng. **13**, 129–141 (2017)
19. Yin, R.K.: Validity and generalization in future case study evaluations. Evaluation **13**, 321–332 (2013)

Evaluation of Agile Team Work Quality

Alexander Poth[1]([⊠]) [iD], Mario Kottke[1], and Andreas Riel[2]

[1] Volkswagen AG, Berliner Ring 2, 38436 Wolfsburg, Germany
{Alexander.Poth,mario.kottke}@volkswagen.de
[2] Grenoble INP, G-SCOP, CNRS, Grenoble Alps University,
38031 Grenoble, France
andreas.riel@grenoble-inp.fr

Abstract. The maturity of organizations is measured with process assessment models like the ISO/IEC 33001. The product quality is aligned with internal and external product quality charactersitics based on models like the ISO/IEC 25010. With the shift from the Tailorism-driven process orientation to a more people centric organization, the two dimensions process and product quality have to be extened by the people or team quality dimension. The presented approach offers aspects for agile Team Work Quality (aTWQ), as well as related measurement indicators. The approach is evaluated in the large enterprise context of the Volkswagen AG. The indicators of aTWQ have been integrated and established in the agile tool box for a sustainable agile transition of the company.

Keywords: Agile team work quality (aTWQ) · Large-scaling agile · Quality assurance (QA) · Agile transformation

1 Introduction

Several big enterprises like Cisco [1], Ericsson [2], and Volkswagen [3] are in the process of agile transformation. Accompanying tools and measures have to scale from individual project teams to bigger organizational entities [4]. The key of agile development is the team who delivers the customer value. However, systematic approaches to team development in software developing industries are rare. They need to cover criteria for the determination of team culture and performance, metrics, as well as recommendations for improvement. In this article, we present the aTWQ (agile Team Work Quality) approach to supporting teams in improving their agile mindset and practices by themselves without external assessments. Given the legislative and cultural context that is typical for large European enterprises, aTWQ shall meet the following particular requirements and constraints:

- The approach shall not use specific roles that are typically fulfilled by a particular person to avoid individual performance measures to be aligned with workers council mindset in enterprises.
- The approach shall be appropriate for integration in project and program reviews to measure transition progress from a governance perspective.

© The Author(s) 2020
M. Paasivaara and P. Kruchten (Eds.): XP 2020 Workshops, LNBIP 396, pp. 101–110, 2020.
https://doi.org/10.1007/978-3-030-58858-8_11

– The approach shall be applicable as a self-service by the teams to ensure scaling without centralized coaching etc. and support the autonomy of the teams during evolving.

The lean and agile approaches most frequently used in industry, Scrum and SAFe®, do not address TWQ explicitly. In SAFe®, one of the four core-values is "Build-in Quality" [5]. In the deep dive documentation [6], however, the focus is product quality and "Flow" as a generic construct for all other aspects of quality. The process quality is implicitly addressed by links to other topics. TWQ is not mentioned at all, and therefore implicit. On the other hand, the consequence of this observation is: everything that is needed for quality is done inherently and not defined in SAFe®. In Scrum, the heart of the value creation is the team, which is supported by the Definition of Done (DoD) for achieving product quality, as well as the team retrospectives for process improvement. The team itself does not get any kind of explicit quality-related instructions and tasks. Instead, the daily, open communication and commitments are essential parts of TWQ. This is motivated by the aspects like mutual trust and performance monitoring which are observed in [7]. Also in [8] aspects like the ability to complete whole tasks or feedback are shown to have an impact to the team work quality. In [9] it is observed that team work quality correlates with performance in some settings which is an important fact for organization development. Also, collocation and diversity in teams [10] helps to improve team work quality.

The particular challenge related to TWQ is the fact that TWQ is part of internal quality aspects that are typically hidden and invisible from the outside. This makes it difficult in lean and agile environments to identify and explicitly "spend effort" on them. The ISO/IEC 25010:2011 makes this more transparent by distinguishing "quality in use" from "product quality". The latter is often directly addressed by regulation and compliance requirements like security or reliability. The process quality is treated as a "first class citizen", because there are powerful and influential (external) stakeholders for legal compliance. Therefore, without some explicit measures and metrics related to TWQ, a systematic development is difficult from the organizational point of view.

2   A Team-Based Approach to Agile TWQ

Team work aspects have been treated to a large extent in literature, e.g. [11] and [12]. Some of this previous work addresses agile team work quality explicitly [13] or [14] some also propose organizational models fostering team work quality [15]. During the design of our approach, we focused on integration of different concepts with a longer evaluation time to not have the work to start from scratch and get benefits form the diversity of the different approaches we are integrating. The three approaches we consider most relevant are the Team Work Quality (TWQ) [14], Team Climate Inventory (TCI) [16] and Group Development Questionnaire (GDQ) [15] because they address both the team development and maturity. The TWQ approach focuses on quality indicators of team work. The TCI approach developed over years and evaluates team indicators related to the teams' working structures for innovation. The GDQ approach focuses on evaluating the teams' alignment with stages of group development. Based on [17], the following empirical observations provide the basis of our aTWQ approach:

a) Team Performance is based on TWQ.
b) TWQ and the TCI have similar "content".
c) TCI works well with GDQ.

Based on [14] and [18], we derived the initial team-level approach covering the six aspects communication, coordination, balance of contribution, mutual support, effort, cohesion. These six quality aspects lead to team performance [19], legitimating economically the effort for measurement and further TWQ improvement. We combined these aspects with those of TCI and defined 19 related questions to come up with a holistic team evaluation questionnaire for aTWQ, see Table 1.

Table 1. aTWQ questionnaire with specific indicators for Scrum and SAFe® and team development level.

Topic	Question (Base Practices)	Scrum	SAFe®	Level
Participative safety	Do we have a "**we** are in it together" **attitude** *driven by the **ability and willingness** to help and support each other in carrying out their tasks?*			IV
	Do people keep **each other informed** about work-related issues in the team *supported by a frequent communication?*	Daily Scrum	Program, team backlog	I
	Do people **feel understood** and accepted by one another?			III
	Are there real attempts to **share information** throughout the team driven *by openness of the information exchange?*	Daily Scrum, Retrospective	Portfolio Kanban, Inspect & Adapt	(I) III
	Is there a lot of **give and take** *by the team members' motivation to maintain the team?*		Innovation and Planning Iteration	IV
	Do we **keep in touch** with one another as a team *by accepting that team goals are more important than individual goals?*		Pairing/frequent review	III

(continued)

Table 1. (*continued*)

Topic	Question (Base Practices)	Scrum	SAFe®	Level
Support for innovation	Is this team always moving towards the development of new answers?			IV
	Is this team open and responsive to change?	Inspect & Adaptation	Innovation and Planning Iteration	III
	Do people in this team always search for fresh, new ways of looking at problems?	Retrospective	Innovation and Planning Iteration, PI Planning	III
	Do members of the team provide and share resources to help in the application of new ideas driven *by team members' ability and willingness to share workload?*	Inspect & Adaptation	Innovation and Planning Iteration	III
	Do team members provide practical support for new ideas and their application by *prioritize the teams' task over other obligations?*	self-organizing	Innovation and Planning Iteration	IV
Vision	How clear are you about what your team's objectives are?	(Product) Vision, Sprint Goal	Vision	I
	To what extent do you agree with these objectives?	Sprint commitment	PI planning	I
	To what extent do you think other team members agree with these objectives?	Refinement	ART commitment	I
	To what extent do you think members of your team are committed to these objectives?	Sprint commitment, DoD	ART commitment	I

(*continued*)

Table 1. (continued)

Topic	Question (Base Practices)	Scrum	SAFe®	Level
Task orientation	Do your team colleagues provide useful ideas and practical help to enable you to do the job to the best of your abilities?		Pairing/frequent review	IV
	Are team members prepared to question the basis of what the team is doing?	Daily Scrum, Refinement		IV
	Does the team critically appraise potential weaknesses in what it is doing in order to achieve the best possible outcome?	Refinement, Retrospective		II
	Do members of the team build on one another's ideas in order to achieve the highest possible standards of performance?	Refinement, Retrospective		(I) IV
Coordination	Is there a **common understanding** when working on parallel subtasks, and agreement on common work breakdown structures, schedules, budgets and deliverables?	Backlog, Stories	Roadmap, Portfolio, ART, Iteration plan, Stories	III

TWQ aspects not explicitly covered by the TCI questionnaire have been added and printed in italics. Terms printed in bold letters signify the most important aspects of the respective question. Column 3 and 4 show the mapping of the questions to Scrum and SAFe®, respectively, based on the specific approach's elements covering the aspects addressed by the questions. Hence, the TCI/TWQ questions represent generic practices, while the associated elements from Scrum or SAFe represent specific practices of either approach. Both combined constitute the practice set of aTWQ in a specific team environment. The sparsely populated columns 3 and 4 indicate that neither Scrum nor SAFe® cover aTWQ aspects well. The indicators of the approaches are based on the current versions of SAFe® 5.0 and the Scrum Guide version of Nov. 2017.

For the integration into the project reviews [20] evaluating individual product teams, a group of teams (like programs), as well as entire organizational units, an extension beyond a typical team size is needed. For the context of aTWQ, a team is constituted by people who have common goals within a purpose. The team size is aligned with the agile definition of 7–9 individuals [21]. A group is a collection of people or teams coordinating outcomes and efforts.

In the aTWQ approach, the extension to groups larger than one team is realized with the Group Development Questionnaire (GDQ) because in scaling agile approaches there is no "one big team". In SAFe®, for example, there exist different types of teams like the technical and business teams sharing a common basic approach. "Both types of teams strive for fast learning by performing work in small batches, assessing the results, and adjusting accordingly" [22]. This leads us to deriving that in SAFe, a group of different types of teams is managed. To handle this appropriately, something beyond TWQ is needed to show that the group which forms a SAFe® environment works fine.

The evaluation of the readiness of organizations is based on the spiral dynamics approach, which is usable in larger social systems like the GDQ. These two models provide the basis for using the aTWQ approach from individual teams to larger organizational units including many teams that work for some shared objectives. Based on this, the Level specification has been made in column 5 of Table 1. These levels represent the following GDQ approach stages: (I) Dependency and inclusion, (II) Counter-dependency and fight, (III) Trust and structure, and (IV) Work and productivity. The numbers in parentheses indicate the rating aligned without the mindset objective primarily based on the formal application of the respective agile aspects only. For example, in the *Scrum theater,* people apply some Scrum methods "mechanically" without actually forming a Scrum team with an agile mindset – this Scrum theater have to be rated with the parentheses level. The levels can be used by the teams to prioritize the improvement actions – start with actions on lower levels to establish a base to build on for higher level actions. The four maturity levels can be easily mapped to ratings used in specific process assessment frameworks such as the ISO/IEC 33001:2015. To have some specific indicators for the rating, column 3 and 4 can be used. Furthermore, the level rating is an indicator for the maturity of teams based on the TCI/GDQ approach.

3   Evaluation and Improvement Iterations

In the first step, the initially designed approach was simulated with the coaches of the Agile Center of Excellence (ACE) [23] which are the Volkswagen Group IT competence center for agile transitions and quality experts from the Quality Innovation Network (QiNET) [24] which is an innovation network for IT quality within the Volkswagen AG. The simulation was realized by virtual application of the aTWO questionnaire to teams coached in the past. For each simulation a point in the past was used as timestamp for answering the aTWO questions based on the situation around the timestamp. During the simulation the answers of the teams were simulated by the coaches/experts based on their knowledge about the team. Based on the answers potential chances and risks for the team development were derived. Then the timestamp was move ahead to check if the chances or risks identified by the aTWO approach are realistic to validate the questionnaire as a starting point for team improvements. An initial Proof of Concept (PoC) was done in the Scrumban aligned product team of TaaS [25]. The self-assessments taken ca. 1.5 h. The team can answer the questions in a way it is most useful and common in the team – bullet points or phrases are valid options to document evidences and indicators as well as for improvement ideas. But it is important to make the rating in the defined NPLF-schema to be able to compare team ratings of different organizations.

Some facts about the TaaS PoC: The concerned service was introduced in 2016 and has been offered in the Volkswagen Group since 2017. Over the years, evolving the team constellations have led to an established devops team with end-to-end responsibly for the service delivery. In April 2020, the team included an internal product owner, two internal software engineers and one external software engineer with a primary focus on product development and third-level ops-support, as well as one external part-time devops engineer with primary focus on first and second-level support and some third-level support activities. The team members' experience levels covers a wide range from junior developer to senior engineer. After a team composition change a few weeks earlier, the team was in a re-balancing phase. The application of the aTWQ questionnaire worked fine and was conducted as a dedicated task of a team retrospective. The identified enhancement potentials were used like retrospective outcomes and lead to actions for team improvement. Some small improvements based on the feedbacks and observations were made about aTWQ and are reflected in the version of Table 1. As an outcome, a spreadsheet was derived with supporting notes and remarks for the teams. This sheet is the core of the aTWQ self-service kit.

Team sizes and self-assessments were similar in the two other applications we investigated. The teams remained stable at least one year before the self-assessment was conducted. All these teams belong to the same organizational unit, which has approximately 25 employees. Furthermore, the organizational unit "shares" experts in the teams. Therefore, in each self-assessment of a team at least one person has two self-assessments. The organizational unit achieves a 2-digit million Euro turnover based on a service-catalog based delivery approach. The service delivery is realized with a few hundreds of external partners. The service are a full stack from management activates, consulting, coding to operations. The evaluation results from this application shows that the self-service kit is ready to use. This leads to the next step to reflect the aTWQ self-service kit in the coach guild of the Volkswagen AG and offer it to the coaches with all brands. In a final step, the integration into the agile tool box was made for a general availability to everybody in the Volkswagen AG. Furthermore, aTWQ was integrated into the *agile project review* [20] in June. This provides the base to compare teams and organizations in the future. To avoid that this approach is used only as a management tool the self-service kit offered to ensure that independent form external triggers the team can work in a safe private environment to improve them.

4   Conclusion

With aTWQ, we proposed a model for the awareness of the team-dimension of the three quality dimensions product-, process- and team-quality. We specified an explicit indicator set for the most popular agile approaches Scrum and SAFe®. First evidences for relevance and added-value for effective team development in Scrumban environments have been given by the self-assessments and the derived team actions.

The key contributions *to theory* can be summarized by the identification of the gap between the current quality-models to the real world in industrial settings which emphasize agile team work which is not explicitly addressed and covered by the established product and process quality models and approaches. The identification of possible approaches reduced this gap by the integration of the TCI, TWQ and DGQ approach to the aTWQ approach with a focus on the application in real world product teams. The initial analysis about the state-of-the-art provides a basis for more sophisticated research about the added value created by the aTWQ approach in the context of team-, multi-team- and organizational-level.

The context of the development and evaluation of aTWQ is a large enterprise setting with a European culture and mindset. This narrows the possibilities and degrees of freedom by design. The evaluation criteria in the questionnaire are not fine grained which lets room for interpretation of what is adequate if no explicit evidences are expected and no indicators are given by the evaluation model. Currently aTWQ has an open design to leave the decision by the teams in case of self-application and by the reviewer from the governance in case of "external" team evaluations. The interpretation by a more or less constant governance reviewer team will give sufficient comparability between the teams within an organization. Really mature agile teams will actively request for external "feedbacks" to get the ranking to other teams and learn from external inspiration for their improvement journey. This kind of limitation is a chance by design to ensure continuous improvement within the teams and organizations because they have not static target like an evidence or indicator list which have to be fulfilled and the *"aTWQ story is done"*.

References

1. Chen, R., Ronxin, R.R., Proctor, D.: Managing the transition to the new agile business and product development model: Lessons from Cisco Systems. Bus. Horiz. **59**(6), 635–644 (2016)
2. Paasivaara, M., Lassenius, C., Heikkilä, V.T., Dikert, K., Engblom, C.: Integrating global sites into the lean and agile transformation at ericsson. In: 2013 IEEE 8th International Conference on Global Software Engineering, Bari, pp. 134–143 (2013)
3. Poth, A.: Effectivity and economical aspects for agile quality assurance in large enterprises. J. Softw. Evol. Process **28**(11), 1000–1004 (2016)
4. Poth, A., Kottke, M., Riel, A.: Scaling agile – A large enterprise view on delivering and ensuring sustainable transitions. In: Przybyłek, A., Morales-Trujillo, M.E. (eds.) LASD/MIDI -2019. LNBIP, vol. 376, pp. 1–18. Springer, Cham (2020). https://doi.org/10.1007/978-3-030-37534-8_1

5. https://www.scaledagileframework.com/safe-core-values/. Accessed 10 June 2020
6. https://www.scaledagileframework.com/built-in-quality/. Accessed 10 June 2020
7. Strode, D.: Applying Adapted Big Five Teamwork Theory to Agile Software Development. arXiv preprint arXiv:1606.03549 (2016)
8. Tessem, B., Maurer, F.: Job satisfaction and motivation in a large agile team. In: Concas, G., Damiani, E., Scotto, M., Succi, G. (eds.) XP 2007. LNCS, vol. 4536, pp. 54–61. Springer, Heidelberg (2007). https://doi.org/10.1007/978-3-540-73101-6_8
9. Lindsjørn, Y., Bergersen, G.R., Dingsøyr, T., Sjøberg, D.I.K.: Teamwork quality and team performance: exploring differences between small and large agile projects. In: XP2018, Porto, Portugal, pp. 267–274 (2018)
10. Melo, C.O., Cruzes, D.S., Kon, F., Conradi, R.: Interpretative case studies on agile team productivity and management. Inf. Softw. Technol. **55**, 412–427 (2013). https://doi.org/10.1016/j.infsof.2012.09.004
11. Moe, N.B., Dingsøyr, T., Røyrvik, E.: Putting agile teamwork to the test – An preliminary instrument for empirically assessing and improving agile soft-ware development. In: Agile Processes in Software Engineering and Extreme Programming: 10th International Conference (XP2009), Pula, Italy, pp. 114–123 (2009)
12. Lingard, R.W.: Teaching and assessing teamwork skills in engineering and computer science. J. Systemics Cybern. Inform. **18**(1), 34–37 (2010)
13. Ramírez-Mora, S.L., Oktaba, H.: Team maturity in agile software development: The impact on productivity. In: IEEE International Conference on Software Maintenance and Evolution (ICSME), Madrid, pp. 732–736 (2018)
14. Hoegl, M., Gemuenden, H.G.: Teamwork quality and the success of innovative projects: A theoretical concept and empirical evidence. Organ. Sci. **12**(4), 435–449 (2001)
15. Wheelan, S.A., Hochberger, J.M.: Validation studies of the group development questionnaire. Small Group Res. **27**(1), 143–170 (1996)
16. Anderson, N., West, M.A.: The Team Climate Inventory: Development of the TCI and its applications in teambuilding for innovativeness. Eur. J. Work Organ. Psychol. **5**(1), 53–66 (1996)
17. Gren, L., Torkar, R., Feldt, R.: Group maturity and agility, are they connected? – A survey study. In: 2015 41st Euromicro Conference on Software Engineering and Advanced Applications, Funchal, pp. 1–8 (2015)
18. Dikert, K., Paasivaara, M., Lassenius, C.: Challenges and success factors for large-scale agile transformations: A systematic literature review. J. Syst. Softw. **119**, 87–108 (2016)
19. Lindsjørn, Y., Sjøberg, D.I., Dingsøyr, T., Bergersen, G.R., Dybå, T.: Teamwork quality and project success in software development: A survey of agile development teams. J. Syst. Softw. **122**, 274–286 (2016)
20. Poth, A., Kottke, M., Riel, A.: Scaling agile on large enterprise level – systematic bundling and application of state of the art approaches for lasting agile transitions. In: 2019 Federated Conference on Computer Science and Information Systems (FedCSIS), Leipzig, Germany, pp. 851–860 (2019)
21. Rodríguez, D., Sicilia, M.A., García, E., Harrison, R.: Empirical findings on team size and productivity in software development. J. Syst. Softw. **85**(3), 562–570 (2012)
22. https://www.scaledagileframework.com/agile-teams/. Accessed 10 June 2020
23. Poth, A.: Effectivity and economical aspects for agile quality assurance in large enterprises. J. Softw. Evol. Process **28**(11), 1000–1004 (2016)

24. Poth, A., Heimann, C.: How to innovate software quality assurance and testing in large enterprises? In: Larrucea, X., Santamaria, I., O'Connor, R.V., Messnarz, R. (eds.) EuroSPI 2018. CCIS, vol. 896, pp. 437–442. Springer, Cham (2018). https://doi.org/10.1007/978-3-319-97925-0_37

25. Poth, A., Werner, M., Lei, X.: How to deliver faster with CI/CD integrated testing services? In: Larrucea, X., Santamaria, I., O'Connor, R.V., Messnarz, R. (eds.) EuroSPI 2018. CCIS, vol. 896, pp. 401–409. Springer, Cham (2018). https://doi.org/10.1007/978-3-319-97925-0_33

A Systematic Approach to Agile Development in Highly Regulated Environments

Alexander Poth[1]([✉]) [iD], Jan Jacobsen[2], and Andreas Riel[3]

[1] Volkswagen AG, Berliner Ring 2, 38436 Wolfsburg, Germany
alexander.poth@volkswagen.de
[2] Volkswagen Financial Services AG, 38112 Brunswick, Germany
jan.jacobsen@vwfs.com
[3] Université Grenoble Alpes, CNRS, Grenoble INP, G-SCOP,
38031 Grenoble, France
andreas.riel@grenoble-inp.fr

Abstract. For established domains within highly regulated environments, a systematic approach is needed to scale agile methods and assure compliance with regulatory requirements. The presented approach works adequately in small agile teams – independently of the underlying method such as Scrum, Kanban, etc. – and is scalable to more and bigger teams or even entire subsidiaries. It is based on a compliance and a quality risk dimension respectively. Both dimensions are needed to fit regulatory requirements in our finance example with more than 100 developers in one subsidiary.

Keywords: Software development management · Agile software development · Regulation compliance · Large scaling agile

1 Introduction

Established industry sectors are more or less regulated. Less regulated sectors solely have to incorporate basic requirements like European Union regulation, i.e. the General Data Protection Regulation (GDPR) [1], and/or national requirements such as the German Commercial Code (HGB) [2]. In highly regulated sectors however, products and services have to comply with further extensive standards and regulations. The financial sector, for example, has to fulfill regulations imposed by the EU countries' national supervisory authorities, as well as Minimum Requirements for Risk Management for financial institutions (MaRisk) in Germany [3]. Many regulations are domain-specific like medical, finance or automotive. However, regulations have some common aspects like quality assurance evidences for verification and validation which demand a more or less stringent traceability and risk management [4].

Our research objective is to design a framework that can be used to derive a specific compliance guideline offering as much autonomy to agile teams as possible by fitting the required specific regulations of the product or service with its organization. In large organizations, specific organizational units have to be aligned with specific compliance requirements. To support this specificity, the approach shall be generic by design. This will enable scaling the approach into different organizations and their units. As for

© The Author(s) 2020
M. Paasivaara and P. Kruchten (Eds.): XP 2020 Workshops, LNBIP 396, pp. 111–119, 2020.
https://doi.org/10.1007/978-3-030-58858-8_12

evidences for the effectiveness of the framework, we want to meet the following three core requirements. First, the external confirmation by audits with focus on compliance shall be facilitated. Second, the delivery of the demanded business value shall not be hampered and remain an essential part of the outcome flow. Third, the framework shall be adaptable to new regulations over time.

2   Related Work and Methodology

A huge body of documentation exists to handle regulation and compliance. However, these works mostly focus on a specific solution or aspect within the respective domain. This leads to partial [5] and inconsistent [6] agile adoptions [7] like ScrumBut. Examples for agile development in regulated domains are [8] for safety related products, [9] for the medical, and [10] for the finance domain. However, it is difficult to find a generic practical framework for regulated domains.

The framework presented here was developed following the design science research approach [11], demonstrating the framework's application in a case study in the financial domain. The framework's general applicability is assured by design thanks to its independence from any specific regulation. Furthermore, it is adoptable by design to different business domain specific demands in large organizations to scale into their units.

3   Scaling Conformity to Regulations via Levels of Done

The development process has to address two dimensions. The domain dimension handles the organizational and procedural compliance requirements. It has to assure that the compliance requirements be fulfilled at least at the latest required point in the product or service life cycle. Earlier assurance of regulatory requirements is possible and a part of the team's self-organization. The product specific dimension helps teams identify and realize their product specific quality-risk requirements. Within this dimension, the team handles product or service specific quality-risks in a structured and transparent manner to assure an adequate risk management. For handling the product specific quality risks, we use the Product Quality Risk (PQR) [12] approach, which focusses on quality risks implied by the specific market chances and opportunities of each service or product. PQR guides the teams from a systematic identification of specific service and product quality risks, and helps them define adequate mitigation actions.

To leverage a lean and agile development process, which teams can apply outcome-specific refinements to, only a minimum predefined framework shall be set while still assuring a systematic handling of the team's refinement work. The process outcome's value is assessed by its (inherent) quality risks. Systematic product or service quality risk identification and handling proposed in [12], can be used to assure that the development process does not lose outcome focus. In [5], the product capabilities and features are used to derive the product specific quality risks. Based on the identified and prioritized quality risks, adequate mitigation actions are scheduled during the development to ensure a compliant and high quality outcome.

To assure that product teams incorporate both dimensions just in time, we propose a Levels of Done (LoD) approach. LoD are an enriched variant of the Definition of Done (DoD) of Scrum that is aligned with requirements [13] at defined milestones in the development process. The LoD approach applies the concept of boundaries [14] beyond the sprint time-box between Definition of Ready (DoR) and DoD to all take-overs in a value chain. This makes it simple and independent from any specific agile approach based on sprints, as well as sufficiently generic to adapt to different regulation domains with the specific check-points they require. This is necessary to fulfill a systematic product and process quality approach demanded by most quality related standards, as well as to allow agile scaling while staying effective [15].

4   The LoD-PQR Approach

While in a traditional compliance scope, the software development life-cycle is clearly defined by a comprehensive set of fixed requirements and deliverables prior to project start, we propose the following four steps to define LoD in agile environments:

Identify all relevant regulations and standards of your enterprise for compliant products and/or services.

Identify how many stages you have for product development via a Kanban board.

The Kanban board helps to identify handover-points in a work stream. These points are the most relevant for LoD.

According to Conway's law [16], the structure of an origination drives their outcomes. Therefore, alignment of the "planned" outcome architecture with the organization shall be considered. This should also drive future changes to an existing LoD to support the transformation in a pull-fashion. The LoD does not refine the internal team organization between two stages. The teams can apply their preferred agile approach like Scrum, Kanban etc. in their self-organized working flows to fit the next stage.

Enabling teams to choose the most effective ways to comply with regulatory relevant outcomes by mapping them to the stages of the Kanban board.

A transparent traceability from the regulation to the LoD will facilitate regulation adoption. However, finding adequate implementations should be delegated to the team to give them freedom to find solutions that fit into their particular context. The openness about how to reach the outcomes give the teams the autonomy to work as it is best for their specific demands and the mastery (responsibility) about their implementations. The traceability from the external requirements to their internal representations – the topics in Fig. 1 – shall be established to avoid interpretations by missing "root" and to avoid non-value adding activities in a lean context.

Reduce the outcomes of "chains" to the last outcome for a shorter list.

To optimize the LoD, chains of dependencies can be reduced to the latest outcome. For example, a separate test protocol is not needed if the test result log and protocols are saved as part of the comprehensive deployment-log and stored in an auditable way. This is covered by an underlying internal control system.

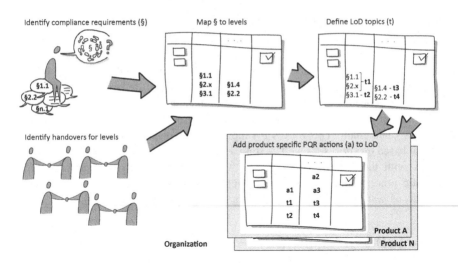

Fig. 1. Schematic picture of a practical LoD-PQR method application scenario.

Provide additional information about practices and work instructions about outcomes for assisting the teams. To help the teams for a fast instantiation, a practice collection can be provided sharing of experiences across the organization. If a new practice is identified, it will be added to the practice collection to leverage continuous improvement and replacement of outdated practices.

Add the PQR dimension to assure that products and services have a comprehensive quality approach. To derive systematically the specific PQR a self-service kit for the teams is recommended as described in [17]. While the LoD covers only formal regulation requirements, the PQR method handles business risks related to deliverables by quality related mitigation actions as described in [12] and [17]. These mitigation actions are mapped to the corresponding stages and handled by the teams. Based on the regulation and quality risk dimension, a holistic quality management system can be established. Figure 1 shows how the actions fit together in a product team specific instantiation. It visualizes the instantiation of the 4 LoDs, the product team specific PQRs actions (a) on top of the organization-wide valid LoD topics (t), as well as the numerous product checks.

The LoD-PQR approach is easily repeatable for the iterative and incremental development in agile product teams. It also foresees cross-team reviews conducted by technical reviewers (IT experts) providing evidence of compliance with the LoD. Quality standards covered in the reviews include: architecture, code quality, PQR, security, documentation, etc. Every topic has its own LoD acceptance criteria. Depending on the technical review result, the accountable role (e.g. Head of IT) grants technical approval for the product release (Fig. 2).

One difference to a DoD is that the latter is typically defined by the team, while a LoD is given by the organization to a team, and team-specific parts are defined via the PQR with a product or service focus. A second difference is that a DoD addresses aspects which are handled by the team, while the LoD-PQR approach ensures an end-to-end view for a delivery of a product or service. Furthermore, the DoD is checked by the team as a kind of a self-commitment, while the LoD is typically checked and ensured by team external reviews initiated by the organization's compliance.

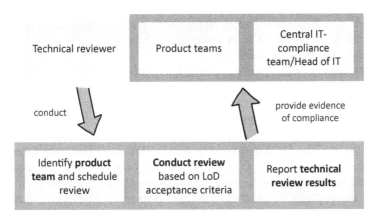

Fig. 2. LoD compliance process and involved stakeholders.

For the review and approval process as well as the LoD, internal criteria shall be derived. The control owner shall establish a monitoring on the whole process against these criteria (via preventive gates and/or detective post-checks) in order to conduct appropriate actions depending on the level of conformance and control effectiveness.

Derivations to the LoD shall be assessed and tracked to sign-off by the risk owners. Teams "pull" experts for specific standards for support in case of new or special issues. Any regulation changes shall be integrated into the LoD as soon as possible and all teams have to ensure to fulfill the current version as soon as possible. Teams can autonomously set synchronization points in case of inter-team dependencies. The time span between the different levels of the LoD in a team mostly depends on the team's delivery frequency, and is independent from a team's delivery cycle duration. Some teams need weeks, others months.

5 Case Study: Instantiation, Deployment and Its Limitations

The Volkswagen Financial Services AG Digital Unit Berlin (DU) identified four stages for their LoD (cf. Fig. 1). First, the business takes over the stories into the team. Second, the team implements the requirements according to compliance for security etc. Third, the product is checked for compliance and business process integration. Finally, the product's functionality is verified during operation. The last stage is interesting for the handover in cases were no DevOps is applied.

The identified regulations and standards for the financial domain are defined by the European Union and are instantiated by German governance and regulation institutions like the MaRisk, BAIT [18] or GDPR. As shown in Fig. 1, a key input to LoD was the experts' collection of LoD-relevant requirements. They derived them from the relevant regulations and collected them in a central document. Subsequently they mapped similar requirements and merged them. They integrated requirements addressing the development process (e.g. independent checks from the business of IT systems in BAIT requirement 41) into the LoD design. These requirements from the *identify compliance aspects* of Fig. 1 have an impact on the team's organization and their interfaces. Hence, regulations impact organization setup and team handovers (*identify handovers for levels* in Fig. 1), in as described in Conway's law. In the given context, this happened for the acceptance testing by the business which is realized in an independent stage in *map § to levels* in Fig. 1. Based on this, all teams have to instantiate this regulation implementation before they can *add product specific PQR actions* in the last step in Fig. 1. Another example is the regulation requirement about systematic requirement documentation of the BAIT requirement 37 "Requirements for the functionality of the application must be compiled, evaluated and documented in the same way as for non-functional requirements." This regulation requirement about requirements is handled in the LoD's first level with the task to refine requirements based on the recommendation to align stories on the INVEST criteria [19]. INVEST stands for Independent, Negotiable, Valuable, Estimable, Small and Testable. The recommendation is given to establish a kind of state of the art for requirements documentation however teams have the option to substitute the recommendation with another more adequate method for the product or service context. Furthermore the BAIT 37 requires "The organisational units shall be responsible for compiling and evaluating the requirements." which leads to assign it to the LoD's first level – responsibility for this level is by the business product owner - and not to the second level with IT responsibility. Both examples show that in a regulated finance environment one team have to has hand-over points which leads to at least three levels of done to be compliant to the BAIT.

Preventive checks of the LoD's correct application are conducted before a productive deployment, while detective compliance check are done after deployment. To assure LoD compliance, the DU adopted the approach from Fig. 2 with some refinements for adequate review sampling and time (pre- or post-deployment). To reduce the direct effects of the LoD procedures on team level, the objective is to reduce the pre-deployment checks, which interrupt the delivery workflow of the team for a compliance task. However, each team has to ensure that in an audit, all relevant artifacts and evidences are available to demonstrate a compliant delivery.

The LoD of the DU has been developed by a cross-functional team. The team incorporated experts from the headquarters compliance, headquarters security, business and development teams, as well as external experts from the Volkswagen AG. Reflections with external consults (agile coaches, auditors etc.) were done cyclically too. Throughout the development period of almost one year, the team allocated approximately 6–7 experts. The initial application (evaluation) in the first teams was done with facilitation by the expert team. After small enhancements and the positive feedbacks of the early adopter teams, a LoD Community of Practice (CoP) was established. This was useful to ensure that the scaling to all teams can be made efficient and quick. The experts are limited resources and in the CoP the teams can help each other too – this helps to reduce bottlenecks by the experts who were focusing on the new issues and questions.

In the last 3 years we established and enhanced the approach for more efficient delivery and to regulation updates with the Scrum masters and the teams. Currently more than 100 developers are working with the LoD-PQR approach, and further locations and organizational units are in the adoption phase.

The application to the DU financial case revealed the following limitations of the LoD-PQR approach with respect to the corporate governance having to assure

- The correct outcomes for the compliance requirements, as well as
- The expected deliverable which creates the customer/user value;
- The update of the LoD by the regulation experts;
- The update of the PQR by the product or service experts.

These limitations are partly addressed by the review procedure (Fig. 2), which however generates a base workload scaling linearly with the delivery frequency of the products and services. To reduce this linear correlation of reviews to deliveries, a team maturity approach can be established. Higher team maturity leads to more autonomy and thus reliefs the team from having mandatory pre-deployment LoD-triggered technical reviews by team-independent reviewers.

6 Discussion and Conclusion

The LoD-PQR approach addresses the demand for a generic approach to handling regulation requirements and product specific quality management in an agile environment. While we have shown the generic LoD-PQR method application to the European finance domain, other domain specific requirements would need to be identified, e.g. for the DO-178 (avionics safety) or ISO 26262 (automotive safety). However, the amount of regulation requirements in finance was lower than initially expected, approximately 50 with direct impact to the software development. The product specific PQRs strongly depend on the outcomes, however the workload which can be handled by a team is a "limiting factor".

The acceptance of our methodology within the agile-teams was encouraged by the committed degree of freedom. In our case, we have witnessed that implementing the LoD-PQR approach supported the teams to navigate through the complex compliance requirements in our domain in a lean way (conformity). Our approach enabled the product teams to realize efficiency by design and to share techniques how to implement compliance requirements in an uncomplicated way. Besides, the genuine learning character of the LoD-PQR approach leads to streamlined development processes of the approach itself, leading to a positive impact on process performance.

References

1. General Data Protection Regulation (GDPR). https://eur-lex.europa.eu/legal-content/EN/TXT/PDF/?uri=CELEX:32016R0679. Accessed 11 June 2020
2. Handelsgesetzbuch (HGB). http://www.gesetze-im-internet.de/englisch_hgb/. Accessed 11 June 2020
3. Mindestanforderungen an das Risikomanagement (MARisk). https://www.bafin.de/SharedDocs/Veroeffentlichugen/DE/Rundschreiben/2017/rs_1709_marisk_ba.html. Accessed 11 June 2020
4. Fitzgerald, B., Stol, K.-J., O'Sullivan, R., O'Brien, D.: Scaling agile methods to regulated environments: an industry case study. In: 35th International Conference on Software Engineering (ICSE), pp. 863–872. IEEE (2013)
5. Karvonen, T., Sharp, H., Barroca, L.: Enterprise agility: why is transformation so hard? In: Garbajosa, J., Wang, X., Aguiar, A. (eds.) XP 2018. LNBIP, vol. 314, pp. 131–145. Springer, Cham (2018). https://doi.org/10.1007/978-3-319-91602-6_9
6. Uludag, O., Kleehaus, M., Caprano, C., Matthes, F.: Identifying and structuring challenges in large-scale agile development based on a structured literature review. In: 2018 IEEE 22nd International Enterprise Distributed Object Computing Conference (EDOC), pp. 191–197. IEEE (2018)
7. Eloranta, V.P., Koskimies, K., Mikkonen, T.: Exploring ScrumBut—an empirical study of scrum anti-patterns. Inf. Softw. Technol. 74, 194–203 (2016)
8. Wolff, S.: Scrum goes formal: agile methods for safety-critical systems. In: 2012 First International Workshop on Formal Methods in Software Engineering: Rigorous and Agile Approaches (FormSERA), Zurich, pp. 23–29 (2012). https://doi.org/10.1109/formsera.2012.6229784
9. Mc Hugh, M., Cawley, O., McCaffery, F., Richardson, I., Wang, X.: An agile v-model for medical device software development to over-come the challenges with plan-driven software development lifecycles. In: 5th International Workshop on Software Engineering in Health Care (SEHC), pp. 12–19. IEEE (2013)
10. Birkinshaw, J.: What to expect from agile. MIT Sloan Manag. Rev. 59(2), 39–42 (2018)
11. Hevner, A., Samir, C.: Design science research in information systems. Design Research in Information Systems, pp. 9–22. Springer, Boston (2010). https://doi.org/10.1007/978-1-4419-5653-8_2
12. Poth, A., Sunyaev, A.: Effective quality management: risk- and value-based software quality management. IEEE Softw. 31(6), 79–85 (2014)
13. Perkusich, M., et al.: A systematic review on the use of Definition of Done on agile software development projects. In: International Conference on Evaluation and Assessment in Software Engineering (EASE) (2017). https://doi.org/10.1145/3084226.3084262
14. Power, K.: Definition of ready: an experience report from teams at Cisco. In: Cantone, G., Marchesi, M. (eds.) XP 2014. LNBIP, vol. 179, pp. 312–319. Springer, Cham (2014). https://doi.org/10.1007/978-3-319-06862-6_25
15. Poth, A.: Effectivity and economical aspects for agile quality assurance in large enterprises. J. Softw. Process: Improv. Pract. 28(11), 1000–1004 (2016)
16. Conway, M.E.: How do committees invent? Datamation 14(5), 28–31 (1968)

17. Poth, A., Riel, A.: Quality requirements elicitation by ideation of product quality risks with design thinking. In: Proceedings of the 28th IEEE International Requirements Engineering Conference (RE 2020), Vienna (2020, in print)
18. BAIT.   https://www.bafin.de/SharedDocs/Downloads/EN/Rundschreiben/dl_rs_1710_ba_BAIT_en.pdf?__blob=publicationFile&v=6. Accessed 11 June 2020
19. INVEST. https://xp123.com/articles/invest-in-good-stories-and-smart-tasks/. Accessed 11 June 2020

Second European Workshop on Serverless Computing and Applications

Summary of the 2nd European Symposium on Serverless Computing and Applications - ESSCA

Davide Taibi[1], Josef Spillner[2], and Feilong Wang[3]

[1] Tampere University, Tampere, Finland
`davide.taibi@tuni.fi`
[2] Zurich University of Applied Science, Winterthur, Switzerland
`josef.spillner@zhaw.ch`
[3] Catalyst Cloud, Wellington, New Zealand

For the second time, a venue in Europe brought together researchers and innovators around serverless technologies. Serverless computing provides a platform to efficiently develop and deploy applications to the market without having to manage any underlying infrastructure. These refer to services, tools and patterns for modular, event-driven and highly scalable application architectures.

After ESSCA @ UCC 2018, which gave the inaugural event a cloud background, ESSCA @ XP 2020 was fitting with a software engineering background. This interdisciplinary nature of serverless topics increasingly tapping into and connecting the cloud, big data and software engineering communities is an ongoing trend that we wanted to debate again, and thus called for submissions in early 2020.

Each submission was reviewed by at least two reviewers from the wider serverless research community. Four papers with positive review scores were chosen to be presented at ESSCA. Authors from five countries were represented at the symposium. The topics focused on application rearchitecting (FaaSification of a web application with database) and execution in FaaS contexts (performance prediction, isolation with WebAssembly, memory autotuning (demo)). The speakers observed that using serverless requires careful planning and design choices, as the associated cost and on-demand serving advantages may otherwise decline or even reverse, making serverless a more expensive choice than necessary.

Contrary to our planning, world-wide travel restrictions led to a pure online event that allowed for sticking with the original date. The virtual symposium took place in two sessions: One for presenting the research results, with space for only few questions, and one more for interactively debating on provocative theses related to the presentations and determining in which directions serverless applications and systems would develop in the future. There was consensus that while FaaS presents the current technology for serverless applications, future technologies will be less constrained and not necessarily function-based.

Overall, we look back to a small but beautiful and certainly not boring event. We take note of the increasing interest by software engineers in serverless application engineering, as evidenced by an upcoming theme issue of the IEEE Software magazine on Serverless Applications Engineering, as well as of growing publishing activity, as evidenced by the Serverless Literature Dataset.

Diminuendo! Tactics in Support of FaaS Migrations

Sebastian Werner[1(✉)], Jörn Kuhlenkamp[1], Frank Pallas[1], Niklas Anders[2],
Nebi Mucaj[2], Olesia Tsaplina[2], Christian Schmidt[2], and Kann Yildirim[2]

[1] Information Systems Engineering, Technische Universität Berlin, Berlin, Germany
{sw,jk,fp}@ise.tu-berlin.de
[2] ProgPrak Team, Technische Universität Berlin, Berlin, Germany
pp1920@ise.tu-berlin.de

Abstract. Function-as-a-Service (FaaS) receives close attention due to highly desirable characteristics, including pay-as-you-go pricing, high elasticity, and its fully managed nature. To leverage these benefits for existing applications, developers face the challenge of migrating legacy code to a FaaS platform (FaaSification). Unfortunately, however, actionable guidance on how to do so for real-world applications does not exist. In this paper, we report on our experience from FaaSifying a data-intensive application, and evaluating different options through extensive experimentation, using approaches such as regression tests and tracing. Based on the obtained results, we present five migration tactics in support of future FaaSification.

Keywords: Serverless · Migration · FaaS · FaaSification

1 Introduction

Function-as-a-Service (FaaS) is a new cloud execution model that receives close attention due to highly desirable characteristics, including pay-as-you-go pricing, millisecond elasticity, or provider-managed operational tasks for, e.g., deployment [6]. To leverage these benefits for existing applications, developers face the challenge of migrating legacy code to a FaaS platform (FaaSification).

While an increasing number of supported programming languages and relaxed limitations, e.g., maximum execution time, give the impression that FaaSification is a trivial task, first exploratory research [4,7] indicates that leveraging the non-functional benefits of FaaS beyond correct execution requires a careful redesign, profiling, and configuration. Unfortunately, little information is available on how these and further subjects are (to be) addressed in the FaaSification of real-world web applications. Thus, many application developers are unaware of the different fallacies of FaaSification.

In this paper, we report on our experience from FaaSifying a data-intensive web application from a VM-based deployment. For the migration, we initially used a naïve migration approach presented in [7] that expectedly resulted in

M. Paasivaara and P. Kruchten (Eds.): XP 2020 Workshops, LNBIP 396, pp. 125–132, 2020.
https://doi.org/10.1007/978-3-030-58858-8_13

failing non-functional end-to-end regression tests. We were able to significantly reduce these degradations by 1) instrumenting application code for tracing purposes, 2) identifying the root-cause for degradation in different third-party libraries and some sections of legacy code, and, finally, 3) refactoring parts of the application architecture and the usage of third-party libraries.

To let others profit from our experiences, we synthesize our insights from the migration and additional previous research into five common migration tactics in support of future FaaSification: *Precompute*, *Reuse*, *Strip*, *Be Lazy*, and *Replace*.

2   Application and Migration Goal

We selected the open participatory data platform OpenSense.network [2] as a use-case to evaluate the effects of legacy code during the migration to FaaS environments. OpenSense.network offers a horizontally scalable, Flask-based API to let users contribute and access sensor data of globally distributed environmental sensors in a uniform, web-friendly way. To provide geospatial capabilities and high-volume sensor data in a performant and scalable manner, it employs a hybrid storage model, comprising a PostGIS database for static metadata and a Cassandra cluster holding timeseries of actual measurements (see Fig. 1). Both the API and databases of OpenSense.network are deployed on the TU Berlin data center premises. For the migration, we were particularly interested in moving the Flask API to a FaaS platform to free up computation resources when the API is not in use while at the same time being able to handle spiking loads in case of, for instance, occasional bulk inserts or data access surges. Further, we were interested in reducing operational overhead, e.g., the management of the Flask API virtual machines.

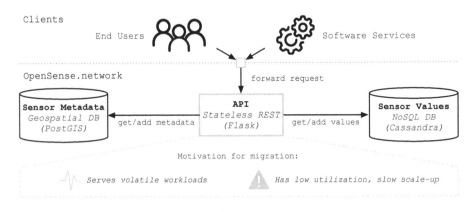

Fig. 1. OpenSense.network architecture with selected component for migration.

We selected Apache OpenWhisk[1] as the target platform and deployed it in the same network as the current OpenSense.network deployment to allow

---
[1] https://openwhisk.apache.org/.

connections to the same databases as the original APIs and, thus, to avoid the need for data migration.

To compare the behavior and responses of the migrated API to those of the original one, we additionally created and continuously extended a rich set of end-to-end regression tests.

3 FaaS Migration Approach

In this section, we outline our approach in migrating OpenSense.network. We start by describing our initial naïve approach, followed by the steps taken to identify root-causes of performance degradations and the subsequent refactoring.

3.1 Naïve Migration

In the first step of the migration, we followed a naïve reuse approach similar to Llyod et al. [7]. Accordingly, we implemented a custom runtime container, based on the OpenWhisk Python runtime[2] with the necessary Python dependencies for OpenSense.network already built-in. These custom runtimes can reduce cold-start problems as less code needs to be downloaded and compiled initially.

Furthermore, we used a modified version of the *flask-openwhisk*[3] wrapper to map OpenWhisk requests to Flask, resulting in a FaaS version of the pre-existing Flask API with almost zero modification.[4] In line with our expectations and previous findings [7], this naïve FaaSification approach was successful on a functional level but exhibited significant performance degradation compared to the original deployment. For instance, a request for a single sensor value for the migrated API took between 2 and 20 s for cold and warm functions, respectively, while it took less than a second on the original API.

In the following, we first describe our approach to identifying the root-causes of this degradation.

3.2 Regression Detection

Determining the root-cause of problems in FaaS applications is challenging [4] since FaaS platforms offer no out-of-the-box facilities for remote-debugging and -profiling. Instead, developers have to rely on application and system log information which can be limited in volume, making debugging and profiling tasks tedious and cumbersome.

As a first step of refactoring towards a more FaaS-aware implementation, we, therefore, created a simple, lightweight profiling tool that instruments Open-Whisk's logging facilities and allows to easily include start- and endpoints of

---

[2] https://github.com/apache/openwhisk-runtime-python.

[3] https://github.com/alexmilowski/flask-openwhisk.

[4] Initially we considered more mature frameworks, e.g., Zappa (https://github.com/Miserlou/Zappa). However, OpenWhisk is not supported in most of them.

```
initialize():
    topen("init")
    topen("flask")
    flask()
    tclose("flask")
    ...
    tclose("init")
```

Fig. 2. Example of instrumented code

relevant functional sections in the code. An accompanying evaluation tool allows to easily analyze respective runtimes[5]. Using these tools, we instrumented the migrated application with a set of tracepoints, see Fig. 2.

We placed each trace-point at potential bottlenecks and points of interest within the code. In particular, we measured object creation, database connection initialization, overall initialization, execution [5], and serialization and deserialization times. Figure 3 shows exemplary results of these measurements for a simple sensor query, before and after refactoring.

We were quickly able to pin down the root causes of the observed performance degradation based on the gathered information. In particular, we observed that in the initial, naïve approach, the API implementation took substantial time to (re-) initialize certain libraries on every single request. Large portions of these initialization overheads could be attributed to Flask and the Cassandra driver. Accordingly, the inefficient pattern of continuous re-initialization for both Flask and the Cassandra driver was a particular subject of refactoring, described further in the next section.

3.3   Refactoring

The data from the regression detection provided a road-map to address the performance issues in the naïvely migrated application. Based on the identified bottlenecks, the following measures particularly helped us to significantly reduce FaaS-specific overheads:

Reuse: We initially focused on reducing the re-initialization of objects and libraries on every single request, see the Reuse tactic in Sect. 4. Specifically, we moved the initialization of most libraries away from the OpenWhisk handler so that initialized libraries remain in memory. We faced some minor challenges as the OpenWhisk runtime did not offer simple mechanisms to execute code before a handler call. However, Python packages allow code execution on imports through including the code to be executed in the __init__ method, which enabled us to shift all expensive initializations to the OpenWhisk runtime creation.

---

[5] https://bit.ly/2Z4TpsR.

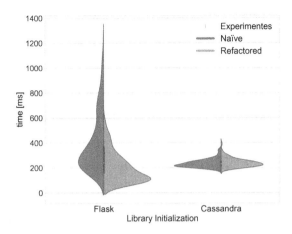

Fig. 3. Comparison of cold-start initialization times. "Naïve" refers to the initial migration, see Sect. 3.1. "Refactored" refers to the code-base after the changes described in Sect. 3.3 (Precompute). Results a based on 200 sensor range queries.

These steps already reduced performance degradations for warm[6] execution environments significantly.

Precompute: Based on a more in-depth analysis of the execution times, we identified that the initialization of both Flask and the Cassandra driver still created notable performance impacts during cold-starts.

For Flask, we managed to precompile most of the Flask object state through the pickle api[7], which we could store as part of the deployment artifact. Using the precompiled object allows that most of the dynamic computation which Flask performs during server initialization can be removed. The effects of this can be seen in the left part of Fig. 3, see the `Precompute` tactic in Sect. 4.

We tried to follow a similar strategy for the Cassandra driver. However, we could not reduce the initialization time significantly with this method. Furthermore, we tried to disable thread-pooling and other functionality that is unnecessary in a FaaS context, but these steps also slightly reduced the initialization time.

Strip: To address the Cassandra driver's performance issues, we observed that the Cassandra driver is not used for every request. For instance, an API method only returning sensor metadata based on several query parameters does not need access to the timeseries data stored in Cassandra and could, therefore, be included in a "Cassandra-less" function. Thus, we decided to `strip` away the Cassandra driver splitting the Flask API into two functions. Of course, this

---

[6] Warm execution environments are functions that were deployed by the platform for a previous event. State in these functions can be reused, reducing expensive initializations, that occur during cold-starts [8].

[7] https://docs.python.org/3/library/pickle.html.

step did not help to reduce the start-up time for Cassandra-related requests but significantly improved the request-response time for all other requests. Significantly decreasing the Cassandra-related overheads for API methods *with* time-series functionality, however, would have required us to `replace` or rewrite the Cassandra library. Even though this would have gone beyond the scope of our migration project, this nonetheless illustrates the need for more lightweight, and possibly less feature-rich libraries and drivers in the FaaS context.

4   Migration Tactics

Beyond those explicitly mentioned above, we also experimented with further approaches of adjusting our code and the underlying runtime to FaaS-specific givens, which mostly took a similar line, albeit with less significant impacts. Altogether, however, our experiences can be synthesized into five general tactics for FaaSification. Each of these tactics implies different prerequisites, the potential for performance improvements, and development costs.

Precompute: This tactic precomputes intermediate results that are included as static content in the deployment package of a function. The tactic requires that the intermediate result does not depend on runtime information and that the size of the intermediate result is comparatively small due to FaaS platform limitations – e.g., 3-250MB for AWS Lambda[8]. In addition, it increases cold-start times with the size of a deployment package [9]. The tactic affects all invocations of a function handler and requires additional development efforts.

Reuse: This tactic caches intermediate results over multiple invocations of a function handler on the same function container. It requires that multiple executions occur on the same function container. This tactic is quite simple to implement by storing intermediate results in global class variables of a function handler or on the ephemeral storage available. However, it benefits only a subset of executions, namely those that actually run on the same function container repeatedly. Thus, Reuse becomes less effective with increasing numbers of cold starts. Different approaches for experiment-driven analysis of cold/warm start ratios [3,5,9] can indicate the effectiveness of this tactic to developers.

Strip: Strip implies that the developer removes source code from the function handler that is initialized but not used on the execution paths of any invocation. It requires that such source code exists and is identifiable by developers. While all invocations benefit, the tactic implies additional development efforts due to profiling and exhaustive testing. We envision that system providers will begin offering specialized lightweight client libraries for short-lived ephemeral compute environments like FaaS platforms.

Be Lazy: This tactic is applicable for function handlers with multiple initializations that are not required on all execution paths. The application developer can conditionally initialize by relying on conditional statements in a function

---

[8] https://docs.aws.amazon.com/lambda/latest/dg/gettingstarted-limits.html.

handler. As an alternative, a developer can decompose a function into multiple focused functions [1]. The potential for performance improvements depends on the distribution of the different execution paths. It implies additional development efforts and potentially changes the application on an architectural level.

Replace: Application developers can resort to re-implementing third-party libraries. A particular form of replacement could be the inclusion of lightweight database connectors within FaaS platforms, allowing FaaS application developers to offload respective functionalities from their code-base. This tactic has no prerequisites and a high potential for improvement but can imply significant development costs. In a FaaS context, the potential additional costs of feature-rich client libraries in terms of higher execution latency and monetary execution costs motivate coexisting lightweight clients with a reduced set of features.

Besides, we argue that a high degree of automation is achievable in order to reduce the development efforts for the different tactics significantly. However, it remains an open question on which level of the technology stack each tactic is applied best. For example, a tactic might be best applied automatically by the cloud platform, integrated with application frameworks, or supported by additional developer tooling in support of FaaSification. We argue that future work should discuss and give guidance on the different associated trade-offs.

5   Conclusion

In this paper, we introduced five tactics in support of migrating legacy--applications to FaaS, that we synthesized from a real-world migration effort. We argue that a high degree of automation is achievable in order to reduce the development efforts for migrations in the future. We additionally see that an extension to current FaaS platforms by offloading expensive operations like database connections to the platform could be an area for investigation. Further, we argue that application framework developers could support FaaS best-practices like lazy loading directly. Lastly, we see an opportunity for third-party library vendors to offer more lightweight options aligned with the FaaS context.

Acknowledgments. The work in this paper was partially performed in the context of the SMILE and BloGPV.Blossom projects. BloGPV.Blossom is partially funded by the German Federal Ministry for Economic Affairs and Energy (BMWi) under grant no. 01MD18001E. SMILE is funded by the German Federal Ministry of Education and Research (BMBF) as part of the Software-Campus 2.0 grand, project number 01IS17052. The authors assume responsibility for the content.

References

1. Baldini, I., et al.: The serverless trilemma: function composition for serverless computing. In: International Symposium on New Ideas, New Paradigms, and Reflections on Programming and Software, Onward 2017, pp. 89–103. ACM, New York (2017)

2. Borges, M.C., Pallas, F., Peise, M.: Providing open environmental data–the scalable and web-friendly way. In: Bungartz, H.J., Kranzlmüller, D., Weinberg, V., Weismüller, J., Wohlgemuth, V. (eds.) Advances and New Trends in Environmental Informatics, pp. 21–37. Springer, Cham (2018). https://doi.org/10.1007/978-3-319-99654-7_2
3. Jackson, D., Clynch, G.: An investigation of the impact of language runtime on the performance and cost of serverless functions. In: 3rd International Workshop on Serverless Computing, WoSC 2018, Zurich, Switzerland, pp. 154–160. IEEE (2018)
4. Kuhlenkamp, J., Werner, S., Tai, S.: The ifs and buts of less is more: a serverless computing reality check. In: Proceedings of The International Conference on Cloud Engineering (IC2E 2020), 21–24 April 2020, Sydney, Australia. IEEE (2020)
5. Kuhlenkamp, J., Werner, S., Borges, M.C., Ernst, D., Wenzel, D.: Benchmarking elasticity of FaaS platforms as a foundation for objective-driven design of serverless applications. In: 34th ACM/SIGAPP Symposium on Applied Computing. Association for Computing Machinery, New York, SAC 2019, pp. 284–291 (2019)
6. Leitner, P., Wittern, E., Spillner, J., Hummer, W.: A mixed-method empirical study of function-as-a-service software development in industrial practice. J. Syst. Softw. 149, 340–359 (2018)
7. Lloyd, W., Vu, M., Zhang, B., David, O., Leavesley, G.: Improving application migration to serverless computing platforms: latency mitigation with keep-alive workloads. In: Proceedings of the 3rd International Workshop on Serverless Computing, pp. 195–200. IEEE (Dec 2018)
8. Manner, J., EndreB, M., Heckel, T., Wirtz, G.: Cold start influencing factors in function as a service. In: International Conference on Utility and Cloud Computing Companion (UCC Companion), pp. 181–188. IEEE (2018)
9. Manner, J., Endreß, M., Heckel, T., Wirtz, G.: Cold start influencing factors in function as a service. In: Proceedings of the 3rd International Workshop on Serverless Computing, WoSC 2018, Zurich, Switzerland, pp. 181–188. IEEE (2018)

Predictable Performance for QoS-Sensitive, Scalable, Multi-tenant Function-as-a-Service Deployments

Andrzej Kuriata[1]([✉]) and Ramesh G. Illikkal[2]([✉])

[1] Intel Technology Poland, Gdansk, Poland
andrzej.kuriata@intel.com
[2] Intel Corp., Santa Clara, CA, USA
ramesh.g.illikkal@intel.com

Abstract. In this paper we present the results of our studies focused on enabling predictable performance for functions executing in scalable, multi-tenant Function-as-a-Service environments. We start by analyzing QoS and performance requirements and use cases from the point of view of End-Users, Developers and Infrastructure Owners. Then we take a closer look at functions' resource utilization patterns and investigate functions' sensitivity to those resources. We specifically focus on the CPU microarchitecture resources as they have significant impact on functions' overall performance. As part of our studies we have conducted experiments to research the effect of co-locating different functions on the compute nodes. We discuss the results and provide an overview of how we have further modified the scheduling logic of our containers orchestrator (Kubernetes), and how that impacted functions' execution times and performance variation. We have specifically leveraged the low-level telemetry data, mostly exposed by the Intel® Resource Director Technology (Intel® RDT) [1]. Finally, we provide an overview of our future studies, which will be centered around node-level resource allocations, further improving a function's performance, and conclude with key takeaways.

Keywords: Performance · Telemetry · Scheduling

1 Introduction

The general Cloud Computing model relies on centralizing computing power and then re-distribution of this computing power among multiple users and tenants. The benefits of such approach, among others, are inherit scalability and, from the end user perspective, simplified resources management.

Additional layers built on top of Cloud Computing, like Function-as-a-Service deployments, release the burden of managing hardware and software resources, from service developers, even further. At the same time, however, resource providers must ensure that performance of services is stable and independent from performance and resource utilization of other services running at the same time on the same set of resources.

M. Paasivaara and P. Kruchten (Eds.): XP 2020 Workshops, LNBIP 396, pp. 133–140, 2020.
https://doi.org/10.1007/978-3-030-58858-8_14

In this paper we investigate the methods for improving services' performance stability, which we view as an important aspect of overall Quality of Service.

1.1 The Importance of Predictable Functions Performance

The predictability of function execution performance (most often function execution time) is important from several reasons. Here are the QoS and performance expectations from Users, Developers/Application Owners and Infrastructure Owners/Admins:

1. End users value performance consistency for practical reasons. Unexpected application slowdown can cause frustration but also can negatively impact important business operations. Positive overall user experience requires assurance that service response time will have low, predictable latency.
2. Developers/Application Owners want predictable billing. Most often Infrastructure Owners charge by millisecond of function execution time. Any churn in function execution time can impact billing negatively. The reason for inconsistent function execution time is only partially in control of Developers/Application Owners (e.g. associated with function logic processing the input). Other issues, like resource contention or noisy neighbor problems in shared-resources, multi-tenant environments, can be solved only by the Infrastructure Owners.
3. Infrastructure Owners want to provide predictable performance for their Users and at the same time maximize resources utilization as this improves their Total Cost of Ownership. As for FaaS, many CSPs adopt sub second billing, which puts stringent SLA requirements in terms of run-to-run variability. When Infrastructure Owners have awareness which resources are most critical for stable functions' performance, they can better optimize their scheduling policies to optimize their computing resources utilization.

In this study we define predictable performance in relation to Coefficient of Variation (CV) for function execution time. The CV itself is defined as [2]:

$$c_v = \frac{\sigma}{\mu} \tag{1}$$

Where, c_v is a coefficient of variation, σ is a standard deviation and μ is a mean.

We consider function to have predictable performance when its CV is less than or equal to 15%. Otherwise, we consider the performance to be unpredictable. When average function execution time is 1 s, and resource utilization billing is done at 100 ms granularity, then 15% execution time churn corresponds to up to 2 billing cycles, which we consider tolerable from function owner perspective.

FaaS deployments are intrinsically multi-tenant and expected to scale rapidly, on-demand. To enable such scaling, without sacrificing performance, we propose to pay special attention to CPU microarchitecture resources utilization, as it directly correlates with functions' performance. Here is the high-level view of resources for Intel Xeon Processor (Fig. 1).

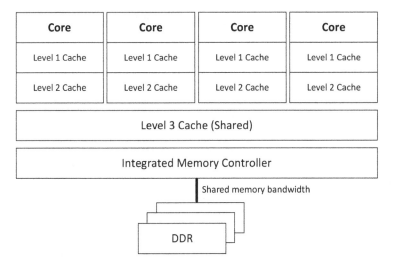

Fig. 1. High level view of Intel Xeon processor

Especially shared resources, like memory bandwidth to DRAM (controlled by the Integrated Memory Controller) and Last Level Cache (i.e. Third Level Cache) should be closely monitored, as minimizing contention on those resources improves overall functions' performance. Also, for multi-socket platforms, crossing socket or NUMA node boundary might be associated with performance penalty (due to narrower remote memory bandwidth). The study analyzing impact of memory latency and memory bandwidth to the workload's performance is described in [3].

In general, the pool of CPU cores is also a constrained resource on which contention might happen. But we leave the task of allocating software threads to CPU cores to the Linux scheduler and did not interfere with that in our study.

2 Analyzing Functions Performance and Performance Predictability

In the following sections we describe how we were analyzing functions performance. We have started with gathering information about functions characteristics, especially resources sensitivity patterns. That enabled us to further analyze performance related problems and propose solutions.

2.1 Test Stack and Test Functions

We've conducted our experiments on a 4-node Kubernetes cluster, with 1 master and 3 worker nodes. All nodes are 2-socket Intel Skylake platforms (Intel® Xeon® Gold 6140 CPU @ 2.30 GHz, with 18 physical cores and HyperThreading enabled).

For the software stack we used: Kubernetes as containers orchestrator, Docker as containers engine/runtime, OpenFaaS as a FaaS framework and Intel Workload Collocation Agent [4] as a main telemetry framework.

In our experiments we are using following functions:

- Incept, which uses Tensorflow for image recognition
- Nmt, which uses Tensorflow for English to German translation
- Sgemm, which does single precision floating General Matrix Multiply
- Stream, the STREAM benchmark [5].

2.2   Introduction to Top-Down Microarchitecture Analysis Methodology

Our test functions have been profiled using Top-Down Microarchitecture Analysis methodology [6, 7]. This approach facilitates finding categories of platform resources, and individual resources, that are most critical to the workload (e.g. function) and can limit performance when not available. The results of the profiling, at high CPU utilization (ranging from 95 to 100%), are presented in the Table 1 below.

Table 1. TMA profiles of the test functions

Function	A	B	C	D	E	F	G
Incept	1.13	60.7	17.0	56.1	22.2	4.7	3.1
Nmt	2.35	52.4	22.8	60.6	10.8	5.8	0.1
Sgemm	0.49	32.8	17.7	25.8	40.8	15.6	29.4
Stream	2.40	71.6	1.5	93.0	5.5	0.1	0.1

Where: A – Last Level Cache Misses per 1000 Instructions, B – Memory Bandwidth Utilization [%], C – Frontend Bound [%], D – Backend Bound [%], E – Retiring [%], F – Bad Speculation, G – Flops Used/Flops Max [%].

This knowledge can be leveraged in optimizing scheduling and load balancing logic, so that functions' performance is not hampered by the lack of critical platform resources. This is specifically important in large scale, multi-tenant deployment where noisy neighbor effects are most prominent.

2.3   Platform Resources Utilization Monitoring

During functions' execution we collect telemetry data to better understand resources utilization patterns. For each function instance, per each call, we are collecting the following:

- Memory bandwidth utilization – exposed by the Linux 'resctrl' filesystem, the source of data is Intel RDT Memory Bandwidth Monitoring technology
- Last Level Cache Occupancy – exposed by the Linux 'resctrl' filesystem, the source of data is Intel RDT Cache Monitoring Technology
- Last Level Cache Misses Per Kilo Instructions – exposed by the platform as a CPU architectural performance monitoring event, can be collected, for example: via Linux perf tool
- CPU utilization – exposed by the Linux CGroup filesystem

We also record function execution times as an indicator of a function's performance.

Having insight into nodes' resource utilization and availability is critical in order to improve placement of functions on the nodes. Here are the most important telemetry data that we collect per each compute node:

- CPU utilization – exposed by the Linux/proc/stat file
- Memory bandwidth utilization – exposed by the CPU Performance Monitoring Unit (of Integrated Memory Controller), can be calculated from events collected, for example via Linux perf tool
- Average memory latency – exposed by the CPU Performance Monitoring Unit (of Integrated Memory Controller), can be calculated from events collected, for example via Linux perf tool.

3   Improving Performance Predictability

3.1   Analyzing Functions' Co-location Cases

In this experiment we use "hey" [8] to stress the test functions. We start from light load (low Request-Per-Second values) and continue stressing functions up to the point where all cores (36 total for 2 sockets, 18 cores per function) on the platform are utilized, thus translating to high RPS values. Theoretically, functions with moderate memory bandwidth consumption should co-exist better on the same node than functions with high memory bandwidth requirements. The reason is less contention on the resource required by both functions. We should also see improved function execution times and lower resources utilization when functions are not competing over the same, shared resource.

The results for the "Incept" function scheduled along with other functions are depicted below (Fig. 2):

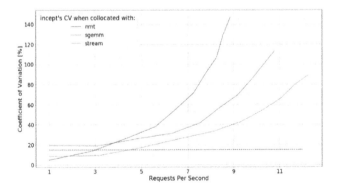

Fig. 2. Incept's CV when scheduled with other test functions (red, dashed line at 15% represents our threshold, below which, we consider function to have predictable performance) (Color figure online)

We can observe that, if Incept is located with Sgemm it achieves the best performance predictability (lowest CV values across the RPS range) and best throughput (lowest average function execution time). An optimal scheduler should co-locate Incept with Sgemm, rather than Nmt or Stream. The worst colocation case is placing Incept and Nmt on the same node, and optimal scheduler should avoid that. Incept and Nmt are poor candidates for colocation because they are heavy memory bandwidth users and natural contenders for this resource.

The table below presents comparison of average node resources utilization when Incept is collocated with Nmt (sub-optimal placement) and when Incept is collocated with Sgemm (optimal placement) in case when all CPU cores on the platform are utilized (Table 2).

Table 2. Comparison of average node resources utilization between optimal (Incept + Sgemm) and sub-optimal (Incept + Nmt) co-location scenarios

Resource	Optimal placement	Sub-optimal placement
Memory bandwidth utilization [%]	30	47
Average memory latency [ns]	41	92
CPU Utilization [%]	55	78
LLC MPKI[a]	50	110

[a]LLC MPKI – Last Level Cache Misses Per Kilo Instructions

Sub-optimal placement results in almost 20% higher memory bandwidth utilization, increased memory latency, and around 20% higher CPU utilization. And as we've seen before, wrong placement decision ultimately impacts function execution time and execution time variability.

3.2   Scheduling Improvements

By leveraging per-container telemetry (especially memory bandwidth utilization) and per-node resource availability we tried to improve the scheduling logic. In Kubernetes, which we are using as our containers' orchestrator, scheduling is a two-stage process. In the first step (filtering) we exclude any nodes without enough available memory bandwidth. In the second step (prioritization) we assign scores to the nodes and select the node with the highest score. Here are the scoring categories:

- Available memory bandwidth – nodes are sorted with available memory bandwidth in descending order. The node with maximum available memory bandwidth is assigned highest score, and the one with the lowest amount of available memory bandwidth is assigned the lowest score.
- Memory Latency – nodes are sorted and assigned scored based on the memory latency (lower values are preferred over higher values)
- CPU utilization – nodes are sorted based on available CPU (more available CPU equals to higher score)

Scores from all categories are summarized per node and the node with highest overall score is selected.

Graph below present comparison of Incept's CV when using default scheduling logic vs scheduling logic which takes memory bandwidth and memory latency into account. Scheduling enhancement were done by leveraging Kubernetes scheduler extender mechanism [9] (Fig. 3).

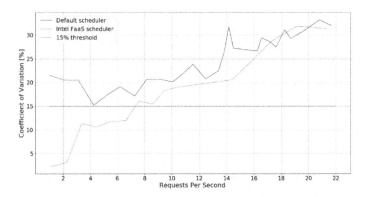

Fig. 3. The comparison of Incept's CV when using default scheduler vs. scheduler which is memory bandwidth and memory latency aware.

For lower RPS (up to around 7), the scheduler extender reduces CV to acceptable level (15%). Execution time also improves slightly, which can result in improved cluster throughput. Those results can be further improved with RDT Memory Bandwidth Allocation feature, which we plan to leverage in future experiments.

4   Future Work

As a next step we plan to research how at-node-level allocation of resources (e.g. by using Intel RDT Memory Bandwidth Allocation and Cache Allocation Technology) impacts functions' performance.

We would also like to deepen studies on differentiated performance for QoS-sensitive workloads. The Service Level Agreements are commonly used for managing QoS. At its simplest form the SLA can be expressed as a two-level function prioritization agreement, distinguishing between high and low priority tasks (e.g. functions). We'd like to research how high-level SLAs can be mapped to resource allocations and how allocations enforcement can be used for improving performance predictability even further.

5   Conclusions

We have demonstrated that low level telemetry data (especially related to memory bandwidth utilization) can be used to improve functions performance predictability, for example by optimizing scheduling logic.

By leveraging memory bandwidth monitoring capabilities of Intel Resource Director Technology, we were able to optimize resource utilization and provide best performance for memory bandwidth sensitive workloads (ML-based inference workloads in our experiment).

References

1. Intel® Resource Director Technology (Intel® RDT). https://www.intel.com/content/www/us/en/architecture-and-technology/resource-director-technology.html. Accessed 10 Mar 2020
2. Everitt, B.: The Cambridge Dictionary of Statistics. Cambridge University Press, Cambridge (1998). ISBN 978-0521593465
3. Clapp, R., et al.: Quantifying the performance impact of memory latency and bandwidth for big data workloads. In: IEEE International Symposium on Workload Characterization. IEEE (2015). ISBN 978-1-5090-0088-3
4. Workload Collocation Agent. https://github.com/intel/workload-collocation-agent. Accessed 10 Mar 2020
5. STREAM benchmark. http://www.cs.virginia.edu/stream/ref.html. Accessed 10 Mar 2020
6. Yasin, A.: A top-down method for performance analysis and counters architecture. In: 2014 IEEE International Symposium on Performance Analysis of Systems and Software (ISPASS). IEEE (2014). ISBN 978-1-4799-3606-9
7. Yasin, A.: Software Optimizations Become Simple with Top-Down Analysis Methodology on Intel® Microarchitecture, Code Name Skylake, Intel Developer Forum, IDF 2015, Intel (2015)
8. Hey GitHub web page. https://github.com/rakyll/hey. Accessed 10 Mar 2020
9. Kubernetes Scheduler Extensions. https://kubernetes.io/docs/concepts/extend-kubernetes/extend-cluster/#scheduler-extensions. Accessed 10 Mar 2020

On the Use of Web Assembly in a Serverless Context

Seán Murphy[1]([⊠]), Leonardas Persaud[2], William Martini[1,2],
and Bill Bosshard[1,2]

[1] Zurich University of Applied Science, Winterthur, Switzerland
murp@zhaw.ch
[2] University of Zurich, Zurich, Switzerland

Abstract. This paper considers how WASM can be run in different serverless contexts. A comparison of different serverside WASM runtime options is considered, specifically focused on `wasmer`, `wasmtime` and `lucet`. Next, different options for running WASM within two serverless platforms – Openwhisk and AWS Lambdai – are compared. Initial results show that a solution which uses the built-in `node.js` WASM supports is found to work better than using the dedicated WASM runtimes but this has limitations and providing more direct integration with WASM runtimes should be explored further.

Keywords: Web Assembly · WASM · Serverless · Runtimes

1 Introduction

Web Assembly (WASM) is a technology that has been receiving considerable interest of late. Originally, developed as a portable runtime for browser contexts, its benefits have been recognized for alternative contexts and there is increasing interest in understanding other environments in which it can be used. Serverless is one such context [2–4] and the use of WASM in a serverless context is the focus of this work.

WASM evolved from `asm.js`[1] – a previous attempt to define a simple assembly like instruction set which could run efficiently within a browser – and was adopted by the Mozilla foundation in 2017 to co-ordinate development and standardization of the technology across all major browser developers.

WASM is designed to be fast, secure, portable and not tied to any specific language or runtime, although realizing all of these aspects is still something of a work in progress. It is characterized by a simple instruction set which can be formally verified, a stack based Virtual Machine which supports functions and control flow abstractions such as loops and conditionals. A good overview of WASM is provided in [1].

---

[1] http://asmjs.org/.

© The Author(s) 2020
M. Paasivaara and P. Kruchten (Eds.): XP 2020 Workshops, LNBIP 396, pp. 141–145, 2020.
https://doi.org/10.1007/978-3-030-58858-8_15

Good support for WASM is provided in today's major browsers but it is still evolving with significant innovations required to provide support for multi-threaded operation, garbage collection GPU and WebGL supports amongst other items[2].

As well as browser support, work has been ongoing on developing supports for execution of WASM outside the browser context. Much of this work has been consolidated under the Bytecode Alliance's work on developing a *Web Assembly Systems Interface* (WASI)[3] which is a set of APIs available within the WASM runtime which can provide POSIX style capabilities (file system access, network access, process management, etc.). This effort and, in particular, the parallel development effort to create WASI compatible execution engines which can run in different environments is creating new opportunities and use cases for WASM, one of which is serverless.

Serverless solutions today are closely coupled to Docker containers; WASM could provide an alternative or complementary runtime environment which is lightweight, works well with different developer toolchains and could potentially be deployed across different serverless platforms. Having some insight into how this could be realized is the focus of this work.

The remainder of this paper is structured as follows. In Sect. 2 there is a brief comparison of different WASM runtimes which can be used on the server side. This is followed in Sect. 3 by a discussion of different solutions for running WASM within serverless platforms. Finally there is a short conclusion and outlook.

2   Evaluation of Serverside WASM in Different Runtimes

Running WASM on the server side requires a means to map from WASM byte-code to native hardware instructions. A number of technologies have been developed to support this: in this work, three were considered – (i) wasmer[4], (ii), wasmtime[5] and (iii) lucet[6].

Both wasmer and wasmtime are runtimes which parse given WASM bytecode, mapping it to native instructions to operate on the host processor using *Just-in-Time* (JIT) compilation mechanisms. The former is under active development by a commercial company, while the latter is developed within the context of a collaborative, standardization activity operated by the Mozilla Foundation. lucet uses a different approach - it performs an *a priori* compilation of the WASM bytecode to produce a standard executable for the host system architecture.

Generating WASM bytecode is generally straightforward although there is some difference in the supports available for different languages and compiler toolchains. Rust and C/C++ currently have the best supports but support for Golang is also good. To compare the different solutions, we chose some reference

---

[2] https://www.w3.org/2020/03/webassembly-wg-charter.html.
[3] https://github.com/WebAssembly/WASI.
[4] https://www.wasmer.io.
[5] https://github.com/bytecodealliance/wasmtime.
[6] https://github.com/bytecodealliance/lucet.

C algorithm implementations as we knew the code was mature and the toolchain supported generation of WASM output; the Clang toolkit was used to generate WASI compatible WASM binaries[7] which could be run directly in `wasmer` and `wasmtime` and compiled to native with `lucet`.

The different approaches were compared using standard memory and compute bound workloads. Figure 1 shows the time taken to determine if a large number is prime using the different approaches.

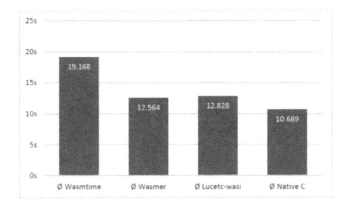

Fig. 1. Time taken to determine if 4294967029 is prime

Here it can be seen that the performance of `wasmer` is similar to `lucet`, both performing faster than `wasmtime`. A number of other comparisons using memory bound and compute bound computation were performed and this conclusion largely held across all the experiments[8]. For this reason, as well as the fact that it has a substantial developer interest, `wasmer` was chosen as the preferred WASM/WASI runtime[9]. It is also interesting to note that the time difference between the WASM executables and native C is not large, with the WASM executables taking approximately 20% longer than native compiled code.

3   Running WASM in Serverless Context

Although the ultimate goal of this work is to understand how WASM can be used as a native runtime in a serverless context, the first priority in this work

---

[7] https://depth-first.com/articles/2019/10/16/compiling-c-to-webassembly-and-running-it-without-emscripten/.

[8] More details are available in the project report [5] and in the project's Github repository at https://github.com/WilliamMartini/WASM.

[9] The bytecode alliance reached out to note the performance of `wasmtime` was due to optimizations being disabled by default in previous versions of `wasmtime`, meaning that similar performance between `wasmer` and `wasmtime` can now be expected.

was to devise a solution which would enable a WASM executable to be run on existing serverless platforms - Openwhisk and AWS Lambda in particular. Hence the initial focus was on the problem of getting WASM code operating in docker container running in different serverless platforms leveraging `wasmer` as the WASM runtime.

The first approach to address the problem focused on using a Python-flask[10] wrapper around the WASM executable; the wrapper provided hooks into the serverless platform, offering a small number of HTTP endpoints which the platform could invoke to initialize the serverless function and to trigger it with some input parameters. Although this approach worked in principle, as it used Python, which typically has a large set of dependencies, it resulted in a large container, thus eliminating one of the potential advantages of considering WASM as a runtime.

The second approach was to leverage WASM capabilities within `node.js`; `node.js` offers the possibility to run WASM binaries directly within the node runtime (rather than needing a standalone WASM/WASI execution environment). As `node.js` is well supported in serverless systems, this approach held some promise.

To compare the different solutions a simple WASM file was generated which performed a calculation of the 42nd number in the Fibonacci sequence. The time taken to execute this function when implemented via the Docker/Python solution was compared with that of the `node.js` solution on different platforms. The results are shown in Fig. 2.

From the figure, it can be seen that using the `node.js` results in lower latency than the docker solution when run on Openwhisk. One limitation of the `node.js` solution, however is that only integer types are supported when communicating between the serverless platform and the executable. The slower execution on AWS is still being investigated.

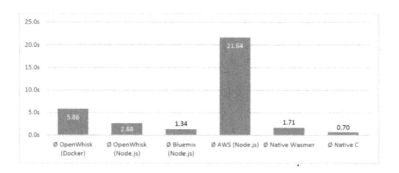

Fig. 2. Time taken to calculate the 42nd Fibonacci number

---

[10] https://flask.palletsprojects.com/en/1.1.x/.

4   Conclusion

In this work, the use of WASM in a serverless context was considered: We compared three different options for running server side WASM: `wasmer`, `wasmtime` and `lucet`. `wasmer` was the best option to proceed with based on the first analysis. Execution of WASM applications within serverless platforms was then considered. One option was to use a container containing glue to the serverless platform, the WASM runtime – `wasmer` in this case – and the WASM application itself. An alternative approach removed the necessity for the WASM specific runtime as standard `node.js` engines provide support for running WASM. An initial comparison of these alternatives showed that using `node.js` can be more efficient than using a dedicated WASM runtime.

Future work will involve deeper comparison of these different approaches for running WASM within different serverless platforms.

References

1. Haas, A., et al.: Bringing the web up to speed with WebAssembly. In: Proceedings of the 38th ACM SIGPLAN Conference on Programming Language Design and Implementation (2017)
2. Hall, A., Umakishor, R.: An execution model for serverless functions at the edge. In: Proceedings of the International Conference on Internet of Things Design and Implementation (2019)
3. Gadepalli, P.K., et al.: Challenges and opportunities for efficient serverless computing at the edge. In: 2019 38th Symposium on Reliable Distributed Systems (SRDS). IEEE (2019)
4. Shillaker, S., Pietzuch, P.: Faasm: lightweight isolation for efficient stateful serverless computing. arXiv preprint arXiv:2002.09344 (2020)
5. Persaud, L., Bosshard , B., Martini, W.: Using WebAssembly to make serverless applications more portable. Project report, Software Maintenance and Evolution Module, University of Zurich, December 2019

Second International Workshop
on Agile Transformations

Agile Transformation (ATRANS) Workshop: A Summary and Research Agenda

Leonor Barroca[1], Noel Carroll[2], Peggy Gregory[3], and Diane Strode[4]

[1] The Open University, UK
leonor.barroca@open.ac.uk
[2] Lero, NUI Galway, Ireland
[3] University of Central Lancashire, UK
[4] Whitireia Polytechnic, New Zealand

Abstract. Agile transformation is a process many organisations undertake to survive and thrive in volatile, uncertain, complex, and ambiguous environments. Global and local challenges such as those caused by COVID-19 have to be embraced at very short notice and impose changes on people, processes, and technology to facilitate an agile transformation. Building on the first international workshop on agile transformation (ATRANS), this year's workshop challenged the scientific community to examine agile transformation across IT functions, business units and whole organisations, focusing in particular on aspects of culture, leadership, people and sustainability. This paper reports on the results of the second international workshop on agile transformation.

Keywords: Agile transformation · Theoretical perspectives · Sustaining agile · Human factors · Research agenda

1 Introduction

Agile transformation is the process of transforming an organisation's socio-technical structures, activities and culture so it can embrace change and thrive in a turbulent and competitive international environment. With a growing global focus on digitalisation, the importance of agility across every sector of society has become paramount to scale and strengthen competitiveness. Within a software context, agile software methods were originally designed for small and collaborative single-team projects with evolving needs. However, given the success of agile methods, many large software organisations have begun to scale these methods to a large-scale and often enterprise-wide context in a hope to mimic their success. As a result, agile transformation has emerged as an important concept within the C-Suite [1]. For example, in 2020, management and leadership commentators report that we are in *"the age of agile"* and *"without agile, human-centered organization is not possible at all"* [2]. Yet, for the practitioner and research communities, there are a number of core challenges which still remain, and which are even more pronounced as a result of the current unprecedented pandemic changes.

Following on from the success of the first Agile Transformation (ATRANS) workshop in 2019 [3], the second ATRANS workshop in 2020 provided an online forum which brought together an excellent mix of practitioners and academics to present and discuss current practice and research, to explore the current challenges, and to pose solutions based on experience and theory [4]. ATRANS 2020 comprised of three sessions. In the first session, four papers on agile transformation were presented on the following topics:

1. *How Employees Experience and Cope with Transformative Change* by Dina Koutsikouri, Sabine Madsen, and Nataliya Berbyuk Lindström;
2. *It's not Easy Being Agile: Unpacking Paradoxes in Agile Environments* by Betting Horlach and Andreas Drechsler;
3. *Agile Transformation; Shifting conceptualization of control in Agile Transformations* by Marius Mikalsen, Viktoria Stray, Nils Brede Moe, and Idun Backer;
4. *Strategy-focused agile transformation: a case study* by Helen Sharp and Katie Taylor.

The second session consisted of three breakout group discussions on agile transformation running in parallel. The third session hosted a four-person panel led by two practitioners and two academics. The panel focused on current research challenges in agile transformation. In the following sections we summarise the key findings from the discussion and the panel sessions.

2   Experience with Agile Transformation

The workshop provided over 80 participants with an opportunity to share their experiences on agile transformation during breakout sessions under the following three categories: (i) theoretical perspectives of agile transformation; (ii) sustaining agile transformation; and (iii) human factors in agile transformation. The three categories were identified, prior to the workshop, by the workshop chairs (the authors of this article) from research and gaps in the literature; we also took into account the topics presented across the workshop research articles. Prior to the breakout sessions, three Metro Retro (an agile retrospective tool) whiteboards were organised, each divided into quarters in order to structure participants' contributions and facilitate discussions during the sessions. During the research article presentations, participants were given the opportunity to indicate which of the three breakout sessions they wished to participate in. There were approximately 25 participants in each breakout session. In each breakout session, participants were asked to identify specific challenges they experienced around the specific topic. Within the Metro Retro site, participants posted virtual post-it notes on various quadrants of a virtual whiteboard which allowed us to probe for more details during discussions and share experiences of participants. The authors of this article facilitated the breakout sessions and summarised the key points from these interactive discussions. All of the key points were also presented back to the main workshop after the breakout sessions for further discussion and debate. We summarise the key takeaway points from each of these sessions in Table 1.

A common theme expressed by participants was a concern with the focus of practitioners and researchers on technical factors (e.g. comparing agile methods and analytics), rather than on the core human elements (e.g. examining the impact of added

Table 1. Summary of discussion in ATRANS Breakout Sessions

Theoretical perspectives of agile transformation	Sustaining agile transformation	Human factors in agile transformation
Examine the complexity of agile transformations using theories such as complex adaptive systems theory Identify new ways to explain changes brought about by agile transformations using theories on coordination, change management (e.g. Kotter's model or Worley's framework), temporality, and dependency Explore the application of control theory and stewardship theory to explain factors which enable or inhibit agile transformations Develop theoretical accounts of the inherently fluid nature of agility as a theory and new norms resulting from agile transformations Identify the paradoxes, tensions, and contradictions which emerge during agile transformation Propose new theoretical and interdisciplinary insights on the management of agile transformation using, for example, institutional theory, leadership theories, adaptation theory, process theory, actor network theory, activity theory, and normalisation process theory	Clearly communicate the rationale, objectives, and benefits of transformation Improve knowledge sharing across the whole organisation Keep the curiosity about what to do next to improve transformation Recognise, identify and manage change fatigue Continuously assess agility, setting expectations, i.e. the time it takes, being a journey not a destination, etc. Educate leaders ahead of the transformation with clear expectations and about how to let go of control (re)Organise the business around value streams Ensure sufficient resources to sustain long term transformation and commitment from leadership, e.g. budget, agile coaches, processes, and tools, etc Inform people about advances in the transformation and celebrate those Inspire and train people, addressing fear of change and insecurity allowing for space and time for improvement Don't try to do it all at the same time, establish priorities	Distinguish between deep transformation and process change Explore how management become agile themselves Investigate how to support people to change to an agile mindset Examine the influence of the certification industry on agile transformation Explore the role of communication between different parts of the organisation, e.g. understanding differences in terminology and aims Consider the role and significance of developing a shared high-level vision Investigate the impact of national and organisational culture on change Explore how to build stakeholder trust during transformation Investigate managers' expectations of agile transformation and how they change over time Explore how individual psychological factors enable or inhibit change and affect embracing an agile mindset Explore how to support staff experiencing resistance to change and fear of job loss

pressures exerted on teams to operationalise agile transformations). Many of the key challenges identified by participants in the discussion were related to human factors throughout the transformation process: e.g., being flexible, trusting, and embracing an agile mindset. Participants also highlighted the need for more novel perspectives on management and coordination of agile and for sustaining transformation through improved communication and training processes.

3 The Panel

The workshop concluded with a panel of four (two academics and two practitioners) reflecting on the future of agile transformation, a research agenda, and key challenges that need to be addressed.

The first panellist, Torgeir Dingsøyr (SINTEF, Norway) highlighted two of the challenges prioritised by participants in the first agile transformation workshop [1], (i) resistance to change and (ii) coordination challenges in multi team environment, as areas in need of further research. Coordination needs to be rethought on several fronts: in personal relations, in teams, when there are higher-level interdependencies, when there is task uncertainty, when many people are involved, and as coordination changes over time. Focusing on agile transformation at the organisation level, the second panellist, Helen Sharp (The Open University, UK) reflected on the drivers for trans-formation and the choices that need to be made (where/how to start? what to trans-form?). Helen highlighted opportunities for interdisciplinary research teams to study, for example, agility from an IT perspective and from a business-oriented perspective, and to test theories from different disciplines in the context of agile transformation. She also pointed to the need to consider appropriate or develop new research methods to study transformation. These need to take into account the fact that the research process is complex, large-scale, and of a long duration. Bringing the voice of practitioners, the third panellist, Parag Gogate (Ascendere, UK) stressed how practice is based on per-sonal experience, advice from colleagues, and knowledge and intuition rather than on findings from the scientific research community. He pointed to the gap between theory and practice that is difficult to bridge, while still acknowledging that it is beneficial to bring theory to practice and vice versa. Focus was placed on the need to consider ways to improve praxis, i.e. the process by which theory can be enacted, embodied, or realized in practice. The fourth panellist, Kjetil Røe (Sopra Steria, Norway) introduced a case study from the Norwegian public sector project highlighting the challenges faced and how they were addressed; initially with a change of focus from process to product, empowering multidisciplinary teams, and then by implementing continuous delivery. One of the decisions taken was not to follow any specific framework. Kjetil reported that more research is needed on the impact of frameworks. During this project they saw the positive impact that continuous delivery had on team culture and processes; yet continuous delivery is another aspect of agile transformation that is not well understood by research.

4 Research Agenda on Main Challenges

Building on the broad themes around paper presentations, workshop participants' insights and experiences, and the panel members contributions, the initial three areas for discussion (in the breakout rooms) were explored in depth resulting in the following proposed research agenda for agile transformation:

- **Theoretical perspectives on agile transformation**: there was a common theme across workshop articles, breakout sessions, and panel discussions on the importance of building new theory and adopting existing theories from other disciplines which can explain facets of the agile transformation phenomenon. There continues to be a gap between theory and practice often due to (i) practitioners' lack of awareness of recent academic developments, and (ii) a lack of open access to academic research outputs, e.g. published journal articles. As part of future research, we propose the need to develop new theoretical accounts across various stages of an agile transformation from the motivation to transform, techniques to manage change and coordination, implementing controls, normalising new agile methods, and evaluating the successes and failures of agile transformations. In addition, academics should consider the importance of praxis to apply and test new theoretical developments in practice. The four panelists highlighted the growing importance of bridging the gap between theory and practice using interdisciplinary viewpoints. The panelists also agreed on the need for academics to target open access publications so practitioners can access research and read about recent initiatives on agile transformation so they can apply and test new research developments.

- **Sustaining agile transformation**: Agile adoption is not the end of the road; recently, agile has extended to larger projects and across the organisation to non-IT areas. Once adopted, agile still needs to be supported, sustained and embedded in the organisation. This raises research questions in a wide range of areas. The papers in this workshop dealt with issues that emerge in the process of sustaining agile transformation, e.g.: managing control in cross-functional teams, identifying tensions in agile environments, understanding how employees sustain confidence in an agile transformation, and bringing a wider organisation perspective to sustaining the transformation, by focusing on strategy. Panel members also highlighted areas that need further research in sustaining the agile transformation: resistance to change; coordination in multi-functional teams; the impact on culture derived from empowering multidisciplinary teams; and implementing continuous delivery. As part of further research, we propose the following questions: how do organisations handle critical incidents (such as COVID-19) and ensure they sustain their agile projects?, What challenges do organisations face when sustaining agile at all levels?, How do organisations overcome challenges in agile transformation concerning leadership, knowledge sharing, communication, organisational structure, motivation, culture and mindset?, How do organisations deal with resistance to change and coordination in multi-functional teams?, Where and how do organisations start transformations and what strategies and choices do they need to make to sustain the transformation?

- **Human factors in agile transformation:** The impact of human factors on agile transformation emerged as a major theme across the workshop articles, breakout sessions, and panel discussion. We propose that future research needs to refocus on this issue. Three key challenges for researchers to investigate were identified during the workshop: conceptualising agile transformation, organisation-level human factors, and individual human factors. Important aspects of agile conceptualisation included the paradox of 'doing agile' versus 'being agile' discussed by Horlach and Drechsler in the second paper presentation. Other issues discussed during the breakout session included how to support people to understand and adopt an agile mindset, the frequent problem of underestimating the size of the task of an agile transformation, and the need for managers to understand that the deep transformation required during an agile transformation includes many changes to management practices. Organisation-level factors include the need for a clearly communicated shared vision and goal for transformation, dealing with the current organisational culture and its diversity, and developing a mutual understanding between people in different parts of the organisation. In the panel discussion Helen Sharp highlighted the need to explore the motivations that organisations have to undertake transformations and how those drivers affect the way in which the transformation is approached. Individual human factors of interest include the different ways individuals respond to and resist change. These factors were also highlighted in the panel discussion. Torgeir Dingsøyr discussed the common phenomenon of resistance to change and Parag Gogate described his experience with practitioners who often find it hard to set aside time to critically reflect even when they know it is an important process.

5   Conclusion

Agile approaches represent a fundamental shift in how we build teams and services to sustain contemporary business practices. Successful agile transformation embeds a deep philosophical change in how ideas are nurtured, how organisations are structured, and how cultures embrace openness and innovation. Yet, as the authors, participants, and panellists reported throughout this workshop, there are many fundamental challenges associated with agile transformation which point to new directions for future research. This workshop demonstrated there is a continuing interest among the research community in agile transformation and a growing body of studies upon which to build. The purpose of the second ATRANs workshop was to explore issues in transformation primarily from the perspective of theory, sustainability, and human factors. The workshop participants explored these issues in depth and based on the submissions, discussions, and insights from practitioners and researchers we propose the following research agenda:

1. To build new interdisciplinary theoretical accounts of agile transformation that are accessible to practitioners and can be applied in practice.
2. To explore how to continuously support, sustain and embed agile within the organisation at all levels (people, processes, products) and throughout time.
3. To enhance our understanding of the complex human factors that influence agile transformation at organisational, team and individual levels.

This second ATRANS workshop built on the first ATRANS workshop [3] and identified in depth areas that constitute a rich research agenda. Going forward, we aspire to two aims for the future of ATRANS. First, that the exchange of interdisciplinary ideas between practice and academia will flourish and support agile software engineering and agile management. Second, that the research agenda developed at the workshop will inspire future studies in this complex and challenging domain and encourage academics and practitioners to build new theoretical perspectives and practical guidelines on how to better manage agile transformation.

Acknowledgement. Thanks to all presenters and participants, to Maria Paasivara for the overall organisation of XP2020 and Hubert Baumeister and Mansooreh Zahedi for chairing the research workshops. Further, we are very grateful to the program committee members: Akim Berkani (Paris Dauphine University, France), Julian Bass (University of Salford, UK), Torgeir Dingsøyr (SINTEF, Norway), Henry Edison (Lero, NUI Galway, Ireland), Christoph Fuchs (Germany), Lucas Gren (Chalmers University, Sweden), Tomas Gustavsson (Karlstadt University, Sweden), Ludvig Lindlöf (Chalmers University, Sweden), Marius Mikalsen (SINTEF, Norway), Sunila Modi (University of Hertfordshire, UK), Nils Brede Moe (SINTEF, Norway) and Helen Sharp (The Open University, UK).

References

1. Dikert, K., Paasivaara, M., Lassenius, C.: Challenges and success factors for large-scale agile transformations: a systematic literature review. J. Syst. Softw. **119**, 87–108 (2016)
2. Denning, S.: The irresistible rise of agile: A paradigm shift in management. Forbes. (2019)
3. Barroca, L., Dingsøyr, T., Mikalsen, M.: Agile tansformation: a summary and research agenda from the first international workshop (ATRANS). In: Hoda, R. (ed.) Agile Processes in Software Engineering and Extreme Programming – Workshops. XP 2019, Springer, Cham (2019)
4. Conboy, K., Carroll, N.: Implementing large-scale agile frameworks: challenges and recommendations. IEEE Softw. **36**(2), 44–50 (2019)

Agile Transformation: How Employees Experience and Cope with Transformative Change

Dina Koutsikouri[1(✉)], Sabine Madsen[2],
and Nataliya Berbyuk Lindström[1]

[1] Department of Applied IT, University of Gothenburg, Gothenburg, Sweden
dina.koutsikouri@ait.gu.se
[2] Department of Politics and Society, Aalborg University, Aalborg, Denmark

Abstract. Modern manufacturing is highly competitive, requiring that organizations reduce lead times and achieve greater organizational flexibility, for example by implementing agile ways of working. However, studies show that incumbent firms have persistent problems with adopting and scaling such practices. In this paper, we present an empirical account of agile transformation in a large manufacturing company that has adopted the SAFe framework. Based on interviews, focus groups, and observation data, we identify three themes for understanding how employees experience and cope with transformative change by: 1) making sense of the new, 2) practicing with peers and 3) letting go of legacy. Key findings are that initially employees are more concerned with making sense of the new rather than with the implementation of agile itself and that implementation of agile happens very gradually over time rather than through major breakthroughs. Thus, it takes time for employees to weather change, become acquainted with the new way of working and stabilize how they work together in the agile teams and across the ARTs (Agile Release Trains). We contribute to extant literature with insight into the human implications of agile transformation.

Keywords: Agile transformation · Software development · Case study · Manufacturing

1 Introduction

Recently, there has been an outpouring of literature that seeks to explain why organizations should strive for agility to be able to respond quickly to change [1]. In larger organizational settings, becoming agile often requires the organization to undergo an agile transformation. Agile transformation refers to how large incumbent organizations change from their existing operating model to an agile way of working. This is accomplished through the adoption of principles, methods and frameworks that facilitate the scaling of agile development [2]. However, agile transformation and agile scaling are considered challenging because they require that employees in an organization change how they think, work and interact [2, 3]. Thus, as organizations attempt to become agile, employees face the challenge of letting go of traditional ways of

M. Paasivaara and P. Kruchten (Eds.): XP 2020 Workshops, LNBIP 396, pp. 155–163, 2020.
https://doi.org/10.1007/978-3-030-58858-8_16

working and embracing the 'new' thereby making agile transformation primarily a 'people transformation' [4]. Yet, main lessons from scholarly research are mostly presented from an *instrumental and managerial view* in terms of identifying, classifying, and mapping solutions onto transition challenges.

In this paper, we look at agile transformation from *the employees' lifeworld perspective* to better understand the effort and agency of employees when their organizations undergo transformative change, for various reasons. For us as researchers, it is *both* a value position to emphasize employee agency rather than managerial drive *and* an avenue for shedding light on what management-initiated transformation 'feels like'. Thus, the aim is to contribute to the emerging research agenda that focuses on the social aspects and human implications of large-scale agile transformations. To this end, we ask: *How do employees experience and cope with transformative change?*

We address this research question using a case study design [5], where we followed the agile transformation for one year by conducting interviews, focus groups and observations in a large Swedish manufacturing company. Thus, we have studied the employees experience of having to adopt the Scaled Agile Framework (SAFe) [2] and to adapt to a new operating model that emphasizes team interaction and agile roles rather than hierarchical power and traditional job titles. The paper advances current knowledge by focusing on agile transformation as a change process, which causes intense experiences that unfold over time as the employees make sense of the change and gradually adjust the way they work, and especially how they work together.

2 Background

Agile transformation and scaling are challenging, because they require transformative change as well as figuring out how to make agile work outside the small-team context, which it was intended for and where it has proven successful [6]. Therefore, researchers as well as practitioners have also demonstrated a significant interest in understanding agile transformation and in supporting agile scaling [e.g. 3, 7–9].

Several frameworks have been proposed for scaling agile in larger organizational settings. The Scaled Agile Framework (SAFe) [2] is the most adopted model for scaling agile across the enterprise. However, there is scarce empirical evidence on how the SAFe framework is deployed (or to what extent it can be fruitfully implemented in a large distributed environment). Further, the existing literature indicates that reaping the benefits of agile principles at a large scale is inherently difficult [3, 8, 9]. Although this do not seem to deter organizations from implementing agile scaling efforts [see, e.g. 7] understanding the contingencies surrounding agile transformation appear more important than ever [10].

Establishing an agile development approach often requires transformation, but many organizations underestimate the efforts required to institute new ways of working [11]. In a recent review of 13 agile transformation cases [9], the authors identified nine key challenges associated with implementing agile methods on a large-scale, including: difficulty in defining concepts and terms, comparing and contrasting frameworks, readiness and appetite for change, top-down vs bottom-up implementation, overemphasis on 100% adherence over value, lack of evidence-based use, balancing organizational structure while adhering to large-scale methods, lack of evidence-based use, maintaining developer autonomy, and misalignment between customer and processes frameworks. They also note that since many problems are 'subtle and can exist under the radar' it is difficult to address all of them. Moreover, they urge researchers to move toward developing theory that captures the dynamic nature of transformation processes and evolution over time.

Paasivaara et al. [8] propose four lessons learnt for large-scale agile transformations: 1) consider using an experimental approach to transformation, 2) consider implementing the transformation step-wise in complex large-scale settings, 3) team inter-changeability can be limited in a complex large-scale product—specialization might be needed, and 4) not using a common agile framework for the whole organization, in combination with insufficient common trainings and coaching may lead to a lack of common direction in the agile implementation. Further, according to the The state of Agile Survey [12] 'internal culture' remains an obstacle to adopting and scaling agile practices successfully in many organizations.

In general, the growing body of literature shows consensus on factors that enable and hinder adoption of agile methods and the challenges of scaling agile practices. However, literature reviews show a lack of systematically conducted studies on large software development organizations adopting agile methods [11, 13]. Given the nascent stage of agile research and theory there is a strong call from the research community for more empirical studies on agile transformation [3, 7, 8].

3   Method

In this paper, we investigate the experience of transformative change, while it is happening. Thus, our study follows the case of an ART (Agile Release Train) implementing the SAFe framework to change from waterfall to agile way of working. When we started collecting the data, the ART had entered the early stages of agile transformation. Data collection in the form of 25 interviews, two focus group sessions and several observations took place over a period of one year at the case company's premises. Specifics regarding the case company have been anonymized for confidentiality reasons.

The interviews lasted 60–90 min and where held with members of the ART, including roles such as systems developers, software testers, system architects, scrum masters, product owners, ART managers and agile coaches. Each of the focus group sessions lasted 90 min. The first session was carried out with four group managers and the second included eight scrum masters. To analyze the empirical data, we have applied Braun and Clarke's [14] phases of thematic analysis. No a priori coding template was used as the purpose was to understand transformative change from the employees' perspective rather than from a pre-existing theoretical point of view. In the first phase, we read the transcribed interviews and noted down ideas in a process of familiarization. Secondly, we conducted open coding to generate the initial codes. Next, the whole data set was grouped together under similar codes and then sorted into initial themes. In the third stage, we considered and conceptualized the themes in relationship to each other. As we examined how the practitioners experienced and were coping with the transition (from waterfall to agile) we began to realize that this emphasized three overlapping processes. We then refined and conceptualized these processes as three overlapping phases, which are illustrated in Fig. 1 (see the conclusion section).

4 Case Study

The organization under study has realized that in order to stay relevant in a highly competitive marketplace, it must be able to respond quickly to change in customer demands and technology. Moreover, the organization's competitiveness is increasingly relying on frequent releases of new/better software that improves the functionality of the physical products, rather than the physical products per se. Therefore, senior management has introduced agile methods and the SAFE framework as a solution that is intended to help the organization's software development employees speed up their ability to release product embedded software often. However, our analysis shows that the shift from the plan-driven waterfall approach to delivery-oriented agile sprints is a major transformative change that involves many elements. These are listed below. The first two elements refer to top management decisions, while the latter three refer to aspects that our interviewees described as particularly challenging.

(1) *Formal training.* Everybody is going through formal training.
(2) *Co-located teams.* The previous departmental/functional area structure is replaced with a cross-functional team structure and if possible, team members are physically relocated to sit together in shared office space.
(3) *Becoming a team.* The team members in the new teams have to get to know each other and figure out how to become a self-organizing team.
(4) *Communication between teams.* The teams must find out if, when and how it is necessary to communicate between teams in the ART.
(5) *Lag time.* Not everybody has switched to the agile way of working yet as it takes a long time for everybody to attend the basic formal training and to be allocated and physically moved into teams. Thus, employees who are trying to learn the new way of working must collaborate with employees, who are still working in the old way.

With the shift to agile nearly everything that the employees could previously take for granted is called into question, meaning that there is much cognitive and practical pressure to create new shared understandings about how to behave, work and relate to each other in the new organization.

4.1 Making Sense of the New

The first process, making sense of the new, is characterized by the employees spending much mental energy on trying to understand the new agile working model. However, "…*it is hard, it is a totally different way of working and thinking…*" (Systems architect).

The employees understand the agile way of working by comparing it with what they are familiar with, namely the waterfall approach. In other words, the old is the frame of reference for making sense of the new. It is also clear from our data that an important step towards understanding the new is to prefer, and even glorify, the past. Thus, the new way of working is initially evaluated rather critically through professional and personal filters based on previous experience. Moreover, agile is subject to continuous individual and shared (re)interpretation and (re)negotiation.

To cope, the employees seek explanations and ask for facts and measurements. However, they still feel that they lack information. Moreover, they express that communication has become more burdensome after the change to agile, because the method prescribes that they must communicate more within the team, but they lack knowledge of who knows what and who can make which decisions.

> "I feel that I lack information. But I have been thinking about this a lot, and I cannot really say what I'm lacking...and that is quite confusing...I hear from a lot of people that we are missing information...but no one really knows what we are missing...I think it is because I have not adjusted..." (Systems architect).

Several interviewees realize that these information and communication challenges are not the real problem, but rather a way of deflecting uncomfortable experiences associated with the change: *"We are still in the uncertainty and they are not really liking this"* (Scrum master). In general, our empirical data suggests that it is the individual's intense experience of confusion, uncertainty and anxiety that carries and colours the sense making processes at the early stages of transformative change.

4.2   Practicing with Peers

The second process, practicing with peers, foregrounds the employees' efforts to, in their own terms, grow into the agile way of working at the coalface, because *"[t]he reality is that you cannot stop [development], because you want to learn how the team has to work together"* (Software developer). This is described positively, as the employees state that it is by trialing and learning agile together in the new teams, that they are able to collectively figure out what the concepts of agile, such as self-organizing teams, rapid feedback, prioritizing backlog and focusing on continuous learning, really mean for their day-to-day work. While the formal training is important for building basic understanding, it is by practicing with their peers that the employees start to adjust to the agile roles and work practices.

> "It is a new thing...so everybody is trying to learn...the Scrum master is new, so he needs to learn more, the Product Owner needs to learn about it, and of course all other parts of the organization...to also even communicate with each other." (Software Developer).

However, it is challenging and time-consuming to practice new relationship types and develop new interaction norms through socializing, while also attempting to do the actual work in another way, using a new language. Consequently, the interviewees experience that because so many things are new for so many people, there is a relatively long period with less productivity; despite the aim being to speed up software development.

> "It takes time, takes time...I just want to go to the same level as before agile. We had a better productivity than now. But I'm expecting it will happen. I'm hoping." (Software Tester).

The employees understand that the software development part of the organization is going through a major learning process. Hoping that people will learn and that things will get better in a foreseeable future seems to be the main coping mechanism. The future-orientation helps the employees deal with the experiences of productivity loss and collaboration challenges that seems to characterize the change at the middle stages.

4.3   Letting Go of Legacy

Once the agile transformation had picked up pace, most employees sought routine in their daily operations and interactions, which contributed to a surge to make it work. Crucial to this 'reorientation' period, is the third process of letting go of legacy. However, some aspects are more difficult to let go of than others, particularly hierarchical structure, cultural values, and identity-defining skills.

> *"What is hard at the moment, is that we are still living in the traditional project management world and this cannot be changed in an afternoon!"* (Product Owner).

Indeed, the interviewees' hierarchical organizational structure difficult to let go of. This challenge is referred to as 'adopting a new mindset'. The employees experience the new agile teams and roles as vastly different from how they used to work. In particular, the team members have to let go of having a boss that they can go to for help. Instead they have to embrace the freedom and responsibility of self-organizing teams. While some employees enjoy this, others find it uncomfortable and feel more alone with the burden of decision-making.

Moreover, some employees who previously had the title of project managers, now have to function as scrum masters. This is a difficult change as old conceptions of what it means to be a manager has to be unlearned in favor of a more facilitating approach. Reminding oneself not to fall back into old habits and encouraging co-workers to remember the new are important coping mechanisms:

> *"I find it difficult to avoid meddling with technical issues since in my old role as group manager I was responsible for the team and technical side. Now I have to let go of the technical responsibility to the product owner. I have to work hard to get myself into this new mindset."* (Group manager).

For the individual employee, the change to agile creates an intense experience of anxiety about the relevance of one's skills and ultimately, one's relevance in the new organization. This is turn means that fear of letting go co-exists with a desire to be *as* or *more* productive than before the shift to agile. Therefore, the task is to keep doing the hard work of understanding agile, its feasibility and its desired outcome, while simultaneously hooking it into the prevailing work system, which is ultimately very difficult to discard.

5   Conclusion

Our research is an attempt to draw on lifeworld interviews with employees to shed new light on why agile transformation presents challenges for established organizations.

In Fig. 1, we summarize our research findings. This process model delineates how the employees experience and cope with transformative change over time through three recursive processes. Thus, initially the employees are more concerned with making sense of the new by comparing it with the past than with the implementation of agile itself. This is a very intense experience propelled by anxiety and uncertainty. Next, an important way for the employees to understand what is required of them and their new roles, is to practice with peers, and despite a drop in productivity due to learning, to hope that things will get better in the foreseeable future. However, it is difficult to let go of the hierarchical structure and identity-defining values and skills and to begin to form a new mindset. Therefore, the implementation of the agile way of working happens very gradually through subtle shifts in meanings and practices rather than through major breakthroughs. At this latter stage, the letting go of legacy is driven forward by the employees' desire for the change to be 'over' and for the new to work as 'normal'.

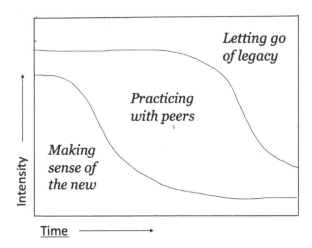

Fig. 1. Three overlapping processes of coping with transformative change

Above all our study highlights that employees will take their time to cope with change, because it is a time- and energy consuming endeavor, both emotionally and practically as well as individually and collectively. We find it interesting that our findings led us to emphasize slowness as key to understanding and perhaps also overcoming some of the challenges of agile transformation. This is of course an uncomfortable insight, for the case company as well as in general, as agile transformation is undertaken to speed up software development and keep up with a competitive marketplace. Overall, the lessons from this case study are relevant for leaders of organizations contemplating large-scale agile transformation.

Future research will assist in determining the extent of generalizability to other organizational contexts facing transformative change. We believe that further research into the three empirically derived phases of change has potential to uncover how members of organisations collectively enact transformative change; thus, acknowledging and normalizing the silent individual struggles, the role of hope when the going gets tough as well as the effort and agency of employees in acquiring new skills and engaging with each other to socialize their way into the new way of working. It will be important to further investigate other types of emotive processes or mechanisms involved in dealing with similar types of transformative change efforts. We hope to have provided a start in this direction.

References

1. Birkinshaw, J.: What to expect from agile. MIT SMR **59**(2), 39–42 (2018)
2. Leffingwell, D.: Scaling Software Agility. Best Practices for Large Enterprises. Addison Wesley, Boston (2007)
3. Carroll, N., Conboy, K.: Applying normalization process theory to explain large-scale agile transformations. In: 14th International Research Workshop on IT Project Management (IRWITPM), 14th December, Munich, Germany (2019)
4. Eden, R., Jones, A.B., Casey, V., Draheim, M.: Digital transformation requires workforce transformation. MIS Q. Executive **18**(1), 1–17 (2018)
5. Eisenhardt, K.: Building theories from case study research. Acad. Manag. Rev. **14**(4), 532–550 (1989)
6. Baskerville, R., Pries-Heje, J., Madsen, S.: Post-agility: what follows a decade of agility. Inform. Softw. Technol. **53**(5), 543–555 (2011)
7. Denning, S.: Why and How Volvo embraces agile at Scale, Forbes, January 2020
8. Paasivaara, M., Behm, B., Lassenius, C., Hallikainen, M.: Large-scale agile transformation at ericsson: a case study. Empir. Softw. Eng. **23**, 2550–2596 (2018)
9. Conboy, K., Carroll, N.: Implementing large-scale agile frameworks: challenges and recommendations. IEEE Softw. **36**(2), 44–50 (2019)
10. Dingsøyr, T., Moe, N.B.: Research challenges in large-scale agile software development. SIGSOFT Softw. Eng. Notes **38**(5), 38–39 (2013)
11. Klunder, J.A., Hohl, P., Prenner, N., Schneider, K.: Transformation towards agile software line engineering in large companies: a literature review. J. Softw. Evol. Process, 1–23 (2018)
12. VersionOne Inc 13th Annual 'state of agile development survey' (2019). https://www.stateofagile.com/#ufh-c-473508-state-of-agile-report
13. Dikert, K., Paasivaara, M., Lassenius, C.: Challenges and success factors for large-scale transformatins: a systematic literature review. J. Syst. Softw. **119**, 87–108 (2016)
14. Braun, V., Clarke, V.: Using thematic analysis in psychology. Qual. Res. Psychol. **3**(2), 77–101 (2006)

Strategy-Focused Agile Transformation: A Case Study

Helen Sharp[1]([✉]) and Katie Taylor[2]

[1] The Open University, Milton Keynes MK7 6AA, UK
helen.sharp@open.ac.uk
[2] University Central Lancashire, Preston, UK

Abstract. Strategic agility enables an organisation to sense and seize opportunities, manage uncertainty and adapt to changes. This paper presents one case study of a traditional charitable organisation taking a strategy-focused approach to agile transformation. Interview data was collected over a 13-month period through interviews at different stages and with different members of the transformation team and Heads of Department. This case study illustrates the challenges faced in such a transformation, and shows that strategic agility requires different time horizons to co-exist: a future vision, a medium term set of objectives and a short term performance monitoring perspective.

Keywords: Culture · Performance measurement · Strategic flexibility

1 Introduction

The implementation of agility outside IT departments and across organisations, often referred to as enterprise agility, is growing in popularity, and is a significant challenge [4]. This is partly driven by the tensions that can arise when agile IT teams interact with non-agile departments in different parts of the organisation [6], and partly by the increasing need for organisations to be responsive to change [7]. Research in the managerial field refers to *flexibility* rather than *agility,* and although the similarities and differences are disputed, literature on flexibility provides a useful viewpoint for analysing enterprise agility. For example, Toni and Tonchia [13] identify four complementary dimensions of flexibility: economic, operational, organisational and strategic. The *economic* dimension has been addressed in conjunction with theories for management of financial buffers against demand uncertainties or external market shocks. The *operational* dimension deals with aspects of manufacturing system flexibility, e.g. ability to adapt the manufacturing system to different environmental conditions and a variety of product features. Agile software development literature [8] captures especially operational aspects related to software component development, e.g. management of rapidly changing business requirements and iterative delivery practices. The *organisational* dimension deals with models of organisation and labour flexibility in rapidly changing environments [13].

The *strategic* dimension may be viewed through culture [10], leadership [5] and dynamic capabilities [12] that enable an organisation to sense and seize opportunities, manage deep business uncertainty and adapt to changes in the business environment.

M. Paasivaara and P. Kruchten (Eds.): XP 2020 Workshops, LNBIP 396, pp. 164–172, 2020.
https://doi.org/10.1007/978-3-030-58858-8_17

From a strategic management perspective [12], strategy is not just a plan but a means to achieve agility through implementation of those plans, hence organisations achieve agility by forming an appropriate strategy and embedding the strategy vision, values, and goals at the operational level across the organisation.

Agile transformation of this kind is referred to using different names, including business agility and enterprise agility [6], but although process guidance for transformation can be found [1], empirical studies are lacking [3]. In particular, there is a lack of evidence illustrating how organisations transform to agility through a strategy focus, and the issues they encounter during this type of transformation. To address this, we conducted a 13-month case study during 2017 and 2018, to answer the research question: What issues arise within organisations focusing on strategic agility? This paper reports the findings of a case study [11], investigating a charitable organisation transforming to agility through a focus on *strategic agility*.

2   Case Background

"What is the role of a Victorian patriarchal provider of services for <disabled> people in an age where funding streams, public expectations, customer expectations, deem that we're actually no longer relevant, fundamentally all of our lead indicators for the business are really unhealthy. Need to fundamentally transform and that makes it really big." Change manager (member of transformation team).

Our case organisation is a traditional charity for disabled people. It was originally two separate organisations with different foci, but over time each took on a wider range of activities and the merged organisation had hundreds of different services and products. As a result they were carrying a lot of cost and their purpose had become confused, both for staff and for customers. Also, their services were not used by the majority of potential customers. Before the transformation reported here, the charity's strategy set an aspiration to reach more potential customers but it wasn't designed to deliver the required step change. To address this, a change programme was initiated but it failed to get sufficient senior management sponsorship, and so the programme started as *skunk works* (a small group of people with autonomy to work on a "secret" project), led by the change management group, with no widespread communication and engaging only with those who had an appetite for change. This was to deliver a change programme for a new agile strategy that focused on a small number of activities. Hence, the change programme encompassed both organisational change and significant strategy change. The change manager, our gatekeeper, was keen to draw on previous Agile Transformation experiences and had self-trained in agile approaches and principles.

Prior to our involvement, an assessment of group culture and a re-structuring of the organisation had taken place. In particular there was an urgent need to improve the financial health of the organisation, and to embed the "lived experience" of disabled people into the organisation, by involving the community more. In April 2017, the organisation was restructured to remove duplicate functions, which resulted in the loss of senior management posts. From July 2017 a series of papers was put to the Board of Trustees setting out the development of a new strategy and delivery plan. Through these papers and ongoing work of the change management group, a new strategy evolved from then until its launch in late 2018.

Strategy development began with identifying an overarching vision and a set of ambitious goals. These were iterated through a group of 10–12 people invited to take part, from a range of different grades, departments, and physical locations around the country. The initial goals and objectives were tested with customer and internal staff stakeholders, and strategy drafts were regularly presented to the Board of Trustees.

Task and finish (T&F) groups were set up to drive the business plan forward. This included a subset of "Heads of Department". Their remit included making sure that others in their department were kept informed of developments. The strategy development process aimed to produce a five-year and a three-year strategy, and a one-year plan. In the end, a five-year strategy, and a one year plan were delivered to the Board of Trustees, and the three-year plan was used as a basis for ongoing improvement.

3   Method

We engaged with this case study from July 2017 to August 2018. The overall approach was to understand the transformation from the participants' point of view rather than to impose any a priori expectations or analytical frameworks [9]. The initial meeting in July 2017 set the scene and agreed subsequent meetings. In Oct 2017 a workshop with the transformation team was held to explore agility and contextual matters including how to assess performance in an agile setting. Short catch-up phone calls (10–20 min) took place in Nov and Dec 2017, and longer interviews and discussions with members of the team (1–2 h) took place in January 2018 and March 2018. During these engagements, the team explained progress and shared their reflections. This data was used to construct a narrative of the transformation from the teams' point of view.

In July 2018 we conducted semi-structured interviews with 9 Heads of Department about the transformation process to identify challenges, successes and next steps. These included Heads of Community Involvement, Customer Service, HR, Finance and Relationship Development. Our interviewees had been with the organisation for between 1 year and 17.5 years, and many were goal owners for the final strategy; none had received formal agile training. In August 2018 we conducted the same semi-structured interview with the Head of Transformation.

Throughout this time, researchers also had access to several documents and versions of the strategy including the one issued to staff in Sept 2018. This included a set of values and behaviours expected from staff and to be used as a guide for recruitment.

All interactive sessions were audio recorded and transcribed, or detailed notes were taken contemporaneously. The documentation, and some aspects of the audio recordings were used to construct the case background above. The views of the journey, including successes and challenges were analysed thematically [2].

4 Results

We present the results from two perspectives: one focusing on the transformation team and the other focusing on the Department Heads. These two are compared in Sect. 5.

4.1 Transformation from Inside the Agile Transformation Team[1]

The main engagements with the transformation team were in Oct 2017, and in January, March and August 2018. During **Oct 2017**, four related issues were discussed:

1. What is agility, and what is it not? Issues included the need for accountability, discipline, empowerment, customer focus, and responsiveness. Common misconceptions about agile that staff in the organisation may have were identified, including that agile isn't chaotic or process-obsessed. A longer list of issues were identified for discussion later, including business readiness, appraisal of team and individuals, agile behaviours and consensus.
2. Performance management in an agile environment. For someone to be accountable, performance needs to be measured, but agile focuses on the team rather than the individual so how can performance of an individual rather than the team be measured?
3. Agile strategy. The strategy needs to be responsive to the environment and hence updated regularly. Discussion included the idea of a three-year rolling plan, and questions such as "where do I start?", "what's sprint 1?", how to keep momentum going – not to just run workshops, get a brilliant "buzz" and then stall. An evidence base for challenging ideas and providing rapid feedback was needed.
4. Sustainability of agile. Agile behaviours and performance management were framed in terms of sustainability "*We can do agile planning, but agile sustainability comes down to what people are motivated to do…and how they are motivated to behave*".

By **January 2018**, there was a sense in the transformation team that the process around the strategy needed to support its continuous improvement, and therefore should be agile. Although the original focus was on an agile strategy, they realised that "*Agile strategy has to be a process*". The organisation had identified a long term vision, and developed a business plan with four priorities and eight cross-cutting objectives. The next step was to change the portfolio management process to adapt to having three-year rolling plans that move towards that long term goal, through three-month cycles to check progress "*is this the right stuff? Yes, move on; no, stop it or cut it*". This will involve test-learn cycles. "*That's your agile strategy, it's your tactical 1-3 year business plan moving towards big significant goals, that get refined*". Creating those business plans was underway, and a template for the business plan for each department had been developed. The culture change that was needed was planned to be driven through the new branding process, which was expected to launch towards the end of the year.

---

[1] All quotes in this sub-section are from a member of the transformation team (one of 3 people).

In **March 2018** (about half way through the transformation process), accountability continued to be a big issue, along with the need to identify and acquire appropriate data for performance management. Difficulties arose from senior managers concerned that they would be accountable for things outside their direct budgetary control. Some people associated accountability with blame, and were concerned about consequences if the objective failed. Although they were still not very agile, the changes so far highlighted the "*massive culture change required*"… "*fundamentally we are not currently built to deliver those goals*". Instead of focusing on changing the culture, the terminology had changed to look at values and behaviours.

Fixed hierarchical structures and fixed timeframes were causing problems, and there was little appreciation that the plan had to drive activities. In the past, the plan was delivered through line management and the budget, and these are structured in silos. In a fixed governance structure it's hard to explain the dynamic nature of the process.

A new operational model was being developed to offer more activities online. Staff and customers had been consulted about the plan and organisational changes; the goals and objectives had also been tested with customers and staff, including potential customers who had not engaged with the organisation before.

People were still working in silos creating their own plans, not talking across departments, and without reference to the overall goals – if it's not in the strategy then "*you really shouldn't be doing it…this isn't about empowerment but discipline*". Overall, the team felt "*it's moving us in the right direction*" but "*we just assumed way too much*" and "*<the process> gently exposed some of the undercurrents of the organisation*".

Highlights from the **Head of Transformation's interview** in **August 2018** include:

> "*the approach we're moving towards is absolutely right – right for <the organisation> specifically but actually generically right for an awful lot of organisations*"… "*the change we're seeing in our external customer environments is just not gonna stop*"

However, he also identified several challenges including

- Senior stakeholders may have buy-in to the process, but they also need to go through a personal change as well as a fundamental organisational transformation "*we didn't appreciate the depth of mindset change basically that it would need.*"
- They needed more stability in terms of leadership
- Agility needs a collaborative way of working, which is counter to a hierarchical organisation with silos. "*half the senior management didn't know what other functions did*" "*A key thing is just understanding what everyone does*".
- Communicating the approach outside the managers involved was limited.
- Difficulty in communicating what accountability means – "*you may not be in control of all the direct levers for an outcome but you are in control of relationships with the people who can pull those levers*"
- Need a real-time (as close as possible) operational dashboard

Two main areas for improvement for the next cycle in the agile process are to:

- Be a bit more creative, e.g. using design thinking, so that people engage in real business change *"we need to focus a lot more on enabling the business change… and probably a bit less on the process itself"*
- Get new senior people up to speed quickly, or find a way to retain senior people. Constant change of personnel created instability.

In his view, strategic agility requires different perspectives to co-exist: a future vision that sets an aspiration, a medium term horizon: *"We now have the purpose statement and the priorities, and we have business plans, but we need to tackle the really important medium-term strategic goals."*, and a short term horizon: *"our major Achilles heel across the whole charity is data … our new performance dashboard is a lot better … we're nowhere near being able to report the real-time heartbeat type metrics that we really need to understand how the business is performing day-by-day"*

4.2   Transformation from the Heads of Department Perspectives

The interviews with the Heads of Department were analysed for themes according to successes, challenges, what could have been done better in the transformation, and next steps. Table 1 summarises the themes emerging from this analysis. Note that the quotes do not represent the full data set; where cells are empty, no interviewee identified anything in that category, e.g. no-one suggested that aspects of Organisational Structure could have been Done Better.

Table 1. Themes from Heads of Department interviews, with illustrative quotes

Theme	Success	Challenge (past)	Challenge (future)	Done better	Next steps
Plan/strategy	"Strategy is great"	"No control or proper oversight"	"Succession planning strategy ownership"		
Org structure	"More manageable organisation"	"Organisation too convoluted"			
Org culture	"Shift in mentality"	"Honesty and openness"	"Morale"		
Org purpose	"Shared organisational goals"	"No guiding narrative or philosophy for decision-making"			"Be clear about Charity's role"
Level of org change		"Degree of organisational change"	"Change fatigue"	"Stability, everything's been changing"	"Get changes embedded"
Transformation process	"Process has been excellent"	"Process took too long"			
External profile	"Responding to external events well"	"Reputation declining for years"	"Need to make sure people know us"		"Launch ourselves as listening"
Operational	"Budget agreed"	"Identifying accountable owners"	"Data difficult to quantify"	"Find effective way to update finances"	"Articulate budget requirements"
Staff buy-in	"Getting senior people on the T&F group"	"People need to buy-in to the philosophy"	"Bring along people across the organisation"		"Excite and energise everyone"

Reading Table 1 left to right provides an overview of the theme and how it plays out across the transformation activities. For example (quotes come from different interviewees, so sentences do not represent any one person's view):

Level of Organisational Change: There was no mention of *success* in this theme. A *past* challenge was the high degree of organisational change, and a *future* challenge will be change fatigue. What could be *done better* is to achieve more stability as everything's been changing, and *next steps* are to get the changes embedded.

External Profile: A *success* was the response to external events. A *past* challenge was that reputation had been declining, and a *future* challenge will be to make sure people know what we stand for; *next steps* are to launch as a listening organisation.

5 Discussion

The meaning of accountability was a concern for the transformation team throughout the process. It was mentioned in every engagement we had with the transformation team, but hardly mentioned at all in the Heads of Department interviews. Other issues raised by the transformation team were recognised by the Heads, but not all the issues raised by the Heads were recognised by the team.

There was a strong support for the progress that had been made up to the new strategy's launch – not just the strategy itself, but also its vision and goals. Other successes related to the organisation's structure, a change in culture and mindset, and the turnaround of the financial situation.

There were several past challenges, but fewer future challenges. Those that were identified relate to keeping staff engaged and energised in the continuing transformation process, succession planning for strategic development, getting the right data available to performance management, aligning the Departments and the strategic goals, and communicating the right external profile.

Areas for improvement in terms of the transformation process were maintaining more stability in the organisation, finding a better way to update finances, being clear and transparent in communications and expectations, and being more creative in how the process unfolds. The next steps identified were in response to the issues raised above, and included embedding changes, articulating clearly the organisation's goals externally, and energising everyone to take the changes forward.

6 Conclusion

"I thought we'd embarked on achieving a destination, but actually what we embarked on was a really long journey" Head of Transformation.

Strategic agility requires three different horizons to co-exist: a long term aspiration, a medium term set of goals, and a short-term response to real-time performance management. The experience of this case study shows that introducing this approach to a traditional, hierarchical organisation requires a number of conditions including: sufficient resources, stable leadership, and suitable performance measurement data.

Although not driven by IT or encompassing traditional Agile frameworks, this case study contributes empirical results to the growing set of transformation studies within the XP community. Future plans in this research include to engage with other organisations using a strategic approach to their transformation, and to compare these findings with organisations who take a different approach to transformation.

Acknowledgements. We thank our participants for taking part, the Agile Business Consortium for funding this work, and our colleagues in the Agile Research Network for their time and support.

References

1. Appelbaum, S.H., Habashy, S., Malo, J.-L., Shafiq, H.: Back to the future: revisiting Kotter's 1996 change model. J. Manage. Dev. **31**(8), 764–782 (2012)
2. Braun, V., Clarke, V.: Using thematic analysis in psychology. Qual. Res. Psychol. **3**(2), 77–101 (2006)
3. By, R.T.: Organisational change management: a critical review. J. Change Manage. **5**(4), 369–380 (2005)
4. Dikert, K., Paasivaara, M., Lassenious, C.: Challenges and success factors for large-scale agile transformations: a systematic literature review. J. Syst. Softw. **119**, 87–108 (2016)
5. Doz, Y.L., Kosonen, M.: Embedding strategic agility: a leadership agenda for accelerating business model renewal. Long Range Plan. **43**, 370–382 (2010)
6. Karvonen, T., Sharp, H., Barroca, L.: Enterprise agility: why is transformation so hard? In: Proceedings of XP2018 (2018)
7. Kuusinen, K., Gregory, A.J., Sharp, H., Barroca, L.: Strategies for doing agile in a non-agile environment. In: Proceedings of ESEM 2016 (2016)
8. Laanti, M., Similä, J., Abrahamsson, P.: Definitions of agile software development and agility. In: McCaffery, F., O'Connor, R.V., Messnarz, R. (eds.) EuroSPI 2013. CCIS, vol. 364, pp. 247–258. Springer, Heidelberg (2013). https://doi.org/10.1007/978-3-642-39179-8_22
9. Robinson, H., Segal, J., Sharp, H.: Ethnographically-informed empirical studies of software practice. Inf. Softw. Technol. **49**(6), 540–551 (2007)
10. Schein, E.H.: Organizational Culture and Leadership. Jossey-Bass, San Francisco (2010)
11. Sharp, H., Barroca, L., Strode, D., Gregory, A.J., Taylor, K.: A strategy-focused agile transformation: planning simultaneously 50 years ahead and 5 minutes ahead (2020). http://agileresearchnetwork.org/publications
12. Teece, D., Peteraf, M., Leih, S.: Dynamic capabilities and organizational agility: risk, uncertainty, and strategy in the innovation economy. Calif. Manag. Rev. **58**, 13–35 (2016)
13. Toni, D.A., Tonchia, S.: Definitions and linkages between operational and strategic flexibilities. Omega **33**, 525–540 (2005)

Shifting Conceptualization of Control in Agile Transformations

Marius Mikalsen[1,2(✉)], Viktoria Stray[1,3], Nils Brede Moe[1],
and Idun Backer[4]

[1] SINTEF, Trondheim, Norway
marius.mikalsen@sintef.no
[2] Norwegian University of Science and Technology, Trondheim, Norway
[3] University of Oslo, Oslo, Norway
[4] Storebrand, Oslo, Norway

Abstract. Agile transformation implies that organizations apply agile methods also outside of software development units. One particular way of doing such transformations is to create cross-functional software development units. This represents new challenges for control for organizations as the unformal agile control mechanisms from the software units meet the more formal, bureaucratic and hierarchical control from other units. The research on how to manage control in agile transformations, however, is scarce. Through a case study of a new, cross-functional unit in a financial institution, we report on their work to implement control in agile transformations. To analyze our results, we draw on new perspectives for control in the digital era, which challenges existing presumptions on control. Our findings indicate how agile transformations require rethinking traditional control mechanisms and experiment with new control perspectives more suitable for the digital era.

Keywords: Agile transformation · Agile program · Empirical · Case study · Control · Stewardship theory · OKRs

1 Introduction

The pressure of digitalization with rapidly changing markets and technology developments drive organizations towards adopting agile ways of working, also outside software development units [1]. Such agile transformation implies that agile methods are used not only in software development teams but also by other parts of the organization, such as business units [3]. Agile transformations deal with challenges such as hierarchical management in waterfall mode, difficulties working across organizational boundaries [1], and units not willing or able to change [3]. One particular form of change aiming to overcome some of these challenges is creating semi-independent, cross-functional units (i.e. consisting of personnel from both business- and software-development units) that use agile methods to improve the value of the software developed [2].

Collaboration across different units while working in new ways represent new challenges for control for organizations. The informal agile control mechanisms from

© The Author(s) 2020
M. Paasivaara and P. Kruchten (Eds.): XP 2020 Workshops, LNBIP 396, pp. 173–181, 2020.
https://doi.org/10.1007/978-3-030-58858-8_18

the software units meet the more formal and hierarchical control from other units. How to implement control mechanisms that enable management to have control while still allowing the autonomy and rapid changes that are required in agile methods remains an open question in the literature of agile transformations. We, therefore, ask the following research question: *How to manage control in agile transformations?*

To answer this research question, we report from a case study of a financial institution that implements a new semi-independent unit, an agile program, consisting of several cross-functional teams working according to agile principles. The teams consist of both software and business developers. In this paper, we report on their work on devising metrics for measuring the teams' performance using Objectives and Key Results (OKRs) [11]. To analyze the results, we draw on new perspectives of control for the digital era, based on stewardship theory. Stewardship argues that our conception of software development control needs to be reinvented in an era in which collaborative value creation is increasingly prevalent [4]. Our analysis indicates how agile transformations allow rethinking control and implementing new control perspectives more suitable for the digital era.

The rest of the paper is organized as follows. Section 2 provides the theoretical background on how agile transformation challenges existing control, using stewardship theory as an alternative theoretical perspective. Section 3 introduces the case and explain how we collected and analyzed data. Section 4 shows the findings from one questionnaire and two retrospectives. In Sect. 5, we discuss our findings in light of a stewardship perspective on control. Section 6 concludes and presents future work.

2   Theory: A Changing Conceptualization of Control

2.1   Agile Transformation and New Challenges of Control

Agile transformation represents new challenges for control for organizations. Previously, large software development projects were controlled by plans, hierarchies and standardization [5]. As this is no longer suitable, new forms of control are introduced, such as large-scale agile frameworks like SAFe and Spotify, with its own set of challenges [6] that again can challenge autonomy [7, 8]. In the digital era, managers face growing pressure to introduce techniques and practices to improve software productivity and reduce such impediments, however, it is unclear how impediments in software practices are controlled, i.e., identified, measured and managed [9]. One technique many organizations use to guide and measure work is OKRs [11].

2.2   Stewardship Theory – Alternative Conceptions of Control

Recent theoretical work suggests that we need new conceptualizations of control for the digital era. Wiener et al. [4] argue that the digital era, with increasingly advanced and pervasive technologies, changes how we develop software. Changes include: new work practices with blurring of roles, a move from delivering commodities to continuous innovation, a move from hierarchical control structures to leveraging dynamic networks, and a changing workforce with increased specialization. Previous research on control has had an agency perspective, which implied that the purpose of control is to ensure that project actors reduce self-interest and work according to a project, program or organization goal. Now rather, the purpose of control shifts towards value creation, which has support in stewardship theory which considers the agent an intrinsically motivated steward working towards a common overall goal [ibid.].

Wiener et al. [4] outline key control questions and digital-era characteristics based on stewardship theory (see the themes of these two aspects in Table 1 below). First, key control questions are concerned with 1) control modes, whether these are formal or informal, 2) control style, and whether this is authoritative or enabling, and 3) whether there is a value appropriation or value-creation purpose to control. Second, digital era characteristics are concerned with: 1) congruence with the common overall goal. 2) information asymmetry is ok, 3) intrinsically motivated actors, 4) long term orientation rather than short term, and 5) dynamic network structures.

3 Case and Method

3.1 Case Background

This study is a part of a longitudinal interpretative case study [10] of agile autonomous teams set in a Norwegian bank (dubbed NorBank for anonymity), with more than 2,000 employees. NorBank initiated in 2017 an agile program (AP) consisting of five cross-functional autonomous teams organized in line with agile principles, with the goal of developing improved software for their business-to-business solutions in the insurance market. The teams consist of resources from both the software and business development side of the organization. The teams deliver software solutions to the business side of the organization, such as sales and settlements. The teams collaborate closely

Fig. 1. The participants discussing OKR implementation

Table 1. Aspects of stewardship theory, themes and questions, from Wiener et al. [4].

Aspect of stewardship theory	Theme	Statements
Key control questions	Formal control or informal control	1) We measure what we produce 2) We control each other and that the team delivers
	Authoritative control style or enabling	3) I have extensive dialogue with those who decide the goals
	Value-appropriation or value-creation purpose	4) We measure to handle insecurity regarding budget, time and functionality 5) We measure to handle insecurities regarding collaborations between actors with different competencies 6) We measure to handle insecurities regarding business value
Digital-era characteristics	Congruence with common goal	7) My goals align with the goal of the program
	Information asymmetry	8) It is ok that others (e.g., experts) have information that I do not have
	Intrinsically motivated actors	9) I am intrinsically motivated by working in the program
	Long-term or short-term focus?	10) We focus on short-term goals 11) We consider the development as part of something that continuously changes
	Dynamic network structures?	12) I collaborate with people outside my team

with organizational units responsible for technology development and innovation. Each team is led by product managers, who is part of the steering-forum of the program, together with managers from the business and technology units. The program has been developing software for a while and is now focusing on delivering value on the business side. Their concern is how to measure and control these processes, while still being agile. In response, the program has decided to use OKRs [11] as a method for goal setting and measurement (Fig. 1).

3.2 Data Collection and Analysis

We collected data through two retrospectives with the program in February 2020. The first retrospective was held with four product managers. The second retrospective was with the steering forum of the program. In this retrospective, a total of 12 people participated. The participants included product managers, the leader of the program, managers from the business units, managers from the technology units, and key IT staff such as architects. Each of the sessions lasted about 1.5 h. The authors facilitated the retrospectives and asked questions for clarifications.

Data was collected by taking pictures, documenting the post-its on the whiteboards, taking notes, and collecting data through a questionnaire. Our data analysis was partly deductive as we asked questions regarding stewardship theory in our questionnaire, but also inductive by analyzing our notes and pictures of the whiteboards for themes emerging in the retrospectives. We operationalized the control questions and digital-era characteristics from [4], as shown in Table 1. The statements were given in Norwegian and rated on a 5-point Likert scale from strongly disagree (1) to strongly agree (5). We collected the questionnaire responses digitally during the second retrospective, and the participants answered from their mobile phones. We decided that we wanted to collect the responses this way so that the participants could think individually in silence and also answer anonymously. Furthermore, the tool we used (Mentimeter.com) gave us the ability to show the answers to the questions in real-time, which sparked a discussion among the participants. As such, we were able to get feedback and better understand the responses. The participants scored the statements on a 5-point Likert scale from strongly disagree to strongly agree.

4   Findings

Key Control Questions Regarding Control Configuration, Enactment and Purpose
In Fig. 2 below, we see the score on key control questions regarding control configuration, enactment and purpose. Team members control each other (Item 2) and have dialogue with those who decide the goals (Item 3). This is in line with a stewardship perspective on control. Still, we see that traditional forms of measurement such as measuring on time and budget (Item 4) and what is produced (Item 1) are in place, indicating the remains of agency rather than value creation perspectives. Measuring on cooperation between different actors is low (Item 5).

Findings Regarding Digital Era Characteristics of Control
In Fig. 3 below, regarding digital-era characteristics of control, we find scores indicating stewardship assumptions. We see a that practitioners are intrinsically motivated (Item 9). We see that their goals align with program goals (Item 7), that information asymmetry among actors is accepted (Item 8), and there is a lot of cooperation with people outside the team indicating dynamic networks (Item 12). Finally, wee see that there is a is a long-term orientation in the work (Item 11), and a lower score on short-term goals (Item 10).

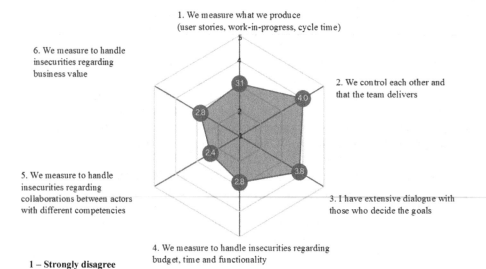

Fig. 2. Key control questions regarding control configuration, enactment and purpose

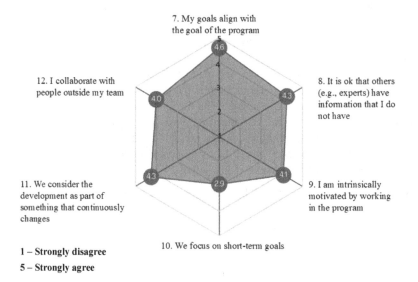

Fig. 3. Digital-era characteristics of control

Findings from the Retrospectives: Collaboration with Business Units

In the retrospective with the product managers, we found that there were collaboration and interdependencies with units outside the agile program. For example, developers in a separate software development unit made architecture decisions that led to the teams needing to rewrite their APIs. Also, they relied on developers from another unit on implementing workflow automation, and these developers were often busy. Moreover, collaboration with actors outside the organization was challenging. Action items identified included increased use of OKRs and continuous OKR reviews as a way to focus the teams, the need for flexibility from the tech side on delivering on what the teams needed, and also get more competence on workflow optimization.

In the retrospective with the program's steering forum, the participants discussed that the most important thing to improve was to better demonstrate to the business side the value of what the program delivered. The second most important was OKRs and how this could be used to engage and involve the business side. The third most important was to keep the steering forum meetings lightweight and short. Action items identified included: OKR reviews, quarterly reviews with regard to overall goals, and clarify roles and responsibilities in the steering forum to make sure everyone could contribute more in future meetings.

5   Discussion

Agile transformations involve that participants from different units, such as software and business, work together using agile methods [1, 3]. Such collaborations challenge traditional conceptions of control found in agile methods. To answer our research question - *how to manage control in agile transformations* – we have reported findings from a cross-functional unit in the midst of an agile transformation.

We used the stewardship theory [4] to shed light on how a cross-functional unit approach control. Our results show that, regarding control configuration, enactment and purpose (Fig. 2), team members control each other and have dialogue with those who decide the goals. This is in line with a stewardship perspective on control. Still, we see that traditional forms of measurement such as measuring time, and budget and what is produced are in place, indicating the remains of agency rather than value creation perspectives. Measuring cooperation is weaker and can be worth focusing on in order to manage known impediments for flow [9].

Regarding digital-era characteristics of control (Fig. 3), we find strong indication of stewardship assumptions [4]. Practitioners are intrinsically motivated, their goals align with program goals, information asymmetry among actors is accepted, there is a lot of cooperation with people outside the team indicating dynamic networks, and there is a long-term orientation. This indicates that the ways of controlling in the agile program keep with the agile principles of mutual adjustment and autonomy [7].

The retrospectives indicated an appreciation of using OKRs as a way to set goals and communicate goals with the rest of the organization, such as the business units in particular, in order to ensure that what is valuable is agreed upon between units, and that value can be delivered. In terms of stewardship theory [4], such dynamic networks are a key characteristic of the digital era and should also be the focus of new forms of control. It is not clear exactly how to control it. In this case OKRs are used as a way to communicate between the cross-functional teams and the business side. What is clear however, is that determining what is a valuable software deliverable will be an element of negotiation between interdependent units [1].

6   Conclusion and Future Work

In this paper, we have used stewardship theory to investigate how cross-functional teams work with OKRs and how new forms of control can emerge in agile transformations. Our results indicate that the members take responsibility for each other and that the team delivers; they also have an extensive dialogue with those who decide the goals. Almost all stated that their goals aligned with the goal of the program, which indicates that the information flow and goal setting works well in this company. The participants also stated that it was ok that others had information that they did not possess. In terms of stewardship theory, this is called information asymmetry. Stewardship assumes that knowledge workers are intrinsically motivated and self-actualizing and that they display a high level of commitment and involvement. The participants in our study reported being intrinsically motivated by working in the program. In sum, our findings indicate the balancing act between new and traditional control in agile transformations.

A key limitation of this study is that it is a single case study. We find indications of stewardship assumptions in the case. However, how and what to measure and control remains a challenge during agile transformations. Future research can investigate how for example, OKRs can be used to support stewardship assumptions rather than older paradigms of control. Also, old paradigms of control are not likely to disappear, so how to incorporate stewardship perspectives with other control regimes is relevant. In sum, agile transformation is about changing practices in organizations, and control seems to us to be a relevant aspect of changing practices.

References

1. Mikalsen, M., Moe, N.B., Stray, V., Nyrud, H.: Agile digital transformation: a case study of interdependencies. In: Thirty Ninth International Conference on Information Systems, San Francisco (2018)
2. Vial, G.: Understanding digital transformation: a review and a research agenda. J. Strateg. Inform. Syst. 28, 118–144 (2019)
3. Barroca, L., Dingsøyr, T., Mikalsen, M.: Agile transformation: a summary and research agenda from the first international workshop. In: Hoda, R. (ed.) XP 2019. LNBIP, vol. 364, pp. 3–9. Springer, Cham (2019). https://doi.org/10.1007/978-3-030-30126-2_1
4. Wiener, M., Mähring, M., Remus, U., Saunders, C., Cram, A.: Moving is project control research into the digital era: the "Why" of control and the concept of control purpose. Inform. Syst. Res. 30(4), 1387–1401 (2019)
5. Barlow, J.B., et al.: Overview and guidance on agile development in large organizations. Commun. Assoc. Inform. Syst. 29, 25–44 (2011)
6. Conboy, K., Carroll, N.: Implementing large-scale agile frameworks: challenges and recommendations. IEEE Softw. 36(2), 44–50 (2019)
7. Moe, N.B., Šmite, D., Šāblis, A., Börjesson, A.L., Andréasson, P.: Networking in a large-scale distributed agile project. In: Proceedings of the 8th ACM/IEEE International Symposium on Empirical Software Engineering and Measurement (2014)

8. Moe, N.B., Dahl, B., Stray, V., Karlsen, L.S., Schjødt-Osmo, S.: Team autonomy in large-scale agile. In: Proceedings of the 52nd Hawaii International Conference on System Sciences (2019)
9. Carroll, N., O'Connor, M., Edison, H.: The identification and classification of impediments in software flow. In: Americas Conference on Information Systems (AMCIS). Association for Information Systems (2018)
10. Klein, H.K., Myers, M.D.: A set of principles for conducting and evaluating interpretative field studies in information systems. MIS Q. **23**(1), 67–88 (1999)
11. Doerr, J.: Measure What Matters: How Google, Bono, and the Gates Foundation Rock the World with OKRs, p. 31. Penguin Publishing Group (2018). ISBN 9780525536239

It's Not Easy Being Agile: Unpacking Paradoxes in Agile Environments

Bettina Horlach[1] and Andreas Drechsler[2(✉)] iD

[1] University of Hamburg, Hamburg, Germany
horlach@informatik.uni-hamburg.de
[2] Victoria University of Wellington, Wellington, New Zealand
andreas.drechsler@vuw.ac.nz

Abstract. In this paper, we outline inherent tensions in Agile environments, which lead to paradoxes that Agile teams and organizations have to navigate. By taking a critical perspective on Agile frameworks and Agile organizational settings the authors are familiar with, we contribute an initial problematization of paradoxes for the Agile context. For instance, Agile teams face the continuous paradox of 'doing Agile' (= following an established Agile way of working) versus 'being Agile' (= changing an established Agile way of working). One of the paradoxes that organizations face is whether to start their Agile journey with a directed top-down (and therefore quite un-Agile) 'big bang' or to allow an emergent bottom-up transformation (which may be more in-line with the Agile spirit but perhaps not be able to overcome organizational inertia). Future research can draw on our initial problematization as a foundation for subsequent in-depth investigations of these Agile paradoxes. Agile teams and organizations can draw on our initial problematization of Agile paradoxes to inform their learning and change processes.

Keywords: Agile teams · Agile organizations · Agile projects · Agile paradoxes

1 Introduction

Agile and hybrid project environments are increasingly becoming the norm within and even beyond the IT industry, and organizations increasingly start scaling Agile[1] beyond IT project teams [1]. There are numerous methodologies for Agile project management and scaling Agile, which claim to embody the Agile Manifesto's principles and values (e.g., Scrum, SAFe, Disciplined Agile etc.). Studies show that embracing Agile leads to generally satisfied individuals and companies, but there are also a variety of obstacles that teams and organizations may face [2–4].

In a more general perspective, "most management practices create their own nemesis" [5 p. 491], and Agile is no exception. As one role of research is to critique the status quo [6], we do so in this paper for the Agile context by outlining areas of tension

---

[1] For brevity, we use the term Agile (with a capital A) in this paper as a term encompassing agile values, principles, methodologies, and techniques, without referring to specific ones.

M. Paasivaara and P. Kruchten (Eds.): XP 2020 Workshops, LNBIP 396, pp. 182–189, 2020.
https://doi.org/10.1007/978-3-030-58858-8_19

which result in paradoxes that Agile teams and organizations running Agile teams may have to navigate. Following Putnam et al. [7], we define paradoxes as "contradictions that persist over time, impose and reflect back on each other, and develop into seemingly irrational or absurd situations because their continuity creates situations in which options appear mutually exclusive, making choices among them difficult" (p. 72).

By providing this critique, we problematize [8] Agile beyond a functionalist view that is centered on performance or effectiveness. Our initial problematization therefore paves the way for future, more in-depth research contributions that investigate each paradox – as an instance of 'the dark side of Agile' – more closely. We see these paradoxes as a starting point for more focused theoretical and empirical investigations how Agile teams and organizations encounter, experience, and cope with these Agile paradoxes. As one key tenet of Agile organizations is continuous learning and change, such in-depth treatments of Agile paradoxes can therefore also contribute to organizational learning and change efforts in practice.

Our analysis draws on a critical reading of selected Agile methodologies and techniques, the Agile research literature, as well as a critical assessment of Agile environments that the authors are familiar with (see Sect. 2). Note that while there is a quite comprehensive dataset that informed the authors' other research in Agile organizational contexts, there was no specific data analysis conducted for this paper to inform our initial problematization of Agile paradoxes. We see such an undertaking as a fruitful endeavor for future research.

In this short paper, we first outline the backdrop against which we provide our critique. We then start discussing sources for agile paradoxes on the levels of the Agile team as well as on the organizational level for those organizations who scaled Agile beyond individual teams.

2 Empirical Background

Both authors are involved in a large-scale cross-industry and cross-country research program on Agile organizational transformation and have collected extensive data across two phases. The first data collection phase consisted of interviews and focus groups with seven executives (e.g., CIO or CDO), whereas the second phase consisted of interviews with lower level managers (e.g. program managers, product owners, enterprise architect) or external consultants. The participants had two essential criteria to fulfill: 1) their organization is undergoing a transformation towards organizational agility, and 2) the participants hold a position with in-depth insights on the overall (agile) organizational system. For the executives group, we conducted three single day focus group workshops [9] and seven semi-structured interviews. For the other group, we conducted 33 semi-structured interviews. Each interview session lasted 45–75 min and was audio-recorded and transcribed.

All gathered data has been qualitatively analyzed to inform research on the implications of Agile for topics such as portfolio management [10], enterprise architecture [11], business/IT alignment [12], and IT governance (currently under review). Beyond these specific topics, however, the authors also observed more general patterns of a paradoxical nature in the Agile organizational contexts the interview and focus group participants gave insight into, and likewise in the (Scaling) Agile frameworks that the interviewees referred to. The following two sections outline the sources for these paradoxes that the authors have identified. Due to space restrictions in this short paper, we are only able to outline and problematize each paradox on a rather general level.

3 Sources for Agile Paradoxes on the Team Level

3.1 Being Agile Versus Doing Agile

The different aspects of Agile such as values, principles, methodologies, or techniques allow us to distinguish between teams that are 'being Agile' (i.e., embrace Agile principles and values in an Agile mind-set and truly focus on delivering customer value while learning continuously) and 'doing Agile' (i.e. adopt an Agile methodology or a set of Agile techniques and simply follow them). Note that 'doing Agile' can be a step on the way of towards fully embracing the Agile mindset [13, 14]. However, there is the danger that an Agile team stops advancing beyond the 'doing Agile' stage, i.e. it keeps trying to 'perfect' their adoption of their chosen Agile approach. In contrast, teams 'being Agile' commit themselves to being accountable for their work, being willing and able to handle uncertainty in their work, and to strive for continuous improvement. The specific way of working (methodology, process, techniques, tools) or any form of adherence is less important. In this sense, the term 'Agile methodology' is already paradoxical in itself, as the term 'methodology' implies a specific prescription. Especially in volatile environments or in environments where an Agile methodology or framework forms the cornerstone of the Agile transformation, there may be a permanent paradoxical tension between 'doing Agile' and 'being Agile' for Agile teams.

3.2 Experience Versus 'Appetite' for Change and Flexibility

Agile environments are built around the assumption that information completeness is never achieved due to ever-changing environments and customer needs. Hence, a high level of readiness for coping with change is a critical factor for Agile team effectiveness. However, a high amount of team members' experience in particular may also be a source for a paradox. A team member's experience can come from traditional project environments (particularly since Agile is still a quite young trend) and therefore include a preference for stable processes and predefined requirements based on detailed planning. Each Agile team member also continuously gains experience in (and may become accustomed to) their particular Agile approach and also regarding the artefact they are working on. Both variants of experience are challenged, however, by Agile's 'permanent uncertainty' in its mindset. Sometimes, a radical change to the way of working or the deliverable may be what the situation or the market requires, and extant experiences may be source for resistance or inertia regarding those changes. The paradox here is therefore that an increase in individual and collective experience may lead to a decreased 'appetite' for future change and therefore to less flexibility for a team.

3.3   Exploration Versus Exploitation

Agile teams are also characterized by a high level of self-organization and decision-making autonomy. In traditional Agile teams, this autonomy mainly concerns the choice of and ongoing changes to the methodology, techniques, and tools [15–17]. In Scaling Agile teams, this autonomy often extends to product or service design changes and future directions for their product(s)/service(s)/area(s) [18, 19]. In the former case, a paradox arises out of the tension between the requirements of getting work done and continuously sharpening (and potentially re-learning) one's – metaphorical and literal – tools. This may pose the danger of splitting a group into those advocating change and those advocating getting things done. Autonomy over one's artefact in the latter case could lead to a similar paradoxical scenario of the well-researched tension between exploration vs. exploitation [20, 21]. Should a team radically re-invent the artefact to adapt to or anticipate market changes, or incrementally refine the artefact to fine-tune it to established customer needs? In both cases, the team's handling of this paradox would enable or constrain future actions.

3.4   Directed Versus Emergent Team Process Change

As the notion of continuous change is built into Agile environments and teams, roles such as the Scrum Masters and Agile coaches are responsible for guiding and supporting the Agile team towards becoming more effective. However, there are two general archetypes how these roles could be set up (or choose by themselves) to fulfill their task: Agile coaches and Scrum Masters could either direct a team's development according to what they perceive as best for the team (to be an 'Agile leader' or even an 'Agile police', so to speak), or could nurture the teams instead (i.e. 'help the people to help themselves') and let any changes to a team's way of working emerge from within the team. In the former case, having change directed and induced from outside the team could potentially undermine a team's autonomy. On the flip side, a team that is perhaps 'too comfortable' with their current Agile approach may not engage in a self-transformation without external direction even though it would benefit from certain changes [22]. Either way, Scrum masters and Agile coaches could even oppose or counteract good Agile practices – perhaps just subconsciously – in order to continuously create their own work in order to be kept employed or contracted and make themselves seemingly indispensable. The underlying paradox here is the one of balancing team autonomy with external directions with respect to changes to the team's way of working.

4   Sources for Agile Paradoxes on the Organization Level

4.1   Starting/Realizing the Agile (Self-)transformation: 'Big Bang' Versus Emergence

When aiming to introduce Agile on a larger scale, organizations have to choose an approach that lies somewhere between an initial 'big bang' top-down transformation towards Agile or an incremental, iterative, and emergent approach where different parts of the organizations can choose whether and how they adopt Agile [23, 24]. In other words, how Agile should the Agile transformation itself be, and how much predefined structures and processes should the first target state have? For instance, in one situation a common way of working across several Agile teams or units may be more effective to successfully transform (parts of) the organization, whereas in another situation self-taught bottom-up experimentation with Agile techniques and tools may be the more effective approach – particularly when considering how to set the stage for 'being Agile' in a longer-term and sustained perspective. As Agile implies a high degree of team autonomy instead of having top-down pre-planned decisions, a 'big bang Agile intro-duction' is therefore paradoxical in itself. The danger of mixed messages during an Agile transformation lies in a regression to a directive (i.e. non-autonomous) way of working and organizational culture, and also would constrain the Agile units' autonomy to self-transform in the future. Simultaneously, unfettered team autonomy right from the start could lead to the danger of an aimless or quickly stalling transformation process.

4.2 Directing Teams Versus Team Autonomy

The tension between directing and simultaneously sustaining autonomous Agile teams may not only occur during the initial Agile transformation but may stay with organi-zations throughout their entire Agile journey. The nature of the resulting paradox, however, shifts to issues related to focus, resources, effectiveness, and efficiency. The *focus* component affects how a team's strategic direction is set and influenced. While each team may know their product's customers best, an organization's top management may wish to change or retire some products. In this situation, the tension arises whether a team should be in charge of a changed purpose or even its own dissolution, or whether an organization wants to override its teams' autonomy in these cases. With respect to *staffing and resourcing*, the Agile idea generally implies that a team would be responsible for the resources they require to fulfill their purpose. However, resource scarcity in organizations, competition for resources across teams, and the willingness to achieve a global optimum across teams may prevent a purely bottom-up decision-making on resources. Again, the organization would paradoxically interfere with a team's autonomy if it denies requested necessary resources. Measuring Agile team *effectiveness or performance* is another source for paradoxes. Measuring performance could have the purpose of identifying the extent to which an Agile team contributes business value, or the purpose of aligning teams with overarching strategic objectives. In both cases an organization would again interfere directly with team autonomy. Finally, *efficiency* concerns the way of working throughout the organization, i.e. should teams be provided with or even have to adhere to a common set of Agile values, processes, techniques, and tools, which would allow team members to be shared or move between teams without having to adjust to fundamentally new ways of working? On the other hand, an organization-wide 'Agile standard' is again a paradox in itself, since one emphasis of Agile lies on continuous change and adaptability, and different Agile approaches may be effective for different teams. All these aspects are manifes-tations of a systemic contradiction of having autonomous teams within a coherent business organization. In a nutshell, any decision above the team level may ultimately undermine the teams' perceived autonomy.

4.3   Team Identity and Purpose Versus the Need for Radical Business Change

When an Agile team in a Scaled Agile environment is made responsible for (a) particular product(s)/service(s)/area(s), it achieves its sustained focus through this purpose. Over time, having a consistent focus and purpose contributes to a team's shared identity. However, being responsible for a specific product or service for quite a long period may lead to a 'blindness' and attachment of teams to their built artefact. Consequently, a team may add unnecessary bells and whistles to 'their' artefact to justify the product's as well as the team's continued existence and resourcing in comparison to other teams. A team may also become protective of 'their' product or service (area) instead of recognizing the need for a radical change or its retirement, in order to fulfill and surpass changed customer needs and support the organization in thriving in the changing business environment. A team's purpose may therefore become a self-referential part of its identity so that strong repressions of or reactions against a radical change to the purpose occur, with the unanticipated consequence of limiting the effective team agility to self-transform when necessary. The paradox here therefore is that the same mechanisms that keep an Agile team together and effective may also hinder its ability to detect the best time and ways to re-invent themselves for their best possible contribution to organizational value.

5   Discussion, Conclusion, Outlook

In this paper, we identified and briefly discussed several potential paradoxes in Agile contexts. Through our discussion of these Agile paradoxes, we contribute a problematization [8] of Agile on a deeper level than a functionalist perspective that analyzes 'what works' [25], a critique of Agile as a management fashion [26], or previous attempts at identifying Agile paradoxes [27]. In our problematization, we interrogated key Agile tenets and found that embracing Agile may produce a number of paradoxes on the team and the organizational level. We do not see these paradoxes' existence as a negative thing. In fact, to harness the true potential of Agile transformations organizations may need to become adept at continuously confronting these paradoxes and utilizing their forces in a constructive and not a destructive way for their ongoing self-transformation. Since learning and change are two key Agile tenets, Agile organizations may be uniquely positioned to incorporate the confrontation with their paradoxes into their 'business as usual', instead of treating tensions and paradoxes as issues that stand in the way of organizational effectiveness and need to be resolved. While we have not investigated each paradox in-depth, our initial problematization may still be useful to guide and inspire [28] learning and change processes in Agile organizations.

Some of the underlying tensions – such as the exploration vs. exploitation one – are already well known in the literature [20, 29]. Others – such as the tensions around Agile team autonomy – may be specific for Agile environments and transformations. They have – to the authors' best knowledge – not been thoroughly investigated yet. Our problematization therefore contributes to a comprehensive research agenda to investigate how Agile teams and organizations encounter, experience, and cope with paradoxes on their Agile journeys. We therefore encourage empirical validation and extension of our findings, as the paradoxes in this paper are limited by being based on general insights from IT organizational roles within two countries. Thus, we also advocate for analyzing tensions perceived by the business side in order to capture a truly comprehensive perspective on the paradoxes.

References

1. Panditi, S.: Survey Data Shows That Many Companies Are Still Not Truly Agile (2018). https://hbr.org/sponsored/2018/03/survey-data-shows-that-many-companies-are-still-not-truly-agile
2. VersionOne: 13th Annual State of Agile Report. https://explore.versionone.com/state-of-agile/13th-annual-state-of-agile-report. Accessed 12 Aug 2019
3. Conboy, K.: Agility from first principles: reconstructing the concept of agility in information systems development. Inf. Syst. Res. 20, 329–354 (2009)
4. Kropp, M., Meier, A., Anslow, C., Biddle, R.: Satisfaction, practices, and influences in agile software development. In: 2018 Proceedings of the 22nd International Conference on Evaluation and Assessment in Software Engineering, pp. 112–121. ACM (2018)
5. Clegg, S.R., da Cunha, J.V., Pina e Cunha, M.: Management paradoxes: a relational view. Hum. Relat. 55, 483–503 (2002)
6. Willmott, H.: Critical Management Studies. SAGE, Thousand Oaks (1992)
7. Putnam, L.L., Fairhurst, G.T., Banghart, S.: Contradictions, dialectics, and paradoxes in organizations: a constitutive approach. Acad. Manag. Ann. 10, 65–171 (2016). https://doi.org/10.1080/19416520.2016.1162421
8. Alvesson, M., Sandberg, J.: Generating research questions through problematization. Acad. Manag. Rev. 36, 247–271 (2011). https://doi.org/10.5465/amr.2009.0188
9. Krueger, R.A., Casey, M.A.: Focus Groups: A Practical Guide for Applied Research. SAGE, Thousand Oaks (2014)
10. Horlach, B., Schirmer, I., Drews, P.: Agile portfolio management: design goals and principles. In: Proceedings of the European Conference on Information Systems, ECIS 2019, Stockholm-Uppsala, Sweden. AIS Electronic Library (AISeL) (2019)
11. Horlach, B., Drechsler, A., Schirmer, I., Drews, P.: Everyone's going to be an architect: design principles for architectural thinking in agile organizations. In: Proceedings of the 53rd Hawaii International Conference on System Sciences (2020)
12. Horlach, B., Schirmer, I., Böhmann, T., Drechsler, A., Drews, P.: Reconceptualising business-IT alignment for organisational agility. In: Proceedings of the 28th European Conference on Information Systems, Marrakesh, Morocco (2020)
13. Denning, S.: Agile's ten implementation challenges. Strategy Leadersh. 44, 15–20 (2016)
14. Dingsøyr, T., Moe, N.B.: Towards principles of large-scale agile development. In: Dingsøyr, T., Moe, N.B., Tonelli, R., Counsell, S., Gencel, C., Petersen, K. (eds.) XP 2014. LNBIP, vol. 199, pp. 1–8. Springer, Cham (2014). https://doi.org/10.1007/978-3-319-14358-3_1
15. Larman, C.: Agile and Iterative Development: A Manager's Guide. Addison-Wesley Professional, Boston (2004)
16. Moe, N.B., Aurum, A., Dybå, T.: Challenges of shared decision-making: a multiple case study of agile software development. Inf. Softw. Technol. 54(8), 853–865 (2012)
17. Moe, N.B., Dahl, B., Stray, V., Karlsen, L.S., Schjødt-Osmo, S.: Team autonomy in large-scale agile. In: Proceedings of the 52nd Hawaii International Conference on System Sciences (2019)

18. Gerster, D., Dremel, C., Kelker, P.: How enterprises adopt agile structures: a multiple-case study. In: Proceedings of the 52nd Hawaii International Conference on System Sciences (2019)
19. Leybourn, E., Hastie, S.: #noprojects - A Culture of Continuous Value. C4Media (2018)
20. Andriopoulos, C., Lewis, M.W.: Exploitation-exploration tensions and organizational ambidexterity: managing paradoxes of innovation. Organ. Sci. **20**, 696–717 (2009)
21. Jansen, J.J., Tempelaar, M.P., Van den Bosch, F.A., Volberda, H.W.: Structural differentiation and ambidexterity: The mediating role of integration mechanisms. Organ. Sci. **20**, 797–811 (2009)
22. Weiner, B.J.: A theory of organizational readiness for change. Implement Sci. **4**, 67 (2009)
23. Dikert, K., Paasivaara, M., Lassenius, C.: Challenges and success factors for large-scale agile transformations: a systematic literature review. J. Syst. Softw. **119**, 87–108 (2016)
24. Paasivaara, M., Lassenius, C., Heikkilä, V.T., Dikert, K., Engblom, C.: Integrating global sites into the lean and agile transformation at ericsson. In: 2013 IEEE 8th International Conference on Global Software Engineering, pp. 134–143. IEEE (2013)
25. Meyer, B.: Agile! Springer, Cham (2014). https://doi.org/10.1007/978-3-319-05155-0
26. Cram, W.A., Newell, S.: Mindful revolution or mindless trend? Examining agile development as a management fashion. Eur. J. Inf. Syst. **25**, 154–169 (2016). https://doi.org/10.1057/ejis.2015.13
27. Wang, X., Conchuir, E.O., Vidgen, R.: A paradoxical perspective on contradictions in agile software development. In: ECIS 2008 Proceedings (2008)
28. Nicolai, A.T., Seidl, D.: That's relevant! Different forms of practical relevance in management science. Organ. Stud. **31**, 1257–1285 (2010). https://doi.org/10.1177/0170840610374401
29. Matook, S., Soltani, S., Maruping, L.: Self-organization in agile ISD teams and the influence on exploration and exploitation (2016)

First International Workshop on Agility
with Microservices Programming

Summary of the First International Workshop on Agility with Microservices Programming

Saverio Giallorenzo[1], Marco Peressotti[1], Filipe F. Correia[2,3], and Kati Kuusinen[4]

[1] University of Southern Denmark, Denmark
{saverio,peressotti}@imada.sdu.dk
[2] Faculty of Engineering, University of Porto, Portugal
filipe.correia@fe.up.pt
[3] INESC TEC, FEUP Campus, Portugal
[4] Technical University of Denmark, Denmark
kakuu@dtu.dk

Abstract. We present the proceedings of the AMP 2020 workshop, co-located with XP 2020, and report our main insights from its conduction. The workshop focused on exploring the interplay between agile methods and microservice architectures. Due to the COVID outbreak, AMP 2020 was moved online, divided into two parts: a live presentation session and a three-week interaction period where authors of accepted papers discussed improvements to their proposals with the PC. The workshop featured four accepted works. More that 30 participants attended the online event. More than 15 people took an active part to the three-week discussion period.

1 Introduction

We are pleased to present the proceedings of the 2020 edition of the *Agility with Microservices* (AMP 2020) workshop, held in affiliation with the annual *International Conference on Agile Software Development* (XP 2020). This was the first edition of the workshop, building on the success of the second International Workshop on Microservices: Agile and DevOps Experience (MADE 18) [1].

The theme of the workshop originates from the realisation that agile architecture does not necessarily emerge from the use of agile practices—it needs to be deliberately sought after—and often results in the style of architecture described as *microservices*. This notion lead us to the theme of the workshop: the interplay between agile methods and the microservices architectural paradigm.

2 Workshop Model and Discussion

Due to the COVID-19 outbreak, the XP 2020 organisation decided to hold the conference online. To adapt to the new medium, we chose to structure the experience of the attendees of the workshop into two distinct moments.

Live Session

The first one was a *live* session through the Zoom platform, provided by the XP 2020 organisation. The session took place on Friday June 12th 2020, lasted 90 minutes, and included the presentation of the accepted works. The workshop attracted more than 30 participants. The works presented included presentations on a wide range of topics: the interplay between the management of shared libraries in microservices and development agility; the effects of the standardisation of communication protocols in microservices agile programming; the industrial experience on the implementation of API binding generators for the agile development of microservices; and the empirical results of using microservices and agile techniques to teach complex system development in undergraduate courses. All presentations followed a 5-10-minute Q/A session. The questions asked by the participants were approached briefly by the present authors, and provided some initial points of discussion for the second phase of the workshop (reported below). The general insight that we gathered is that the interplay between microservices and agile methods happens at many levels (from tooling to architecture and even education), all of interest to the community of involved experts.

Open Interactive Review

The second moment was a three-week period of *open interactive review*. This period started in the week after the workshop and had the goal of promoting interaction with the authors—which is often hindered in online events—and to help them to improve their work further. The discussion happened via a mailing list with all authors and PC members. Some members of the Program Committee were invited to assume the role of *chaperone* for one of the accepted papers. Chaperones played the role of moderators and fostered the online discussion with the authors. This resulted in more than 15 people interacting with several empathetic, intelligent, and inspiring discussions among the participants. We summarise below the main points of discussion (and improvement) developed during the interactive review period of the accepted contributions.

Improving Agility by Managing Shared Libraries in Microservices. Full paper by *Saulo S. de Toledo, Antonio Martini and Dag I. K. Sjøberg*. Questions asked and address by the authors regarded including more insight on how the organisation chart influences the awareness of shared libraries and their agile development process, eliciting the distinctive characteristics of shared-library management in microservices architectures (w.r.t. the other existing architectural paradigms), and clarifying the possible open challenges of shared-library management (e.g., addressable through new tools or organisational configurations).

Certification as a Service. Full paper by *Sebastian Copei, Manuel Wickert and Albert Zündorf*. The main improvement included a more detailed discussion on the empirical evidence on the discrepancies between protocol-standardisation processes and agility, the definition of the elements that let the proponents of new (or updated) protocols declare their specification "complete" to proceed with implementations, and the expansion of the relationship linking microservice architecture development and the agile standardisation of protocols.

Multicloud API Binding Generation from Documentation. Extended abstract by *Michaĺ, J. Gajda, Victor Vitali Barrozzi and Gabriel Araujo*. The main points of improvement centred on expanding the description of the agile process used to create their proposal, refining the presentation of the stages that characterise their solution, and how the generated tool fits into agile processes for microservices development.

Teaching Complex Systems based on Microservices. Extended abstract by *Renato Cordeiro, Thatiane Rosa, Alfredo Goldman and Eduardo Guerra*. The improvements included details on the concrete applications, useful to other teachers/researchers. That encompassed the characteristics of the services the students developed (architecture, functionalities, codebase metrics) and how much of the course time was spent in the microservices design and implementation vs other activities.

3   Acknowledgements

We want to thank everyone who contributed to this workshop and all the participants to the online event. We thank Florian Rademacher for his work as Publicity Chair and the PC members that acted as chaperones: Florian Rademacher, Jonas Sorgalla, Rebecca Wirfs-Brock and Stefano Pio Zingaro. We also thank the members of the programme committee who made essential contributions to the workshop, in the form of reviews to the submitted works before the presentations took place, and by participating of the open interactive reviews.

Ademar Aguiar	Alceste Scalas	Alfredo Goldman
Andrea Melis	Antonio Bucchiarone	Blagovesta Kostova
Cees de Groot	Eduardo Guerra	Florian Rademacher
Gustavo Petri	Jacopo Soldani	Jessica Díaz
Jonas Sorgalla	José Luiz	Justus Bogner
Ka I Pun	Larisa Safina	Nuno Santos
Pooyan Jamshidi	Rebecca Wirfs Brock	Stefano Pio Zingaro
Tiago Boldt Sousa		

We would also like to thank our institutions for their support, as well as the Microservices Community, an international NPO aimed at fostering research on microservices and collaboration between academia and industry.

Reference

1. Taibi, D., Mandić, V., Jabangwe, R., Giallorenzo, S.: Session details: MADE'18: second international workshop on microservices: agile and devops experience. In: Proceedings of the 19th International Conference on Agile Software Development: Companion. XP'18. Association for Computing Machinery, New York (2018). https://doi.org/10.1145/3329526

Improving Agility by Managing Shared Libraries in Microservices

Saulo S. de Toledo(⊠), Antonio Martini, and Dag I. K. Sjøberg

{saulos,antonima,dagsj}@ifi.uio.no

University of Oslo, Oslo, Norway

Abstract. Using microservices is a way of supporting an agile architecture. However, if the microservices development is not properly managed, the teams' development velocity may be affected, reducing agility and increasing architectural technical debt. This paper investigates how to manage the use of shared libraries in microservices to improve agility during development. We interviewed practitioners from four large international companies involved in microservices projects to identify problems when using shared libraries. Our results show that the participating companies had issues with shared libraries as follows: coupling among teams, delays on fixes due to overhead on libraries development teams, and need to maintain many versions of the libraries. Our results highlight that the use of shared libraries may hinder agility on microservices. Thus, their use should be restricted to situations where shared libraries cannot be replaced by a microservice and the costs of replicating the code on each service is very high.

Keywords: Cross-company study · Multiple-case study · Software quality · Qualitative analysis · Architectural technical debt

1 Introduction

A microservices architecture may be considered a kind of agile architecture. Over the years, large companies such as Amazon and Netflix shared their success histories with microservices on dozens of presentations[1], always highlighting how such architectural style helped them to be agile and surpass many of the limitations and impediments they had in their previous monolithic software solutions. Since then, many other companies and practitioners tried to learn about microservices and adopted them in their projects.

However, systems that use microservices may become more complex than monolith systems [8]. Practitioners are still struggling with the adoption of this architectural style in their projects, and there is not much knowledge about Architectural Technical Debt (ATD) in microservices [10].

---

[1] Examples of presentations are "Mastering Chaos" by Josh Evans (Netflix, 2016), "Amazon and the Lean Cloud" by Werner Vogels (Amazon, 2011) and "What We Got Wrong: Lessons from the Birth of Microservices" by Ben Sigelma (Google, 2018).

© The Author(s) 2020
M. Paasivaara and P. Kruchten (Eds.): XP 2020 Workshops, LNBIP 396, pp. 195–202, 2020.
https://doi.org/10.1007/978-3-030-58858-8_20

ATD is a metaphor used to describe architectural suboptimal decisions that, in exchange of benefits in the short term, incurs future additional costs for the software. There are many studies on ATD in general but few on ATD in microservices and no discussion about agility. Our previous study [10] investigates what is ATD in microservices through a qualitative case study in a single company, Lenarduzzi and Taibi [5] presents a position paper about code debt on microservices, also in a case study in a single company, Bogner et al. [3] performed a qualitative case study in 10 companies to explore evolvability assurance processes for microservice-based systems. The three studies have distinct scopes.

In this study, we investigate the practice of using shared libraries in companies that use microservices, and how do these companies manage such libraries in order to improve agility. We define a *shared library* as a piece of software developed in-house containing a collection of resources used by several components. Externally developed components such as frameworks and language support extensions are not considered shared libraries in this study. Shared libraries are used as a black box by the different components, have their own version management and are copied and bundled together with the components.

Taibi and Lenarduzzi [9] have shown that the use of shared libraries may be a microservice bad smell and have proposed solutions for removing the smell. We extend that work by presenting an expanded list of issues and solutions, and do it in the context of different companies.

We pose the research questions as follows:

RQ1: Which practical issues when using shared libraries in microservices hinder agility in organizations?

RQ2: Which solutions do developers apply to solve such issues?

In order to answer these questions, we conducted a multiple-case study in four large international companies that use microservices. The remainder of this paper is structured as follows: Sect. 2 presents our background, Sect. 3 our methodology, Sect. 4 our results, Sect. 5 our discussion and threats to validity. Section 6 concludes and outlines future work.

2   Background

Using microservices architecture is an approach that decomposes a single application into a collection of small and loosely coupled services; such services are autonomous, independent of each other and run on separate processes [6]. A few other characteristics are also taken in consideration while defining microservices, such as loose coupling, organization around business capabilities and ownership by small teams.

Microservices may improve agility by allowing teams to focus on small pieces of software, facilitating aspects like change, scalability and testing. As it raises new ways of developing software, it also raises new kinds of ATD [10]. If properly managed, the accumulation of ATD may be beneficial to the software development, but it is necessary to know when the debt should be avoided and how to prevent its accumulation [7].

ATD is based on financial terms and has three main concepts [2]: *debt*, which describes a sub-optimal solution that yields short-term benefits, but recurring to the later payment of some interest; *interest*, which is the additional cost that has to be paid because of the accumulation of debt; and *principal*, which is the cost of refactoring in order to remove the debt.

3   Methodology

We conducted a multiple-case study in four large international companies, with more than 1000 employees. For confidentiality reasons, the companies are named *A*, *B*, *C* and *D*, respectively. The studied projects operate in the domains as follows, respectively: financial systems, healthcare systems, city management and transport mobility.

We interviewed six architects: one from Company A, two from each of Companies B and C, and one from Company D. We conducted semi-structured interviews that lasted from 30 min to one and a half hours. We discussed several aspects of architecture beyond the scope of this investigation, such as architectural issues and solutions while using microservices. The questions in the interview guide relevant to this study are available at https://bit.ly/ImprAgilitySL. Three of the interviews were conducted face-to-face. The three other ones were conducted through remote audio calls due to the physical distance between the parts.

4   Results

4.1   The Issues Caused by Using Shared Libraries

Table 1 shows which issues related to shared libraries were found in which companies. We refer to the those issues by using their IDs between parenthesis in the following paragraphs. The context related to the issues discussed below is illustrated in Fig. 1, an example reported by Company B: A team is assigned to create and maintain a library for authentication and authorization. Versions of the library are regularly released with fixes or new functionalities. Other teams are assigned to develop microservices. Eventually and due to several reasons, several microservices end up using distinct versions of the library. We present below the causes and implications of such circumstances for each company in the context of the projects we investigated.

Company A could not migrate all the clients to a newer version of a library right after its release. Distinct teams have different priorities: some services are critical, some are secondary, some have more urgent updates (1). Such a scenario required libraries maintainers to be active in supporting previous versions of their libraries that were still being used in production (2). Even in situations where

ID	Issue	Company			
		A	B	C	D
1	Impossibility to update library in service due to priorities	X		X	
2	Need to maintain too many versions of the library	X		X	
3	Impossibility to update library in service due to breaking changes			X	
4	Delays while waiting for fixes		X	X	X
5	Early adopters refusing to migrate	X			
6	Failures due to unknown use cases		X	X	
7	Failures after library upgrades		X	X	
8	Overhead to library maintainers		X	X	X
9	Dependent agile teams	X	X	X	X

Table 1. Issues reported by companies as the result of using shared libraries

the library was supposed to be updated soon, the company experienced delays in the process due to other priorities (1). In addition, the company also identified situations where early adopters resisted to migrate (5), since a new version of the library was released right after they finished the integration of the previous version in their project.

In Company B, the developers experienced a number of system breaks. Later they identified that part of the breaks were caused by the use of libraries in many unforeseen and untested situations (6). In addition, Company B also noticed an overhead on library maintainers (8) and consequent delays. Since the functionality was provided by the libraries, the teams using them had to wait for the fixes, which caused delays in new microservices releases (4). In some situations, the new versions of the libraries caused new issues that prevented the microservices to be released in production right away (7).

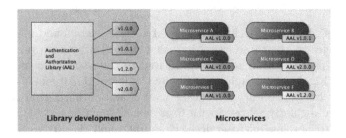

Fig. 1. Shared libraries example

Company C, similarly to Company A, found itself in a situation where it was not possible to migrate all the clients, which required teams to support many deprecated versions of libraries (2). Breaking changes and internal roadmap priorities were some of the factors that prevented developers to use new versions of the libraries (3 and 1). The use of shared libraries became a bottleneck, causing failures on microservices (6 and 7), delays while waiting for fixes (4) and an unexpected amount of extra work for library developers (8).

Company D reported delays in delivering new functionalities as the most damaging issue connected to the use of shared libraries (4). The library developers had to handle an extensive amount of change requests, including requests for additional features and fixes (8). The microservices developers were frequently blocked while waiting for the arrival of the new versions of the libraries.

In all four companies, there was a clear dependency (coupling) among the microservices developers and the library teams (9).

4.2   How to Manage Issues Regarding the Use of Shared Libraries

All the companies reported that the use of shared libraries should be reduced as much as possible. Company B reported that many libraries implemented trivial functionality that could be implemented by the microservices themselves, and the fixes could be implemented by the teams, reducing the delays caused by third-party developers. Company D suggested that well-defined and well-documented interfaces of their own implementations were important for guiding practitioners when they did not use shared libraries to provide required functionality.

Figure 2 shows solutions proposed by the companies for the issues caused by the use of shared libraries. Considering the example presented in Fig. 1, simple functionalities, such as extracting an ID or user name from a token, could be implemented by the services themselves. Such a functionality is easy to implement, usually by using a well-known technique that can be learned by the developers, and that does not require the use of an entire library. On the other hand, some functionalities are complex and could involve, as in our example, many security steps. In such circumstances, an external microservice with a well-defined interface, good documentation and a versioning policy should be maintained by a separate team. Well-defined interfaces should not be changed unless in exceptional cases, meaning that internal bug fixes may be conducted without the other services noticing it, and new functionality may be added without breaking previous behavior unless a breaking change is strictly necessary. Such a scenario reduces the need for changes in the other microservices that are using the aforementioned interfaces. Finally, if there are important reasons for not using one of the approaches above, the use of shared libraries may be acceptable. Similar approaches may be found in other migration reports. Balalaie et al. [1], for example, moved common libraries to microservices when they migrated to such an architecture style. Hasselbring et al. [4] argue that code should not be shared among microservices because teams and applications should be as independent and loosely coupled as possible.

5   Discussion and Threats to Validity

Our results suggest that using shared libraries in some contexts impacts on the development flow, causing delays, reducing development velocity and hindering

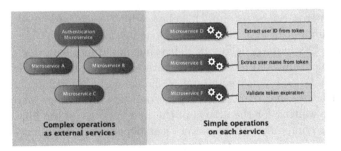

Fig. 2. How to handle shared functionality

agility. In such cases, shared libraries are an ATD that may lead to costly interest if not managed properly. By sharing the experience from other practitioners on issues and solutions, we can prevent others from having to pay high software maintenance costs later.

We answer the research questions introduced in Sect. 1 by listing the issues (RQ1) raised by the use of shared libraries and by presenting corresponding solutions (RQ2). The issues we identified do not seem connected to any specific application domain; the practitioners from the different companies complained about similar issues and solutions. We do not claim that shared libraries should never be used. However, their use should be controlled to prevent high costs. There are also drawbacks of such an approach. For example, it may incur additional latency; performance may decrease due to network as opposed to in-memory invocations; reliability may decrease since the service might not be reachable; and complex functionality may not be possible to be implemented in a distributed system. Such drawbacks should be carefully considered in practical situations.

Companies should also consider the reasons for replacing their shared libraries. There may be alternative solutions, such as improving processes for development, testing and quality assurance, which should be considered when the drawbacks of moving to services may be more costly than using shared libraries.

Regarding the validity of this study, we consider the following threats: (i) The interviewees may have interpreted the concept of shared libraries differently. We mitigated this threat by asking the interviewees to clarify if they were talking about libraries developed internally or about external dependencies; (ii) Our sample of interviewees was small from each company, we do not know how representative the opinions in this study were for the investigated companies. Still, the sample was heterogeneous and the practitioners were located in three different countries, with projects from four different companies; (iii) There might be factors that the interviewees were not aware of or did not express in the interviews, such as the quality of the implementations and management issues.

6   Conclusions and Future Work

In four Europe-based companies, we identified a set of issues that reduce development velocity and hinder team agility while using shared libraries in microservices. We highlighted two solutions: creating additional microservices or implementing the code in the microservices themselves. Although these solutions have been reported by Taibi and Lenarduzzi [9], we went beyond their work by presenting and discussing a more comprehensive list of issues, and relating them all to the different companies. Our results suggest that the use of shared libraries may increase the complexity of the system, which in turn decreases development agility, cause delays and raises maintainability costs. Our results do not indicate that shared libraries should not be used at all, but if there are no acceptable alternatives, they should be used rather carefully as they often generate costly interest. As an alternative to the use of shared libraries, simple functionalities should be implemented by each microservice, whereas complex functionalities should be implemented by external microservices with well defined interfaces, good documentation and adequate versioning policies.

As future work, we propose a further investigation of the problem, increasing the size of the sample and looking for practitioners with different experiences. As part of this investigation, we propose to look for a decision process supported by the factors that influence the trade-off between using a shared library and a microservice. We would also like to investigate the problem and their solutions with other architectural styles, like Service Oriented Architecture, in order to identify whether there are other solutions proposed by practitioners that could be used in microservices. In addition, we would like to investigate the external dependencies and how moving to them could affect our results.

References

1. Balalaie, A., Heydarnoori, A., Jamshidi, P.: Microservices architecture enables DevOps: migration to a cloud-native architecture. IEEE Softw. **33**, 42–52 (2016)
2. Besker, T., Martini, A., Bosch, J.: Managing architectural technical debt: a unified model and systematic literature review. J. Syst. Softw. **135**, 1–16 (2018)
3. Bogner, J., Fritzsch, J., Wagner, S., Zimmermann, A.: Assuring the evolvability of microservices: insights into industry practices and challenges. In: IEEE International Conference on Software Maintenance and Evolution (ICSME) (2019)
4. Hasselbring, W., Steinacker, G.: Microservice architectures for scalability, agility and reliability in e-commerce. In: Proceedings - IEEE International Conference on Software Architecture Workshops (ICSAW): Side Track Proceedings (2017)
5. Lenarduzzi, V., Taibi, D.: Microservices, continuous architecture, and technical debt interest: an empirical study. Euromicro SEAA. Work in Progress (2018)
6. Lewis, J., Fowler, M.: Microservices: a definition of this new architectural term (2014). https://www.martinfowler.com/articles/microservices.html
7. Martini, A., Bosch, J.: An empirically developed method to aid decisions on architectural technical debt refactoring: AnaConDebt. In: Proceedings of the 38th International Conference on Software Engineering Companion (ICSE) (2016)

8. Soldani, J., Tamburri, D.A., Van Den Heuvel, W.J.: The pains and gains of microservices: a systematic grey literature review. J. Syst. Softw. **146**, 215–232 (2018)
9. Taibi, D., Lenarduzzi, V.: On the definition of microservice bad smells. IEEE Softw. **35**(3), 56–62 (2018)
10. de Toledo, S.S., Martini, A., Przybyszewska, A., Sjøberg, D.I.K.: Architectural technical debt in microservices: a case study in a large company. In: 2019 IEEE/ACM International Conference on Technical Debt (TechDebt) (2019)

Certification as a Service

Sebastian Copei[1]([✉]), Manuel Wickert[2], and Albert Zündorf[1]

[1] Kassel University, Kassel, Germany
{sco,zuendorf}@uni-kassel.de
[2] Frauenhofer IEE, Kassel, Germany
manuel.wickert@iee.frauenhofer.de

Abstract. The development of industry 4.0 and smart energy IT-Components relies on highly standardized communication protocols to reach vendor-independent interoperability. In innovative and fast-changing environments, the support of standard protocols increases the time to market significantly. In the energy domain, the business models and the regulatory frameworks will be updated more often than the protocols. Thus agile development and supporting standardized protocols at the same time seems to be an issue. Here we will present a new proposal for standardization and certification processes as well as an architecture for a certification platform. Both will improve the support of agile development in the industry and energy domain.

Keywords: Microservices · Standardization · Certification · Agile

1 Motivation

In the energy and industry domain, vendor-independent scaling of distributed systems is a key challenge. To provide interoperability between different systems or integrated electronic devices (IED) the use of standardized communication protocols (such as OPC UA [11], IEC 61850 [8], IEC 60870-5-104 [7], etc.) is very common. While vendor independence is crucial for IEDs, which stay in operation for years or decades, for IED vendors itself selling certified products may also be a sales argument.

Fig. 1. Classic standardization and product development processes

---

S. Copei and M. Wickert—These two authors contributed equally.

© The Author(s) 2020
M. Paasivaara and P. Kruchten (Eds.): XP 2020 Workshops, LNBIP 396, pp. 203–210, 2020.
https://doi.org/10.1007/978-3-030-58858-8_21

Figure 1 shows a classical standardization and certification scenario divided into two processes. The first (upper) process shows a view on developing a new version of a standard. The second process shows a classical waterfall model for applications where the certification is part of the testing phase. Note, both process views are very coarse overviews and do not provide a detailed look at a certain complex standardization or certification scenario.

The standardization typically begins with the specification of standard documents for a collection of requirements. Usually, the communication standard only describes the communication of a particular layer of the ISO/OSI communication stack. After publishing a finished version, conformance tests may be specified, and test suites may be implemented. E.g. The OPC Foundation offers a conformance test suite for its members [12]. The development of compliant products and the certification of them are illustrated as a classical waterfall model, where the certification is done in the test phase.

The key message of Fig. 1 is that the development process typically starts after (a new version of) the standard has been published. An earlier start of software development may result in incompatibilities with the standard. From a new requirement for the communication standard to a certified software version in operation, it may easily take several years. E.g., the Protocol IEC 61850-1 was published in 2003 in version 1.0 and 2013 in version 2.0. In the meantime, a lot of extensions were developed e.g., [1,14]. From our practical experience with such communication standards, we see a lot of vendor-specific deviations. Therefore we assume that standardization approaches are often designed for classical and not for agile development processes.

Smart Energy Applications and Industry 4.0, are connecting classical industrial monitoring and control solutions with modern IoT-based technologies. Thereby modern software development processes are applied to address fast-changing requirements in both sectors to provide fast feedback cycles. Therefore we reconsidered how standardization and certification processes can be integrated into an agile product development process. It can be argued that stability is an essential requirement for communication protocols. But from our experience with more than 15 different projects, we see an upcoming preference for regular updates in operation over stability.

This paper presents two proposals to support agile standardization and certification processes. We propose a new standardization and certification process for communication protocols. For both process, proposals will use the terms standardization and certification. Our second proposal is an architecture for cloud-native certification services. The aim of the architecture is to support our idea of future agile certification processes. The proposals were developed with a background in smart energy systems and industry 4.0. However, our aim was to specify the process very generic to achieve transferability.

2   Related Work

Agile standardization and certification processes have already been examined in various domains. Examples are high security system certification for aviation

[4] and railways [2]. The authors of [4] present a way to certify security-critical components in a transportation system. They focus on high-level certificates. To provide the credibility of the certificates, the authors use a semi-formal description language. [2] shows a way to certify security-critical aerospace components. The authors use UML as a modeling tool to provide an incrementally changeable model description to achieve an agile certification process. However, the solutions presented in both papers are very domain-specific and focused on security certification. The given solutions only fit into their use cases and can not be used as a general approach. Furthermore, the solutions only cover the certification process on a client-side. Our solution wants to cover the whole process from developing a standard to certifying implementations of it.

An evolutionary standardization approach for file-based data is presented in [5]. The considered standardization focus is the engineering of automation systems. The basic idea is to start from an existing proprietary file format of one vendor and change it evolutionary to a neutral and later on to a common format, apparently often XML in that context. Similar to our process, this approach proposes a stepwise standardization. Nevertheless, the evolutionary approach is not intended to support agile development processes and focuses on file-based communication.

In [3] an agile standardization was performed for Process Control Equipment (PCE). The domain is close to the considered domain of this work. The authors require that standardization has to be done agile and "should proceed stepwise". However, the focus of [3] is the concrete standardization of PCE Requests, not the standardization process itself.

3   The Agile Standardization and Certification Processes

Fig. 2. Agile standardization process

We propose an agile standardization and certification process that has two intertwined development cycles, cf. Fig. 2. As in other agile approaches, standardization and certification should be performed in small increments. The basic idea is to start with a minimal set of communication protocol features (e.g., establish a connection or login to a server) and add feature by feature in several iterations. Every iteration ends with a minor version change in the standard. The corresponding part of the overall standard is published e.g., via Github or some other configuration management service. Based on the publication of the standard for some features, the standard conformance tests that certify compliance with these features are extended or adapted and again published via a configuration management service. The standardization process runs iteratively, i.e., as soon as one feature has been completed, subsequent application development may start while the standardization continues with the next features.

The product development cycle, including the certification of a product, is shown on the right side of Fig. 2. The development of standard-compliant products may start with the requirements definitions for specific product features. The implementation of these product features may follow this. As soon as some feature is available, the feature implementation may try to pass the corresponding protocol conformance tests for a specific communication standard version. When the new product version is certified, it may be released and operated in production.

Each time a new version of the standard is exposed, and the corresponding conformance tests are deployed a test-driven development iteration of the products is ready to begin. Obviously, the conformance test will not be able to provide a complete test set for a product. However, these tests will support the product development relating to the communication interfaces. This approach has the advantage that first conformance tests will be available soon after the first iterations of the standardization process have completed. Thus, product development and standard development may be intertwined. Thereby, standard-compliant products will be available soon after the standard has reached a sufficient level of completeness. Besides, product development may provide feedback to the standardization process. Product development may e.g, point to overly complex conformance tests or inconvenient APIs or missing details, etc. This feedback may be used by the standardization process to enhance the standardization of the corresponding features and to come up with improved versions of the conformance tests. The importance of such feedback is also discussed in [5].

On the other hand, new versions of the standard lead to changes in the conformance test. This may result in failing tests for the new standard version and triggers the adaption of existing features. Such changes to already defined conformance tests may also happen when following features or later standardization iterations require previously standardized features to evolve. This is an infrequent problem inherent in agile software development. If a product development team wants to avoid such issues, it may wait until the standardization process has reached a sufficient level of completeness and stability. One can argue that this may be a drawback of our approach since stability is a critical requirement for communication devices in operation. However, since we have also to consider security for such field devices, we have to provide easy mechanisms to provide software updates in operation.

4 Certification as a Service Architecture

For a certain standard, a certification service will support the agile standardization and certification process. Here we propose a microservice [6,10] based certification as a service architecture. This architecture should support the understanding of our agile standardization and certification process on the one hand. An implementation of this architecture is currently work in progress and part of our future work.

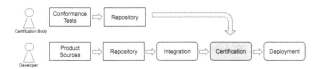

Fig. 3. Continuous certification pipeline

Continuous integration and continuous deployment are methods to support fast feedback during agile development. A Certification as a service implementation extends a typical continuous deployment pipeline, as shown in Fig. 3. The certification step should be performed after the integration phase (which includes integration testing). The certification step consists of the execution of the conformance tests and the creation of a certificate. An implementation of our certification as a service platform will perform this step. This allows the deployment of certified products in every continuous deployment cycle. If conformance tests fail, the pipeline stops at the certification step, just like a failure during integration tests will stop the pipeline.

Each certification pipeline certifies a product according to a particular standard version. Whenever a new standard version is published, the respective conformance tests will be adapted or extended for this version of the standard. The certification bodies will add the standard to a repository. As soon as the new tests have uploaded, a product can be certified for the new standard version.

The certification service itself should be hosted as a service by the standardization or depending on organizational aspects, a certification body. As software as a service (SaaS), it should be compatible with a typical build pipeline software such as Jenkins. That allows an independent certification of products even with fast development cycles.

Our proposal for the certification service architecture is shown in Fig. 4. We defined five microservices, two repositories, and an event broker.

The repositories are responsible for storing a product for certification (artifact repository) and the conformance tests (conformance test repository). Both artifacts and conformance tests should be available in different versions. To perform the conformance tests, an instance of the artifact should be up and running for certification. The "Artifact runner Service" is responsible for running this artifact and configure it correctly. The "Test Service" will do the execution

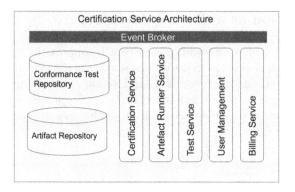

Fig. 4. Certification service architecture

of the conformance tests. It will also provide test results for the "Certification Service". The certification service will create a certificate for the artifact if all tests are passed successfully. The "User Management" and "Billing Service" have administrative responsibilities. Since the business model of a certification body is to issue certificates, it is necessary to implement user management and billing functionalities. The communication to the product development should be done by RESTful HTTP, to integrate with existing build pipelines easily. For internal communication, event sourcing should be used. Therefore we suggest making use of an event broker like Apache Kafka.

Our architecture aims to provide a proposal for certification as a service solution. Typical container orchestration tools can support implementations. Therefore an implementation of our service should be cloud-native [13].

5   Conclusion and Future Work

We presented a new way to achieve a more agile process during the standardization and certification steps. We provide an architecture that should support the affected stakeholders during the whole process. On the one hand, this means that a standardization organization should have the possibility to provide fast incremental updates of their standards. On the other hand, we enable companies to use agile development processes for their certified implementation of standardized communication interfaces.

In the next steps, we will implement the architecture for a new communication standard for e-mobility use cases. We will examine how agile standardization approaches will work in that context. Furthermore, we will evaluate how this approach will support the agile development of prototypes for e-mobility use cases.

Acknowledgement and Disclaimer. This Publication is part of a
project [9] that has received funding from the European Union's Horizon 2020 research and innovation programme under grant agreement
N°857237. The sole responsibility of this publication lies with the author. The European
Union is not responsible for any use that may be made of the information contained
therein.

References

1. Bergmann, J., Glomb, C., Götz, J., Heuer, J., Kuntschke, R., Winter, M.: Scalability of smart grid protocols: protocols and their simulative evaluation for massively
distributed DERs. In: 2010 First IEEE International Conference on Smart Grid
Communications, pp. 131–136 (2010)
2. Bezzecchi, S., Crisafulli, P., Pichot, C., Wolff, B.: Making agile development
processes fit for V-style certification procedures. CoRR, abs/1905.06604 (2019).
arXiv:1905.06604
3. Bigvand, P.G., Drath, R., Scholz, A., Schüller, A.: Agile standardization by means
of PCE requests. In: 2015 IEEE 20th Conference on Emerging Technologies Factory
Automation (ETFA), pp. 1–8 (2015)
4. Coe, D.J., Kulick, J.H.: A model-based agile process for DO-178C certification.
In: Proceedings of the International Conference on Software Engineering Research
and Practice (SERP), p. 1. The Steering Committee of The World Congress in
Computer Science, Computer Engineering and Applied Computing (WorldComp)
(2013)
5. Drath, R., Barth, M.: Concept for managing multiple semantics with automationml
— maturity level concept of semantic standardization. In: Proceedings of 2012
IEEE 17th International Conference on Emerging Technologies Factory Automation (ETFA 2012), pp. 1–8 (2012)
6. Fowler, M., Lewis, J.: Microservices (2014). http://martinfowler.com/articles/
microservices.html
7. IEC 60870-5-104: Telecontrol equipment and systems. Standard, International
Electrotechnical Commission, Geneva, CH (2006)
8. IEC 61850 Standard Series: Communication networks and systems in substations.
Standard, International Electrotechnical Commission, Geneva, CH (2020)
9. Interconnect project - homepage. https://interconnectproject.eu/. Accessed 20 Apr
2020
10. Newman, S.: Building Microservices, 1st edn. O'Reilly Media Inc., Sebastopol
(2015)
11. OPC Unified Architecture, IEC 62541, Standard Series. Standard, OPC Foundation, International Electrotechnical Commission, Scottsdale, USA (2008)
12. OPC foundation test tools. https://opcfoundation.org/developer-tools/certification-
test-tools/opc-ua-compliance-test-tool-uactt. Accessed 20 Apr 2020
13. Pahl, C., Jamshidi, P., Zimmermann, O.: Architectural principles for cloud software. ACM Trans. Internet Technol. **18** (2017). https://doi.org/10.1145/3104028
14. Ustun, T.S., Ozansoy, C.R., Zayegh, A.: Implementing vehicle-to-grid (V2G) technology with IEC 61850-7-420. IEEE Trans. Smart Grid **4**(2), 1180–1187 (2013)

Third International Workshop
on Autonomous Agile Teams

A Decade of Research on Autonomous Agile Teams: A Summary of the Third International Workshop

Nils Brede Moe[1] and Viktoria Stray[1,2]

[1] SINTEF, Trondheim, Norway
nilsm@sintef.no
[2] University of Oslo, Oslo, Norway
stray@ifi.uio.no

Abstract. Ever since the agile manifesto was created in 2001, the research community has devoted attention to autonomous teams. This article first examines publications on autonomous agile teams to illustrate how the research has progressed in the last ten years and next summarizes the result of the Third International Workshop on Autonomous Agile Teams. The workshop's goal was to capture what practitioners and researchers in the field of agile software development believe are emergent research themes and update the research agenda. We found that the top-rated research questions are related to autonomy in large-scale agile software development. Further, the number of relevant scientific publications is increasing, and there is widespread interest in the topic at various conferences.

Keywords: Autonomous teams · Agile software development · Team design · Self-organizing teams · Self-managing teams · Coordination · Large-scale frameworks

1 Introduction

To succeed in solving complex projects, agile organizations have to find ways to support and regulate teams' autonomy according to environmental demands. Furthermore, agile organizations have to take into consideration the degree of change and uncertainty and that there is no one-size-fits-all autonomy approach [1]. The process of forming and implementing autonomous teams, as well as the effective coordination of such teams, are not yet adequately addressed or understood [2]. Common barriers for such teams are 1) too much dependence on others, 2) lack of trust, and 3) part-time resources [3]. In large-scale agile development, autonomous teams struggle to handle organizational dependencies, set and communicate goals, establish a shared direction [4], and implementing tools like Slack to increase team awareness [5]. Further, even in the same large-scale agile projects, teams have individual needs for coordination with experts and other teams [6]. Thus, there is a need for new knowledge on how organizations should organize for the right level of team autonomy and utilize autonomous teams to attain better performance, productivity, innovation, and value creation.

Next, we introduce research on autonomous teams and present findings from a literature search in the Scopus database. Then, we introduce the papers and results from the workshop. Finally, we present the updated research agenda.

2   Research on Autonomous Teams

Autonomy refers to control over the way a task is carried out [7] and can simultaneously reside at the team level and the individual level [8, 9]. While autonomy can have a positive impact on a team, an important question to answer is when—and how much—autonomy is appropriate under the specific conditions the team and organizations are facing. Hackman [10 p.92] discusses the relationship between self-management and autonomy, where the self-managing team has *a certain but limited amount of autonomy*. More precisely, the self-managing team is given responsibility for executing its tasks and monitoring and management of its work processes. As autonomy increases, the team is given responsibility for both designing the team and setting the overall direction. When a software development company maintains or develops a product or service, the work is assigned to several teams, and each team needs to align many decisions regarding the tasks and process with the rest of the unit. As a result, the team's autonomy will be reduced in large-scale agile software development.

First-generation large-scale agile methods combine agile methodology, such as Scrum, with project management frameworks, such as Prince2. Today, many second-generation large-scale frameworks, such as the Scaled Agile Framework (SAFe) and the Large-Scale Scrum (LeSS) have been implemented. The SAFe is a comprehensive framework that requires the introduction of many predefined roles and processes, and the goal is establishing stable processes. Stable roles and processes provide control but reduce the flexibility required to solve complex tasks and experiment with ideas. The SAFe is based on daily team meetings and cross-team meetings as well as planning ahead with "big room planning." Empirical studies suggest that these practices are insufficient when coordination is complex and changes over time [11]. The LeSS is based on the principles in Scrum related to product queue and defined sprints (time-boxing). Although the LeSS is more flexible than the SAFe, it does not support the need for team members with a high degree of autonomy and high responsibility to make decisions on a continuous basis when solving problems. The Spotify model is inspired by the Nordic model with a high degree of autonomy. However, the model is designed for a born digital company, built on an entirely separate platform without legacy systems and with many thousands of developers.

To better understand current research on autonomous agile teams, we conducted a literature search in the Scopus database. This search identified 170 research papers from journals and conferences that were published in the last ten years—between 2009 and 2019 (Fig. 1). After conducting the initial search, we added 2020 (until July 1) to check if the trend continued. We used the following search string: TITLE-ABS-KEY = ("autonomous team*" OR "self-managing team*" OR "empowered team*" OR "team autonomy" OR "self-organizing team*") AND (computer science). We carefully read all titles and excluded articles that were not about teamwork. When in doubt, we read abstracts to make the decision. Seventy-four papers were excluded, and 96 were kept.

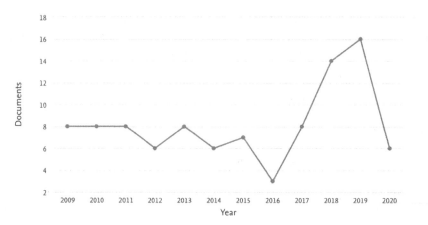

Fig. 1. Publication per year on autonomous teams in the field of computer science until July 1 2020

Most were conference articles (66%); however, 30% were journal articles, indicating the field is maturing. The ten most productive authors on the topic are shown in Fig. 2, and the four most productive institutions are SINTEF (Norway), University of Auckland (New Zealand), University of Oslo (Norway) and Victoria University of Wellington (New Zealand). However, as many as 33 countries are represented (Fig. 3). The top conference for research on autonomous teams is the XP conference, and many articles can be found in Springer proceedings.

Fig. 1 shows that the number of publications per year is increasing, and one reason for this is the XP conferences and the International Workshop on Autonomous Teams. There are a low number of publications recorded for 2020 because the search was conducted July 1. We estimate that 2020 will have more publications on autonomous teams than the previous years. The post-conference workshop proceedings from XP 2020 include five articles and will be summarized in Section 3.

We investigated the use of theories and the construction of theories in the articles included in the literature review by adding "AND (*theory OR *theories)" to the search

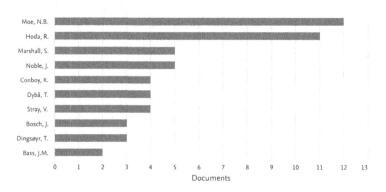

Fig. 2. Publication per authors on autonomous teams in the field of computer science

Fig. 3. Publication per authors on autonomous teams in the field of computer science

string earlier presented. We found a total of 12 articles (13%) and these articles reported using Agile Matching Theory, Modern Sociotechnical Theory, Control Theory, Complex Adaptive Systems Theory, Big Five Teamwork Theory, and Grounded Theory.

3   Summary of the Workshop

The 2020 workshop was an online event (because of COVID-19) as part of XP2020. The main conference had 900 registered participants, and the workshop on autonomous agile teams had 120 participants attending via Zoom. The workshop included five presentations by researchers who had had their papers peer-reviewed. After each presentation, the workshop participants gave feedback and asked questions. Finally, there were two interactive sessions.

In the first interactive session, attendees were divided into breakout rooms using Zoom, with 4–5 participants in each room (a total of 24 rooms), to discuss two questions: "What are the real-world problems that need to be solved (for autonomous teams)?" and "What are the research questions that should be answered?" In the second session, a silent writing session was conducted using Metro Retro to collect ideas. Forty-two ideas were posted on the virtual board and synthesized into a list of research questions by the organizers of the workshop. Because XP 2020 and the workshops were held online, the timeslots for all sessions and workshop were reduced. As a consequence, there was no time to discuss the identified research questions. The day after the workshop, the research questions were posted on the conference's Slack channel for the workshop participants to vote on the most important questions.

3.1   Research Themes on Autonomous Agile Teams

All of the papers presented at the workshop were based on investigations of autonomous teams in the context of large-scale agile frameworks. In the workshop, Gren [12] presented a paper using two popular theories from social psychology to better understand team autonomy in a large-scale setting: Group Socialization Theory and Social

Identity. Gren argues that the two social theories can be useful in explaining complexities to help one gain a better understanding when building autonomous agile teams, such as the social-psychological components of the team-based workplace or group dynamics. Group Socialization Theory explains patterns of behavior in retrospective meetings, and the Social Identity Theory explains why stand-up meetings within cross-functional teams decrease intergroup bias.

Salameh and Bass [13] explored how architectural governance increases team autonomy in a case study of a multinational fintech organization. The authors identified tailored practices that promote effectiveness in autonomous teams using the Spotify model. One important practice was introducing new roles and responsibilities within the team, such as the architect with a focus on facilitating decision-making regarding the architectural aspect and sharing architectural knowledge among teams.

Theobald and Schmitt [14] highlighted some challenges faced by agile teams when working on large, complex projects; in such projects, agile teams are often required to collaborate with other organizational branches, such as marketing and human resources. Moreover, safety-critical products still utilize traditional system engineering processes and mindsets, which may cause issues in collaboration between teams and their surrounding environments. In their study on the SAFe, the authors found that the framework does not provide enough details on how an efficient collaboration should be set up.

Mohagheghi et al. [15] highlighted challenges of autonomous teams within the governmental sector, such as inexperience with agile methods, large and complex projects, and reliance on traditional approaches. The authors examined a team in the Norwegian Labor and Welfare Administration that adopted agile methods while backsourcing. Defining a clear product boundary, reducing dependencies on other teams, and developing necessary skills were critical factors for team autonomy. Furthermore, changes such as adding product owners to the team; abandoning a stage-based software development process with handovers between business, IT, and vendors; and having the team refine its portfolio for better cohesion supported agile adoption.

Doležel [16] collaborated with a global antivirus company to provide more clarity on the coined term "TestOps." The author analyzed a set of practitioner videos on YouTube using thematic analysis and found that TestOps was understood as either a collaborative behavior associated with a shift in test personnel's mindset or as a technology-intensive set of software practices. The first perspective is a people-centric view that binds with culture and sharing elements in DevOps, while the second is a technical view denoting TestOps as new tools, workflows, and processes supporting DevOps teams, highlighting automation and measurement elements. Doležel argued that both perspectives should be combined.

4   Revised Research Agenda

During the 2019 workshop, we asked participants about the best team size for autonomous agile teams; 23% answered four to five members, 23% answered eight to nine members, and 54% answered six to seven members. In the 2020 workshop, 9%

answered two to three members, 18% answered four to five members, 55% answered six to seven members, and 18% eight to nine members.

The actual performance of an autonomous agile team depends not only on the competence of the team itself in managing and executing its work but also on the organizational context of the teams. In the 2018 workshop, eight barriers to team autonomy were identified [2], and in 2019, these eight barriers were rated on a scale from 1 to 10. "Too much dependence on others" was rated as the main barrier [3]. One explanation could be that agile methods are applied increasingly often in a large-scale context.

The 120 participants of the 2020 workshop generated 42 ideas for research questions and these questions were synthesized into a list of eight questions. The workshop participants were then invited to rate these questions on a scale from 1-10. The top two questions are related to the challenges of autonomy in large-scale agile frameworks. Below is the ranked list:

1. How can autonomy and alignment be balanced?
2. How does a top-down approach to agile (e.g., SAFe) affect autonomy?
3. How can relationships and good communication habits be established?
4. How can teams be autonomous within a hierarchy?
5. What are the limits to the level of autonomy?
6. How can the dependencies between teams be reduced?
7. How can autonomous BizDevOps teams be implemented?
8. How can autonomy be measured?

5   Conclusion

It should be apparent from this introductory article that the research community is paying greater attention to issues related to autonomous teams in software development. There is an increasing number of scientific publications and widespread interest in the topic at various conferences; in addition, many countries (33) have engaged in research on autonomous teams in the field of computer science. This paper presents an overview of what practitioners and researchers in the field of agile software development believe are emergent research themes for autonomous teams. Top-rated research questions are related to autonomy in large-scale agile frameworks.

Acknowledgement. The work was funded by the A-team project, supported by the Research Council of Norway through Grant 267704 and the companies Kantega, Sbanken, Storebrand, and Knowit. We would like to thank the program committee members, workshop participants for engaging discussions, Lucas Paruch and Marthe Berntzen for valuable input to the analysis, and the reviewers of this article for their constructive feedback.

References

1. Bass, J.M.: Future trends in agile at scale: Chen, J., Neubaum, D.O., Reilly, R.R., Lynn, G.S.: The relationship between team autonomy and new product development performance under different levels of technological turbulence. J. Oper. Manag. **33**, 3483–3496 (2015).
2. Stray, V., Moe, N.B., Hoda, R.: Autonomous agile teams: challenges and future directions for research. In: Proceedings of the 19th International Conference on Agile Software Development: Companion, pp. 1–5. ACM, Porto (2018).
3. Moe, N.B., Stray, V., Hoda, R.: Trends and updated research agenda for autonomous agile teams: a summary of the second international workshop at XP2019. In: Agile Processes in Software Engineering and Extreme Programming – Workshops, Montreal, Canada, pp. 13–19 (2019).
4. Moe, N.B., Dahl, B., Stray, V., Karlsen, L.S., Schjødt-Osmo, S.: Team autonomy in large-scale agile. In: Proceedings of the 52nd Hawaii International Conference on System Sciences, pp. 6997–7006 (2019)
5. Stray, V., Moe, N.B.: Understanding coordination in global software engineering: a mixed-methods study on the use of meetings and slack. J. Syst. Softw. **170** (2020). https://doi.org/10.1016/j.jss.2020.110717
6. Sablis, A., Smite, D., Moe, N.: Team-external coordination in large-scale software development projects. J. Softw. Evol. Process (2020)
7. Hackman, J.R., Oldham, G.R.: Work redesign (1980)
8. Langfred, C.W.: The paradox of self-management: Individual and group autonomy in work groups. J. Organ. Behav. **21**(5), 563–585 (2000)
9. van Mierlo, H., Rutte, C.v., Vermunt, J., Kompier, M., Doorewaard, J.: Individual autonomy in work teams: the role of team autonomy, self-efficacy, and social support. Eur. J. Work Organ. Psychol. **15**(3), 281–299 (2006)
10. Hackman, J.R.: The psychology of self-management in organizations. In: Pallack, M.S., Perloff, R.O. (eds.) Psychology and work: Productivity, change, and employment. American Psycological Association, Washington, DC (1986)
11. Moe, N.B., Dingsøyr, T., Rolland, K.: To schedule or not to schedule? An investigation of meetings as an inter-team coordination mechanism in large-scale agile software development. Int. J. Inf. Syst. Project Manag. **6**(3), 45–59 (2018)
12. Gren, L.: Understanding work practices of autonomous agile teams: a social-psychological review. In: XP2020. Springer (2020)
13. Salameh, A., Bass, J.: Spotify tailoring for architectural governance. In: XP2020. Springer (2020)
14. Theobald, S., Schmitt, A.: Dependencies of agile teams – an analysis of the scaled agile framework. In: XP2020. Springer (2020)
15. Mohagheghi,P., Lassenius, C., Bakken, I.: Enabling team autonomy in a large organization. In: XP2020. Springer (2020)
16. Dolezel, M.: Defining TestOps: collaborative behaviors and technology-driven workflows seen as enablers of effective software testing in DevOps. In: XP2020. Springer (2020)

Dependencies of Agile Teams – An Analysis of the Scaled Agile Framework

Sven Theobald$^{(\boxtimes)}$ ⓘ and Anna Schmitt ⓘ

Fraunhofer IESE, Fraunhofer-Platz 1, Kaiserslautern, Germany
{Sven.Theobald,Anna.Schmitt}@iese.fraunhofer.de

Abstract. *Context:* Agile teams are small teams with 3 to 9 members. In complex development endeavors such as systems engineering, an agile team has many dependencies, since it is not possible to incorporate all specialist skills into one team. Frameworks like the Scaled Agile Framework (SAFe) describe how agile teams operate in a larger setting. *Objective:* The aim of this study is to analyze how agile teams collaborate with their organizational environment. *Method:* We analyzed SAFe to investigate how much guidance it provides concerning the collaboration between agile teams and their environment. *Results:* The results show that many different organizational parts exist with which agile teams have to collaborate. SAFe mentions concepts like shared services, system teams, or business teams, but there is no further guidance on collaboration with the agile team. *Conclusion:* We motivate future research into guidelines for efficient collaboration of agile teams with their organizational environment.

Keywords: Agile team · Dependency · Interface · Scaled Agile Framework

1 Introduction

Many software development teams already use agile development approaches like Scrum, eXtreme Programming or Kanban [1]. In an ideal agile environment, agile teams are small cross-functional teams that have all the competencies needed to ship product increments in regular short time intervals. They are self-empowered and can work without external dependencies. However, this ideal team setup is not always possible. For the development of large, complex products, many specialized skills are required that cannot all be part of a small agile team. Most of those roles are not required full-time, but only contribute in certain phases of the product development.

Therefore, agile software development teams have to collaborate with many different parties. In addition, teams need the support of different organizational functions like marketing, sales, or the human resources department [2]. Especially in established large companies, it is difficult to change the existing hierarchical structures, silo knowledge, and traditional mindset. For the development of safety-critical products like cars, traditional systems engineering processes are still in use and define a framework for the underlying agile, hybrid, or traditional subprojects [3]. This gap between the agile way of working of development teams and the traditional approach of the surrounding organization leads to problems regarding the collaboration between an agile

M. Paasivaara and P. Kruchten (Eds.): XP 2020 Workshops, LNBIP 396, pp. 219–226, 2020.
https://doi.org/10.1007/978-3-030-58858-8_22

team and its environment, so-called interface problems [2]. Since the environment is important in order to allow agile teams to thrive [4], efficient collaboration between agile teams and the environment on which they depend is important.

In this work, we analyze what guidance the Scaled Agile Framework (SAFe) provides regarding collaboration at the interface between an agile team and its environment. In Sect. 2, we provide further motivation for research on the collaboration between agile teams and their environment, and present the research question as well as our research approach. Section 3 presents the concepts of SAFe for synchronizing agile teams with their environment. In Sect. 4, we discuss how much guidance is provided and what guidance is lacking, and summarize the need for further research on this topic. Finally, we conclude the paper with suggestions for future work in Sect. 5.

2   Motivation and Research Approach

Challenges mentioned at the workshop A-Teams in 2019 [5] were that teams have "too many dependencies to others", a "lack of organizational support", and "part-time resources", which are all "interface problems" [2]. In the 2018 A-teams workshop [6], concerns like "coordination", "organizational context supporting autonomy", or "leadership" also address interface problems and were rated as having the highest priority.

The large-scale agile workshop [7] also identified "inter team communication" as a challenge, e.g., whether formal interfaces are needed or whether new or special roles need to be defined that intermediate between interface partners. "Agile transformation and business agility" was another challenge that deals with the alignment between business and IT, and "Scaling Agile" dealt with agile beyond software development.

Participants of the Agile Transformation workshop (A-Trans) 2019 [8] reported challenges like "hierarchical management and organizational boundaries", "integrating non-development functions", or "coordination challenges in multi-team environment".

The research themes from these workshops show the need to investigate how autonomous teams collaborate with their organizational environment. Every team is dependent on organizational functions, independent of whether they are part of a scaled agile project or working as a single team. In the scaled context, additional dependencies occur. Team-level agile methods like Scrum, Kanban, or XP only discuss a few of these dependencies, namely the interface to the customer in the form of the Product Owner, as well as the Scrum Master, who shields the team from negative influences from the organization or resolves impediments caused by the environment.

In order to get a more complete picture, we wanted to investigate so-called scaling agile frameworks in terms of their support of those interfaces. We initially considered the list collected for a comparison of scaling agile frameworks [9]. We then focused on the frameworks that not only deal with scaled product development (e.g., Scrum of Scrums, LeSS, or Nexus), but also offer solutions for a complete agile organization. The expectation was that these frameworks provide support when synchronizing agile teams with their environment.

We selected the Scaled Agile Framework (SAFe), the Disciplined Agile (DA) Framework, Scrum at Scale (SaS), and the lesser known Recipes for Agile

Governance (RAGE). These frameworks had the largest scope, thus we hoped to identify the most complete list of dependencies between agile teams and the rest of the organization.

For this work, we decided to focus on SAFe [10] as the most popular and most commonly used scaling framework [1]. Thus we defined the following research question:

RQ1. What guidance does SAFe provide for the collaboration between an agile team and its environment?

In order to answer this research question, the existing documentation on SAFe version 4.6 [10] was analyzed. The "Full SAFe" configuration was considered, covering all four levels (Team, Program, Large Solution, Portfolio). For each level, all concepts such as roles and practices are investigated by reading the information provided for each concept. In addition, "the foundation" of SAFe includes information about core values, the lean-agile mindset, SAFe principles, or guidelines for the implementation of SAFe. The "competencies for a lean enterprise" define five competencies regarding lean-agile leadership, team and technical agility, DevOps and release on demand, business solutions and lean systems engineering, and lean portfolio management. Finally, the "spanning palette" contains additional aspects that influence several levels, e.g., metrics, shared services, communities of practice, roadmap, or system teams.

First, a student researcher systematically went through all these parts of SAFe to identify all mentioned dependencies between an agile team and its environment and noted down all dependencies in a document. Independently, the two authors investigated SAFe regarding concepts that align the agile team with dependent organizational parts. This was not done systematically, but based on previous experiences of the authors with scaling agile frameworks in general and SAFe in particular. Afterwards, the two authors checked the dependencies found by the systematic analysis of the student researcher and had a closer look into the information that is provided by SAFe on how to handle these dependencies.

3 Results

Our analysis of SAFe [10] identified several concepts regarding the collaboration of agile teams with their organizational environment. We will present and explain the identified concepts in this section.

In SAFe, cross-functional agile teams are called **technical teams** – they have all the necessary skills to define, build, test, and deliver products. We will discuss how these technical teams are supported by their environment, explain the differences in the concepts of system teams, shared services, and business teams, and discuss how they collaborate with the technical team to generate value.

The **Agile Release Train (ART)** is the mechanism used to synchronize different agile teams when it comes to joint development of a product increment. Different teams work on parts of the solution and have joint planning, daily standups, reviews, and retrospectives. **Solution trains** coordinate multiple ARTs to build complex solutions. Solution trains include organizational functions in the form of business teams.

Both system teams and shared services work in an ART to support value generation. **System teams** provide support in building and maintaining the proper environment for development, testing, or integration. System teams are usually not cross-functional teams, since they only focus on one aspect, e.g., taking over end-to-end testing. A system team can be dedicated to supporting one ART, or it could support all ARTs in a solution train.

Shared services are specialist roles that are needed in an ART, but that cannot be dedicated to a team full-time. Examples are data security experts or database administrators. Shared services may be responsible for supporting a certain ART, or even multiple ARTs across the enterprise. One way of working with the ART is that shared service staff join a team for a short period of time, which also has the advantage that knowledge is shared, so dependencies on the shared service team might be reduced in the future. Shared services occasionally form a separate team. Anyway, they join in all synchronization events of an ART and help resolve all issues related to backlog items where their experience is needed.

Thus, the difference is that system teams are incorporated as a team into the ART, while shared services are not dedicated to a specific team, but rather flexibly support an ART by providing their experience when and where it is needed.

Business teams provide support regarding infrastructure, contracting, supplier management, legal guidance, marketing, security, compliance topics, etc. They collaborate with technical teams and are aligned via shared objectives and the same cadence.

SAFe defines a **three-step process** for aligning business teams with technical teams. Business teams have to first adopt the agile mindset by applying the principles of the Agile Manifesto to their work. This allows for a shared value system in the whole company and an increased understanding on how technical teams work. Teams also apply the typical Scrum practices, like sprint planning, daily scrum, demo, and retrospective, and use the Scrum roles (Scrum Master and Product Owner). If the business teams have understood and live the mindset, they join the value stream. This means the way they work has to change; e.g., business teams have to collaborate more closely with the technical teams. This could happen by including a whole business team into an ART, having a business team work in a separate ART within a solution train, or by including single experts into an agile team. Finally, business teams need to identify their own agile way of working by defining specialized principles and practices. The old processes that conflict with the nature of agile need to be evolved to allow for better integration of the way of working of agile teams and the ART.

SAFe also mentions **other ways to handle dependencies** between an agile team and its environment. One specific interface appears between the development team and **operations**. DevOps is mentioned as the agile product delivery competency that is used in ART and solution trains. However, the operation side is not further explained. Another specific interface mentioned for solution trains is the one towards **suppliers**. Suppliers are part of the solution train, so they are required to work in an agile way, sharing the same cadence and participating in all events of the ART. They are treated like an individual ART that develops a subsystem or capabilities for the value stream. Another important dependency is towards **customers** that are involved at every level, e.g., with the help of the role of the Product Owner.

4   Discussion and Related Work

In this section, the identified concepts for the collaboration between an agile team and its environment will be discussed and contrasted with related work. We will first discuss whether the existing guidance provided by the proposed concepts from SAFe is sufficient, especially highlighting any lack of guidance. Then we will discuss how SAFe provides guidance for the stepwise improvement of collaboration at the interface between technical and business teams aimed at agile collaboration. Finally, we will summarize the need for further research on collaboration between agile teams and the environment on which they depend.

Guidance Regarding Collaboration. In SAFe, the agile development team's autonomy depends on support by shared services, support by system teams, and collaboration with business teams. SAFe defines these concepts with different levels of involvement in the development processes of an agile team. Some constraints are defined, such as working in the same cadence, or that synchronization happens throughout the events of the agile release train, such as joint planning, daily synchronization, product demonstration, and retrospectives. Thus, SAFe provides concrete guidance on the synchronization mechanisms that can be used.

However, it remains unclear whether the information and collaboration needs of all related stakeholders can be fulfilled by participating in these joint events. Some stakeholders might not benefit from participating in every event. On the other hand, satisfying the needs of all additional stakeholders might extend the scope and the intention of the normal sprint events, leading to increased time effort to conduct these meetings. Since product development happens in a cadence, it might not always be possible for shared service staff or business teams to attend multiple sprint events of several teams within the same ART.

There is also no concrete guidance on synchronization between a cross-functional agile delivery team and a functional system team, e.g., on how an agile software development team coordinates testing with one or multiple system teams that are responsible for end-to-end testing.

When setting up an ART, there is no help regarding the decision on what expertise has to be incorporated into the agile teams, or generally into the ART, and what expertise only collaborates with the agile team, e.g., in the form of business teams or shared services. This was also identified as a challenge in [11]. Developing criteria on when to use one or the other concept could be beneficial to practitioners. DevOps could be an example of how to bring two different functional teams closer together, and similar concepts could be developed for the collaboration between the agile team and other organizational functions.

Guidance is also needed on how agile teams should coordinate activities such as architecture or testing within a scaled product development. As an example, [12] investigated the collaboration between architects and agile teams - similar guidance is needed for other aspects.

SAFe only prescribes how to synchronize in the process, but does not talk about how to manage the information or products that are shared at the interface between an agile team and another party. Explicitly defining such so-called boundary objects that are exchanged across team borders [13] could improve collaboration, as SAFe does not provide information on what artifacts need to be exchanged or on which concrete information is shared.

Transition to Agile Collaboration. SAFe provides an example of how business teams align with the agile teams they support within an ART. A three-step process for integrating business functions into the ART is defined (cf. Sect. 3, business teams). First, business teams are required to understand agile and live the mindset themselves. In practice, companies that start with an agile transformation using SAFe adapt the framework to their own purpose and situation. Often, the surrounding organization is not touched and business functions continue to work in their established processes. A survey of SAFe adoptions also reported challenges regarding mindset change [14]. Guidance for assessing and improving the agility of teams is provided by [15].

As a second step, agile business teams need to join the ART in order to have a shared cadence and synchronization points. There is not much guidance on the way business functions have to collaborate with agile teams, or whether this collaboration is feasible for every business function.

Finally, business teams are supposed to improve their process in order to create their own agile way of working that harmonizes with the development flow of the ART. Guidance is missing for different business functions on what this collaboration could look like in detail.

Summarizing the Need for Further Research. In summary, the autonomy of an agile team highly depends on its environment. [16] also claims that the organizational culture and structures need to be adapted in order to increase the autonomy of an agile team. When synchronizing agile teams with their environment, the production and control structures influence the autonomy of agile teams [17]. Thus, it is important to be aware of the environment of an agile team, explicitly considering how to synchronize and what information to share.

Hence, it must first be understood with what parties an agile team has to collaborate. SAFe already mentions some dependent functions and responsibilities, but does not try to provide a complete view. More interfaces not explicitly addressed by SAFe exist, e.g., synchronizing agile development with a product line approach [18]. An initial overview of the dependencies of agile teams on their environment is provided by [2]. A possible next step for research would be to refine this classification of interfaces to understand what concrete dependencies exist in order to be able to find solutions.

SAFe provides synchronization concepts that could be used to improve the collaboration between an agile team and its environment, but there needs to be further research on when a certain concept is suitable for solving a certain dependency. In addition, SAFe does not provide guidelines about the content of the synchronization. Providing guidelines on what information to exchange or which artifacts to share at a certain interface could benefit practitioners. A final step would be to combine the "what" and the "how" to explain how the collaboration mechanisms can be used to convey certain information or artifacts.

5   Conclusion and Future Work

Autonomous agile teams often have dependencies on their organizational environment. In order to improve the efficiency of these agile teams, collaboration with their environment has to be improved. The Scaled Agile Framework (SAFe) was reviewed to analyze what guidance exists for managing the dependencies of agile teams. SAFe provides concepts like system teams, business teams, or shared services that define different levels of involvement, but does not provide details on what efficient collaboration should look like.

In future work, we want to list existing dependencies by analyzing all scaling frameworks. It would also be interesting to look at other sources, such as PMBOK or CMMI, and evaluate how their recommendations are applicable to handling dependencies. Based on the results, those dependencies that need most research can be prioritized in order to find solutions for specific interfaces or identify strategies or patterns for collaboration that are commonly applicable.

Acknowledgments. This research is funded by the German Ministry of Education and Research (BMBF) as part of a Software Campus project (01IS17047). We would like to thank Sonnhild Namingha for proofreading the final version of this paper.

References

1. VersionOne: 12th Annual State of Agile TM Report (2018) https://www.versionone.com/
2. Theobald, S., Diebold, P.: Interface problems of agile in a non-agile environment. In: Garbajosa, J., Wang, X., Aguiar, A. (eds.) XP 2018. LNBIP, vol. 314, pp. 123–130. Springer, Cham (2018). https://doi.org/10.1007/978-3-319-91602-6_8
3. Marner, K., Theobald, S., Wagner, S.: Release planning in a hybrid project environment. In: Przybyłek, A., Morales-Trujillo, M.E. (eds.) LASD/MIDI -2019. LNBIP, vol. 376, pp. 19–40. Springer, Cham (2020). https://doi.org/10.1007/978-3-030-37534-8_2
4. Krieg, A., Theobald, S., Küpper, S.: Erfolgreiche agile Projekte benötigen ein agiles Umfeld. In: Mikuzs, M., Volland, A., Engstler, M., Hanser, E., Linssen, O. (eds.) Projektmanagement und Vorgehensmodelle 2018 - Der Einfluss der Digitalisierung auf Projektmanagementmethoden und Entwicklungsprozesse, pp. 217–222. Gesellschaft für Informatik, Bonn (2018)
5. Moe, N.B., Stray, V., Hoda, R.: Trends and updated research agenda for autonomous agile teams: a summary of the second international workshop at XP2019. In: Hoda, R. (ed.) XP 2019. LNBIP, vol. 364, pp. 13–19. Springer, Cham (2019). https://doi.org/10.1007/978-3-030-30126-2_2
6. Stray, V., Moe, N.B., Hoda, R.: Autonomous agile teams: challenges and future directions for research. In: Proceedings of the 19th International Conference on Agile Software Development: Companion, pp. 1–5. ACM, Porto (2018)
7. Bass, J.M.: Future trends in agile at scale: a summary of the 7th international workshop on large-scale agile development. In: Hoda, R. (ed.) XP 2019. LNBIP, vol. 364, pp. 75–80. Springer, Cham (2019). https://doi.org/10.1007/978-3-030-30126-2_9
8. Barroca, L., Dingsøyr, T., Mikalsen, M.: Agile transformation: a summary and research agenda from the first international workshop. In: Hoda, R. (ed.) XP 2019. LNBIP, vol. 364, pp. 3–9. Springer, Cham (2019). https://doi.org/10.1007/978-3-030-30126-2_1

9. Diebold, P., Schmitt, A., Theobald, S.: Scaling agile: how to select the most appropriate framework. In: Proceedings of the 19th International Conference on Agile Software Development: Companion (XP 2018), pp. 1–4. Association for Computing Machinery, New York (2018). Article 7. https://doi.org/10.1145/3234152.3234177

10. Scaled Agile Framework (2019). http://www.scaledagileframework.com/. Accessed 01 Dec 2019

11. Putta, A., Paasivaara, M., Lassenius, C.: How are agile release trains formed in practice? A case study in a large financial corporation. In: Kruchten, P., Fraser, S., Coallier, F. (eds.) XP 2019. LNBIP, vol. 355, pp. 154–170. Springer, Cham (2019). https://doi.org/10.1007/978-3-030-19034-7_10

12. Uludağ, Ö., Kleehaus, M., Erçelik, S., Matthes, F.: Using social network analysis to investigate the collaboration between architects and agile teams: a case study of a large-scale agile development program in a german consumer electronics company. In: Kruchten, P., Fraser, S., Coallier, F. (eds.) XP 2019. LNBIP, vol. 355, pp. 137–153. Springer, Cham (2019). https://doi.org/10.1007/978-3-030-19034-7_9

13. Wohlrab, R., Pelliccione, P., Knauss, E., Larsson, M.: Boundary objects in Agile practices: continuous management of systems engineering artifacts in the automotive domain. In: Proceedings of the 2018 International Conference on Software and System Process (ICSSP 2018), pp. 31–40. Association for Computing Machinery, New York (2018). https://doi.org/10.1145/3202710.3203155

14. Laanti, M., Kettunen, P.: SAFe adoptions in Finland: a survey research. In: Hoda, R. (ed.) XP 2019. LNBIP, vol. 364, pp. 81–87. Springer, Cham (2019). https://doi.org/10.1007/978-3-030-30126-2_10

15. Guckenbiehl, P., Theobald, S.: Assessment of agile culture. In: PVM 2019, p. 165 (2019)

16. Spiegler, S.V., Heinecke, C., Wagner, S.: The influence of culture and structure on autonomous teams in established companies. In: Hoda, R. (ed.) XP 2019. LNBIP, vol. 364, pp. 46–54. Springer, Cham (2019). https://doi.org/10.1007/978-3-030-30126-2_6

17. Mikalsen, M., Næsje, M., Reime, E.A., Solem, A.: Agile autonomous teams in complex organizations. In: Hoda, R. (ed.) XP 2019. LNBIP, vol. 364, pp. 55–63. Springer, Cham (2019). https://doi.org/10.1007/978-3-030-30126-2_7

18. Hohl, P., Theobald, S., Becker, M., Stupperich, M., Münch, J.: Mapping agility to automotive software product line concerns. In: Kuhrmann, M., et al. (eds.) PROFES 2018. LNCS, vol. 11271, pp. 409–421. Springer, Cham (2018). https://doi.org/10.1007/978-3-030-03673-7_32

Understanding Work Practices of Autonomous Agile Teams: A Social-psychological Review

Lucas Gren[1,2(✉)]

[1] Chalmers | University of Gothenburg, Gothenburg, Sweden
lucas.gren@lucasgren.com
[2] Volvo Cars, Gothenburg, Sweden

Abstract. The purpose of this paper is to suggest additional aspects of social psychology that could help when making sense of autonomous agile teams. To make use of well-tested theories in social psychology and instead see how they replicated and differ in the autonomous agile team context would avoid reinventing the wheel. This was done, as an initial step, through looking at some very common agile practices and relate them to existing findings in social-psychological research. The two theories found that I argue could be more applied to the software engineering context are social identity theory and group socialization theory. The results show that literature provides social-psychological reasons for the popularity of some agile practices, but that scientific studies are needed to gather empirical evidence on these under-researched topics. Understanding deeper psychological theories could provide a better understanding of the psychological processes when building autonomous agile team, which could then lead to better predictability and intervention in relation to human factors.

Keywords: Programming · Social psychology · Agile practices · Teams

1 Introduction

The importance of understanding team autonomy has increased in the last decades due to agile development processes [1]. There have been studies on the barriers of self-organization in agile teams [2], the emerging roles of self-organizing agile teams and how these roles enable agility [3], and the role of senior management [4] to just mention a few. Some authors, like Moe et al. [5], suggest using theories from social psychology to better understand team autonomy. They refer to studies on self-organization in psychology but here are many more theories in that field that would make sense to use in the software development context. The two theories from social psychology, namely Social Identity Theory and Group Socialization Theory where selected from a textbook on social psychology [6]. I do not consider these theories more important

M. Paasivaara and P. Kruchten (Eds.): XP 2020 Workshops, LNBIP 396, pp. 227–235, 2020.
https://doi.org/10.1007/978-3-030-58858-8_23

than others, they were only selected based on the vast number of studies on them in the last decades. Therefore, they seem to be quite robust and relevant to investigate in the software development context. Some results might replicate, but others might not.

In order to theoretically analyze these two theories from social psychology and their connection to agile teams, I use the study by So [7] in which the author divide common agile practices into *core, technical, team interaction,* and *customer interaction* practices. Due to saving space, I selected only the *core* and *team interaction* practices (five in total) for this paper. I do not consider these practices to cover all aspects of agility nor to be the most important agile practices, however, the practices chosen are widely used in industry [8].

I will describe the general agile work practices and connect these to existing social, management, and organizational psychology findings, but I will start by presenting the two important psychological theories that are in focus.

2 Important Psychological Theories

I have chosen to focus on two popular theories in social psychology on which none or very few studies exist in software engineering research. The first one is group socialization, which can be defined as the "dynamic relationship between the group and its members that describes the passage of members through a group in terms of commitment and of changing roles" [6]. The idea is that a new team members will go through a certain set of phases through the group's lifespan. The group as a whole will evaluate a new member first by assessing how much a potential new member can contribute to the group's goal-fulfillment. The individual will also assess how much the group can fulfill their personal needs. Step two is commitment, which takes the outcome from the evaluation as input and is an assessment of both parties' beliefs about the rewadingness (i.e. the quality of being rewarding) of the relationship (and other alternative ones). The last phase is role transition in which the commitment reaches a critical level and the relationship thereby changes. These three phases are continuously depending on the result of the assessment. The individual goes through five phases of group socialization: (1) Investigation, (2) Socialization, (3) Maintenance, (4) Resocialization, and (5) Remembrance. These phases have transition steps in-between that are: (1) Entry, (2) Acceptance, (3) Divergence, and (4) Exit [9].

Group socialization is separate from stages that the whole group goes through together. The most famous and used model of group development was introduced in 1965 by Tuckman [10]. He integrated many theories and research findings into a model with the four stages Forming, Storming, Norming, and Performing. The forming stage is when the group is new and need to set the stage and figure our what it is supposed to do and who can do what. Storming is a conflict stage where people now feel safe to question the other team members, which is needed to figure out good group goals and good strategies of work. The Norming phase is when the group starts to set group norms of their collaboration and know how to organize to be productive, and the final stage, Performing, is when the team can focus the most of being productive because they have created a system of good collaboration and effective conflict resolution techniques. These phases are similar to the ones suggested by Agazarian and Gantt [11] in systems centered theory, and what Wheelan [12] also suggested as an integrated model of group development.

Another well-researched approach to explaining many group phenomena is the social identity theory (see e.g. Hewstone et al. [13] or Hogg [6]). Not only has the theory gained empirical evidence in social psychology research but also in quite recent research in social neuroscience (see e.g. van Bavel and Cunningham [14]). To understand that theory, we first need to understand the concepts on which it is based. Social categorization is the classification of people into different social groups, which is a deeply-rooted human trait, and a person's social identity is the part of the self that is derived from the various memberships we have in social groups. Social identity theory is, therefore, the theory of group membership and intergroup relations based on self-categorization, social comparison and a self-definition regarding in-group[1] properties (i.e. a prototype[2]). Self-categorization is how we categorize ourselves and thereby construct a social identity [15]. According to the minimal group paradigm [16], even explicitly random group assignments trigger discriminatory behavior against an out-group[3]. The idea is that a successful intergroup bias creates or protects (high) in-group status, which provides a positive social identity (which in turn satisfies group-members' need for positive self-esteem[4]). Researchers have successfully explained how groups gain positive self-esteem through intergroup bias but have been less successful when explaining intergroup bias motives due to threats or depressed self-esteem [13]. However, Hogg and Williams [15] suggest that competition for positive social identity characterizes intergroup behavior.

3   Agile Practices and Social Psychology

3.1   Iterative Development – A Core Practice of Agile Development

Delivering in short iterations has high face validity, but when broken down, these ideas include a diversity of competences and dynamics needed by the agile team to deliver value in such short iterations. In more general management research, there has been more thorough research on which general work practices contribute to performance (see e.g. Combs et al. [17]) and to successfully implement iterative development, the team must have a high degree and maturity of, for example, staffing, decentralized decision-making, and communication [18]. So to understand the dynamics of iterative development, we should consider these confounding factors before we, as researchers, jump to conclusions about other found effects.

---

[1] A group that an individual is a member of [6].
[2] Cognitive representation of the typical/ideal defining features of a category [6].
[3] A group that an individual is not a member of [6].
[4] Feelings about and evaluations of oneself [6].

3.2   Iteration Planning – A Teamwork Practice

Obtaining empowered and motivated individuals that have the needed support to solve any given task together with high levels of trust, are all aspects known to be necessary [19] but are not always in place [20]. Creating a shared vision has also been shown in research to be a key for success since the beginning of the 1990s and is one of the main components of transformational leadership [21]. A shared vision is necessary since the team needs an overall goal to break down when planning the upcoming iteration. Regarding the importance of simplicity in agile is somewhat connected to the concept of reducing waste in lean manufacturing, together with the continued avoidance of doing unnecessary activities in the project (or process) life-cycle [22]. To plan in such a way, the team must know the members' real competences and abilities, which also implies maturity in the development process and that the members of the group are committed and fully integrated into the group. With such prerequisites, understanding the group socialization process then becomes paramount when understanding how teams plan in short iterations.

3.3   Stand-Up Meetings – A Teamwork Practice

Developers, but also business people and testers, should be on the same team and collaboratively work together through the whole project life-cycle (i.e. having cross-functional teams). When connecting the popularity of having cross-functional teams in the modern workplace (see e.g. Denison et al. [23]) to social identity theory, it becomes clear that it, in fact, decreases intergroup bias. Having these various organizational functions share their chores and issues often, would be expected to increase cohesion and understanding of the whole project through shared mental models, which have also gained initial empirical support [24]. Having social identity theory and intergroup bias as factors in software engineering research would then probably increase the explained variance.

3.4   Retrospectives – A Teamwork Practice

The idea of a retrospective meeting is that the team should reflect on possible improvement points about their teamwork at the end of each iteration [25]. More generally, such reflective meetings are often called *team debriefs*, and have been shown with scientific rigor to increase effectiveness [26]. McHugh et al. [19] found that these types of meeting need work and careful guidance to function in their intended way also in software development. In a recent longitudinal study, Lehtinen et al. [27] showed that, initially, newly formed teams focus more on task progress and task outcome and, as the teams mature, they focus to a larger extent on process and cooperation. Such findings also relate the "agility" of a team to group socialization and group development since members of the group will behave differently depending on how well integrated they are in the team [9], meaning that a well-integrated individual will be more likely to perform retrospectives in the way they are intended. If the socialization process is not a part of understanding the dynamics of retrospective meetings, studies will have difficulty explaining and predicting patterns of behavior.

3.5   Co-location – A Teamwork Practice

Having the team co-located in the same room with requirements as sticky notes on physical boards have been promoted by the agile community in order to, again, increase the velocity of the development in a rapidly changing environment. Many cases have been reported where the communication challenges of distributed teams have been satisfactory dealt with using modern technology and slightly different practices (see e.g. Berczuk [28]). Another study showed that both agile and traditional projects have the same issues regarding co-location [29]. All-in-all, every social aspect of building relationships will become more cumbersome with distance and implies that more effort is needed to mitigate these challenges [30]. Since the social problems are amplified with distance, failing to understand their influence in distributed agile teams will have even larger negative effects on teamwork. And since agile processes are dependent on the team as a working unit, understanding the social aspects of both distributed and co-located teams are a key to building effective agile teams.

4   Discussion and Implications

As we have seen in this review, there is a lot of overlap between existing knowledge of, and research on, the workplace in general and the agile practices. A few internal organizational examples being decreasing inter-group bias through cross-functional teams [23], striving towards self-organization of teams in order to increase responsiveness to change [18], creating organizational citizenship behavior through shared visions [21], empowerment and trust [31], and removing *waste* in the process [22]. All these aspect are of interest to agile software engineering researchers when trying to understand the development of software using agile teams because these theories might add explanatory power to the observed behaviors.

However, the theory could be seen as complex and hard to grasp for people without any behavioral science education, which means researchers must first run experiments to gather empirical evidence in order to eventually build a theory of "agility," and then provide scientifically founded and validated guidelines to practitioners. One large hurdle of achieving this, though, is the fact that an overwhelming majority of human factors research in software engineering is conducted by software engineering researchers interested in psychology and not psychology researchers interested in software engineering, which often means that the research findings have little depth and offer little new insights from a psychological perspective. I will not cite any studies here due to the fact that such studies were conducted with the best of intentions and do have high value in that they have highlighted the importance of looking at psychological factors in the software engineering domain, which was not the case at all before.

Social identity theory could be utterly useful when navigating through the added complexity of the different social relationship surfacing in an agile project. Hogg and Williams [32] explicitly suggest a set of propositions for how social identity and self-categorization relate to the organizational context. One of their propositions is that changes in which out-groups the in-group compares itself to, will change the view of the group's own identity, including the properties of the ideal member (i.e. the prototype). Another proposition is that harmonious relations between different subgroups of the organization is best kept by recognizing both the subgroups (e.g. Quality Assurance Engineer, Software Developers, Software Tester, etc.) and other organizational constellations, including the teams and the company as a whole. This means that the cross-functional agile teams must recognize both the value of the team as a whole but also the different roles and make distinctions between them. All these aspects should be part of agile team measurements in the future in order to fully make sense of the agile team context.

When looking at the descriptions of the agile practices overall, many of the internal practices seem to assume full group-membership seen from a group socialization perspective [9]. They also assume the entire work-group to be mature from a developmental perspective [10]. In order to fully understand the social-psychological components of the team-based workplace in general, and the agile context in particular, we also need to investigate the temporal perspective of the interplay between group development, group socialization, and the agile approach to projects by setting up autonomous teams.

As have also been shown in this short review, the prescribed behavior in these agile practices are well-founded in social psychology, which provides social-psychological reasons for their popularity. The reason for this is that if the agile practices enable mechanisms known to work well for people in other contexts, it is likely that they would also be appropriate in some variation in the agile context. One example is the decrease of intergroup bias by having cross-functional teams. Therefore, I argue for that these theories should be applied more to the study of autonomous agile teams. In the review by [33], they also call for more theory-based research since the current status of the field mostly comprises method-specific case studies, which is particularly the case in software engineering studies on human factors. In this present study, I have explained some social-psychological underpinnings in relation to five common agile practices, which contributes to founding agile practices in more general social psychology theories. An understanding of such underpinnings can help abstract the essentials of agile software development as opposed to other approaches, but also guide researchers in conducting experiments using theory from social psychology in the software development context. Many of the agile principles are far from new in relation to human knowledge of work-groups. However, what might be considered as having gotten a stronger acceptance is the implementation of being responsive to change. The reasons for not relating agile software development to any existing science outside of software engineering might be due to lack of research knowledge from practitioners, but it might also reflect the difficulty of interdisciplinary research.

5   Conclusion

Without understanding the psychology of groups, agile maturity survey findings are hard to use in order to improve one's own practices. Relating agile practices to deeper psychological theories, like in this study, could instead provide a deeper understanding of the psychological processes of implementing autonomous agile teams.

References

1. Moe, N.B., Stray, V., Hoda, R.: Trends and updated research agenda for autonomous agile teams: a summary of the second international workshop at XP2019. In: Hoda, R. (ed.) XP 2019. LNBIP, vol. 364, pp. 13–19. Springer, Cham (2019). https://doi.org/10.1007/978-3-030-30126-2_2
2. Moe, N.B., Dingsøyr, T., Dybå, T.: Understanding self-organizing teams in agile software development. In: 19th Australian Conference on Software Engineering (ASWEC 2008), pp. 76–85. IEEE (2008)
3. Hoda, R., Noble, J., Marshall, S.: Self-organizing roles on agile software development teams. IEEE Trans. Softw. Eng. **39**(3), 422–444 (2012)
4. Hoda, R., Noble, J., Marshall, S.: Supporting self-organizing agile teams. In: Sillitti, A., Hazzan, O., Bache, E., Albaladejo, X. (eds.) XP 2011. LNBIP, vol. 77, pp. 73–87. Springer, Heidelberg (2011). https://doi.org/10.1007/978-3-642-20677-1_6
5. Moe, N.B., Dingsyr, T., Kvangardsnes, O.: Understanding shared leadership in agile development: a case study. In: 2009 42nd Hawaii International Conference on System Sciences, pp. 1–10. IEEE (2009)
6. Hogg, M.A., Vaughan, G.M.: Social Psychology, 7th edn. Pearson, Harlow (2014)
7. So, C.: Making Software Teams Effective: How Agile Practices Lead to Project Success Through Teamwork Mechanisms. Peter Lang, Frankfurt am Main (2010)
8. Licorish, S.A., et al.: Adoption and suitability of software development methods and practices. In: 23rd Asia-Pacific Software Engineering Conference (APSEC), pp. 369–372, December 2016
9. Levine, J.M., Moreland, R.L.: Group socialization: theory and research. Eur. Rev. Soc. Psychol. **5**(1), 305–336 (1994)
10. Tuckman, B.W.: Developmental sequence in small groups. Psychol. Bull. **63**(6), 384–399 (1965)
11. Agazarian, Y., Gantt, S.: Phases of group development: systems-centered hypotheses and their implications for research and practice. Group Dyn. Theory Res. Pract. **7**(3), 238 (2003)
12. Wheelan, S.: Group Processes: A Developmental Perspective, 2nd edn. Allyn and Bacon, Boston (2005)
13. Hewstone, M., Rubin, M., Willis, H.: Intergroup bias. Annu. Rev. Psychol. **53**(1), 575–604 (2002)
14. van Bavel, J.J., Cunningham, W.A.: A social neuroscience approach to self and social categorisation: a new look at an old issue. Eur. Rev. Soc. Psychol. **21**(1), 237–284 (2010)

15. Hogg, M.A., Williams, K.D.: From I to we: social identity and the collective self. Group Dyn. Theory Res. Pract. **4**(1), 81 (2000)
16. Tajfel, H., Billig, M.G., Bundy, R.P., Flament, C.: Social categorization and intergroup behaviour. Eur. J. Soc. Psychol. **1**(2), 149–178 (1971)
17. Combs, J., Liu, Y., Hall, A., Ketchen, D.: How much do high-performance work practices matter? A meta-analysis of their effects on organizational performance. Pers. Psychol. **59**(3), 501–528 (2006)
18. Evans, W.R., Davis, W.D.: High-performance work systems and organizational performance: the mediating role of internal social structure. J. Manag. **31**(5), 758–775 (2005)
19. McHugh, O., Conboy, K., Lang, M.: Agile practices: the impact on trust in software project teams. IEEE Softw. **29**(3), 71–76 (2012)
20. Buchanan, D.A.: You stab my back, I'll stab yours: management experience and perceptions of organization political behaviour. Br. J. Manag. **19**(1), 49–64 (2008)
21. Bass, B.M.: From transactional to transformational leadership: learning to share the vision. Organ. Dyn. **18**(3), 19–31 (1990)
22. Hicks, B.J.: Lean information management: understanding and eliminating waste. Int. J. Inf. Manag. **27**(4), 233–249 (2007)
23. Denison, D.R., Hart, S.L., Kahn, J.A.: From chimneys to cross-functional teams: developing and validating a diagnostic model. Acad. Manag. J. **39**(4), 1005–1023 (1996)
24. Stray, V., Sjøberg, D.I., Dybå, T.: The daily stand-up meeting: a grounded theory study. J. Syst. Softw. **114**, 101–124 (2016)
25. Derby, E., Larsen, D.: Agile Retrospectives: Making Good Teams Great. Pragmatic Bookshelf, Raleigh (2006)
26. Tannenbaum, S.I., Cerasoli, C.P.: Do team and individual debriefs enhance performance? A meta-analysis. Hum. Factors **55**(1), 231–245 (2013)
27. Lehtinen, T.O., Itkonen, J., Lassenius, C.: Recurring opinions or productive improvements – what agile teams actually discuss in retrospectives. Empir. Softw. Eng. **22**(5), 2409–2452 (2017)
28. Berczuk, S.: Back to basics: the role of agile principles in success with a distributed scrum team. In: Agile Conference (AGILE), 2007, pp. 382–388. IEEE (2007)
29. Noll, J., Beecham, S., Richardson, I.: Global software development and collaboration: barriers and solutions. ACM Inroads **1**(3), 66–78 (2010)
30. Alzoubi, Y.I., Gill, A.Q., Al-Ani, A.: Empirical studies of geographically distributed agile development communication challenges: a systematic review. Inf. Manag. **53**(1), 22–37 (2016)
31. Wat, D., Shaffer, M.A.: Equity and relationship quality influences on organizational citizenship behaviors: the mediating role of trust in the supervisor and empowerment. Pers. Rev. **34**(4), 406–422 (2005)
32. Hogg, M.A., Terry, D.I.: Social identity and self-categorization processes in organizational contexts. Acad. Manag. Rev. **25**(1), 121–140 (2000)
33. Dingsøyr, T., Nerur, S., Balijepally, V., Moe, N.B.: A decade of agile methodologies: towards explaining agile software development. J. Syst. Softw. **85**, 1213–1221 (2012)

Spotify Tailoring for Architectural Governance

Abdallah Salameh$^{(\boxtimes)}$ and Julian M. Bass

University of Salford, 43 Crescent, Salford M5 4WT, UK
a.salameh@edu.salford.ac.uk, j.bass@salford.ac.uk

Abstract. Organisations usually tailor Agile methods to fit their needs best. Spotify has developed its own Agile culture to facilitate software development for hundreds of developers across multiple cities. The Spotify model has become influential among agile proponents and hence formed the basis of methods used in other organisations. We have identified a lack of research into agile architecture using the Spotify model.

To explore *How can architectural governance increase the autonomy of teams when using the Spotify model?*, an intervention embedded case study was conducted in a multinational FinTech organisation, using the Spotify model. New processes were introduced by developing and evaluating an approach to Agile architectural governance. This approach incorporates a structural change and a change management process. We conducted 6 semi-structured open-ended interviews and direct observations of Agile practices. The collected data was analysed using Thematic Analysis and informed by some Grounded Theory techniques.

The practitioners in our study report benefits of this evaluated approach. These benefits include transforming architectural based decision into decentralised based decision-making, strengthening the autonomy of squads through aligning architectural based decisions, sharing the architectural knowledge among the squads, and other benefits.

We identify the characteristics and benefits of our evaluated approach to Agile architectural governance using the Spotify model. Also, we identify guidelines and challenges for those wishing to adopt this approach.

Keywords: Spotify tailoring · Architecture governance · Autonomous teams · Large-scale · FinTech · Intervention embedded case study

1 Introduction

The introduction of agile software development has shifted the focus from the individual level into the team level by employing self-organising autonomous teams [8]. These teams should be aligned with each other and to common product development objectives to enable their autonomy [9]. Previous research has identified the topic of autonomous teams as immature within software engineering because of some identified challenges that need addressing [12].

© The Author(s) 2020
M. Paasivaara and P. Kruchten (Eds.): XP 2020 Workshops, LNBIP 396, pp. 236–244, 2020.
https://doi.org/10.1007/978-3-030-58858-8_24

The Spotify model is an example of an agile approach that is driven by creating autonomous, yet aligned squads (i.e., teams) [6]. In our previous work on Spotify Tailoring, we have identified tailored practices that promote effectiveness in autonomous squads [9] and have revealed a novel approach to agile tailoring using the Spotify model, which we called Heterogeneous Tailoring [11]. Two key features characterise this approach. Firstly, each autonomous cross-functional squad is empowered to select and tailor its development method. Secondly, each squad is aligned with other squads and to common product development goals.

One of the identified challenges to the Heterogeneous Tailoring approach is the need for aligning and governing architectural decisions across autonomous squads [11]. In the same way, previous research on the topic of autonomous teams has identified the coordination of system architecture among autonomous teams as a challenge that needs exploration [12]. Often, positions are linked to individuals, which leads to a bottle neck since one person bears many responsibilities and has to reply to many different demands simultaneously [4]. External dependencies to one person decreases team autonomy and its innovation. We found that our case study organisation utilises a centralised architectural decision-making while using the Spotify model.

Our research question in this study is: *How can architectural governance increase the autonomy of teams when using the Spotify model?* To answer this question, we have conducted an intervention embedded case study in a multi-national FinTech organisation uses the Spotify model with a large-scale project. In this intervention, we develop and evaluate an approach to architectural governance. In this approach, we introduce specific roles in each squad to increase autonomy within squads instead of relying on one person (i.e., architect) who is responsible for all teams. Also, we introduce a change management process to streamline the agile architecture process among the stakeholder. During this intervention trial, we have conducted a direct observation of 23 ceremonies over 9 weeks. After that, 6 semi-structured interviews were conducted.

The practitioners in our study report benefits of this approach such as transforming architectural decision-making into decentralised based decision-making, resolving conflicted architectural decisions and mitigating key technical risks across autonomous squads, strengthening the autonomy of squads through aligning architectural based decisions, and other benefits.

In this paper, we identify the characteristics and benefits of our evaluated approach to architectural governance. Also, we identify guidelines and challenges for those wishing to adopt this approach using the Spotify model.

2   Background

2.1   The Spotify Model

The Spotify model, which was introduced by Henrik Kniberg [6,9], has been developed to utilise agile development with hundreds of developers that are distributed among many squads and across 4 cities. The overall structure consists, mainly, of Squads, Chapters, Guilds and Tribes. A Tribe is a collection of co-located squads with less than 100 members and aims to promote collaboration among the squads. Within the same Tribe, there are small groups of people, called Chapters, that work within the same competency area and have similar skill sets. While Chapters are always located within a specific Tribe, there are groups of people, called Guilds, who are wide-reaching with a desire to share knowledge across the whole organisation.

A squad leader is responsible for communicating what problem needs to be solved and why. Squads' job is to collaborate to find a solution [6]. A Squad has access to a coach, which is responsible for improving squads' ways of working. Each squad has a Product Owner, who is responsible for prioritising the work, matching product backlog for each squad, and maintaining a high-level roadmap for the organisation.

2.2   Agile Architecture

Iterative and incremental way of architecture evolution is recognised by previous research as an agile way to reduce Big Design Up-Front and to keep a project synchronised with the latest changing conditions [7]. Previous research realised the coexistence of software architectures and agile development in the utilisation of identified architecting activities and approaches, as well as agile architecting practices [13]. Yang et al. [13] identified 41 agile architecting practices. However, only a few of these practices have been widely employed in practice and discussed in the literature – such as Backlog, Sprint, Iterative and Incremental Development, Just Enough Architectural Work, and Continuous Integration.

Neglecting certain architectural considerations even early in the software development process can make architectural refactoring costly [2]. What teams build is influenced and constrained by how they build it. Yet, how teams build something is affected and also constrained by their design and architecture [2]. Hence, agile practitioners need to focus on *"what architectural issues block a team's agility"* to achieve technical excellence, good design and improve the agility of software development [2]. For instance, modular architecture and microservices are identified as prerequisites for applying agile practices [5].

3   Research Design and Methodology

Our case study is carried out in a multinational FinTech organisation that employs around 650 people in 60 markets. This organisation processes around 60 billion € per year. Our case study project is considered as an offshore outsourced FinTech project, which manages hundreds of autonomous financial services. The development programme of our case study project is of large-scale size (<100 people). The developers are distributed over 6 squads. Also, there is 1 Architect, 3 Key Account Managers, 5 Product Owners, 2 Agile Coaches, and 1 Test Lead.

The intervention embedded case-study was conducted in one squad and two Chapters within the case study organisation. This squad consists of 6 developers – 2 of them are Chapter Leaders. The data were collected through direct observation of agile practices for 9 weeks, during which 23 ceremonies were observed. After the intervention trial, 6 semi-structured open-ended interviews were conducted and continued for around 50 min. After the second interview, the questions were revised. After conducting each interview, the recording was transcribed verbatim and analysed in a continuous basis.

The collected data was analysed using Thematic Analysis [1] and informed by some Grounded Theory techniques [3]. Our analysis was carried out by following the six steps proposed by Braun and Clarke [1]: (1) familiarising with the data, (2) generating initial codes, (3) searching for themes, (4) themes review and refinement, (5) defining and naming themes, and (6) writing the final report. During these steps, we utilised some Grounded Theories techniques such as continuous memoing, open coding, constant comparison, and sorting [3]. Furthermore, the observations were analysed and compared to the derived themes from the analysed interviews. In result, minor contradictions were identified, which were explored and accommodated accordingly.

4   Findings

This section presents the findings of our study, before and after conducting the intervention embedded case study. Also, this section describes the characteristics of our introduced architecture governance approach, which incorporates an organisational structural change and a change management process. Moreover, this section describes the reported benefits and challenges of the evaluated approach.

4.1   Before Conducting the Intervention – Baseline

Before starting this intervention embedded case-study, our case-study organisation was utilising Spotify's organisational structure while exercising a centralised based architectural decision-making because of the complexity of this FinTech project. Practitioners say: *"Despite having chapters communities, I was the main reference for all squads when it comes to any architectural based change because of the complexity of the project"*–P2, Enterprise Architect. Also,   *"we (developers) were always turning to our architect when it comes to architectural based decisions to figure out the best way to perform an architectural change"*–P4, Senior Developer and Chapter Leader. However, our case study organisation had challenges in aligning and governing architectural decisions across autonomous squads. *"The size of the development programme is now much larger than what it was 3 years ago... I'm overloaded with many responsibilities, which in turn causes a delay in taking architectural decisions and impacts squads autonomy"*–P2, Enterprise Architect.

4.2   After Conducting the Intervention – The Evaluated Approach

Organisational Structural Change: This intervention introduced a change to the organisational structure. This change aims to facilitate the alignment architectural decisions across autonomous squads and ultimately to strengthen the autonomy of squads. The structural change is presented in (1) empowering Chapter Leaders and other developers with the role of Architecture Owners, (2) changing the responsibilities of the architect to be of Enterprise Architectural focus, and (3) locating all Architecture Owners in a virtual squad that is led by an Enterprise Architect.

The role of *Architecture Owners* is assigned to Chapter Leaders. Since Chapters are formed based on competency areas, and Squads are aligned on the product-level, the Architecture Owners were aligned accordingly. Practitioners say: *"Giving me the role of Architecture Owner facilitates taking architectural decisions within my Chapter"*–P4, Senior Developer and Chapter Leader. Also, *"breaking down the role of the architect into Architecture Owners roles and distribute it among Chapter Leaders, based on their competency areas transforms decisions into the operational level, which is beneficial in aligning architectural based decisions"*–P1, Agile Coach.

The role of *Enterprise Architect* is assigned to the architect. The architect's responsibilities are changed to be of enterprise nature. Practitioners say: *"The architect has great knowledge about the technical and the business roadmaps of our organisation... He should continue focusing on the Enterprise architectural tasks"*–P1, Agile Coach. This Enterprise Architect should support and help Chapter Leaders in tackling architectural based decisions. A practitioner says: *"It is vital to have the required commitment and support from our the Enterprise Architect in taking enterprise architectural decisions such as integrating two intercorrelated components or even specifying how to expose some APIs"*–P5, Senior Developer and Chapter Leader.

A virtual architecture squad, which consists of Architecture Owners and Enterprise Architect, was created to facilitate the technical and architectural governance and alignment among autonomous squads. Architecture Owners should have "willing" to collaborate closely with the Enterprise Architect and other Architecture Owners. This is to get the best out of the Architecture Squad and to utilise better alignment across the organisation. A practitioner says: *"The main reason behind creating this virtual architecture squad is to have proper technical and architectural based alignment through the organisation... Meeting whenever needed is important to resolve encountered obstacles"*–P1, Agile Coach.

Change Management Process: Our introduced change management process was adapted throughout the intervention trial. This evaluated change management process aimed to guide the involved stakeholders – including the developers, Architecture Owners, Enterprise Architects and Product Owners – in governing and aligning architectural based decisions. This process is comprised of those activities illustrated in the figure shared online in [10].

When a developer encounters a possible architectural change, the developer will determine the impact of the architectural change, create a Kanban card describing the change request and visualise it as a WIP in the analysis phase. Then, the architecture owner and the involved developers should understand the nature of the change and determine its potential architectural impact. The Architecture Owner updates the Kanban card with more accurate technical specifications. If the work requires an enterprise architectural change, the architecture owner should discuss the required change with the enterprise architect and if needed within the architecture squad. An iterative impact analysis process can be conducted based on the encountered challenges. In case of identifying newly impacted components, the architecture owner will create new user story for unpredicted changes. If the change request was approval by the architecture squad and the architecture owner, the Kanban card should be available for the planing and development. Consequently, POs can plan the implementation of this change request and forward the user story and its tasks to the relevant squads for implementation. The squads utilise a hybrid process of Behaviour Driven Development and Test Last Development. Also, the developers utilise the continuous integration to avoid delays caused by integration problems. Also, the scope of testing is extended from test cases to behaviour requirement. Based on the testing results, a new release can be planned for deployment on production.

4.3   Benefits and Challenges of the Evaluated Approach

The practitioners in our case study reported benefits of this introduced approach. Firstly, it has shifted the boundaries and transformed the architectural based decisions into decentralised decision-making. A practitioner says: *"I do not need to wait for the architect anymore... Instead, I can get in touch directly with our Chapter Leader (Architecture Owner)"*–P6, Senior Developer. However, enterprise architectural decisions need to be discussed within the architecture squad. A practitioner says: *"Taking decisions about how to integrate different components, or APIs might require a deep investigation by multiple Architecture Owners and the Enterprise Architect"*–P4, Senior Developer and Chapter Leader. Secondly, our approach has facilitated resolving conflicted architectural decisions and mitigating key technical risks across autonomous squads. Developers might encounter conflicted architectural decisions and not always come to an agreement. A practitioner says: *"Many developers are smart and strong-willed where they do not always come to an agreement... Someone should lead and facilitate the evolution of the architecture"*–P4, Senior Developer and Chapter Leader. Thirdly, our approach has facilitated sharing architectural knowledge among the squads. A practitioner says: *"Our Enterprise Architect started arranging and conducting workshops to train and coach our squads in architectural related aspects"*–P4, Senior Developer and Chapter Leader. Fourthly, our approach has improved software quality and mitigated obstacles to aligning architectural decisions across autonomous squads. Practitioners say: *'Conducting proper architectural analysis within our Chapter and then evaluating and discussing the results, if needed, with the Enterprise Architect improves the quality of our produced work"*–P4, Senior Developer. Yet, *"overlooking some aspects that can be considered at the time being might cause a lot of waste because of the need for refactoring"*–P6, Senior Developer.

The practitioners in our case study reported a challenge of this introduced approach. This challenge is presented in prioritising user stories without considering the technical and architectural aspects, which can in turn impact the planning activity negatively. The introduced change management process does not support a process for screening the user stories by the Architecture Squad before conducting the planning. A practitioner says: *"Right now, we do not go through the user stories, in our Architecture Squad, before planning... Yet, sometimes we discuss them informally upon POs request"*–P5, Senior Developer and Chapter Leader. However, the introduced change management process handles such situations when discovering unpredicted architectural changes. This is achieved by moving from Step 6 to Step 1, as illustrated in [10]. The case study organisation considers a spike as an investment to figure out what needs to be built and how. A practitioner says: *"We allocate some resources for complicated work items, ahead of the targeted delivery deadline, to find out what needs to be done... Such investments are considered as necessity to solve architectural issues, which work as enabler for the next Sprint"*–P3, Product Owner.

5   Discussion and Conclusion

The topic of autonomous teams is immature within software engineering since there are challenges that need to be addressed [12]. One of these identified challenges that need exploration is how system architecture can best support the coordination of autonomous teams [12]. Our previous research on the Spotify model has revealed a novel approach to agile tailoring, which we called Heterogeneous Tailoring [11]. One of our identified challenges to the Heterogeneous Tailoring approach is the need for aligning and governing architectural decisions across autonomous squads [11].

We conducted an intervention embedded case study to overcome the challenge of aligning architectural decisions across autonomous squads. In this intervention, we developed and evaluated an approach to agile architectural governance, which comprises a structural change and a change management process.

Our findings demonstrate that team-external (i.e., architect) influence over architectural based decisions is negatively related to teamwork quality and team autonomy. The external dependencies to one person decrease team autonomy and lead to a bottleneck since one person bears many responsibilities and has to reply to many different demands simultaneously. In fact, team-external dependencies to individuals should carefully consider any interference with operational project decisions since it is negatively related to important collaborative processes in the teams [4,11]. Therefore, we have introduced Architecture Owners roles within Chapters to devolve architecture decision making to the operational level. Also, we have changed the responsibilities of the Architect to be of Enterprise Architectural focus to facilitate enterprise architecture decision making, resolve conflicted architectural decisions, and mitigating key technical risks across autonomous squads.

Our evaluated change management process comprises a set of activities, which cover 7 activities out of 11 that have been identified by Yang et al. [13]. These activities are Architectural Analysis and Synthesis (Activity 1 and 2), Architectural Evaluation and Impact Analysis (Activity 3), Architectural Refactoring (Activity 6), and Architectural Maintenance and Evolution (from Activity 6 back to Activity 1). However, Architectural Description and Understanding are used to some extent at the enterprise level. In addition, Architectural Reuse is observed within the squads and encouraged by Architecture Owners.

In this paper, we identified the characteristics and benefits of our evaluated approach to Agile architectural governance using the Spotify model. Also, we identified guidelines and challenges for those wishing to adopt this approach.

References

1. Braun, V., Clarke, V.: Using thematic analysis in psychology. Qual. Res. Psychol. **3**(2), 77–101 (2006)
2. Buschmann, F., Henney, K.: Architecture and agility: married, divorced, or just good friends? IEEE Softw. **30**(2), 80–82 (2013)
3. Glaser, B.G.: Doing Grounded Theory: Issues and Discussions. Sociology Press, Mill Valley (1998)
4. Hoegl, M., Parboteeah, P.: Autonomy and teamwork in innovative projects. Hum. Resour. Manag. **45**(1), 67–79 (2006)
5. Kilu, E., Milani, F., Scott, E., Pfahl, D.: Agile software process improvement by learning from financial and fintech companies: LHV bank case study. In: Winkler, D., Biffl, S., Bergsmann, J. (eds.) SWQD 2019. LNBIP, vol. 338, pp. 57–69. Springer, Cham (2019). https://doi.org/10.1007/978-3-030-05767-1_5
6. Kniberg, H.: Spotify squad framework - part II, April 2014. https://medium.com/project-management-learnings/spotify-squad-framework-part-ii-c5d4b9398c30
7. Kruchten, P.: Software architecture and agile software development: a clash of two cultures? In: 2010 ACM/IEEE 32nd International Conference on Software Engineering, vol. 2, pp. 497–498, May 2010
8. Moe, N.B., Dingsøyr, T., Dybå, T.: Overcoming barriers to self-management in software teams. IEEE Softw. **26**(6), 20–26 (2009)
9. Salameh, A., Bass, J.M.: Spotify tailoring for promoting effectiveness in cross-functional autonomous squads. In: Hoda, R. (ed.) XP 2019. LNBIP, vol. 364, pp. 20–28. Springer, Cham (2019). https://doi.org/10.1007/978-3-030-30126-2_3
10. Salameh, A., Bass, J.M.: Spotify tailoring for architectural governance, March 2020. https://salford.figshare.com/articles/Spotify_Tailoring_for_Architectural_Governance/11960835/1
11. Salameh, A., Bass, J.M.: Heterogeneous tailoring approach using the spotify model. In: Proceedings of the Evaluation and Assessment in Software Engineering, EASE 2020, pp. 293–298. Association for Computing Machinery, New York (2020)
12. Stray, V., Moe, N.B., Hoda, R.: Autonomous agile teams: challenges and future directions for research. In: Proceedings of the 19th International Conference on Agile Software Development: Companion, XP 2018, pp. 16:1–16:5. ACM, New York (2018)
13. Yang, C., Liang, P., Avgeriou, P.: A systematic mapping study on the combination of software architecture and agile development. J. Syst. Softw. **111**, 157–184 (2016)

Enabling Team Autonomy in a Large Public Organization

Parastoo Mohagheghi[1(✉)], Casper Lassenius[2,3],
and Ingrid Omang Bakken[1]

[1] The Norwegian Labour and Welfare Administration, Oslo, Norway
{parastoo.mohagheghi, ingrid.omang.bakken}@nav.no
[2] Simula Metropolitan Centre for Digital Engineering, Oslo, Norway
casper@simula.no
[3] Aalto University, Aalto, Finland

Abstract. This paper describes how autonomy emerged in a team in a large public organization and which factors were important in this process. The organization has back sourced software development and abandoned a stage-based software development process with many handovers between business, IT and vendors. We collected data in four semi-structured interviews and analyzed information on changes in the structure and responsibilities of the team. The team has refined its portfolio for better cohesion, stepwise taken over the responsibility for software development from the vendor and in parallel recruited software developers, UX designers and testers. Product owners have joined the team as well. Supported by changes to the financing model, the team has transformed from mediating between business and vendors to a cross-functional product team with autonomy over its budget, backlog and software development process. As a result, the team can better balance between delivering new features and quality improvements, continuously deliver software with less overhead and focus on its mission to deliver user-friendly services with increased involvement of domain experts. Defining a clear product boundary and reducing dependencies on other teams, developing necessary skills and changing the financing model are recognized as the main success factors, as well as the main challenges in the transition process.

Keywords: Agile · Autonomous team · Backsourcing · Outsourcing

1 Introduction

Agile software development has become the norm in the industry and is increasingly getting a foothold in the public sector, albeit so far not as an exclusive approach [1]. Public sector organizations adopt agile to solve several problems, including faster value delivery, better end-user satisfaction, better collaboration between business and IT, and cost reduction [2]. However, several factors in the government sector, such as lack of experience with agile methods, IT megaprojects and reliance on traditional procurement have been reported to make the adoption difficult [2]. When agile method adoption is combined with a change from outsourcing to insourcing, additional challenges arise such as recruiting, competence transfer and contractual negotiations [3].

M. Paasivaara and P. Kruchten (Eds.): XP 2020 Workshops, LNBIP 396, pp. 245–252, 2020.
https://doi.org/10.1007/978-3-030-58858-8_25

In this paper, we present a single case study of a team in the Norwegian Labour and Welfare Administration (NAV) that adopted agile methods while taking ownership of previously outsourced IT systems. We describe how the team evolved from supporting product owners for the acquisition of systems from an external vendor to an autonomous agile team with full ownership of the applications it is responsible for.

2 Related Work

A systematic literature review on agile methods in the public sector citing 17 primary studies reported several benefits, including faster value delivery, increased end-user satisfaction, lower cost, better collaboration between business and IT, reduced dependency on contractors, and improved team morale. Factors making adoption difficult included an unsuitable organizational culture, lack of experience with agile methods, the ingrained use of prescriptive approaches, and big bang deliveries. In addition, the public sector often runs "IT megaprojects" and relies heavily on traditional procurement and contracts, which make agile adoption challenging [2].

The 1990s and early 2000s saw a wave of outsourcing when organizations, often in the pursuit of cost savings, outsourced IT, oftentimes to low-cost countries. Lack of client involvement and competence is reported as a major challenge. A more recent trend, spurred by factors such as the recognition of IT as a core competence, unmet goals with outsourcing, and the need for better control of the IT systems, is *backsourcing (or insourcing)*, i.e. bringing the outsourced components back in-house [3].

There is an extensive amount of literature on autonomous teams and different types of autonomy such as autonomy over product, people and planning decisions [4]. Autonomy has some pre-conditions, among them having the right skills in the team as well as a redundancy of skills (since it affects the team's capability to adapt to changing situations), culture such as team orientation, sharing of information and management support in order to create the right environment for the teams [4, 5]. Team autonomy has furthermore been identified as a success factor for agile transformations [8].

3 Context and Method

NAV was founded in 2006 by merging three large organizations in the public sector. NAV has 19000 employees including an IT department of over 700 employees and administers a third of the Norwegian national budget through various benefit schemes such as pension, unemployment and child-care benefits. The end-users of IT applications are twofold: organizations and individuals in Norway on the one hand, and the employees of NAV who manage the benefits on the other. Since the establishment of NAV, IT development and maintenance has mainly been outsourced to several vendors, with NAV responsible for requirements specification, acceptance testing and operation of services. In 2017, due, e.g., to high development costs and the growing need for digitalization of services, NAV decided to backsource most of the IT development. In addition, the organization has gradually adopted agile development to achieve better commitment, motivation to perform and desire for responsibility in the organization.

In previous work [7], we described a pilot study on autonomous agile teams at NAV. The experience described therein was considered successful and encouraged the organization to initiate a move towards increased cross-functionality, and to have NAV employees and vendor resources working shoulder to shoulder.

The team in this case study develops and maintains the information and user interfaces intended for the general population provided via the organization's main website nav.no, apps and in other channels. The team is also responsible for developing organization-wide guidelines for publishing information online.

The research presented here is a single qualitative case study and part of a larger study into agile adoption and backsourcing in NAV. We selected the case due to the insights it provides on enabling team autonomy in a complex setting. We collected data through four semi-structured interviews [6], which forms the main unit of analysis. We interviewed the team leader, one product owner, a member of the team performing test, and a representative from the vendor; all being involved in the team since 2017. The interviews lasted between 60 and 90 min and were recorded and transcribed for analysis. In addition, we had a workshop with the team leader to analyze changes in the team structure and responsibilities and validated our findings with her.

4 Results and Discussion

In this section, we present the results, first discussing the transition of the team, followed by discussing factors that enabled the transition towards an agile autonomous team.

4.1 Steps in the Transition Process

Before backsourcing, over 50 applications covering a broad range of user interfaces were managed by a group of employees organized in an office in the IT department. The office managed the contract with the vendor, provided support to the business side, and followed testing, deployment, and operations of the applications. The employees of the office had roles such as functional experts, technical experts, team leaders and project leaders. Functional experts had deep domain knowledge, while technical experts focused on non-functional aspects and technology. The business side, organized in other departments in NAV, specified the requirements, prioritized the backlog, financed changes (often via projects), evaluated the estimations and design, and tested the final applications. The vendors estimated the costs of changes and designed and developed the solutions. The process thus required many handovers between business, IT and vendors. Changes were often delivered in a few large deliveries per year to manage dependencies between services.

In the first step in the backsourcing process, the portfolio covered by the office was divided and assigned to multiple teams. In this process, the team "Self-services" was established, consisting of a team leader, six functional experts and one technical expert. The vendor had its own team collocated at NAV, with seven developers and one team leader. Figure 1 shows the changes in the team structure and roles from 2017 to 2020. The term "IT team" refers to a team managed by the IT department which has an own budget for maintenance, but depends on the business side for prioritization and financing of major changes.

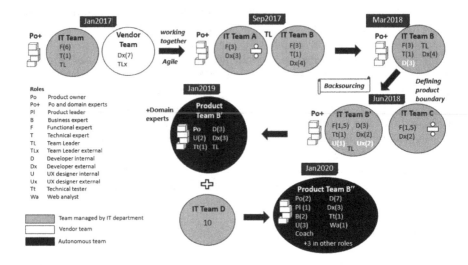

Fig. 1. Changes in the team structure and roles for enabling team autonomy.

The situation was changed gradually, through the following steps:

1. *Building internal development capability.* Before backsourcing, the team consisted of functional and technical experts while the developers were on the vendor side. The business department owning the applications financed recruiting 3 developers in 2018, the first one starting in February. This was considered a major step towards insourcing software development.
2. *Competence transfer.* The team had little knowledge of the code prior to the backsourcing. The IT-team and the vendor team started working together on software development for the purpose of competence transfer; including working shoulder to shoulder and pair-programming.
3. *Analyzing the applications and planning the handover.* The outsourcing contracts included steps for handover to other vendors but not to NAV. The team and the vendor performed an analysis of applications regarding their status (functionality, technical debt, security concerns and remaining failures) and developed a roadmap with milestones and actions for a stepwise handover of applications.
4. *Defining the product boundary in steps.* The old contract model put many applications to be developed by a single vendor in the same contract. As a result, the contract included over 50 applications, all related to user interfaces but managed by different stakeholders. By September 2017, the portfolio of applications was divided between two teams with a shared team leader: "Team A" (services for unemployment) and "Team B" followed here, named "Team Insight". Some applications were

handed over to other teams as well. The purpose was to separate concerns and avoid communication with multiple product owners.

5. *Transfer of ownership and responsibility; becoming self-sufficient competence-wise.* By June 2018, the team had the full responsibility for software development. A User experience (UX) designer was recruited in addition to getting support from two external UX designers. A new tester, who used to be a functional expert, was added to the team as well. Thus, the team included all necessary skills for software development. The team changed its name to "Personal users" to highlight its focus. Some functionality was left out to be handled by "Team C".

6. *Becoming an autonomous product team.* By January 2019, the team was fully financed by the business side and one functional expert became a product owner, enhancing his competence by taking courses and participating in product owners' fora. This type of team is called a "cross-functional product team" (in short Product Team) and the team owns its budget, product backlog and its prioritization.

7. *Enhancing the portfolio.* In January 2020, the team merged with an IT team responsible for the information on web pages, which had backsourced its applications as well ("Team D" in Fig. 1). The whole team working receives a yearly budget covering the personnel costs in full, instead of receiving funds for the changes to be implemented. The team covers two areas of functionality with team members almost 50-50 divided between these two and the possibility to assist each other when needed.

The focus of this paper has been on "Team B" and its evolution. For information, "Team A" and "Team C" are still IT Teams with some changes in their portfolio as well.

4.2 Factors Important for Enabling Team Autonomy

The transition from an IT team mediating between product owners and vendors towards an autonomous team required several changes. We identified the following seven factors that were necessary to enable team autonomy:

1. *Full product ownership.* NAV had made a strategic decision to backsource the development of its systems and decided not to renew the contract with the vendor. Taking ownership of both the systems and the teams developing them was a precursor to creating autonomous teams. The case team has full ownership of its product and prioritizes, implements, and delivers features based on urgency and capacity.

2. *An agile mindset and way of working.* Teams can now choose their own development processes and tools, and the whole organization is developing an agile mindset, which is a profound change. The case team started to use Kanban almost overnight in September 2017. The whole team sits together and delivers continuously.

3. *Building all needed competences.* Building all the skills necessary for working autonomously was a major challenge for the organization. This included recruiting software developers in a highly competitive market, and knowledge transfer and continued collaboration with the vendor. NAV has recruited over 130 software

developers since 2017 by improving its image as a high-skilled software development organization and emphasizing its role in the society. After the contract expired, a transition period was necessary for knowledge transfer and preparing the NAV team for taking charge of software development. In the team discussed here, newly recruited software developers applied pair-programming with peers from the vendor for six months. Some employees in the IT department have changed their roles and developed skills to become product owners, testers, software developers and coaches. The team leader is, e.g., now a coach for this team and other teams. The relation with the vendor was and continues to be professional with good collaboration. A new contract type is now in place to hire resources from 2–3 vendors when necessary by paying per hour.

4. *Empowerment and trust.* Without trust between the team and the surrounding organization, as well as empowerment to make and execute product and process related decisions, a team cannot function autonomously. Developing this in a large organization with a long history of traditional management can be extremely challenging.

5. *Resource-based financing.* The organization is gradually abandoning large projects and its traditional portfolio management process, and giving some teams, such as the team in this case their own budgets, which facilitates their autonomy.

6. *A manageable team portfolio.* The old contract model put many pieces to be developed by a single vendor in the same contract. It was necessary to focus the portfolio to reduce dependencies and give the team autonomy over the product.

7. *The right team size.* Like many organizations, NAV had challenges cutting the team size down to the optimal one, which their experience is 7–9 people, just in line with most recommendations in the team and agile literature.

4.3   Benefits and Challenges

The team leader, product owner and the team member participating in this research reported many subjective benefits of the autonomy. The feeling of ownership and mastery had led to increased employee satisfaction. The team could now respond faster to changes since there are no handovers in the development process. Since they have product ownership, the team members can think strategically, and better balance between functional and technical improvements. This has made it possible to significantly reduce the technical debt. Cost-wise an internal employee costs less than half of an external one, and the savings are invested in new technology and in further development.

The reported challenges were mainly related to 1) the *people factor;* it was difficult to recruit enough software developers and develop skilled product owners; 2) the *product factor:* i.e. defining suitable product teams with fewer dependencies on other teams and a more coherent portfolio. In this process, it has been challenging to handover legacy applications to other teams with limited budget and capacity; and 3) the *financing model* is still not homogenous and creates challenges in prioritization and planning.

4.4   Discussion

In this paper, we understood team autonomy in agile software development as having the power to plan and prioritize the work of the team according to budget, resources, roadmaps and constraints, and to have ownership of the processes and practices employed. This required several changes in the organizational structure and processes, and even the financing model. The autonomy to plan and prioritize work was implemented through incorporating the product ownership in the team. In this case, the organization was able to design the work of the team to have a rather independent portfolio, making it possible to have a high degree of autonomy. Our findings about how to enable team autonomy are well in line with what other cases have reported, as summarized in [8]. In particular, similar results with respect to increased morale was reported by [9, 10].

Our finding regarding the need for changing the financing model points to the importance and challenges of portfolio management in large-scale agile development, an area which currently has a lack of research. Furthermore, our findings indicate that outsourcing relationships can lead to a high degree of technical debt if there are lack of financing to remove technical debt and lack of mechanisms to incentivize high code quality.

The findings in this paper are based on four interviews with practitioners in the studied team in different roles, as well as of an analysis of other documents such as presentations. While this limits the generalizability of the findings, they are well in line with existing literature, and point toward a need for deeper understanding not only of how autonomous teams can work, but of the surrounding organizational context. Two of the authors are employees of NAV, which could introduce bias. However, the first author works in an independent role, and the findings are based on an analysis done jointly by the first two author.

5   Conclusions and Future Research

We presented a case study of how team autonomy was enabled in a single team in a large public organization. We discussed that many factors are required to enable autonomy, both in the team and in the organization. The team members agreed on the benefits of the transformation that happened over the course of three years and experience increased employee satisfaction, faster response to changes and more strategic thinking.

By now, we have interviewed 35 employees in different roles and from different teams in NAV, as well as representatives from vendors. This paper is based on an initial analysis of the data from one team. We are extending our analysis to multiple teams with focus on backsourcing of software development and large-scale agile development.

We thank NAV and the interviewees for the possibility to perform the research and for sharing valuable data and insights with us.

References

1. Viechnicki, P., Kelkar, M.: Agile by the numbers: a data analysis of Agile development in the US federal government. In: Kaji, J., Rao, A., Garia, N., Khan, A. (eds.) Agile in Government: A Playbook from the Deloitte Center for Government Insights, Deloitte, pp. 42–47 (2017)
2. Vacari, I., Prikladnicki, R.: Adopting agile methods in the public sector: a systematic literature review. In: The 27th International Conference on Software Engineering and Knowledge Engineering (2015). https://doi.org/10.18293/seke2015-159
3. Von Bary, B., Westner, M.: Information systems backsourcing: a literature review. J. Inf. Technol. Manag. **29**(1), 62–78 (2018)
4. Moe, N.B., Dingsøyr, T., Dybå, T.: Understanding self-organizing teams in agile software development. In: 19th Australian Conference on Software Engineering, pp. 76–85 (2008)
5. Nerur, S., Mahapatra, R., Mangalaraj, G.: Challenges of migrating to agile methodologies. Commun. ACM **48**(5), 72–78 (2005)
6. Patton, M.Q.: Qualitative Research & Evaluation Methods: Integrating Theory and Practice. SAGE Publications, Thousand Oaks (2014)
7. Lundene, K., Mohagheghi, P.: How autonomy emerges as agile cross-functional teams mature. In: XP2018, Workshop on Autonomous Agile Teams (2018). https://doi.org/10.1145/3234152.3234184
8. Dikert, K., Paasivaara, M., Lassenius, C.: Challenges and success factors for large-scale agile transformations: a systematic literature review. J. Syst. Softw. **119**, 87–108 (2016)
9. Long, K., Starr, D.: Agile supports improved culture and quality for healthwise. In: Agile 2008, pp. 160–165 (2008)
10. Moore, E., Spens, J.: Scaling agile: finding your agile tribe. In: Agile 2008, pp. 121–124 (2008)

Defining TestOps: Collaborative Behaviors and Technology-Driven Workflows Seen as Enablers of Effective Software Testing in DevOps

Michal Doležel[(✉)] ⓘ

University of Economics, Prague, 130 67 Prague, Czech Republic
michal.dolezel@vse.cz

Abstract. **Context:** DevOps is an increasingly popular approach to software development and software operations. Being understood as mutually integrated, both activities have been re-united under one single label. In contrast to traditional software development activities, DevOps promotes numerous fundamental changes, and the area of software testing is not an exception. Yet, the exact appearance of software testing within DevOps is poorly understood, so is the notion of TestOps. **Objective:** This paper explores TestOps as a concept rooted in industrial practice. **Method:** To provide a pluralist outline of practitioners' views on *What is TestOps*, the YouTube platform was searched for digital content containing either "TestOps" or "DevTestOps" in the content title. Through a qualitative lens, the resulting set was systematically annotated and thematically analyzed in an inductive manner. **Results:** Referring to DevOps, practitioners use the notion of TestOps when characterizing a conceptual shift that occurs within the area of software testing. As a matter of fact, two dominant categories were found in the data: (i) TestOps as a new organizational philosophy; (ii) TestOps as an innovative software technique (i.e. process supported by technology). A set of high-level themes within each of these categories was identified and described. **Conclusion:** The study outlines an inconsistency in practitioner perspectives on the nature of TestOps. To decrease the identified conceptual ambiguity, the proposed model posits two complementary meanings of TestOps.

Keywords: Continuous testing · Testing in production · Shift-left testing · Shift-right testing · Software testers · Software-testing skills · Collaboration

1 Introduction

During the past years, the concept of DevOps (Development-Operations) has firmly established itself as an important landmark in the software domain. DevOps can be defined in a number of ways, including a "set of practices", a "development methodology", a "cultural movement", an "organizational approach", and "infrastructure" [1]. Hence, little clarity around DevOps exists, and many see DevOps representing more than one of these aspects. Bringing a sort of consensus and partly clearing the "buzz"

© The Author(s) 2020
M. Paasivaara and P. Kruchten (Eds.): XP 2020 Workshops, LNBIP 396, pp. 253–261, 2020.
https://doi.org/10.1007/978-3-030-58858-8_26

[2], four DevOps dimensions were proposed to describe DevOps as a multifaceted phenomenon. Specifically, *Culture, Automation, Measurement* and *Sharing* (CAMS) have been viewed as the key focus areas when adopting DevOps [3, 4].

Regarding *Sharing,* i.e. one of the organizational vehicles crucial for DevOps, practitioner literature claims that team members should be encouraged to share knowledge and practices to make DevOps successful [1]. In essence, DevOps teams are considered autonomous, and exhibit more blurred responsibilities of software professionals than in traditional teams [5]. For example, previously independent functions, such as independent software testers, may become embedded in DevOps teams in an attempt to strengthen the teams' autonomy, self-sufficiency and cross-disciplinarity [6].

Not only due to the *Sharing* element in DevOps, software testing is an area which is expected to become significantly influenced by the adoption of DevOps principles (cf. [7]). In fact, new test approaches and strategies are needed for DevOps, along with the new skills of test personnel [8]. The emergence of *continuous testing* is one particular facet of this shift, being enthusiastically promoted as "the key for DevOps" [9]. Yet, from an overall perspective, the possible synergy between software testing and DevOps is still poorly understood, having been discussed in only a handful of empirical studies [10] and practitioner reports [6, 9] so far. Also, in practitioner forums, the discussion seems to be somewhat fragmented. Two salient topics related to DevOps have emerged – the notion of *shifting left,* and the notion of *testing in production.* Simply put, the former is an idea of involving testers early in the software development life cycle [11]; the latter idea proposes to start "using real users and real environments to find bugs that matter" [12].

In addition to the previous ideas, some practitioners recently coined the term *TestOps* [12, 13]. Nevertheless, this broad notion seems to add even more confusion on the top of the already ambiguous DevOps concept. Presently, there is little clarity about what the term TestOps means to practitioners today, or could mean in the future. This gap in knowledge has motivated the present exploratory qualitative study. Using an inductive approach, a thematic analysis of available YouTube content related to TestOps was carried out. As a result, a conceptual map was constructed, rendering an inconsistency in practitioner perspectives on the nature of TestOps. By exploring the influential, yet in Software Engineering (SE) research an under-used digital media [14], the study reports on the significance of TestOps, as being promoted by early adopters in the field. The paper contributes to the emerging line of research on software testing in DevOps.

The paper is organized as follows. Following Introduction, the research approach is described in Sect. 2. Section 3 presents a summary of findings. Section 4 concludes the paper by discussing the principal takeaways and limitations of the study.

2   Research Approach

The practice-driven research described in this paper took part within a broader collaborative initiative between academia and a global antivirus company. Our common focus has been on increasing the understanding of the changing role of software testers nowadays (see also [8]). The main aim of this small-scale study was to propose a provisional definition of TestOps/DevTestOps by analyzing how practitioners across the world characterize this emerging concept. The study was motivated by a lack of clarity in how the concept fits into a broader picture of DevOps and continuous practices studied earlier [2–4]. The research question posed here therefore is: *How do early-adopters define and promote TestOps/DevTestOps as a concept?*

YouTube as Data Source. We used YouTube – a content-sharing media platform – as the main source of empirical evidence. While software practitioners follow a plethora of knowledge sources to learn about new technologies and influential ideas, media platforms like YouTube seem to be particularly popular among them [14]. In fact, these platforms represent an inexpensive, easily accessible option for staying updated about the latest trends in the field. Presently, only a small portion of SE researchers use this type of research data [14]. Arguably, this is because these platforms are not viewed by the academic part of the SE community as a credible-enough source of information. Yet, Garousi, Felderer, and Mäntylä [15] explicitly categorize audio-video media within the same category as blogs, both exhibiting "moderate outlet control and credibility". So far, only the merit of the latter data source has been clearly articulated by SE researchers [16]. Fortunately, regarding the use of YouTube, inspiration can be taken from other disciplines, e.g. from medicine. In this field, YouTube is considered a legitimate source of research data, for example when exploring specific topics with limited existing knowledge [17], or when mapping emerging sources of information available to patients [18].

In our view, publicly available video platforms offer a vivid, pluralist view on coming SE trends rooted in practice. Having said that, an important methodological aspect should be taken into consideration. That is, the content available at these platforms may be significantly shaped by marketing activities of software companies (e.g. tool-producers). Similarly, additional individual actors may cause that the obtained perspective will fundamentally differ from a mainstream one, i.e. from a hypothetical view of an "average" software practitioner. To label these actors with influence, we propose the term *brand evangelists* borrowed from marketing research. The term denotes individuals who act on their own with the intention to persuade others to adopt a product or idea [19]. Typically, brand evangelists do so via social media platforms.

Regarding the material included in this study, the majority of videos was recorded at practitioner conferences focused on software testing, or during software testing webinars. In SE, both the above mentioned platforms represent crucial vehicles for knowledge dissemination among practitioners [20]. In this study, we did not attempt to identify brand evangelists nor categorize the analyzed content by involving any similar criteria. In general, we hold that it is presently unclear how practitioners judge the credibility of conference speakers in terms of sensing them as possibly *selling* or *evangelizing*. Indeed, many practitioners consider conference speakers to be highly influential figures and *de-facto* thought leaders of industrial practice [21].

Data Collection. Using two keywords ("TestOps", "TestDevOps"), a search for relevant content at YouTube was performed. The search results were sorted according to relevance, which is the default setting. All content displayed in the main result section and containing "TestOps" or "DevTestOps" [and variants such as Dev(Test)Ops] in the title was considered. The results listed in the sections "Related to your search" and "For you" were not included. After an initial screening, further excluded was: (i) trade content dealing solely with a technological aspect of commercially available solutions; (ii) all content in different languages than English; (iii) post-conference interviews with the presenters. Additionally, the most recent presentation from the same author presenting the topic at more than one venue was selected. Whenever possible, the decision was based on the examination of the presentation details (e.g. the first slide), not YouTube metatags of the videos.

Possible Replicability Issues. With regard to the nature of data, full replicability cannot be guaranteed, as researchers have generally little control over media ranking algorithms embedded in the platforms like YouTube [15]. In the present study, this was partly mitigated by using a 'clean' browser, carrying out the search with the same keywords multiple times, and focusing only on the non-personalized search results. Also, the consistency of the results was checked using a different computer homed in a different network infrastructure. The final list of included content is available in on-line Appendix (https://cutt.ly/ciQgedC).

Data Analysis. The principles of inductive thematic analysis [22, 23] were followed to analyze the material, which comprised of 8 h and 19 min of recordings. To get familiar with the data, we firstly played every recording in full-length. During this process, memoing [22] was used to capture preliminary ideas about the data. This phase was followed by a systematic annotation (open-coding) of the content using the video analysis feature in our qualitative data analysis software (MAXQDA Plus 2020, r. 20.0.7). The descriptive codes derived from individual recordings were than cross-compared and re-organized into larger categories. The resulting conceptual map was constructed in an inductive manner through constant comparison [22].

3   Results: What Is TestOps?

Based on our analysis, a level of disagreement among practitioners regarding the meaning of the term TestOps was identified. While concise definitions of the term were rarely given in the analyzed talks, it was still possible to derive two broad super-categories of meanings that practitioners attribute to TestOps (Fig. 1). These are as follows.

TestOps as a Pattern of Collaborative Behavior Associated with a Shift in the Test Personnel's Mindset and Organization. This super-category covers the human and organizational aspects of TestOps described by the following high-level themes. To begin with, the theme *Testers [need to be] involved early* was central to the discussion. While this is not a new claim, it is in contrast with the everyday reality of sequentially-managed software projects, in which independent testers dominate a separate testing phase near the end of the software development lifecycle. Inversely, TestOps-inspired testers were encouraged to leave silo-ed test centers and move back to development teams *(Testing is activity, not [organization] function)*. Highlighting the aspects of collaboration, testers were further encouraged to *Act as "bridge" [or "glue"] between Dev and Ops* (hence the term Dev*Test*Ops). Also, they were asked to offer their testing-

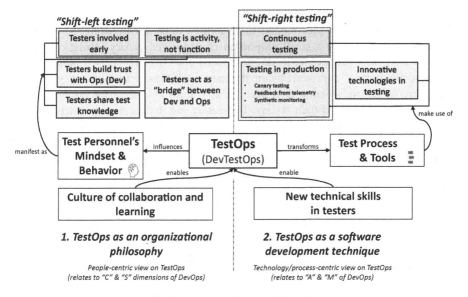

Fig. 1. Conceptual map of TestOps

related expertise to both developers and operations specialists, and to guide these professionals through software testing problems *(Testers share test[ing-related] knowledge)*. Proactive trust and relationship building *(Testers build trust with Ops/Dev)* initiated by testers was promoted as a mean for lowering existing organizational barriers (e.g. issues related to organizational structures). The practitioners also held that the described patterns of behavior did not happen automatically. Therefore, creating a *Culture of collaboration and learning*, resulting in the "right mindset" of people, was suggested as a key enabler.

TestOps as a Technology-Intensive Set of Software Practices. In contrast to the previous view, this super-category covers the technology-related aspects of TestOps summarized as the following high-level themes. First and foremost, the practitioners argued that software testing in TestOps needed to be conducted in a rapid and holistic way. Again, this new form overarches the traditional (phase-based) understanding of software testing. In that sense, *Continuous testing* was promoted as a key practice that was to introduce automated tests as an integral part of deployment pipelines (i.e. automated processes driving the integration, building and deployment of software versions). As the professionals argued, while testers did not need to become DevOps engineers, they needed to acquire skills allowing them to support DevOps engineers and/or developers in their effort. In addition, another impactful shift was discussed: The scope of software testing was claimed as newly ranging beyond test (or non-production) environments. To label this new phenomenon, the term *Testing in production* (TiP) was introduced. The TiP theme was conceptually rich. Interestingly, some practitioners explicitly cited the work of Seth Eliot [12] as a source of the ideas presented by them. Therefore, Eliot's categorization informed also our analysis.

Eliot's "TestOps model of software testing" [12] promotes three TiP-related activities discussed by the practitioners to a varying extent: 1) evaluating the impact of new features provided to a small proportion of end-users (canary testing); 2) using telemetry data from production to design better tests; 3) using "active monitors" or "synthetic monitoring" at production environments. All these activities were suggested as a source of rich production data that could be used by testers for improving test coverage and the depth of their testing. Differently put, by increasing testers' understanding of end-user interactions with the application, testers could do their job better.

Finally, varying significantly in depth and focus, some practitioners discussed the impact of new technologies on TestOps (e.g. cloud, big data, and artificial intelligence being the technologies that caused "digital disruption" in many segments) (*Innovative technologies in testing*). Details regarding this theme are considered beyond the scope of this paper. Taking into consideration all the above technology-related aspects, the key enabler was conceptualized as *New technical skills in testers*.

While not explicitly defined in the analyzed video sample, the notions of *Shift-left* and *Shift-right testing* are conceptually related to TestOps. The proposed understanding is portrayed in the conceptual map as well, and further discussed in Sect. 4.

4   Discussion and Conclusion

Exploring the views of TestOps advocates, this paper brings initial insights into the nature of TestOps. The presented analysis demonstrates that according to the practitioners, the notion comes with a set of powerful ideas. When embraced by industry, the ideas may cause a shift in the field of software testing, which was previously dominated by manual testing [8]. Using a conceptual map, two meanings of TestOps were explored. First, a people-centric view was conceptualized as the cornerstone of TestOps. This perspective binds TestOps with the *Culture* and *Sharing* dimensions in DevOps. In contrast to this view, it was proposed that some practitioners used the term "TestOps" to label a different area of interest: the emerging field of software technology concerned with new tools, workflows and processes for effective test automation supporting DevOps teams. The latter meaning of TestOps goes back to the *Automation* and *Measurement* DevOps dimensions. This is to highlight that a potential for bringing significant technological innovations to the SE field exists by establishing synergies between test tools and other tools used by either developers or operations.

As portrayed in the conceptual map, the term *Shift-left testing* transcends the boundary between the two perspectives, i.e. refers both to people and technology. This is due to the term being a conceptual umbrella for both an organizational approach (*Testers involved early [and continually]*) and a related technology-driven practice (*Continuous testing*). By contrast, the term *Shift-right testing* refers to the aspects connected with two technology-related concepts – *Continuous testing* and *Testing in production*. Interestingly, while the term *Shift-left testing* originated from a 2001 vision [11], the term *Shift-right testing* appears to be of a more recent origin. The suggested metaphor of "right" vs. "left" becomes obvious when one considers a V-shaped lifecycle model, such as the one proposed by Rook in the late 1980s [24]. In Rook's model, the logical beginning (i.e. requirement specification) of SE activities was located on the left side, and the logical end (i.e. software operation and maintenance) on the right side. Therefore, shift-left means *earlier* than during the separate testing phase following coding. In contrast, shift-right means *later* than during that phase, i.e. in production.

Regarding the two high-level perspectives of TestOps (i.e. people vs technology), this paper does not suggest either of them as dominating. Quite to the contrary, SE practice can possibly take the best from the TestOps-related ideas by combining both views [25]. However, as our data show, not all the TestOps promoters followed this route. Not only that – some of the presentations seemingly made use of the term TestOps (DevTestOps) only as of a catchy title to attract the attention of conference audience (see Sect. 2). Likewise, it is important to mention that TestOps overlaps with already existing concepts such as continuous testing [4] and testing in production [9, 12]. As made clear in one of the analyzed videos by Lisa Crispin, a software testing thought leader, one of the reasons for using the term TestOps/DevTestOps is: "People see the word DevOps ... [and they may think there is] no tester in DevOps". Accordingly, the terms TestOps and DevTestOps were coined to highlight the importance of software testing in the DevOps world. Differently put, software testing, as a domain of expertise, is not to cease to exist. Yet, testing activities may become cross-fertilized into the total of development and operational activities performed by autonomous DevOps teams [26].

Methodologically speaking, this study has important limitations. First and foremost, exploring grey literature relates to a specific set of challenges [15] outlined in Sect. 2. Regarding the scope of this study, the YouTube content was considered for our analysis only when explicitly containing the word "TestOps" or "DevTestOps" in the title. This approach to acquiring empirical data was chosen to mimic the behavior of practitioners performing an initial mapping of a new phenomenon by searching through available YouTube videos. However, the chosen approach obviously did not cover the complete landscape of software testing in DevOps, as only a fraction of available knowledge was mapped. In our subsequent research, we plan to conduct a broader, multi-vocal study focused on getting a more comprehensive perspective on the state of software testing in DevOps.

Acknowledgement. I thank Vladimír Falada from AVAST for sharing his thoughts on TestOps. This research was supported by the University of Economics, Prague (F4/23/2019).

References

1. Erich, F.: DevOps is simply interaction between development and operations. In: Bruel, J.-M., Mazzara, M., Meyer, B. (eds.) DEVOPS 2018. LNCS, vol. 11350, pp. 89–99. Springer, Cham (2019). https://doi.org/10.1007/978-3-030-06019-0_7
2. Stahl, D., Martensson, T., Bosch, J.: Continuous practices and DevOps: beyond the buzz, what does it all mean? In: SEAA, pp. 440–448 (2017)
3. Lwakatare, L.E., Kuvaja, P., Oivo, M.: Dimensions of DevOps. In: Lassenius, C., Dingsøyr, T., Paasivaara, M. (eds.) XP 2015. LNBIP, vol. 212, pp. 212–217. Springer, Cham (2015). https://doi.org/10.1007/978-3-319-18612-2_19

4. Fitzgerald, B., Stol, K.-J.: Continuous software engineering: a roadmap and agenda. J. Syst. Softw. **123**, 176–189 (2017)
5. Moe, N.B., Stray, V., Hoda, R.: Trends and updated research agenda for autonomous agile teams: a summary of the second international workshop at XP2019. In: Hoda, R. (ed.) XP 2019. LNBIP, vol. 364, pp. 13–19. Springer, Cham (2019). https://doi.org/10.1007/978-3-030-30126-2_2
6. Roche, J.: Adopting DevOps practices in quality assurance. Commun. ACM **56**, 38–43 (2013)
7. Cruzes, D.S., Moe, N.B., Dyba, T.: Communication between developers and testers in distributed continuous agile testing. In: ICGSE, pp. 59–68 (2016)
8. Florea, R., Stray, V.: The skills that employers look for in software testers. Softw. Qual. J. **27**(4), 1449–1479 (2019). https://doi.org/10.1007/s11219-019-09462-5
9. Zimmerer, P.: Strategy for continuous testing in iDevOps. In: ICSE, pp. 532–533 (2018)
10. Cruzes, D.S., Melsnes, K., Marczak, S.: Testing in a DevOps era: perceptions of testers in Norwegian organisations. In: Misra, S., et al. (eds.) ICCSA 2019. LNCS, vol. 11622, pp. 442–455. Springer, Cham (2019). https://doi.org/10.1007/978-3-030-24305-0_33
11. Smith, L.: Shift-Left Testing. Dr. Dobb's J. **26**, 56 (2001)
12. Eliot, S.: The future of software testing. Part Two - TestOps. Test. Planet. **3**, 1–5 (2012)
13. Dracup, B.: DevOps and the emergence of TestOps! https://www.devopsonline.co.uk/devops-and-the-emergence-of-testops/
14. MacLeod, L., Storey, M.A., Bergen, A.: Code, camera, action: how software developers document and share program knowledge using YouTube. In: ICPC, pp. 104–114 (2015)
15. Garousi, V., Felderer, M., Mäntylä, M.V.: Guidelines for including grey literature and conducting multivocal literature reviews in software engineering. Inf. Softw. Technol. **106**, 101–121 (2019)
16. Rainer, A., Williams, A.: Using blog-like documents to investigate software practice: benefits, challenges, and research directions. J. Softw. Evol. Process. **31**, e2197 (2019)
17. Linkletter, M., Gordon, K., Dooley, J.: The choking game and YouTube: a dangerous combination. Clin. Pediatr. **49**, 274–279 (2010). (Phila)
18. Kallur, A., et al.: Doctor YouTube's opinion on seasonal influenza: a critical appraisal of the information available to patients. Digit. Health **6**, 1–6 (2020)
19. Cestare, T.A., Ipshita, R.: The tribes we lead: understanding the antecedents and consequences of brand evangelism within the context of social communities. J. Mark. Dev. Compet. **13**, 10–26 (2019)
20. Garousi, V., Felderer, M.: Worlds apart: industrial and academic focus areas in software testing. IEEE Softw. **34**, 38–45 (2017)
21. Bride, E.: The media are the message: "the influencers". IEEE Ann. Hist. Comput. **28**, 74–79 (2006)
22. Stol, K.-J., Ralph, P., Fitzgerald, B.: Grounded theory in software engineering research: a critical review and guidelines. In: ICSE, pp. 120–131 (2016)
23. Braun, V., Clarke, V.: Using thematic analysis in psychology. Qual. Res. Psychol. **3**, 77–101 (2006)
24. Rook, P.E.: Controlling software projects. Softw. Eng. J. **1**, 7–16 (1986)
25. Luz, W.P., Pinto, G., Bonifácio, R.: Adopting DevOps in the real world: a theory, a model, and a case study. J. Syst. Softw. **157**, 110384 (2019)
26. Stray, V., Moe, N.B., Hoda, R.: Autonomous agile teams: challenges and future directions for research. In: XP Companion (2018)

Doctoral Symposium

Investigating Agile Adoption in Saudi Arabian Mobile Application Development

Fahad S. Altuwaijri[1,2(✉)] and Maria Angela Ferrario[1]

[1] School of Computing and Communications, Lancaster University, Lancaster, UK
{f.altuwaijri,m.ferrario}@lancaster.ac.uk
[2] Department of Information Technology, College of Computer, Qassim University,
Buraydah, Saudi Arabia
f.altuwaijri@qu.edu.sa

Abstract. Mobile app development has been considered as one of the fastest growing segments of the software industry both worldwide and in Saudi Arabia. Due to their pervasiveness, mobile applications call for consideration of complex and rapidly changing requirements given the diversity of their environments. Therefore, agile is considered the most suitable methodology for developing mobile apps. However, little research has investigated agile adoption in mobile app development in the real context. Therefore, the purpose of this PhD is to investigate the factors that have a significant impact on agile adoption in mobile app development by small and medium-size software organisations in Saudi Arabia. The expected key contribution of this research will be a deep insight into agile adoption in mobile app development, and the design and development of tools and techniques that may support agile adoption within Saudi context.

Keywords: Agile software development · Agile methods · Agile · Mobile application development · Mobile apps · Software engineering

1 Introduction

The aim of this PhD research is to investigate the factors influencing agile adoption in mobile application development sector in Saudi Arabia. Mobile app development has been considered as one of the fastest growing segments of the software industry both worldwide [1], and in Saudi Arabia [2] with mobile devices now becoming integral parts of our lives across domains such as health, entertainment, education and marketing. Due to their pervasiveness and ubiquity, mobile applications call for careful consideration of complex and rapidly changing requirements given the diversity of the environments of their use in terms of user experience, user interface, and reception quality [3,4].

Although there have been several studies that concluded that agile is a natural fit for mobile app development [4–7], there is a need for empirical evidence-based research that investigates the specific factors (e.g. cultural, technical and

M. Paasivaara and P. Kruchten (Eds.): XP 2020 Workshops, LNBIP 396, pp. 265–271, 2020.
https://doi.org/10.1007/978-3-030-58858-8_27

environmental) that support or challenge the agile adoption in mobile app development by small and medium-size software organisations. To the best of the author's knowledge, there are no studies about that in Middle Eastern countries, particularly in Saudi Arabia.

In the following subsections, the research aims and objectives are presented as well as the research questions. Section 2 briefly summarises the related work. The research methodology design is provided in Sect. 3, covering a description of each step of the research process. Section 4 discusses the validity threats. The last section outlines the current status of my PhD and some future works.

1.1 Research Aims and Objectives

This research aims to investigate the key factors that can either support or hinder agile adoption in mobile app development by software organisations in the Kingdom of Saudi Arabia. It is intended that the key research contribution will be twofold: (1) a deeper insight into agile adoption in Saudi mobile app development; and (2) the development of tools and techniques that support agile work in Saudi Arabia. These aims will be achieved through the following objectives:

1. Review current literature about the adoption of agile, particularly in mobile app development.
2. Investigate the awareness, current usage, and perception of agile by Saudi mobile app practitioners through empirical research.
3. Obtain a deeper insight into the factors that may influence agile adoption in Saudi Arabian mobile app development through empirical research.
4. Design and develop tools and techniques that can support agile adoption in Saudi Arabia's mobile app industry.

1.2 Research Questions

The main research questions that motivated this research are:

RQ1. What are the types of factors that support or hinder agile adoption in mobile app development in the context of Saudi Arabian software organisations?

The main research question is divided into four sub-research questions:

RQ1.1 What is the state-of-art research in agile adoption in general and particularly its adoption in mobile app development?

RQ1.2 What is the level of awareness of agile amongst mobile app practitioners in Saudi Arabia? How is it perceived?

RQ1.3 What are the enabling factors and the challenges of adopting agile in mobile app development in the context of Saudi Arabia?

RQ1.4 What are the mechanisms (including software tools and techniques) that can support agile adoption in Saudi Arabian mobile app development?

2   Related Work

2.1   Agile Software Development Adoption

It is important to investigate the facilitating factors and the challenges related to the adoption of agile principles and practices in developing software projects. This is because such understanding will help determine to what extent agile can be adopted and how it influences the success of projects. In this regard, scholars have advocated that the suitability of agile adoption by software organisations depends on the practitioners'cultural background, hence, agile is dependent on several human factors [8,9]. Studies have found that practitioners' culture, communication, skills and experiences are considered as the most important factors that influence the adoption of agile [10,11]. Furthermore, organisational aspects are considered as one of the most significant aspects of agile adoption [9,11]. On the other hand, Chow and Cao [8] argued that besides the importance of organisational and people aspects, technical factors have a significant impact on agile adoption, including the agile software techniques and delivery strategies.

All of the studies mentioned above advocate that the practice of agile is mainly influenced by human factors. This means that people or organisations in different countries practice agile differently according to their cultural differences. Therefore, this research will investigate the factors identified in previous studies to determine whether they can be considered as the main aspects affecting the adoption of agile in Saudi mobile app development. Although there are numerous studies that focused on identifying the factors influencing agile adoption [10,12,13], there is a lack of studies on the adoption of agile in Middle Eastern countries, particularly its adoption in mobile app development in Saudi Arabia. With regards to investigating agile adoption in mobile app development, several studies have focused on identifying the benefits and challenges of the adoption and discussing the proposed agile-based mobile methodologies such as Mobile-D [5,6]. However, these studies did not investigate the factors influencing agile adoption in mobile app development.

2.2   Agile Awareness and Perceptions

The initial step in investigating the factors influencing agile adoption by software organizations is to examine practitioners' awareness and perceptions of agile. Several research efforts about this topic, however, most of these studies were conducted in developed countries such as [14–16] and only a handful were conducted in the context of developing countries such as Brazil [17], Paraguay [18] and India [19]. Unfortunately, none of these studies is focused on agile perceptions and usage in mobile app development in the Middle Eastern countries, especially Saudi Arabia. In the context of Saudi Arabia, Bin-Hezam et al. [20] studied to what extent agile has been adopted by SMEs in Saudi Arabia. This study was applied to different enterprises (i.e. technical and non-technical) and did not target mobile software organisations.

Some existing research examined the awareness and perception on a global scale. An example is the work of Begel and Nagappen [14] who investigated that among Microsoft employees. On the other hand, even though this study was considered global because the data was collected from three continents (i.e. North America, Asia and Europe), it only concentrated on one company that has similar aspects across the world. Therefore, to the best of the author's knowledge, there has been no study about the level of awareness among Saudi mobile app developers towards agile, the reasons for agile adoption and non-adoption from their point of view, their perceptions towards agile methods and the tools and techniques used to support their agile teams and their limitations.

3   Research Methodology

The design of this research will be explorative and inspired by interdisciplinary research framework [21], which is agile, people-focused and reflective. Using an agile approach in managing our PhD research will help us move forward quickly and reflectively through the research process. Hence, the results from each study will be used to inform and shape the subsequent studies of the research.

3.1   Empirical Investigation Design

This research is divided into three cycles, which are explained below and summarised in Fig. 1. Each cycle will last for 7–9 months and involves three iterative stages (i.e. plan, act and reflect). In each cycle, there are several sprints each of which will last for 2–4 weeks.

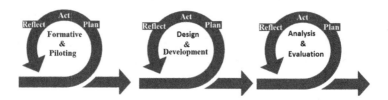

Fig. 1. Research cycles

The First Cycle: Formative and Piloting. This cycle aims to study the current related work and to understand the current usage and perception of agile in Saudi Arabia. Expert interviews will be conducted to take the experts' viewpoint about the perception of agile and take their opinions before designing next studies. In addition, a survey questionnaire will be conducted to identify the awareness and perception of software development in general, particularly agile among Saudi mobile app developers who either adopt or do not adopt agile methods.

The Second Cycle: Design and Development. This cycle aims to conduct in-depth investigation to obtain a deep insight into the key factors that may influence agile adoption in Saudi mobile app development and the tools and techniques used. This investigation will be achieved through three data collection methods (i.e. interviews, observation and a focus group). The results of each activity will be used to inform and shape the next one. In addition, a prototype of tools or techniques that can support agile team within Saudi context will be designed and developed. If there are certain tools and techniques that widely acceptable in agile in western context, but may not be suitable in Saudi context, we will investigate what mechanisms could support the outcome of these tools and techniques in Saudi context.

The Third Cycle: Analysis and Evaluation. This cycle aims to analyse and evaluate the factors and tools, as well as to conclude the writing up of the thesis. A questionnaire will be utilised in this study to analyse the relationships between variables with a statistical technique (i.e. Factor Analysis). In terms of the tools and techniques developed, they will be evaluated based on the interviews with the agile team members who will use them.

3.2 Data Analysis

The data collected from the quantitative methods will be analysed using a statistical software (i.e. SPSS). This will determine the relationships and trends in the data and illustrate them through graphs and cross-tabulated formats. In addition, Factor Analysis (FA) will be used to analyse the relationships between variables [22]. With regards to the data collected from qualitative methods, NVivo software will be used for organising and coding the data. In addition, the data will be subjected to the approach of thematic analysis that helps in developing themes and patterns from the data collected [23].

4   Validity Threats and Control

The validity threats are discussed in this research to explain how to reduce these threats. Using the empirical research method, I will reduce my bias by applying mixed research methods as different data collection methods will be used. A pilot test for each data collection method will be conducted to avoid the threat of having questions that can be hard to understand by the participants. In terms of the research context, the study will not be limited to a specific software organisation and data will be collected from different teams from different organisations to represent organisations throughout Saudi context. Furthermore, my supervisor has strong experience in empirical research methods, thus, she could be a reference point to ensure the validity of the study.

5 Current Status

This research is still in the early phase, thus, we have not started the fieldwork yet. Several tasks have been completed over the last months. First, we have reviewed the current literature. Second, we have designed the research methods that will be used throughout this research. Third, we have contacted mobile app developers in Saudi Arabia to participate in our study, and they agreed to collaborate with us. Finally, we have designed the first empirical study (i.e. expert interviews) that is seeking approval from the ethics committee. The next step will be conducting expert interviews. A survey questionnaire will be designed and shaped based on the finding of the expert interviews to the awareness and perceptions of agile. After that, we will begin to investigate the key factors influencing agile adoption through empirical research.

References

1. Ahmad, A., Li, K., Feng, C., Asim, S.M., Yousif, A., Ge, S.: An empirical study of investigating mobile applications development challenges. IEEE Access **6**, 17711–17728 (2018)
2. Ernst & Young Global Limited. Unlocking the digital economy potential of the Kingdom of Saudi Arabia, Technical report, Ernst & Young Global Limited (2019)
3. Aldayel, A., Alnafjan, K.: Challenges and best practices for mobile application development: review paper. In: ACM International Conference on Compute and Data Analysis Proceeding Series, vol. Part F1302, pp. 41–48 (2017)
4. Wasserman, T.: Software engineering issues for mobile application development. In: Proceedings of the ACM Workshop on the Future of Software Engineering Research FoSER, pp. 397–400 (2010)
5. Corral, L., Sillitti, A., Succi, G.: Software development processes for mobile systems: is agile really taking over the business? In: 2013 IEEE 1st International Workshop on the Engineering of Mobile-Enabled Systems (MOBS), pp. 19–24. IEEE (2013)
6. Kaleel, S.B., Harishankar, S.: Applying agile methodology in mobile software engineering: android application development and its challenges. Computer Science Technical Reports, pp. 1–11 (2013)
7. Francese, R., Gravino, C., Risi, M., Scanniello, G., Tortora, G.: Mobile app development and management: results from a qualitative investigation. In: Proceedings - 2017 IEEE/ACM 4th International Conference on Mobile Software Engineering and Systems MOBILESoft 2017, pp. 133–143 (2017)
8. Chow, T., Cao, D.B.: A survey study of critical success factors in agile software projects. J. Syst. Softw. **81**(6), 961–971 (2008)
9. Misra, S.C., Kumar, V., Kumar, U.: Identifying some important success factors in adopting agile software development practices. J. Syst. Softw. **82**(11), 1869–1890 (2009)
10. Cockburn, A., Highsmith, J.: Agile software development: the people factor. IEEE Comput. **34**(11), 131–133 (2001)
11. Gandomani, T.J., Nafchi, M.Z.: Agile transition and adoption human-related challenges and issues: a grounded theory approach. Comput. Hum. Behav. **62**, 257–266 (2016)

12. Conboy, K., Coyle, S., Wang, X., Pikkarainen, M.: People over process: key challenges in agile development. IEEE Softw. **28**(4), 48–57 (2011)
13. Iivari, J., Huisman, M.: The relationship between organizational culture and the deployment of systems development methodologies. Mis Q. **31**(1), 35–58 (2007)
14. Begel, A., Nagappan, N.: Usage and perceptions of agile software development in an industrial context: an exploratory study. In: The First IEEE International Symposium on Empirical Software Engineering and Measurement (ESEM), pp. 255–264 (2007)
15. Pikkarainen, M., Salo, O., Kuusela, R., Abrahamsson, P.: Strengths and barriers behind the successful agile deployment-insights from the three software intensive companies in Finland. Empirical Softw. Eng. **17**, 675–702 (2012)
16. Rodríguez, P., Markkula, J., Oivo, M., Turula, K.: Survey on agile and lean usage in finnish software industry. In: International IEEE Symposium on Empirical Software Engineering and Measurement, pp. 139–148 (2012)
17. de O. Melo, C., et al.: The evolution of agile software development in Brazil. J. Braz. Comput. Soc. **19**(4), 523–552 (2013). https://doi.org/10.1007/s13173-013-0114-x
18. Salinas, M.R.N., Neto, A.G.S.S., Emer, M.C.F.P.: Concerns and limitations in agile software development: a Survey with Paraguayan Companies. In: Santos, V.A., Pinto, G.H.L., Serra Seca Neto, A.G. (eds.) WBMA 2017. CCIS, vol. 802, pp. 77–87. Springer, Cham (2018). https://doi.org/10.1007/978-3-319-73673-0_6
19. Nazir, N., Hasteer, N., Bansal, A.: A survey on agile practices in the Indian IT industry. In: Proceedings of the 2016 6th International Conference - Cloud System and Big Data Engineering, Confluence 2016, pp. 635–640 (2016)
20. Bin-Hezam, R., Bin-Essa, A., Abubacker, N.F.: Is the agile development method the way to go for small to medium enterprises (SMEs) in Saudi Arabia? In: 21st IEEE Saudi Computer Society National Computer Conference NCC 2018, pp. 1–6. IEEE (2018)
21. Ferrario, M.A., Simm, W., Newman, P., Forshaw, S., Whittle, J.: Software engineering for 'social good': Integrating action research, participatory design, and agile development. In: Companion Proceedings of the 36th International Conference on Software Engineering, pp. 520–523. Association for Computing Machinery (2014)
22. Field, A.: Discovering Statistics Using IBM SPSS statistics, 4th edn. Sage publications, CA (2013)
23. Boyatzis, R.: Thematic Analysis and Code Development. Sage Publications Inc. (1998)

Crowd Agile Model for Effective Software Development

Shamaila Qayyum[1]([✉]), Salma Imtiaz[1], and Huma Hayyat Khan[2]

[1] International Islamic University, Islamabad, Pakistan
shamaill1a@gmail.com, salma.imtiaz@iiu.edu.pk
[2] National University of Modern Languages, Islamabad, Pakistan
humakhan0@gmail.com

Abstract. Crowd Sourced Software Development (CSSD) is becoming popular in software development industries due to reduced cost and efficiency. Many companies are moving towards crowdsourcing, and have already adopted Agile Software Development (ASD). However, CSSD differs from ASD in many ways due to its distributed nature. Although there is little research on the integration of these two approaches, whereas at the same time the combination of the two is advocated by some. It is deemed necessary to identify and resolve the issues emerged while integrating CSSD and ASD. This study hence intends to explore the issues emerged as a result of integrating agile and CSSD and propose a Crowd Agile model that will help in effective software development.

Keywords: Agile · ASD · Scrum · Crowd source software development · CSSD

1 Introduction

With the growth of software industry, traditional software development practices are getting old [1–3]. Internet and social media have provided ways for developers and employers to reach each other across the globe to get their task done [1, 3]. This approach of developing software which utilizes people around the globe for various kind of tasks is known as crowdsourcing [4, 5]. Recently Crowd Sourced Software Development (CSSD) has taken over the software industry [6]. The phenomenon involves outsourcing the tasks to the crowd consisting of unknown, heterogeneous people by an open call [4, 7]. The crowd, coordinates via any online platform [8] such as Amazon Mechanical Turk and Topcoder, to complete the tasks given by the employer [7]. This technique has said to improve the quality of tasks by increasing response time and reducing the cost [9].

CSSD enables the abilities of assorted individuals to be incorporated into a single venture [12]. It is commonly used for coding [13–16] and testing [17–23] in software development. In crowdsourcing, people performing tasks are heterogeneous gatherings, who do not know each other. As the software requirements are becoming unpredictable and researchers are emphasizing on more communication within team [24], CSSD is facing the challenges of team development [4, 9], developing volunteers' network [8],

M. Paasivaara and P. Kruchten (Eds.): XP 2020 Workshops, LNBIP 396, pp. 272–279, 2020.
https://doi.org/10.1007/978-3-030-58858-8_28

task decomposition, trust among the crowd working on same project [14] and coordination.

On the other hand agile methodology is also a very popular software development methodology [25, 26] as it enables software teams to deliverable valuable services in flexible manner [27, 28]. It has been established that many companies adopting CSSD are also following ASD [29]. Companies, such as TPI, that use TopCoder as a platform, are shifting towards crowdsourcing and are already following agile methods [30]. The combination of crowd sourced software development and agile is one of an interesting and latest research area. As stated by Mishra [29], lately practitioners are following crowd source approach while working in agile environment, but research lacks sufficient articles on the effective integration of these two approaches. Stol [30] also highlighted the importance of effective combination of crowd and agile. The research is still very new and limited. Therefore, we aim to conduct an exploratory research to determine what are the challenges faced when CSSD is used within agile environment and what strategies can be followed to reduce these challenges, followed by an explanatory research in which we will validate our proposed model.

The rest of the document is divided into following sections; Sect. 2 gives the background on CSSD and agile. Section 3 provides literature review and recent state of art of agile and CSSD. Section 4 contains the objectives of this study and research questions this study intends to follow. Section 5 states detailed research methodology. Section 6 presents the contribution of this research and Sect. 7 provides a timeline in which this research will be completed.

2 Background and Motivation

In the recent years a new trend of software development has become popular in industry that lets the organizations involve isolated group of developers to develop software projects [1–3]. This concept is known as crowdsourcing. The term crowdsourcing was initially defined by Howe [10] in 2006. Social networking is one reason behind this globalization [1, 3]. A crowd can be any group of large number of anonymous people, which may comprise of experts as well as fresh graduates and inexperienced people. Crowdsourcing helps utilizing the skills of different people to be integrated into a single project [12].

At the same time, companies are widely adopting agile software development methodology [33]. Interestingly, some of the characteristics that are faced as challenges by CSSD are the benefits achieved as a result of following ASD. Agile not only keeps the team productive and motivated, but provides quality products [34]. ASD emphasizes on face to face communication [35, 36] and works in iteration with close collaboration of team, project manager and business people [27, 37]. Trust development among team members is another strength of ASD [38]. A daily meeting is held to discuss the progress of the project [34, 39]. ASD also helps in lowering cost of project as there is increased communication which decreases the chances rework and therefore cost overrun and project delay [24]. However, it is problematic executing CSSD in an agile environment [33].

Agile Software Development (ASD) has been adopted by the organizations doing Global Software Development (GSD) [27, 40–43]. GSD leads software developing companies, develop the software across remotely located teams [44]. Since many practices of agile are thought to solve different challenges of the organizations working across the globe [44–46]. CSSD is different from GSD, in GSD there are designated teams and CSSD comprise of a large group of unknown people who do not know each other neither are they designated employees of the organization [33]. Since agile practices can benefit GSD [33] we suggest they can be integrated and used during CSSD. How both can be effectively integrated needs to be explored [4]. This motivated us to conduct a research on exploring how agile and CSSD can be used together in a way that the maximum benefits of both the approaches can be achieved.

3   Related Work

3.1   State of Knowledge on Crowd Sourced Agile Development

After reviewing recent literature we found a few studies on crowd sourced agile development. The most recent study among them on crowd source agile development was conducted by Klass Jan Stol [30] in 2019. They conducted interviews and found that the managers, who were involved in CSSD as well as agile, faced many problems because of these contradictory approaches. Researchers emphasized the need to investigate how these two approaches can be combined effectively. Likewise, another study by Klass Jan Stol is conducted in 2014 [4], where the researchers reported the significance of crowdsourcing. Mishra and colleagues in 2017 [29] conducted a study that reports the importance of integrating CSSD and ASD. The researchers highlighted the recent trends towards investigating agile development with crowd sourcing.

CSSD [1] and ASD [34] are widely adapted by the companies today since there are some key issues in following these both simultaneously as many characteristics of agile and crowdsourcing are contradicting each other. As [30] stated:

> *"Given the widespread adoption of agile approaches to software development (in particular Scrum) that emphasize regular face-to-face communication, how can the crowdsourcing approach (which resembles a waterfall-style approach to software development with an emphasis on documented requirements) be effectively combined and coordinated?"*

Literature shows that ASD is also used by organizations doing GSD [40], [60]. Since GSD also has many characteristics that contradict with the principles of ASD. However, it has been established that agile practices are used for mitigating many challenges of GSD [44–46]. GSD differs from CSSD as in GSD there are designated teams but in CSSD a large group of unknown people is working on same task [33]. However, in CSSD the workers are globally dispersed as the designated teams in GSD are working from remote locations, so geographical difference is a commonality among both. If agile practices can be used for GSD, where teams are geographically apart from each other, it can also be used within CSSD for effective software development.

4 Research Questions

The study aims to explore the challenges of CSSD when used with ASD and the solutions that help reduce these challenges. This motivated us to design our research questions, as follows:

RQ1:
How can Crowd Sourced Software Development (CSSD) be effectively integrated with Agile Software Development (ASD) to achieve maximum benefits of both?

RQ 1.1: What are the challenges when ASD is used with CSSD?

RQ 1.2: What strategies could be used to overcome the challenges of ASD and CSSD integration?

RQ 1.3: How can the crowd agile model help CSSD teams be more successful in their use of ASD?

5 Methodology

To answer each research question of the study, following research methodology will be adapted. Table 1 gives a detailed research summary along with the methodology.

Table 1. Research summary

Research question	Objective	Methodology	Outcome
RQ 1.1	To identify the challenges of integrating CSSD and ASD from literature as well as industry	- Literature review - Survey	List of issues faced by companies following crowd source approach with agile software development
RQ 1.2	To identify the practices that can address the identified challenges of CSSD and ASD	- Literature Review - Survey	- List of solution strategies adapted by companies to resolve issues while using crowd sourcing approach within agile environment
	To propose a Crowd Agile model		- a model based on the issues and solutions identified in previous phases
RQ 1.3	To evaluate how crowd agile model helps in effective software development	- Case study - Plan B - Experiment	An evaluated model

Literature review (LR) will be conducted in order to find the reported issues while working together with crowd sourcing and agile. LR will also be carried out to find the solutions and strategies for the issues emerged that are given in the literature.

A *survey* will be conducted to find out what issues practitioners are facing when they use crowdsourcing while working in an agile environment. This survey will also figure out what strategies these practitioners adopt to overcome the issues faced by combining crowdsourcing with agile. The survey will be *exploratory* as we will be identifying issues and the strategies that are faced by industry. Guidelines for conducting survey by Kasunic [47] will be followed. *Type of survey:* This survey will be self-administered. Self-administered surveys are those which are sent online through web based surveys or emails. The survey will be a mix of both open and closed questions. *Target audience:* The targeted audience for our survey is the software development practitioners and managers working with crowdsourcing and agile. The target audience will be approached by different platforms which allow crowdsourcing. It will be first confirmed through email/any other contact medium that they are also following agile.

Case study: The evaluation of the model proposed in this study, will be done with a case study. For carrying out case study effectively, guidelines for conducting and reporting case study research in software engineering by Runeson [48] will be followed. Case study will be *explanatory*. This study intends to find how CSSD and agile can be integrated and what benefits can be achieved from this integration. *Case definition*: The case of any software development company will be considered who carry out software engineering activities through crowdsourcing while working in agile environment. *Unit of analysis:* Our unit of analysis will be the software project and the practitioners that will develop software using our model. *Data Collection:* Data collection from the case study will be done through second level technique. The researchers will directly collect raw data by monitoring the use of the model. This will be done using *interviews*. *Data analysis:* Qualitative data analysis will be done. Narrative analysis and discourse analysis will be used for this purpose. As the data will be received in the form of different responses from the respondents" so it will be better analyzed in the form of respondents' stories, talks and texts.

We understand the issues in identifying an organization for case study, as a plan B, we will conduct an experiment for the evaluation of our proposed model.

6   Research Framework

Theoretical Perspective of Research: The theoretical perspective of this study is based on organizational theory as it focuses on the improvement in organizational performance. A positivist approach is being followed as the research aims to study human behavior and results are produced on empirical basis.

Methodological Perspective of Research: This is *applied research* as the sole purpose of carrying out this research is to address the problems of an organization which is using ASD along with CSSD. The type of applied research this study follows is *evaluation research*, as we intend to study the impact of our suggested model.

7 Expected Outcomes

The outcome of this study will be in the form of a model. In this model guidelines will be provided for effective use of CSSD with ASD. These guidelines will be in the form of challenge-strategy pair. This pair will specify that for any particular challenge (while integrating CSSD with ASD), what strategy can be followed so that the benefits of both can be achieved. The contribution of this research will be; the identification of issues while using CSSD with agile, the identification of solutions for the issues identified while using CSSD with agile, a crowd agile model for effective usage of CSSD and agile and validation of the model.

References

1. Begel, A., Bosch, J., Storey, M.I.: Social networking meets software development: perspectives from github, msdn, stack exchange, and topcoder. IEEE Softw. **30**(1), 52–66 (2013)
2. Tamburri, P., Vliet, H.: Organizational social structures for software engineering. ACM Comput. Surv. **46**(1), 1–35 (2013)
3. Storey, M.A., Singer, L., Filho, F.F., Zagalsky, A., German, D.M.: How social and communication channels shape and challenge a participatory culture in software development. IEEE Trans. Softw. Eng. **41**(7), 185–204 (2015)
4. Stol, K.J., Fitzgerald, B: Two's company, three's a crowd: a case study of crowdsourcing software development. In: Proceedings of the 36th International Conference on Software Engineering, pp. 187–198 (2014)
5. Ågerfalk, P.J., Fitzgerald, B., Stol, K.J.: Software Sourcing in the Age of Open. SCS. Springer, Cham (2015). https://doi.org/10.1007/978-3-319-17266-8
6. Mao, K., Capra, L., Harman, M., Jia, Y.: A survey of the use of crowdsourcing in software engineering. J. Syst. Softw. **126**, 57–84 (2017)
7. Mooty, M., Faulring, A., Stylos, J., Myers, B.A.: Calcite: completing code completion for constructors using crowds. In: 2010 IEEE Symposium on Visual Languages and Human-Centric Computing, pp. 15–22 (2010)
8. Schenk, E., Guittard, C.: Towards a characterization of crowdsourcing practices. J. Innov. Econ. Manag. (**1**), 93–107 (2011)
9. Hosseini, M., Phalp, K., Taylor, J., Ali, R.: Towards crowdsourcing for requirements engineering (2014)
10. Howe, J.: The rise of crowdsourcing [Електронний ресурс] (2006)
11. Brabham, D.: Crowdsourcing. MIT Press, Cambridge (2013)
12. Vander Schee, B.A.: Crowdsourcing: why the power of the crowd is driving the future of business. J. Consum. Mark. **26**(4), 305–306 (2009)
13. Latoza, T.D., Zhao, M., Van Der Hoek, A., Chen, M., Jiang, L., Van Der Hoek, A.: Borrowing from the Crowd: A Study of Recombination in Software Design Competitions Microtask Programing View Project Merge Nature View Project Borrowing from the Crowd: A Study of Recombination in Software Design Competitions (2015)
14. Oi, D., Doan, A., Ramakrishnan, R., Halevy, A.Y.: Crowdsourcing systems on the world-wide web. Commun. ACM **54**(4), 86–96 (2011)
15. Morisaki, S., Usui, Y.: An Approach for crowdsourcing software development. In: Proceedings Joint Conference of the 21st International Workshop on Software Measurement and the 6th International Conference on Software Process and Product Measurement, pp. 32–33 (2011)

16. Xu, X., Wang, Y.: Crowdsourcing software development process study on ultra-large-scale system. In: Advanced Materials Research, pp. 4441–4446 (2014)
17. Schneider, C., Cheung, T.: The power of the crowd: performing usability testing using an on-demand workforce. In: Information Systems Development. Springer, New York (2013). https://doi.org/10.1007/978-1-4614-4951-5_44
18. Liu, D., Bias, R.G., Lease, M., Kuipers, R.: Crowdsourcing for usability testing. Proc. Am. Soc. Inf. Sci Technol. **49**(1), 1–10 (2012)
19. Nebeling, M., Speicher, M., Grossniklaus, M., Norrie, M.C.: Crowdsourced web site evaluation with crowdstudy. In: Brambilla, M., Tokuda, T., Tolksdorf, R. (eds.) ICWE 2012. LNCS, vol. 7387, pp. 494–497. Springer, Heidelberg (2012). https://doi.org/10.1007/978-3-642-31753-8_52
20. Meier, F., Bazo, A., Burghardt, M., Wolff, C.: Evaluating a web-based tool for crowdsourced navigation stress tests. In: Marcus, A. (ed.) DUXU 2013. LNCS, vol. 8015, pp. 248–256. Springer, Heidelberg (2013). https://doi.org/10.1007/978-3-642-39253-5_27
21. Speicher, M., Nebeling, M., Norrie, M.C.: CrowdStudy: general toolkit for crowdsourced evaluation of web interfaces In: Proceedings of the 5th ACM SIGCHI symposium on Engineering interactive computing systems, pp. 255–264 (2013)
22. Teinum, A.: User testing tool towards a tool for crowdsource-enabled accessibility evaluation of websites (2013)
23. Gomide, V.H.M., et al.: Affective crowdsourcing applied to usability testing. Int. J. Comput. Sci. Inf. Technol. **5**(1), 575–579 (2014)
24. Bowes, J.: Kanban vs scrum vs XP–an agile comparison. Kanban vs Scrum vs xp (2015)
25. Williams, L., Cockburn, A.: Underlying values (2003)
26. Boehm, B.: Get ready for agile methods, with care. Computer **35**(1), 64–69 (2002)
27. Hossain, E., Ali Babar Lero, M.A.: Using scrum in global software development: a systematic literature review Hye-young Paik. In: 2009 Fourth IEEE International Conference on Global Software Engineering, pp. 175–184 (2009)
28. Sutherland, J., et al.: Distributed scrum: agile project management with outsourced development teams. In: 2007 40th Annual Hawaii International Conference on System Sciences (HICSS 2007) (2007)
29. Mishra, A., Garbajosa, J., Wang, X., Bosch, J., Abrahamsson, P.: Future directions in agile research: alignments and divergence between research and practice. J. Softw. Evol. Proc **00**, 1–5 (2017)
30. Stol, K.J., Caglayan, B., Fitzgerald, B.: Competition-based crowdsourcing software development: a multi-method study from a customer perspective. IEEE Trans. Softw. Eng. **45**(3), 237–260 (2019)
31. Latoza, T.D., Ben Towne, W., Van Der Hoek, A., Herbsleb, J.D.: Crowd development. In: 2013 6th International Workshop on Cooperative and Human Aspects of Software Engineering (CHASE), pp. 85–88 (2013)
32. Greengard, S.: Following the crowd. Commun. ACM **54**(2), 20–22 (2011)
33. Li, W., Tsai, W.T., Wu, W.: Crowdsourcing for large-scale software development. In: Li, W., Huhns, M.N., Tsai, W.T., Wu, W. (eds.) Crowdsourcing. PI, pp. 3–23. Springer, Heidelberg (2015). https://doi.org/10.1007/978-3-662-47011-4_1
34. Profile, S., Alyahya, S., Alsahli, A., Khan, H.: Agile development overcomes GSD challenges: a systematic literature review. Int. J. Comput. Sci. Softw. Eng. **6**(1), 7 (2017)
35. Newkirk, J.: Introduction to agile processes and extreme programming. In: Proceedings of the 24th International Conference on Software Engineering. ICSE 2002, pp. 695–696 (2002)

36. Damian, D., Lassenius, C., Paasivaara, M., Schröter, A., Borici, A.: Teaching a globally distributed project course using Scrum practices NaPiRE: Naming the Pain in Requirements Engineering View project Need for Speed View project Teaching a Globally Distributed Project Course Using Scrum Practices (2012)
37. Srivastava, A., Bhardwaj, S.: SCRUM model for agile methodology. In: 2017 International Conference on Computing, Communication and Automation (ICCCA), pp. 864–869 (2017)
38. Kniberg, H., Skarin, M.: Kanban and Scrum-Making the Most of Both. Lulu. com, Morrisville (2010)
39. Rubin, K.: Essential Scrum: A Practical Guide to the Most Popular Agile Process. Addison-Wesley, Boston (2012)
40. Holmström, H., Fitzgerald, B., Ågerfalk, P.J., Conchúir, E.Ó.: Agile practices reduce distance in gloral software development. Inf. Syst. Manag. 23(3), 7–18 (2006)
41. Beecham, S., Noll, J., Richardson, I.: Using agile practices to solve global software development problems - a case study. In: Proceedings International Computer Software and Applications Conference, 18–21 August 2014, pp. 5–10 (2014)
42. Hossain, E., Babar, M.A., Verner, J.: How can agile practices minimize global software development co-ordination risks? In: O'Connor, R.V., Baddoo, N., Cuadrago Gallego, J., Rejas Muslera, R., Smolander, K., Messnarz, R. (eds.) EuroSPI 2009. CCIS, vol. 42, pp. 81–92. Springer, Heidelberg (2009). https://doi.org/10.1007/978-3-642-04133-4_7
43. Shrivastava, S.V., Date, H.: Distributed agile software development: a review, June 2010
44. Herbsleb, J.D.: Global software engineering: the future of socio-technical coordination, in FoSE. Future Softw. Eng. 2007, 188–198 (2007)
45. Bannerman, P.L., Hossain, E., Jeffery, R.: Scrum practice mitigation of global software development coordination challenges: a distinctive advantage?. In: Proceedings of the Annual Hawaii International Conference on System Sciences, pp. 5309–5318 (2012)
46. Hossain, E., Bannerman, P.L., Jeffery, D.R.: Scrum practices in global software development: a research framework. In: Caivano, D., Oivo, M., Baldassarre, M.T., Visaggio, G. (eds.) PROFES 2011. LNCS, vol. 6759, pp. 88–102. Springer, Heidelberg (2011). https://doi.org/10.1007/978-3-642-21843-9_9
47. Kasunic, M.: Designing an Effective Survey DISTRIBUTION STATEMENT a Approved for Public Release Distribution Unlimited (2005)
48. Runeson, P., Höst, M.: Guidelines for conducting and reporting case study research in software engineering. Empir. Softw. Eng. 14(2), 131–164 (2009)

Continuous Information Monitoring in Software Startups

Usman Rafiq$^{(\boxtimes)}$ ⓘ and Xiaofeng Wang ⓘ

Faculty of Computer Science, Free University of Bozen-Bolzano, Bolzano, Italy
{urafiq,xiaofeng.wang}@unibz.it

Abstract. Software startups are central nowadays and considered primary drivers of economy and innovation. Lean and agile approaches are suggested for software startups to continuously build and validate the product. Thereby, they need to balance between the speed to deliver product and the quality of the product. It further urges startups to continuously monitor the versatile information, adjust their directions, and keep the bird's-eye view. However, the preliminary literature review highlights that software startups, especially at the early stages, are not even aware of the need for information monitoring. This research project aims to identify how software startups decide what information needs to be monitored. The research plan proposes to utilize multiple case-study and surveys as data collection methods while grounded theory and factor analysis as data analysis procedures. Overall, both qualitative and quantitative research methods are expected to be implemented. The prospective research results encompass a framework to decide what information needs to be continuously monitored.

Keywords: Software startups · Information monitoring · Metric monitoring

1 Introduction

Startups have peculiar characteristics and are human organizations aiming to innovate and grow under extreme conditions of uncertainty [6]. They strive to develop and offer new services or products. A rough estimate indicates that about 100 million new startups are created each year around the world [3]. Among them, there is a large pool of software startups. The venture capital group of IBM [17] states that software-based startups are central nowadays among the pool and considered primary drivers of economy and innovation. Success stories of many existing and successful startups like Facebook, Instagram, Dropbox, Airbnb and etc. are primarily contributing towards this radical uplift. Despite this latest trend, very little is known about failures. The statistics given in [4] show about 98% of startups that aim to present new products end up with failure. Whatsoever we may think of a startup failure reason, the statistics still remain alarming for all definitions of failure. For instance, Nobel and Carmen [5] reported that 90–95% of startups fail in the conception phase, 70–80% fail to see a return on projection, and 30–40% fail by losing everything.

Software startups share a lot with other types of startups; however, they are also required to cope with the frequently changing technological wave [7]. Time pressure is

© The Author(s) 2020
M. Paasivaara and P. Kruchten (Eds.): XP 2020 Workshops, LNBIP 396, pp. 280–287, 2020.
https://doi.org/10.1007/978-3-030-58858-8_29

also critical when a software startup is at an early stage [11]. A software startup is at an early stage when it struggles to conceptualize the idea and float it to the market for the first time [11]. These all factors urge software startups to balance between the speed and the quality of the product [14]. Pantiuchina et al. [14] also indicate that software startups combine agile and lean startup approaches to build the product. Similar results are reported in [2, 8]. While agile helps to manage product development, the lean startup approach helps to continuously validate product ideas with the help of potential customer collaboration [8]. These pieces of evidence suggest that "moving fast" is a compulsion for software startups. While doing so, a software startup continuously communicates with various stakeholders including the team itself to meet both short and long-term goals [2].

Gislaine Camila et al. [2] highlight that communication, direct or indirect, brings a lot of changes in the original idea and startups need to continuously adjust their product and business models to conform to the requirements of their customers. The team needs to continuously communicate and discuss the day-day operations and also look at past decisions to make better ones in the future [2]. The early-stage startup teams are usually small, and decisions are taken by the team as a whole, involving co-founders, playing multiple roles in startup [13].

There is still uncertainty, however, how software startups, especially, at early stages, continuously monitor the versatile information and keep the bird's-eye view. The study [12] reveals that the majority of the startups, especially at early stages, are not even aware of the dire need for information measurements. Whilst the body of literature on software startups is growing, however, most studies are conducted on software development methodologies [7, 16]. A search of the literature only revealed limited studies that discussed a few aspects of the information monitoring in software startups. However, the studies we found, such as [12, 13], only discuss the importance of monitoring metrics and benefits of measuring it. Despite the listed benefits, software startups are also not using consolidated information measurement tools [3]. Therefore, software startups must utilize information monitoring to deliver better quality products, maintain good momentum, and stay competitive, while moving fast [2, 12]. The term 'information' refers to the sum of data and associated meaning, which holds further power to generate knowledge [23].

2 Aim and Objectives

The aims of this study are to understand what startups are currently doing regarding information monitoring and investigate how information monitoring could serve them better. Our initial literature review highlights the lack of studies on the utilization of information monitoring in startups. Regarding the second aim, we did not find how software startups decide what key information they shall monitor. Both qualitative and quantitative methods will be utilized to meet the research aims. The resultant framework will ease software startups to decide what is really important for them to monitor according to their needs. This will further enable them to filter the flood of available information to grow and take corrective action when required.

3   Research Questions

The main research question that we plan to answer is:

RQ1: How to identify what information a software startup needs to monitor continuously?

This main research question is decomposed into the following aspects of continuous information monitoring in software startups:

RQ1.1: What information is available for startups to monitor?
RQ1.2: What are the enablers and inhibitors of information monitoring in software startups?
RQ1.3: How do software startups decide what information they need to monitor continuously?

The initial literature review reveals a lot of results about the large pool of information on measurements in software startups i.e. RQ 1.1. On the other hand, it clearly lacks on how the startups decided what is really important for them and what makes them do so.

Expected Results:

- Enablers and inhibitors of information monitoring in software startups.
- A framework enabling a particular software startup to identify the key information that needs to be monitored continuously.
- A Goal Question Metric for software startups based on the prospective framework.

We also foresee that the information monitoring process inside software startups would be iterative, flexible, and robust i.e. continuous. This indicates that once the key information is identified and monitored then the startup may decide to look for the additional information again in the next iteration. As a result, a modification in the required key information will occur. According to [19], the process of learning and discovery brings changes in a startup and takes it to the different life-cycle stages. This process goes in parallel with the product development process [19]. A startup is also divided into different stages according to the product development state. These stages are concept in-development, working prototype, functional product with limited users, functional product with high growth, and mature product [19]. When a startup moves to the next stage as a result of learning then there seems to be the need to monitor additional or different perspectives. Accordingly, this research proposes to monitor the key information continuously i.e. across all life-cycle stages of a startup.

4   Related Work

The key studies were identified using multiple search strings. The initial search string was based on the keywords, or their synonyms, used in the research questions. However, reading the search results revealed additional keywords that were later added to the list. The sources selected for this search were Scopus, Google Scholar, and IEEE

Xplore. The search was performed in the title, abstract, and keywords fields. Likewise, search strings were developed by merging keywords information monitoring and startup. We did not particularly look for information monitoring in software startups as we were expecting a few results on the topic. Therefore, all the articles ranging from general startup organizations to software startups, in particular, were also undertaken.

The search results were first examined using the titles of the articles. However, in some of the cases, the abstracts were also used to know whether the particular article answers any of the research questions. Articles were also excluded if the word startup or start-up did not refer to the startup organization. Our search stems up from two sources i.e. information monitoring and startups. For information monitoring, we used keywords like information monitor, metric monitor, knowledge monitor, performance analysis, performance monitor, knowledge acquisition, performance indication, key performance indication, key performance data, monitor, and dashboard. Similarly, for the startup, we used startup, start-up, software startup, and software start-up.

4.1 Findings

The literature review findings are classified and discussed according to the research questions. It is also found that the results were mainly discussing a few or none of the aspects of information monitoring.

Identification of key information that needs to be monitored is the very first and crucial challenge of this research. The initial literature review revealed very few published studies that discussed some aspects of information identification. The found studies provide a long list of recommended measurements and metrics in software startups while what is not clear is how software startups decide the most relevant information that needs to be monitored continuously. In the same vein, we did not find factors that motivate or restrict startups to monitor information. For instance, recently Kamulegeya et al. [12], studied 19 nascent software startups of the East-African region and concluded that software startups are measuring or wish to measure relevant information and also aware of the benefits of measurements. A similar conclusion has been echoed by [13] while stressing the use of data in the form of metrics to make better decisions. While performing a multi-vocal literature review and considering the practitioner's opinions, available on the web, Kemell et al. [13] produced more than 100 different metrics. However, these metrics are not validated with the software startups and we also believe that a major portion of this list of metrics is applicable for more mature software startups. In contrast to Kemell et al. [13], Kamulegeya et al. [12] also studied software startups, particularly at early stages, and also produced a list of metrics that is important for software startups. The list seems comprehensive and well-classified. However, we found a limited similarity in the results of [12, 13].

Kamulegeya et al. [12] based their study on the measurements in large and established software companies [18] and compared their results with a practitioner's book, known as "Lean Analytics" [10] that motivates software entrepreneurs to start measuring. While highlighting the paucity of studies on measurements in software startups, authors [12] conclude that software startups are using several measurements. The word metric and measurements are used interchangeably in this article. They classify the metric, being measured, or wish to be measured in software startups, into five categories. These categories include business-oriented, product-oriented, organizational performance-oriented, project-oriented and design-oriented metrics. This categorization is originally discussed in the study of measurements in large organizations [18]. Overall, 28 metrics were found belonging to one of these categories. It is interesting to relate that most software startups (17 out of 19) were using at least one of the business-oriented metrics while no one was using or wish to use design-oriented metrics. Likewise, what stands out in [12] is that the majority of startups, 12 out of 19, were not satisfied with what they were measuring and believed that they shall measure several aspects of software startups more adequately.

Based on the results discussed in [12], a multiple case-study report, we present categories and a list of associated key information that software startups, particularly at early stages, are measuring or wish to measure. The first category is related to business and associated key metrics include customer analytics (number of people using platform, customer behaviour), product delivery process time estimation, rate of customer/partner acquisition/growing customer base, revenue growth/generated revenue/activities that generate revenue, using a telemetry tool, tracking market indicators/market events, set and review business targets, product awareness/customer interest, using market as a benchmark, customer feedback measurement, reaching key business milestones (patents, tax registration, incorporation). The second category, product-oriented information, covers product/feature usage, production process time estimation, system reliability, ability to build a complete product, feedback from friends about product features (peer endorsement), product maintenance/support, and comparing product versions (added features). The third category, organizational performance measures, set and evaluate key performance indicators, time-based task setting, tracking and review for progress of project and time-based project performance appraisal. The fourth category, project metrics, monitors monetary value of time spent on task/activity, set and evaluate tasks, activity completion time, process adherence by the team, tools usage by team, product maintenance/support, documenting, and reviewing activities for progress. Lastly, not a single startup was found measuring design metrics.

Together, these studies [12, 13] indicate that data is worthwhile and provides deep insights if measured properly. Alongside, in another study, Kamulegeya et al. [13] interestingly, glimpsed a little about the Goal Question Metric (GQM) approach and concluded that GQM can also be used to identify the data required to be measured during business operations. While highlighting the limitations of GQM in only revealing productivity and quality metrics, they concluded that software startups are also required to look at other aspects such as business and technical activities. On that basis, we propose to build a GQM for software startups, including but not limited to product quality and team productivity.

A significant contribution to the use of data in software startups was introduced by Croll and Yoskovitz [10] in their book on lean analytics. The book explained to grow the startup faster and better by using measurements and metrics. Croll and Yoskovitz [10] categorized software startups according to six different business models and the relevant metrics were defined and associated with each kind of model. The business models include e-commerce, Software as a Service (SaaS), free mobile app, two-sided marketplaces, media sites, and startups providing user-generated content. Startups were also classified using the stages of software startups when startups sell to the enterprise.

The stages referred to as empathy, stickiness, virality, revenue, and scale. The book [10] further defined the criteria to make sure that the startup is choosing the right metrics. Here, metrics were classified into five categories (qualitative versus quantitative metrics, vanity versus actionable metrics, exploratory versus reporting metrics, leading versus lagging metrics, and lastly correlated versus causal metrics). On the other hand, in contrast to the practitioner's opinion [6], Kamulegeya et al. [12] claimed that the startup models which are listed in [10] are not sufficient to cover the types of startups in the market. They also pointed out that the metric provided by the lean analytics framework [10] specifically targets established software startups in developed economies and does not apply to emerging and nascent ecosystems.

5 Research Methods

The research design consists of both qualitative and quantitative research methods. This research study aims to have a thorough understanding of what startups are currently doing regarding information monitoring. It highlights the nature of the study i.e. exploratory nature, particularly at initial stages; therefore, multiple case study method [22] is considered as the appropriate research method. Moreover, we also consider multiple case study approach as suitable due to the startup context and limited existing literature on the topic. The decision of using a multiple-case study approach is inspired by the recommendations provided by Easterbrook et al. [21]. A major advantage of using a multiple-case study is that it brings greater generalizability and validity control. Consequently, it is much easier to conclude strong and reliable results by investigating multiple cases.

To select the sample for our study, we propose to stratify cases according to the product type or business model and product development stages. Six classifications of software startups are indicated in [10] based on the product type and business models. Overall, therefore, we expect a combination of semi-structured interviews and observations to explore the cases for further analysis. Accordingly, interpretivist approach [20] is found suitable for this investigation based on the focus of research, nature of startups, and the use of interviews and observations as data collection methods. Going in the same vein, survey research is also being proposed to bring methodological triangulation for the initial findings. We also propose to conduct multiple interview sessions with startup representatives by involving multiple researchers to control validity threats.

Similarly, we plan to utilize both inductive and deductive data analysis approaches to analyze the data. In the inductive analysis, Grounded Theory (GT) [20] is proposed to analyze the qualitative data. It has been suggested that GT should be considered when there are no existing theories, or the explanation of a phenomenon is inadequate [20]. On the other hand, for deductive analysis, we will explore the relationships between variables using factor analysis [20].

6 Conclusions

Software startups are different from other software development organizations, as they need to handle business aspects as well along with the technical challenges, in a very limited time. They are required to monitor information continuously to make better decisions in the future, adjust their directions in finding the right product idea, maintain the momentum and balance between speed and quality. While the literature on software startups is growing, there is still uncertainty, however, how software startups need to monitor the key information continuously. Likewise, existing software engineering tools and practices are considered heavy for software startups. Therefore, the current research project aims to address the challenge of understanding how software startups decide what information needs to be monitored continuously. To conduct the study, we plan to employ multiple case studies using interviews and observations, and survey. Similarly, to analyze the data, we plan to implement grounded theory and factor analysis approaches. Taken together, the research will take an interpretivist approach to execute the work.

References

1. Mackinlay, C.: Readings in Information Visualization: Using Vision to Think. Morgan Kaufmann, San Francisco (1999)
2. Leal, G.C.L., Prikladnicki, R., Ebert, C., Balancieri, R., Pompermaier, L.B.: Practices and tools for software start-ups. IEEE Softw. **37**(1), 72–77 (2020)
3. Worldwide business start-ups. MKM Research Web site. http://www.moyak.com/papers/business-startups-entrepreneurs.html. Accessed 30 June 2020
4. Mullins, J.W., Mullins, J.W., Mullins, J., Komisar, R.: Getting to Plan B: Breaking Through to a Better Business Model. Harvard Business Press, Boston (2009)
5. Nobel, C.: Why Companies Fail–and How Their Founders Can Bounce Back. Harvard Business School, Boston (2011)
6. Ries, E.: The Lean Startup: How Today's Entrepreneurs Use Continuous Innovation to Create Radically Successful Businesses. Currency, New York (2011)
7. Unterkalmsteiner, M., et al.: Software startups–a research agenda. e-Inf. Softw. Eng. J. **10**(1), 89–123 (2016)
8. Bosch, J., Holmström Olsson, H., Björk, J., Ljungblad, J.: The early stage software startup development model: a framework for operationalizing lean principles in software startups. In: Fitzgerald, B., Conboy, K., Power, K., Valerdi, R., Morgan, L., Stol, K.-J. (eds.) LESS 2013. LNBIP, vol. 167, pp. 1–15. Springer, Heidelberg (2013). https://doi.org/10.1007/978-3-642-44930-7_1
9. Cockburn, A.: Agile Software Development: The Cooperative Game. Pearson Education, Upper Saddle River, NJ (2006)
10. Croll, A., Yoskovitz, B.: Lean Analytics: Use Data to Build a Better Startup Faster. O'Reilly Media Inc, Sebastopol (2013)
11. Giardino, C., Paternoster, N., Unterkalmsteiner, M., Gorschek, T., Abrahamsson, P.: Software development in startup companies: the greenfield startup model. IEEE Trans. Softw. Eng. **42**(6), 585–604 (2015)

12. Kamulegeya, G., Mugwanya, R., Hebig, R.: Measurements in the early stage software start-ups: a multiple case study in a nascent ecosystem. Found. Comput. Decis. Sci. **43**(4), 251–280 (2018)
13. Kemell, K.-K., Wang, X., Nguyen-Duc, A., Grendus, J., Tuunanen, T., Abrahamsson, P.: 100+ metrics for software startups – a multi-vocal literature review. In: CEUR Workshop Proceedings, vol. 2305, pp. 15–29 (2018)
14. Pantiuchina, J., Mondini, M., Khanna, D., Wang, X., Abrahamsson, P.: Are software startups applying agile practices? the state of the practice from a large survey. In: Baumeister, H., Lichter, H., Riebisch, M. (eds.) XP 2017. LNBIP, vol. 283, pp. 167–183. Springer, Cham (2017). https://doi.org/10.1007/978-3-319-57633-6_11
15. Paredes, J., Anslow, C., Maurer, F.: Information visualization for agile software development. In: 2014 Second IEEE Working Conference on Software Visualization, pp. 157–166. IEEE (2014)
16. Paternoster, N., Giardino, C., Unterkalmsteiner, M., Gorschek, T., Abrahamsson, P.: Software development in startup companies: a systematic mapping study. Inf. Softw. Technol. **56**(10), 1200–1218 (2014)
17. Srinivasan, S., Barchas, I., Gorenberg, M., Simoudis, E.: Venture capital: fueling the innovation economy. Computer **47**(8), 40–47 (2014)
18. Staron, M., Meding, W.: Mesram–a method for assessing robustness of measurement programs in large software development organizations and its industrial evaluation. J. Syst. Softw. **113**, 76–100 (2016)
19. Blank, S.: The Four Steps to The Epiphany: Successful Strategies for Products that Win. Wiley, Hoboken (2020)
20. Creswell, J.W.: Research Design: Qualitative, Quantitative, and Mixed Methods Approaches. Sage Publications, Thousand Oaks (2013)
21. Easterbrook, S., Singer, J., Storey, M.A., Damian, D.: Selecting empirical methods for software engineering research. In: Shull, F., Singer, J., Sjøberg, D.I.K. (eds.) Guide to Advanced Empirical Software Engineering. Springer, London (2008). https://doi.org/10.1007/978-1-84800-044-5_11
22. Yin, R.K.: Case Study Research: Design and Methods. Sage Publications, Thousand Oaks (2013)
23. Floridi, L.: Information: A Very Short Introduction. OUP, Oxford (2010)

Agile Education and Training Track

Is It Possible to Apply Agile Methods to Contribute to the Linux Kernel?

Thatiane de Oliveira Rosa[1,2](✉) and Alfredo Goldman[2]

[1] University of São Paulo, São Paulo, SP, Brazil
{thatiane,gold}@ime.usp.br
[2] Federal Institute of Tocantins, Paraíso do Tocantins, TO, Brazil

Abstract. In this document, we describe the experience of teaching Agile Methods for developing projects related to the Linux Kernel, during the XP Lab course. In 2018, the first project related to this context emerged. This project had the objective of making adjustments to the driver for Linux IIO subsystem. The second project was developed in 2019 and aimed to refactor the Ethernet driver used in the kernel of a Brazilian Single Board Computer. Based on 19 years of experience offering the XP Lab course, we consider the development of these projects to be a challenging teaching activity, which deserves to be presented and discussed with students, educators, and professionals. Our aim is to show that it is possible to adapt Agile Values to different software development settings.

Keywords: Agile methods · Linux kernel · Low-level programming · XP Lab · Teaching challenges

1 Introduction

There are several challenges related to the teaching-learning process of Agile Methods in the academic context. The ideal is that students learn the theoretical concepts and have a practical experience close to the industry reality. Since 2001, the Institute of Mathematics and Statistics of the University of São Paulo annually offers the eXtreme Programming Laboratory (XP Lab) course, which aims to teach Agile Methods in practice, where students deal with real customers and projects and follow the XP values and principles [4]. From the offer of this course, we can deal with different teaching challenges, contexts, and development projects, as well as to evolve and continuously improve.

Recently, we were faced with a new challenge: to teach the adoption of Agile Methods to develop projects that deal with low-level programming. In 2018, we had a project in our Agile Methods course related to the Linux Kernel IIO Staging Drivers. In 2019, we had another project that the goal was to refactor the Ethernet driver of a new device. In this paper, we describe how we adapted our mindset to do Agile in these particular software development environments.

The rest of this experience report is organized as follows. Section 2 presents our XP Lab course. Sections 3 and 4 describe the two projects developed during

© The Author(s) 2020
M. Paasivaara and P. Kruchten (Eds.): XP 2020 Workshops, LNBIP 396, pp. 291–297, 2020.
https://doi.org/10.1007/978-3-030-58858-8_30

2018 and 2019 related to low-level programming. Section 5 discusses how we adapted to support the development and present some lessons learned. The last section presents some final thoughts and remarks.

2   XP Lab Course

XP Lab (eXtreme Programming Laboratory) is a course offered annually by IME/USP (Institute of Mathematics and Statistics of University of São Paulo) since 2001 for undergraduate and graduate students in Computer Science. The main goal is to teach Agile Methods in practice, providing the student with real knowledge and experience [3]. To achieve this goal, during the course, students develop real projects with real customers. The projects are developed by the students following the XP (eXtreme Programming) values - communication, simplicity, feedback, respect, and courage - and principles such as continuous improvement, incremental changes, and mutual benefit [1].

Furthermore, students use the original XP practices such as pair programming, shared code, stand-up meetings, and simple design, and other practices such as whole-class retrospectives in fishbowl format, lightning talks at lunchtime, rotation of team members across teams, brainwriting, coding dojos, test day, and refactoring day. During the first classes and in a punctual and opportune manner during the course, lectures and practical activities are held on relevant subjects such as Agile Methods and practices, DevOps, software architecture and patterns, continuous integration, technological stack, software testing, and technical debt. During the course, it is possible to notice that learning evolved, and students started to continuously learn and share technical knowledge, projects, Agile Methods, and skills [3].

Since 2001, over 500 students have been taught to adopt Agile Methods, 89 projects were executed, and over 10 companies attended [4]. During 19 years of offering, we had to adapt to several different contexts and situations.

In the last two years, we have faced the challenge of developing projects to contribute to the Linux Kernel. In the two next sections, we present an overview of these projects, outline the development process, some practices used, challenges faced, outcomes, and the evaluation process adopted.

3   IIO Staging Drivers Project

This project was proposed by Rodrigo Siqueira[1], an autonomous Linux Kernel contributor. The purpose was to create a development and contribution cycle to the Linux Kernel, disseminating the desired procedures to collaborate with the Linux Kernel's evolution, in partnership with Kernel maintainers in Brazil. The main planned tasks were: basic contributions such as preparation of the development environment, aiming the code style adjustments; intermediary contributions such as minor bug fixes and refactorings; and advanced contributions, such as adjustments to the driver for the IIO subsystem [2].

---

[1] https://www.linkedin.com/in/rodrigosiqueirajordao/.

Since XP Lab students did not know about Linux Kernel development, it was proposed contributing to staging drivers (drivers that need more adjustment, before being added to the live Kernel tree). Therefore, during the XP Lab course, students adopted Agile Development Methods to improve Linux test drivers. Furthermore, adjusted drivers should meet quality requirements to be appropriately added to the Linux Kernel.

The team of this project was formed by six students and two external coaches (Linux Kernel contributors). The customer was the Linux Kernel Community. During the project development, different face-to-face meetings with the customer were held to discuss and plan tasks. At the beginning of each class (twice a week), a stand-up meeting was held. Once a week, a member selected by the team participated in a stand-up meeting with the coaches of other projects that were being developed in the course. The purpose of this meeting was to share experiences among the teams. The team held regular meetings with the customer to discuss and plan tasks and priorities. Furthermore, at the end of each sprint, the team held a retrospective meeting. One of the most useful and used Agile Practices was pair programming.

As reported by the team members, the main challenge faced during the project development was the distance or unavailability of customers. The strategy adopted to mitigate this challenge was reading the available documentation to minimize the impacts of the lack of interaction with the customer.

At the end of the project, the team members reported that they could learn fundamental concepts of FLOSS (Free/Libre and Open Source Software) development. The main concepts learned were: the importance of clear and complete documentation and the importance of searching information in this documentation; recognize the importance of code reviews; use of tools that facilitate software development for Linux; workflow and development process in the Linux Kernel; and importance of sharing the code with the community. Furthermore, the team emphasizes that communication between developers, specialists (external coaches), and the community is essential for successful FLOSS development.

Another relevant outcome is that during the course, the team accounted for 20% of the contributions to the Linux IIO Subsystem. Furthermore, at the end of the course, the team members founded an extension group called FLUSP[2], which aims to contribute to FLOSS projects. Among their main achievements we have: FLUSP was one of the top contributors for the kernel drivers for a while; one of our former students is now contributing to GCC as a committer; one of our former students was responsible for parallelizing the grep command of GIT. More details and information about this project is available in the following GitHub repositories: github.com/rodrigosiqueira/kworkflow and gitlab.com/groups/kernel-usp/.

---

[2] https://flusp.ime.usp.br/.

4 Labrador Project

The Labrador is a Brazilian Single Board Computer (SBC) developed by Caninos Loucos that works with open hardware and software. Caninos Loucos is an organization that develops SBCs with an open structure (hardware and software) for the Internet of Things (IoT). It is an initiative of the Technological Integrated Systems Laboratory (LSI-TEC) with the support of Polytechnic School of the University of São Paulo (Poli-USP) and Jon "Maddog" Hall, Board Director of the Linux Professional Institute [5].

The proposed project for the XP Lab course was to adopt Agile Development Methods to refactor the Ethernet driver used in the Labrador Kernel. This driver used obsolete Linux Kernel functions and must be updated. Such updates were necessary to enable the wide distribution of Labrador SBC.

The team of this project was formed by two students and three external coaches (domain specialists). The customers were the Caninos Loucos members. The development process and practices adopted in this project were very similar to the IIO Staging Drivers Project. At the beginning of each class (twice a week), a stand-up meeting was held. Once a week, the two members participated in a stand-up meeting with the coaches of other projects that were being developed in the course. The team held regular face-to-face meetings with the customer to discuss and plan tasks and priorities. Furthermore, at the end of each sprint, the team held a retrospective meeting.

According to the team, the main challenges faced are related to communication with the customers and the complexity of the legacy architecture and code. Communication with the customer was unsatisfactory, and it was difficult to get constant feedback. Given the complexity of the legacy architecture and code, it was difficult to define objectives and dimension the sprints. This last problem hindered the measurement of the progress of the driver refactoring work. Furthermore, given the difficulties listed, students were unable to adopt strategies to automate tests or carry out effectively continuous integration.

In order to mitigate the communication problem, the team sought other information sources. Thus, the students tried to use discussion forums and sought members of the Labrador project with higher availability. Regarding the complexity of the legacy architecture and code, the team readjusted expectations and broke the work into smaller issues.

At the end of the project, the team members reported that they could learn about the importance of efficient communication, constant feedback, clear and complete documentation, and proper software architecture.

The main results of this project include the refactoring of a part of the Labrador Ethernet driver and redefining the used software architecture. Furthermore, students resolved a Linux Kernel bug (approved patch), which influenced the Labrador driver's refactoring. More details and information about this project is available in the following GitHub repository: github.com/r0zbot/labrador-linux.

5 Lessons Learned

In the XP Lab course, the students are assessed continuously and incrementally. The final grade is defined based on the analysis of the following elements: Class attendance; Compliance with four extra hours per week; Self-evaluation; The internal coach's evaluation of each team member (coach is a team member with greater knowledge of Agile Methods); Team evaluation by the customer; Team evaluation by meta-coach (graduate student with deep knowledge of Agile Methods, who supports the professor and guides the students).

The team evaluation by meta-coach is divided into three stages, where different requirements are analyzed. During stage 1, it is analyzed if the infrastructure has been installed and if the team is organized. In stage 2, the meta-coach analyzes the internal and external communication of each team and observes the activities' planning and recording. Furthermore, the meta-coach monitors the rotation of pairs, the use of repositories, the realization of commits and tests, and the initialization of the continuous integration practice. In the last evaluation stage, elements such as tracking documentation, continuous integration, implementation of test-driven development, test coverage index, deliveries made to the customer, self-organization of the team during the course, and publication of "artifacts" to ensure the project continuity are considered.

However, when trying to adopt the same criteria for evaluating projects related to the Linux Kernel, we realized some could be adopted, and others could not. Among the inadequate criteria, we can mention continuous integration, test-driven development, test coverage, and deliveries. It is because, considering the development close to the hardware, it is very complex to create a continuous integration pipeline or obtain a good test coverage index. Therefore, it was necessary to adjust the criteria evaluated by the meta-coach.

To adapt the evaluation process, we return to the origin of Agile Methods; that is, we consider adherence to the values and principles of the Agile Manifesto [6]. For that, we monitored the teams' work closely and made a checklist, composed by items such as customer satisfaction through valuable software, team adaptation to late changes, working software after a few weeks of development, team members engagement, face-to-face communication, simplicity of design, and self-organize ability. In the end, we were surprised at how the Agile Values were present.

We believe that the main lessons learned from the development of the projects presented were:

- Is recommended that the team has at least one coach (internal or external) who is a member of the FLOSS community and knows the Linux Kernel workflow and development process;
- It is fundamental to adopt the original Values and Principles of the Agile Manifesto to assist in the evaluation of projects developed in agile contexts.

6 Final Remarks

The main objective of this document was to share the experience of adopting Agile Methods to develop software that deals with low-level programming. This type of project is especially challenging because it is not trivial to combine the teaching of Agile Methods with development close to the hardware.

We consider that our experience was successful, and we could provide relevant contributions to educators and the Agile and Free Software Communities. Furthermore, we were quite happy to leave our comfort zone and see that it is possible to apply Agile Principles and Methods to different environments. Therefore, the main conclusion we reached with the development of this work was to realize the simplicity, relevance, versatility, and transversality of the Agile Values and Principles.

We hope to have the opportunity to adopt and teach Agile Methods in new projects that deal with low-level programming and in other challenging contexts.

Acknowledgment. We would like to thank to Diogo Pina, meta-coach in 2018; Joe Yoder, who suggested adopting Agile Principles for adjusting the assessment; to customers Rodrigo Siqueira, Giuliano Belinassi, and Marcelo Schmitt; and to the students who developed the projects: Bruno Almeida Carneiro da Cunha, Daniel Martinez, Gabriel Capella, Lucas Moreira Santos, Matheus Tavares Bernardino, Renato Lui Geh, and Victor de Oliveira Colombo.

References

1. Beck, K.: Extreme Programming Explained: Embrace Change. Addison-Wesley Professional (2000)
2. FLUSP: Flusp - floss at USP - linux kernel - IIO. https://flusp.ime.usp.br/projects/
3. Goldman, A., de Oliveira Rosa, T., Santos, V.A.: Having fun doing research on agile methods. In: Meirelles, P., Nelson, M.A., Rocha, C. (eds.) WBMA 2019. CCIS, vol. 1106, pp. 147–164. Springer, Cham (2019). https://doi.org/10.1007/978-3-030-36701-5_12
4. Goldman, A., Santos, V.A.: Continuous improvement of an XP laboratory course: An 18 year history. In: 2019 Agile Conference (2019)
5. Loucos, C.: Caninos loucos. https://caninosloucos.org/en/program-en/
6. Manifesto, A.: Principles behind the agile manifesto. https://agilemanifesto.org/principles.html

Forming and Assessing Student Teams in Software Engineering Courses

Henrik Hillestad Løvold$^{(\boxtimes)}$, Yngve Lindsjørn, and Viktoria Stray

Department of Informatics, University of Oslo, Oslo, Norway
{henrihlo,ynglin,stray}@ifi.uio.no

Abstract. In software development projects, working in teams is essential. Therefore, software engineering courses often require the students to be working in teams to learn about team work behaviors and practices. The instructors of software engineering courses are presented with several challenges when teaching courses that require teamwork. For example, how to form high-performing student teams, and how to assess their work. The aim of this study is to evaluate whether there are differences in performance whether the students form the teams themselves, or if the teams are formed by the instructor. We evaluated a course involving agile software development by 200 students working in 39 teams. A total of 76% of the students chose to form their own teams, the remaining 24% were placed in teams by the instructors. Our findings indicate that teams formed by the students perform slightly better than the teams formed by the instructors.

1 Introduction

To better prepare software engineering students for real work-life, it is important to let them experience developing software in project teams. A main goal with teamwork is that the participants value working together and learning from each other. Teamwork in software engineering projects is harder than the students expect [1]. A common problem with teamwork is a lack of commitment and contribution of one or more members of the team [4] and communication challenges among the team members [3]. Therefore, understanding how to form teams that experience successful teamwork where everyone learns and contributes is of vital importance.

There are many ways to form teams, ranging from the simple randomizing of teams, to hand-picking students for each team based on their qualifications. Research within the field of formation of teams (also called team composition [3] and group selection [2]) within software engineering courses at the undergraduate level is scarce. Some research on team formation within software engineering in general has been carried out in the US, pointing instructors towards forming teams themselves, without the involvement of the students [9]. Other research points to using algorithm-based tools to automatically match students [5], or by using personality tests to match team members [8].

M. Paasivaara and P. Kruchten (Eds.): XP 2020 Workshops, LNBIP 396, pp. 298–306, 2020.
https://doi.org/10.1007/978-3-030-58858-8_31

Oakley et al. [9] found that simply putting students in groups to work on assignments is not a sufficient condition for achieving the benefits of cooperative learning and working in teams. One of the findings in this study is that the teams should establish policies that will govern their operation and get them to formulate their own expectations of one another using a *Team Policies Statement and the Team Expectations Agreement.*

There seems to be no consensus on which way actually leads to more learning and better results in terms of students' overall performance. Motivated by this, we aimed to investigate the topic of team formation in a large software engineering course.

2   Methods

In the spring of 2019, the University offered a software engineering course involving a major agile project where the students worked in teams to develop a mobile application. The course was 20 ECTS credits; equivalent to a total workload of 33% of one full academic year in Norway. The course was made mandatory for second-year undergraduate students following three study programmes; *Programming and Systems Architecture (ProSA), Design, Use and Interaction (Design)* and *Digital Economy and Leadership (DigØk)*. This study was carried out using the data recorded from the teams participating in this course.

2.1   Course Design

During a project period of 13 weeks, students were assigned to write an app for the Android operating system involving API data gathered from the Institute of Meteorology. The students were given introductions to agile methods of software engineering, Scrum and Kanban in particular. All work was to be logged and end up in a report which was then assessed together with the final product and scored on a scale of 0–50 points. The report and product were assessed using the criteria presented in Table 1.

In our course, all the teams followed an agile project model. While Scrum was the process model most focused on in the lectures, this was not the most used process model among the teams. Scrum was chosen by 17 teams. However, the majority of the teams incorporated Kanban elements into their Scrum process models. This process model, ScrumBan, was chosen by 21 teams. The two most popular tools to use in the teams were Trello (used by 24 teams) and Slack (used by 20 teams). Trello was used to keep track of tasks and visualize the workflow. Slack was used to communicate and coordinate, and this tool has been shown to increase team awareness and communication in agile teams [10]. In our teaching, we aimed to focus both technical and soft skills. This applies in the learning elements of the course such as lectures, weekly tasks and mandatory assignments, as well as in the assessment of the report and product as seen in Table 1.

Table 1. Criteria for the evaluation of student reports and products, and their percentage of total score.

Criteria	% of score
Title, abstract, team presentation, introduction	4
User documentation	11
Requirements analysis, modelling, patterns	15
Technical product documentation	15
Testing and test documentation	8
Process documentation, reflection on process	19
Overall impression, language, context	12
References, sources, appendices	4
Product and functionality	12

The report and product accounted for 50% of the final grade given to students, the other half being the result of a final individual written exam. The questions on the exam were both from theory presented in lectures and group sessions and from the project they were a part of in the teamwork.

As we can see from Table 1, we assessed the product and functionality of the projects. This includes the source code written by the teams; an aspect which is inherently difficult to assess. In many courses where students write code, only the final outcome and the product is assessed. We found it important not only to look at the outcome and product, but also the source code, as this gives us better insight in the architecture and design patterns chosen by the students, and how this is reflected on in their final report.

2.2   Forming Teams

Early on in the process of designing the course, the question about how teams were to be formed, and how involved in the forming of teams the instructors were to be, arose. Initially, we aimed to minimize the work required by the lecturers, and wanted all students to form their own teams consisting of 4–6 students. We quickly became concerned about the students forming too homogeneous teams in terms of study programme, gender and workload capacity. We were also concerned that students who did not have a social network at the campus would fall behind and not find other students to work together with. To solve these problems, we went with a middle-ground solution where students could choose to either form teams on their own, or be placed in a group manually by the lecturers, based on the following: study programme, ambitions, and availability.

We initially aimed to make the teams as diverse as possible with regards to study programme and gender, whilst minimising the distance between group members level of ambition. This is in line with previous studies within the field with successful results [11]. The students were also instructed to report to the instructors immediately if any signs of dysfunction occurred. This would then lead to a conversation with the course administration in order to solve the problems as they arose.

3   Results

In total, 76.3% of the students opted to organise teams by themselves, without the involvement of the instructor. The rest of the students who answered wanted to be placed in teams by the instructor. We were not surprised that the students opting to be placed in teams by the instructor were outnumbered by students opting to form teams on their own; these are second-year students who know each other well and many have already formed study groups.

Unsurprisingly, most students (68.7%) answered that their ambitions were to aim for grades A-B. About a third answered (31.3%) that they aimed at an average grade, and no students answered that they were happy about just passing the course. Furthermore, it is interesting to note that no students were happy as long as they passed.

3.1   Group Formation Outcome

The instructors assessed the results of the survey and put together nine teams of five to six individuals. Six of the teams were within the A-B ambition level, and three of the teams were in the average grade ambition level.

As we see from Table 2, three teams formed by the instructors consisted of only males, and males were over-represented in all but one team formed by the instructor. For the 9 teams formed by the instructors 27% of the students were female. For the 30 teams formed by the students themselves 31% of the students were female. While some research suggests the gender balance within the team is irrelevant in regards to result [6], we wanted our teams to be diverse. We made it a rule that teams formed by the instructors should at least have two students of each gender, or otherwise be a single-gender team. This was to prevent one student from becoming the "odd one out", and thus purely for social reasons. However, in the student-formed teams, five of the teams chose to have only one female. The average team size across all teams was 5.21.

As for study programme, on the other hand, we wanted diversity. Mishra et al. state that most of the tasks of software development organizations are diverse in nature, and suggests that Software Engineering educators should seek diversity

Table 2. Gender distribution of teams formed by the instructors and teams formed by the students. M denotes male, F denotes female.

	M only	F only	One F	Mixed
Instructor formed	3	0	0	6
Student formed	9	2	5	14

302   H. H. Løvold et al.

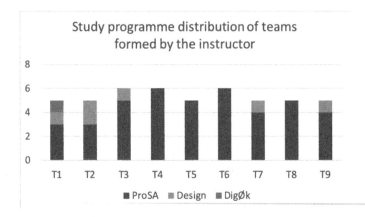

Fig. 1. Distribution of students from each study programme grouped by team, from the teams formed by the instructors.

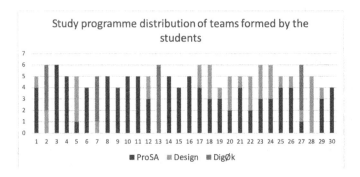

Fig. 2. Distribution of students from each study programme grouped by team, from the teams formed by the students themselves.

when preparing students for the industry [7]. Figure 1 shows the distribution of students with regards to study programme, grouped by teams. We can read from the figure that students from the programme *ProSA* were over-represented. This comes as no surprise as this by far is the largest study programme at the department with regards to number of students.

For the self organised teams, as we can read from Fig. 2, there were 99 from *ProSA*, 37 from *Design* and 17 from *DigØk*. 12 of the 30 teams had team members from a single study programme, 10 of them were from *ProSA*, 1 from *Design*, and 1 from *DigØk*. It is interesting to note that the student-made teams seem to be just as diverse as the teams formed by the instructors in terms of study programme. This is likely a result of the students signing up to be placed in groups by the instructors mainly coming from a single study programme (ProSA).

Table 3. Team project score and individual exam score grouped by student-formed and instructor-formed teams.

	Average points	Standard deviation
Team score		
Student-formed teams	42.5	4.70
Instructor-formed teams	40.3	4.27
Individual exam score		
Student-formed teams	40.1	6.47
Instructor-formed teams	38.5	7.55

3.2 Project Performance

The first section of Table 3 shows the average final points on a scale between 0 and 50 for all teams, grouped by those formed by students and those formed by the instructor, as well as the standard deviation within the teams. As we can see from the results, the teams formed by the students themselves performed slightly better than the teams formed by the instructor. The difference is, however, well within one standard deviation, and with a p-value of $p = 0,114$ we cannot draw a clear conclusion from our data.

Although the data is somewhat inconclusive, it is interesting to note that the results seem to indicate that teams formed by the students themselves perform slightly better than teams formed by the instructor. The implications of these results will be further analysed in Sect. 4.

3.3 Individual Exam

In addition to the project report and the software product, all students had an individual exam with questions from the curriculum and from the project and teamwork. The second section of Table 3 shows the average points for the individual exam on a scale from 0 to 50 for all teams, grouped by those formed by students and those formed by the instructor, as well as the standard deviation within the teams. For each team we calculated the average of the points (exam results) for all the individual team members in the team. The results are similar to the results presented in Table 3 for average team score, but with a higher standard deviation due to the differences in the results of the individual team members within the teams.

4 Discussion

In this study we have analysed the results of student teams in a large 20 ECTS course on software engineering. The students were given the choice to either form teams on their own, or be placed in a team by the instructors based on a small questionnaire at the beginning of the semester. The instructors' goal was to make teams as diverse as possible, as previous studies seem to support the claim that diverse teams perform better overall than homogeneous teams [11].

We found that 31% of the students chose to be placed in teams by the instructor, while the majority (69%) formed their own teams. Many of the students who opted to form their own teams probably knew each other well on beforehand. This course was offered exclusively to students in their 4th semester of computer science studies, and it is not unlikely that many of the students already had a group of 4–6 peers with which they have collaborated with on other courses. This means that the students who formed teams on their own had the advantage of already knowing they work well together with their teammates, compared to the students who were placed in teams by the instructor.

Furthermore, our analysis might indicate that individuals in teams formed by the students themselves performed slightly better than the individuals in teams formed by the instructors, both on the team evaluation, and the individual final exam.

4.1   Study Limitations

Although we aimed to make the teams as diverse as possible, we do not know the level of diversity, both professionally and in terms of gender and study programme of the teams that the students created themselves. In other words; we cannot be sure whether the teams created by the instructor are, in fact, more diverse than the teams created by the students themselves. We did, though, find it plausible to assume that the general level of diversity probably was in fact lower, as students from the same programmes usually attend the same lectures and spend spare time together.

Although more than 200 students attended the course, and with 39 teams included in our study, there were only 9 teams formed by the instructors. A sample size this small makes it hard to draw definite conclusions, as personal factors of each student within the teams affect the final result.

5   Conclusion and Future Work

We studied 39 teams in a major software engineering course. Our results suggest that teams formed by the instructors intended to be as diverse as possible, do not necessarily perform better than teams formed by the students themselves. Our data indicate that the teams formed by the students perform slightly better, but there is no significant difference between the teams in each group. We have no conclusive evidence of why this is the case, but we assume that the social factor plays a major role in this regard. Teams consisting of peers who know each other on beforehand have an advantage over teams who have to get to know each other before starting to work.

Future research should go deeper into investigating if and why student-formed groups perform better, as well as to analyse the effect of diversity. Furthermore, it is a need to understand how this diversity affects the quality of the different parts of the project (such as testing, documentation, usability and maintainability). It would also be interesting to investigate how teamwork quality, meeting frequency and agile practices differed with regards to how the teams were formed. As other research shows promising results using algorithm-based tools to match students [5], this might also be something worth looking further into.

This course was offered again in spring 2020 with a different approach to forming teams. Students could not select all team members by themselves, but were instructed to suggest 1–3 peers they wanted to have in their team. Based on their wishes, we put together teams of 5–6 members, and thus all students had to work with at least one team member they did not know beforehand. This approach has shown promising results, which might be worth looking further into.

References

1. Bastarrica, M.C., Perovich, D., Samary, M.M.: What can students get from a software engineering capstone course? In: 2017 IEEE/ACM 39th International Conference on Software Engineering: Software Engineering Education and Training Track (ICSE-SEET), pp. 137–145 (2017). https://doi.org/10.1109/ICSE-SEET.2017.15
2. Dugan Jr., R.F.: A survey of computer science capstone course literature. Comput. Sci. Educ. **21**(3), 201–267 (2011)
3. Dzvonyar, D., Alperowitz, L., Henze, D., Bruegge, B.: Team composition in software engineering project courses. In: 2018 IEEE/ACM International Workshop on Software Engineering Education for Millennials (SEEM), pp. 16–23. IEEE (2018)
4. Iacob, C., Faily, S.: Exploring the gap between the student expectations and the reality of teamwork in undergraduate software engineering group projects. J. Syst. Softw. **157**, 110393 (2019)
5. Jahanbakhsh, F., Fu, W.T., Karahalios, K., Marinov, D., Bailey, B.: You want me to work with who?: stakeholder perceptions of automated team formation in project-based courses. In: Proceedings of the 2017 CHI Conference on Human Factors in Computing Systems, pp. 3201–3212. ACM (2017)
6. Lingard, R., Berry, E.: Teaching teamwork skills in software engineering based on an understanding of factors affecting group performance. In: 32nd Annual Frontiers in Education, vol. 3, pp. S3G–S3G. IEEE (2002)
7. Mishra, A., Mishra, D.: Industry oriented advanced software engineering education curriculum. Croatian J. Educ. **14**(3), 595–624 (2012)
8. Rodríguez Montequín, V., Mesa Fernández, J.M., Balsera, J.V., García Nieto, A.: Using MBTI for the success assessment of engineering teams in project-based learning. Int. J. Technol. Des. Educ. **23**(4), 1127–1146 (2012). https://doi.org/10.1007/s10798-012-9229-1
9. Oakley, B., Felder, R.M., Brent, R., Elhajj, I.: Turning student groups into effective teams. J. Stud. Cent. Learn. **2**(1), 9–34 (2004)
10. Stray, V., Moe, N.B., Noroozi, M.: Slack me if you can! Using enterprise social networking tools in virtual agile teams. In: 2019 ACM/IEEE 14th International Conference on Global Software Engineering (ICGSE), pp. 111–121. IEEE (2019)
11. Tafliovich, A., Petersen, A., Campbell, J.: Evaluating student teams. In: Proceedings of the 47th ACM Technical Symposium on Computing Science Education - SIGCSE 2016, pp. 181–186. ACM Press, New York (2016). https://doi.org/10.1145/2839509.2844647, http://dl.acm.org/citation.cfm?doid=2839509.2844647

Panel

COVID-19's Influence on the Future of Agile

Dennis Mancl[1][✉] [iD] and Steven D. Fraser[2] [iD]

[1] MSWX Software Experts, Bridgewater, NJ 08807, USA
dmancl@acm.org
[2] Innoxec, Santa Clara, CA, USA
sdfraser@acm.org

Abstract. As a result of the global COVID-19 pandemic, the way the world works, collaborates, and plays has changed. Commerce has stalled with travel, hospitality, education, retail, and health sectors particularly affected. This paper is based on an XP 2020 panel organized by Steven Fraser and featuring Aino Corry, Steve McConnell, and Rachel Reinitz. The panel discussed the impact of COVID-19 on knowledge workers, the acceleration of digital workplace transformation, and anticipated long term effects from the pandemic in the context of agile practices. Four key observations emerged from the discussion: First, virtual collaboration between those working from home is enabled by a variety of communication tools – substituting for face-to-face interactions. Second, agile work practices are harder to perform given the virtual nature of meetings and interactions. Third, communication tools are not always adequate for high-bandwidth or informal interactions, such as brainstorming, side discussions, or hallway conversations. Fourth, forming new teams and onboarding staff is challenging in a virtual work environment.

Keywords: Agile · COVID-19 · Digital transformation · Virtual collaboration

1 Setting the Context: COVID-19's Impact on Agile

In March 2020, the world changed due to the pandemic, which necessitated quarantines that impacted most if not all individuals, communities, and countries around the world. The pandemic had an almost immediate effect on the software community by limiting face-to-face collaborations and meetings.

Other consequences of the pandemic included supply chain and business continuity interruptions. The delivery of goods and services were affected by transportation challenges, including border closures, quarantines, and the need to prioritize medical supplies. COVID-19 has impacted many sectors of the global economy, including hospitality (restaurants, hotels, cruises, casinos, theme parks, etc.), travel (airlines, trains, buses, etc.), education (school and university), retail, and health. All of these sectors have struggled to adapt to a world where most people-to-people interactions are virtual.

Additionally, we now have virtual rather than face-to-face conferences. Technical interactions catalyzed by internationally recognized conferences such as ACM/IEEE's ICSE and the Agile Alliance's XP conference have been transformed to virtual experiences. Without face-to-face presence, the opportunity for interesting personal

M. Paasivaara and P. Kruchten (Eds.): XP 2020 Workshops, LNBIP 396, pp. 309–316, 2020.
https://doi.org/10.1007/978-3-030-58858-8_32

hallway conversations, which have long been a hallmark of such international exchanges, is lost. It is likely that virtual experiences will be *de rigueur* for the foreseeable future. The widespread adoption of work-from-home environments has accelerated the digital workplace transformation. A serendipitous consequence includes issues related to workforce compensation (based on location) and the move to wide-spread virtual interaction channels between work teams and with customers. In some ways, this move to mostly remote staff accelerates the possibility of offshoring and outsourcing, since if geography is removed as a limiting constraint, team members need not be co-located. Previously mandated face-to-face interactions have transformed to digital interactions through necessity – and knowledge workers are enjoying the benefits of reduced commute time while shifting employer expenses (e.g. real estate, heat, light, power, IT infrastructure) to personal home "overhead" costs.

The panel session began with an online poll of conference participants. The audience members were asked if they attended XP 2020 only because it was an online conference. Of the 80 conference attendees who responded, 30 indicated they had planned to attend the in-person conference, in contrast to 50 who indicated their attendance was enabled by the virtual nature of the conference. A similar response was elicited regarding plans to attend XP 2021: 47 participants said they would attend XP 2021 if it were virtual, in contrast to 31 who indicated that they would attend an in-person conference. This result suggests that conference organizers of the future should consider hybrid virtual-physical conferences to increase conference geographic reach even if COVID-19 is no longer a factor.

The three XP 2020 panelists, Aino Corry, Steve McConnell, and Rachel Reinitz, expressed their personal views on the world of virtual work in a discussion facilitated by Steven Fraser. Aino Vonge Corry is an agile software expert, a teacher, technical conference editor, and retrospectives facilitator working for her own consultancy company, MetaDeveloper. Corry is the author of a forthcoming book, *Retrospectives Antipatterns*, that is planned for release in fall 2020 [1]. Steve McConnell is CEO and Chief Software Engineer at Construx, a worldwide software consulting and training company. McConnell is also the author of *Code Complete* [2], the classic book on software development practices, as well as the recent *More Effective Agile* [3], a roadmap for software leaders. Rachel Reinitz is an IBM Fellow, and the CTO and Founder of the IBM Garage, an organization that consults with clients to define, build, and deploy cloud applications.

The panel impresario and co-author of this paper, Steven Fraser (Innoxec), advises on open innovation strategies to accelerate the development and adoption of technologies based on his work at HP, Cisco, Qualcomm, Nortel, and the Software Engineering Institute (SEI) at Carnegie Mellon University. Dennis Mancl, panel recorder and co-author of this paper, is an independent consultant on software technology and practices. He worked for many years for AT&T, Lucent, and Alcatel-Lucent. In his role as an internal software technology expert, he supported the ongoing education of developers in many technologies.

There were four main conclusions from the panelists. First, COVID-19 has made drastic changes in the way we do our daily work – it has affected our work schedule, our collaborations and travel, and we are still working to readjust our work-life balance. Second, agile work practices are harder to perform since casual conversations are limited due to the online nature of meetings and interactions. Third, although virtual collaboration tools for video chat and online meetings have improved since the turn of the century, current communications tools are still not as good as face-to-face for performing high-bandwidth and informal interactions, such as brainstorming, whiteboarding, side discussions, and hallway conversations. Finally, the process of forming new teams and onboarding new employees is challenging in a virtual work environment.

2   COVID-19 Impact on Daily Work

Early in the panel discussion, McConnell presented a few results from a recent Construx study based on a survey of his clients' recent experiences with a work-from-home environment [4]. McConnell noted that for most people, routine communications continue to work well in the new all-virtual environment, and some people feel more productive because they have fewer distractions. High-performing teams continued to do well in a virtual environment, however if a team suffered from interpersonal friction prior to COVID-19, the friction was exacerbated by working from home. McConnell further explained that the survey suggested that virtual collaborators felt discussions were more to the point, attendees weren't distracted by side conversations, and meetings started on time and ran more efficiently.

Reinitz observed that the organization of work activities needed to be modified in the new virtual regime. She observed that one needs to resist merely "taking what you do face-to-face and now doing it virtually." For example, her team used to run multi-day face-to-face workshops with clients. But in the new virtual COVID-19 environment, they made one important change to their process by spreading their workshops over additional days – scheduling a series of half-day sessions. Reinitz explained that a multi-day schedule made it easier for team members to schedule workshops since schedules were more flexible and not tightly constrained by travel logistics. Participants also had time for daily mini-retrospectives: "When we do workshopping, we usually do them in the morning – then in the afternoon, the team reflects and discusses what's working."

Corry added to Reinitz's points, agreeing that we need to adjust the way we run some of our work activities. She observed that it is essential to discover what can be done in virtual meetings that would provide added benefits over being physically together. For example, Corry has frequently used "round robin" in virtual meetings – where each participant gets to speak in turn. It is more socially acceptable to use a round robin when virtual than in a face-to-face setting.

The panel discussion turned to speculation about back-to-work protocols when the dangers of COVID-19 diminish. Corry explained that many offices in Denmark had reopened in May and June, but that "some people thrived so much on working from home" that they would prefer to remain virtual.

McConnell echoed this observation. "I agree with Corry that we are seeing people who really don't want to go back to work from the office. I see that in my own company. Some of that is about avoiding a potentially risky work environment, and some of it is just a work practice preference. I think right now it is impossible to separate which is which." McConnell noted many tech workers have worked virtually (from home) for years, but the pandemic increased the use of online collaboration tools by less technical business partners. The increased familiarity with online collaboration likely will increase future acceptance for virtual work.

McConnell raised the issue of how virtual working might erode trust between team members. A lack of trust within a team might not be a serious problem in the short term, but McConnell was unsure of long-term consequences if work-from-home practices were to be mandated for six months or more.

Reinitz voiced concern for work-life balance issues, noting emergent issues with overwork and Zoom (conferencing) fatigue. Reinitz has observed team members working long hours without breaks, even though in the office they would formerly take regular breaks to play ping pong. Reinitz also observed benefits working from home – since it gives her more face time with her teenage daughter and the two often play cards during breaks. Reinitz has also observed other team members interacting with their children while in virtual meetings.

3 Impact on Agile Practices

The panelists reflected on the changes in agile practices in an all-virtual work environment. McConnell observed that many agile teams are somewhat conservative and old-fashioned, using agile practices the way they were defined at the turn of the century, in the days before global distributed teams. McConnell believes that working from home and using virtual collaboration tools has "forced" teams to adopt more state-of-the-art communication practices. One area where many agile teams are progressing is in innovative uses of remote collaboration technology.

Reinitz's team pair programmed for much of their coding work, but with the COVID-19 constraints they use a combination of approaches with some solo coding, some pairing, and some mob programming. Reinitz addressed the challenges of "mixed mode" meetings, where some attendees are face-to-face and others are remote. Her experience is that hybrid meetings require much more advance preparation. She explained that they made careful choices to select the right tools for their interactive sessions, including interactive drawing and distributed note taking. She found it beneficial to have facilitators as remote participants.

Overall, the lessons shared by the three panelists suggested that remote collaboration should be embraced. McConnell emphasized a key point from the Construx work-from-home report – "It's really helpful to have the entire team working from home, if they're going to work from home." Corry agreed that all face-to-face or all virtual would be ideal, but in her experiences in Denmark, there have been more hybrid meetings. Corry warned of challenges if management creates multi-national distributed teams as a cost saving measure – merely to take advantage of differential pay scales based on geography.

4   Whiteboarding and Other High-Bandwidth Collaborations

The panelists shared experiences with virtual brainstorming tools for remote collaboration. McConnell reported that many participants in the Construx work-from-home survey had mentioned the word "whiteboarding" in their text responses to the survey, so it was clear that many respondents struggled with virtual brainstorm as a replacement for face-to-face whiteboard interactions. McConnell noted that respondents characterized early design activities for conceptualization and other high-bandwidth interactions with project stakeholders as particularly challenging.

Reinitz explained that she uses multiple alternatives to traditional in-person communications including a small physical whiteboard in her home office which she uses for brainstorming and is visible via video. Participations also create drawings on paper, scan (digital photo), and then share with meeting participants. Another useful tool for shared drawings is MURAL (mural.co). Reinitz advised to be "agile" – try different approaches, leverage what works, and iterate and adjust as necessary.

Which collaboration tools are best? Simplicity and functionality are attributes often admired when assessing collaboration tools. Collaboration platforms such as Zoom, WebEx, GoToMeeting, Microsoft Teams, Skype, etc. combined with software development environments and visioning tools such as MURAL, Box Notes, Slack, and MentiMeter were important enablers for virtual work. As an aside, the XP 2020 conference applied a simple set of tools for remote collaboration: Zoom for presentations (sometimes with breakout rooms for tutorial activities), MentiMeter for quick surveys, Zoom "chat" for audience questions, and Slack for follow-up discussions.

Reinitz explained that many people find text-based communication tools such as Slack useful, but she warned that text exchanges should not be considered a replacement for face-to-face conversation. McConnell believed that people generally communicate with greater fidelity face-to-face, although introverts may communicate more readily by text with a degree of anonymity. Text interactions complemented by emojis can both avoid and cause awkward interactions.

Audience members for this virtual panel contributed to the discussion of online drawing tools and text-based communications tools. One attendee noted that drawing isn't easy with a mouse or a touch screen. Another comment noted that groups turn to text-based collaboration tools like Slack for casual conversations in their everyday work. Slack-based dialogs are generally less effective than the conversations that co-workers would have face-to-face over lunch or in hallways, because text-based communication lacks body language cues and may be harder to interpret. It was also noted that text communication using emojis can be misinterpreted since so much depends on personal interpretation.

5   Spinning up New Teams and On-Boarding New Employees

McConnell reported that the Construx survey respondents found that spinning up new teams in an all-virtual environment is difficult. New team members require high-touch interactions (a mix of coaching and mentoring) to learn and excel at their new jobs. Reinitz shared experiences for new hires at IBM's Garage organization, explaining that their training takes more effort. Training in a remote collaboration environment requires integration of online and virtual training experiences to be effective. Virtual training is exhausting due to long hours of "screen time" – a similar challenge to that experienced by virtual conference attendees such as XP 2020 participants.

Reinitz further reflected on the training process for new employees, observing that we learn how to shape our work by watching and emulating others. In a distributed online work environment, it is necessary to be very deliberate about the act of watching others work. Reinitz believes that a technique of immersive learning for new employee onboarding can be achieved through virtual work shadowing.

6 Summary

In the short term, many organizations are rediscovering Plato's [5] observation that "necessity is the mother of invention." The primary conclusion of the panel was that tech workers will continue to work from home and use virtual collaboration technology for the foreseeable future. High-performing teams will do well, but teams with interpersonal communication challenges will likely struggle. Many (as expressed in the popular press [6]) prefer to work in a virtual collaboration environment from their home without the need for a physical office and the overhead of commute, even if the COVID-19 crisis subsides.

Although the virtual work environment will be appealing to many knowledge workers and companies, the popular press is also beginning to warn about some of the risks and problems of a transition to a virtual environment [7, 8]. Employees are now taking personal responsible for issues usually administered by their company: e.g., office furnishings, network and compute infrastructure, workplace safety, heat, light, and power. As an aside, press reports [9] attribute world-wide shortages in toilet paper to differences in supply chains for commercial and home use.

Some companies may follow the lead of Facebook, whose CEO indicated the possibility that "employee compensation will be adjusted based on the cost of living in the locations where workers choose to live. [10]" Virtual workers are often very isolated, they have more pressure to work unpaid overtime, and it is more difficult for virtual workers to organize collectively to oppose unfair management practices. Unequal and potentially unfair compensation policies are not consistent with agile values [11]. Related issues of outsourcing and offshoring have been previously discussed at XP [12] and ACM's OOPSLA/SPLASH [13, 14] conferences in the not so distant past.

Teams that excel in the application of agile development practices will likely succeed with the integration of virtual collaboration practices and tools into their distributed work environment. High-bandwidth interactions such as design discussions and dialogs with stakeholders will drive teams to replace standard "discussions catalyzed by a whiteboard" with new kinds of virtual interactions. Some meetings will use tools including digital cameras and physical whiteboards, while others will rely on a mix of collaborative software, digital drawing tools, and distributed annotation tools.

Meeting the challenge of building new teams and onboarding employees will require better strategies for virtual training and knowledge sharing. In many ways,

COVID-19 has accelerated the adoption and deployment of network-based digital collaboration tools and new practices to ensure team and company agility – however, many of the team challenges described in Peopleware [15] and Brooks' treatise on development practices [16] endure – and teams would be well advised to remember past lessons in the still short history of software development.

References

1. Corry, A.: Retrospectives Antipatterns website. http://retrospectiveantipatterns.com. Accessed 29 June 2020
2. McConnell, S.: Code Complete, 2nd edn. Microsoft Press, Redmond (2004)
3. McConnell, S.: More Effective Agile. Construx Press, Bellingham (2019)
4. McConnell, S., Stuart, J.: WFH in the Age of the Coronavirus: Lessons for Today and Tomorrow (2020). https://www.construx.com/resources/wfh-in-the-age-of-coronavirus-report/. Accessed 29 June 2020
5. Plato: The Republic (375 BC)
6. Zippia, P: Half of American workers would rather work from home forever. https://www.zippia.com/advice/coronavirus-remote-work-survey/. Accessed 2 July 2020
7. Turits, M: Why are some people better at working from home than others? BBC News website. https://www.bbc.com/worklife/article/20200506-why-are-some-people-better-at-working-from-home-than-others. Accessed 2 July 2020
8. The future of the remote worker. https://us.directlyapply.com/future-of-the-remote-worker. Accessed 2 July 2020
9. What Covid-19 toilet Paper shortages tell us about supply chains, Financial Times, 7 June 2020. https://www.ft.com/video/6e5acf3e-511b-48d1–948c-ff7c94f3ba1b. Accessed 2 July 2020
10. Conger, K.: At Facebook, Home Work Could Be Permanent. New York Times, p. B1, 22 May 2020
11. The Agile Manifesto (2001). https://agilemanifesto.org/. Accessed 2 July 2020
12. Fraser, S., et al.: Off-Shore agile software development. In: Baumeister, H., Marchesi, M., Holcombe, M. (eds.) XP 2005. LNCS, vol. 3556, pp. 267–272. Springer, Heidelberg (2005). https://doi.org/10.1007/11499053_43
13. Fraser, S., et al.: Challenges in outsourcing and global development: how will your job change?. In: OOPSLA 2004 Companion, pp. 145–147 (2004). https://doi.org/10.1145/1028664.1028722
14. Fraser, S., Mancl, D., Namioka, A., Salama, R., Wirfs-Brock, A.: East meets west: the influences of geography on software production. In: SPLASH 2014 Companion, pp. 41–42 (2014). https://doi.org/10.1145/2660252.2661293
15. DeMarco, T., Lister, T.: Peopleware: Productive Projects and Teams, 3rd edn., p. 2013. Addison-Wesley, Upper Saddle River, New Jersey (2013)
16. Brooks, F.P.: The Mythical Man-Month: Essays on Software Engineering. Addison-Wesley Longman Inc., Cambridge (1995)

Author Index

Printed in the United States
By Bookmasters